UITGAVEN VAN HET
NEDERLANDS HISTORISCH-ARCHAEOLOGISCH INSTITUUT TE ISTANBUL

Publications de l'Institut historique-archéologique néerlandais de Stamboul
sous la direction de
E. van DONZEL, Machteld J. MELLINK, C. NIJLAND,
J. J. ROODENBERG et K. R. VEENHOF

LXVI

A MUSLIM PRINCIPALITY IN CRUSADER TIMES

The early Artuqid State

A MUSLIM PRINCIPALITY IN CRUSADER TIMES

The early Artuqid State

by

CAROLE HILLENBRAND

NEDERLANDS HISTORISCH-ARCHAEOLOGISCH INSTITUUT
TE ISTANBUL
1990

CIP-GEGEVENS KONINKLIJKE BIBLIOTHEEK, DEN HAAG

Hillenbrand, Carole

A muslim principality in crusader times: the early artuqid state / Carole Hillenbrand. — Istanbul: Nederlands Historisch-Archaeologisch Instituut; Leiden: Nederlands Instituut voor het Nabije Oosten [distr.]. — (Uitgaven van het Nederlands Historisch-Archaeologisch Instituut te Istanbul; 66)
Met bibliogr., index.
ISBN 90-6258-066-1
SISO 929.1 UDC 95-011 NUGI 941
Trefw.: Nabije Oosten; geschiedenis.

To Robert

Acknowledgements

This book has benefited in many ways from the help I have received from a number of people and institutions and I am happy to record my debt to them.

I should like to thank John Walsh for acting as my thesis supervisor and for his infectious enthusiasm for Turkish history. My sincere thanks also go to Victor Ménage and Alan Jones who gave me crucial encouragement at the beginning of my research.

I should like to acknowledge with gratitude the financial support of the University of Edinburgh towards the costs of the preparation of this book for publication. I also wish to express my thanks to the University of Oxford Computing Service for producing the Arabic text and to the Director of the Netherlands Institute for the Near East, Dr. Emery van Donzel, and to his colleague Dr. Kees Nijland, for publishing this book.

I have also benefited from the help of 'Abd al-Raḥīm 'Alī and Jāsim Ḥusain who discussed cruces in the Arabic text with me, Ian Morrison and Ray Harris who were responsible for the map of the Jazīra, Murray Campbell who typed the genealogical tables, Stuart and Bronwen Campbell who took on the task of typing the English part of this book, John Cooper who put the Arabic text onto computer and Edmund Bosworth who has never failed to give me encouragement and support.

Finally I should like to thank my husband for all his valuable criticisms and support since I began work on this subject. This book is dedicated to him.

A note on transliteration

The transliteration of Arabic adopted in this work is that of the Encyclopaedia of Islam (2nd edition) with the following modifications:

d̲j̲	is rendered as	j
k̲h̲		kh
d̲h̲		dh
s̲h̲		sh
g̲h̲		gh
ḳ		q

The ending -iyya has been preferred to -īya /-iyyah /-īyah.

For Turkish names, the system used in *The Cambridge History of Iran, Volume 5*, ed. J. A. Boyle (Cambridge, 1968) has been adopted as a general guide, with minor exceptions.

A note on conventions used in the translation

1. denotes a possible missing vowel.

2 ( ) denotes a word or words added for stylistic or semantic reasons.

3 ¶ denotes *qīla* in the text.

Chapter 1

Prolegomena

i) Introduction

The value of the *Tārīkh Mayyāfāriqīn wa Āmid* of Ibn al-Azraq as a source for the history of the Jazīra has long been recognised. Amedroz,[1] who first drew attention to this text, subsequently transcribed some relevant sections of it in the footnotes to his edition of Ibn al-Qalānisī.[2] V. Minorsky translated and analysed Ibn al-Azraq's account of İl-Ghāzī's campaign to Tiflīs in 515/1121,[3] whilst Cahen, in an early article, sketched the major political outlines of the part of the *Tārīkh Mayyāfāriqīn wa Āmid* which deals with Artuqid

1. H.F. Amedroz, "Three Arabic MSS. on the History of the City of Mayyāfāriqīn", *Journal of the Royal Asiatic Society* (1902), 785-812.
2. Ibn al-Qalānisī, *Dhail Tārīkh Dimashq*, ed. H.F. Amedroz (Leiden, 1908).
3. V. Minorsky, "Caucasica in the History of Mayyāfāriqīn", *Bulletin of the School of Oriental and African Studies* XIII/I (1949), 31-5. Part of that account and other subsequent passages in Ibn al-Azraq which refer to Georgia are also published in an Arabic reader for Georgian students: *Arabuli Krest'omathia*, ed. G.V. T'seret'heli (Tiflis, 1949), 68-72. Minorsky later returned to the text, giving translations of later passages of Ibn al-Azraq which deal with Caucasian affairs (*Studies in Caucasian History* [London, 1953], 79, 87-8, 95, 97, 106 and 157). He also translated an account by Ibn al-Azraq of his visit to Darband in 549/1154-5 (*A History of Sharvān and Darband* [Cambridge, 1958], 170-3).

history.[4] The section of the text concerned with the Marwānids has been edited and published by ʿAwaḍ.[5]

It has not been the intention in this book to edit the whole section of Ibn al-Azraq's work which is concerned with the Artuqids. A conscious decision has been taken to restrict the material edited to those folios of Ibn al-Azraq's text which deal with the activities of the first two Artuqid rulers, İl-Ghāzī and Temür-Tash, whose reigns cover a time-scale of roughly fifty years (c.1100-c.1150), from the establishment of İl-Ghāzī at Mārdīn to the death of his son Temür-Tash. The reign of Najm al-Dīn Alpï, which concludes the *Tārīkh Mayyāfāriqīn wa Āmid*, has been omitted.

Instead of a longer edition, a translation of the text has been provided. Although a good portion of the chronicle is easy to read, certain sections remain obscure. Translating such passages will, it may be hoped, clarify them or at least stimulate discussion as to alternative meanings. Moreover, this text, although unreliable in its chronology and full of unexplained allusions, contains a wealth of material which deserves to be better known both to Islamic historians of the Jazīra and of the late Saljuq empire and to Western historians interested in the Muslim world at the time of the First Crusade and the establishment of Frankish power in the Near East.

The translation is accompanied by a detailed commentary which sets out to explain some of the background to the text. The *Tārīkh Mayyāfāriqīn wa Āmid* presents many unfamiliar place-names and numerous references to little-known people, and the footnotes of the commentary attempt to clarify some of this problematic material. They also discuss the better-known episodes of the period by a comparison with other contemporary sources.

This book began as a Ph.D. thesis in the University of Edinburgh.[6]

4. C. Cahen, "Le Diyār Bakr au temps des premiers Urtuḳides", *Journal Asiatique* CCXXVII (1935), 219-76. Cf. also M. Canard, who gives an extract from Ibn al-Azraq's text in his *Sayf al-daula: Recueil de textes* (Algiers, 1934), 284-5.
5. B.A.L.ʿAwaḍ, rev. M.S. Ghorbal, *Tārīkh al-Fāriqī* (Cairo, 1959).
6. Those chapters of the original thesis which have formed the basis of separate articles already published have been omitted from this book. Cf. C. Hillenbrand, "Some medieval Islamic approaches to source material", *Oriens* 27-28 (1981), 197-225; *eadem*, "The career of Najm al-Dīn İl-Ghāzī", *Der Islam* 58/2 (1981), 250-292; *eadem*, "The establishment of Artuqid power in Diyār Bakr in the twelfth century", *Studia Islamica* LIV (1981), 129-53. The one remaining unpublished chapter in the thesis deals with the language of Ibn al-Azraq and will appear in print separately in due course.

Since its completion in 1979 a number of important new studies on related subjects have appeared and information from these has been included in the present work. Eddé's book is a mine of information on Northern Syria[7] and Ilisch's study of the later Artuqids, although its scope is well outside the purview of this book, illuminates a good many problems, especially those of a topographical nature, raised by the text of Ibn al-Azraq.[8]

ii) The Near East at the beginning of the twelfth century

At the beginning of the twelfth century, the Near Eastern world was in disarray.[9] The Saljuq dynasty, which had ruled the eastern Islamic world since 447/1055, was no longer as strong or as centralised as it had been. Weaknesses inherent in the Saljuq system of government - which was based on the divisive principle of family rule - had become more blatant and debilitating since the deaths in quick succession of Niẓām al-Mulk and Sulṭān Malikshāh in 485/1092-3. Petty scions of the Saljuq family, whose power was concentrated in such key cities of Syria as Damascus and Aleppo as well as Akhlāṭ, Mārdīn and Mayyāfāriqīn in eastern Anatolia, were being replaced or manipulated by ambitious Turkish *amīrs* who served as their *atābegs* and then seized power for themselves.

The Saljuqs had been engaged, ever since their assumption of supreme power, in a long struggle with the Ismā'īlī Shī'ite rulers of Egypt, the Fāṭimids. This conflict was both ideological and territorial, and the main theatre of war had been Syria and Palestine. The situation in this area was further complicated from the first decade of the sixth/twelfth century onwards by the presence of the Assassins, the breakaway group of the Ismā'īlīs who had seceded from the Fāṭimids after the death of al-Mustanṣir in 487/1094. Their power rested not only on an extensive network of castles but also on their covert or open supporters in the cities. Although they were numerically small,

7. A.M. Eddé, *'Izz al-Dīn Ibn Šaddād. Description de la Syrie du Nord* (Damascus, 1982).
8. *L. Ilisch, Geschichte der Artuqidenherrschaft von Mardin zwischen Mamluken und Mongolen 1260-1410 A.D.* (Münster, 1984).
9. For a detailed background to the historical situation in the Near East at this time, cf. C.E. Bosworth, "The political and dynastic history of the Iranian world (A.D. 1000-1217)", in *The Cambridge History of Iran, 5. The Saljuq and Mongol Periods*, ed. J.A.Boyle (Cambridge, 1968), 1-202.

the Assassins wielded disproportionately large influence on the politics of Syria and the Jazīra, as well as further east, working as much by threats and pressure behind the scenes as by outright assassination.

These dissensions within the Islamic world contributed to the ease with which the Crusaders, who had set out in 1096 for the Holy Land, captured Jerusalem from the Fāṭimids in 492/1099.[10] The Crusaders quickly set up a series of small principalities centred on cities like Jerusalem and Edessa. There then began a steady and complicated power struggle both within Crusader ranks and with the rival Muslim rulers in Northern Syria. Aleppo, in particular, became a major focal point for both Muslim and Christian territorial ambitions.

Byzantium had been seriously weakened by its defeat at Saljuq hands in 464/1071 at Manzikert on its eastern borders. Thereafter the process of nomadic infiltration had intensified and eastern Anatolia was divided up amongst rival nomadic Turcoman *amīrs* who subjected it to a long period of anarchy and devastation. On the north-eastern border of the Saljuq empire another Christian state, Georgia, had profited from Byzantine and Armenian weakness to consolidate its political power and even to extend its territories at the expense of its Christian neighbours. It now entered a new phase of internal stability and revived national sentiment. These factors, coupled with the decline of Saljuq power, encouraged the Georgians to adopt a new policy of aggression towards their Muslim neighbours after the death of Malikshāh in 485/1092. King David the Restorer (1089-1125) had by the end of his reign substantially extended the frontiers of Georgia, and Georgian troops were a power to be reckoned with even in distant Jerusalem.

In the heart of Mesopotamia were situated the last bastions of the Arab Bedouin dynasties who had wielded considerable power in Syria and the Jazīra more than a century before. The 'Uqailids held a few citadels on the Euphrates while the Mazyadids were based at Ḥilla. The decline of Saljuq power offered the Bedouin dynasties a last chance to retrieve their former fortunes, and their proximity to Baghdad favoured this ambition. Nevertheless, their power base was too limited for them to strike out independently. Thus they sought to exercise power and retain their autonomy by setting up a complex system of alliances directed against the Saljuqs. The Mazyadid Dubais b. Ṣadaqa was to be a thorn in the side of successive Saljuq *sulṭāns;* but with his death in 529/1135 the political power of the Bedouin in this period was extinguished.

10. The Fāṭimids had within recent memory held the city for only a year, having taken it from the Saljuqs in 491/1098.

Within the heartland of the Saljuq empire, the caliphate at Baghdad was beginning to enjoy a greatly improved status after the low ebb which it had reached in the Būyid period. The well-known Sunnī religious revival, whose roots may be traced in that period, had reached fruition under the Saljuqs and its impetus was felt long after. It was during the reign of an astute and vigorous caliph, al-Mustarshid (512-529/1118-35), that the first signs of resurgent caliphal power appeared. This power was centred on Baghdad and is better defined as that of a small, geographically circumscribed principality than as a pan-Islamic force.

It is against this background of political fragmentation and turbulence that the achievements of the first two Artuqid rulers of Mārdīn and Mayyāfāriqīn, İl-Ghāzī and Temür-Tash, as related in the chronicle of Ibn al-Azraq al-Fāriqī, must be evaluated.

iii) The life of Ibn al-Azraq al-Fāriqī

A certain amount of autobiographical information is given by the author in the *Tārīkh Mayyāfāriqīn wa Āmid.* He was born in 510/1116-7[11] and died some time after 572/1176-7. He began travelling around neighbouring territories in 529/1134-5.[12] In 531/1136-7 he was in the Jazīra and whilst at Naṣībīn saw Zangī.[13] He visited Baghdad several times, once in 534/1139-40 when he lived there for six months and studied with some of the prominent *'ulamā'* of his time.[14]

Ibn al-Azraq held administrative posts of some importance. He was *mutawallī ishrāf al-waqf* - supervisor of charitably endowed property - outside Mayyāfāriqīn in 543/1148-9.[15] In the previous year he must have been in the employ of the Artuqid ruler Temür-Tash, since he mentions how in 542/1147-8 he went to al-Ma'dan to buy copper for Temür-Tash to mint coins.[16] Again in 562/1166-7 he was in charge of charitably endowed property in Mayyāfāriqīn,[17] an office which he

11. F. 160a.
12. F. 167b.
13. F. 168a.
14. F. 169a.
15. F. 174a.
16. F. 172b.
17. F. 190b.

held a year later at Damascus.[18] Ibn al-Azraq visited Georgia in 548/1153-4 and worked for its king, Dimitri.[19]

So far as his literary output is concerned, Ibn al-Azraq appears to have written only the *Tārīkh Mayyāfāriqīn wa Āmid*. For this chronicle he wrote two texts, one in 560/1164-5 and the other, a more extended version of the first, in 572/1176-7. It seems reasonable to assume that Ibn al-Azraq was not an important personality in his own right. He was certainly not considered as such by later biographers. Ibn Khallikān, who uses the work of Ibn al-Azraq extensively in his famous biographical dictionary, sees no need to grant Ibn al-Azraq even a few lines in his lists of famous men.

The *Tārīkh Mayyāfāriqīn wa Āmid* gives several hints as to its author's religious, political and ethnic background. The exact religious allegiance of Ibn al-Azraq is difficult to determine. Minorsky describes him as having "pro-Alid inclinations"[20] but he gives no corroborative evidence for this assertion. In fact, this view would appear to be wrong. Ibn al-Azraq relates in some detail Temür-Tash's brief but energetic flirtation with Ismā'īlī beliefs, but he is at pains to underline the eventual disenchantment of his master and the loss of public approval experienced by the Ismā'īlī *shaikh*.[21] Moreover, Ibn al-Azraq mentions with obvious pride his own contact at Baghdad with the moṣt prominent Shāfi'ite *'ulamā'* of his time, stating that he studied works of *fiqh* with them.[22] Most probably, the author favours Sunnī beliefs but is no great proselytiser. Only on one occasion does he make an explicit statement in favour of the 'Abbāsid caliphate and that is when he is denouncing the Fāṭimids.[23] It would be unwise to make much of this statement, for such denunciations were often voiced by Sunnī historians when dealing with Shī'ite history.

Politically, the views of Ibn al-Azraq are biased primarily in favour of the Artuqids. His attitude towards the Saljuq *sulṭān* Mas'ūd and the three 'Abbāsid caliphs who set out to oppose him remains unclear. The Almohads are treated without the venom poured on them by Ibn al-Qalānisī[24], but no significant inferences should be drawn from a probably borrowed narrative which Ibn al-Azraq seems barely to have understood.

18. F. 191b.
19. F. 161b.
20. Minorsky, *Sharvān and Darband*, 170.
21. F. 171b.
22. F. 169a.
23. F. 164a.
24. *Dhail*, 291-3.

It is difficult to ascertain the linguistic and ethnic background of Ibn al-Azraq. A wide variety of languages - Turkish, Syriac, Armenian, Kurdish and Arabic - were spoken in Diyār Bakr in the sixth/twelfth century. An analysis of the language of the text reveals that the author's grounding in classical Arabic was poor, but that was not particularly unusual at the time when he wrote. It seems unlikely that Ibn al-Azraq knew Syriac since he mentions that he needed a Syriac text translated for him before he could include it in his history.[25] His ethnic origin can therefore be narrowed down no further than one of the following possibilities: Kurdish, Armenian, Arab or Turkish. The evidence permits no definite conclusion, although the fact that Ibn Khallikān gives him the Muslim names of Aḥmad b. Yūsuf b. 'Alī suggests that he was not an Armenian.

iv) The historiographical value of Ibn al-Azraq's chronicle

a) Twelfth-century Arabic chronicles on Northern Syria and the Jazīra

There is a notable dearth of roughly contemporary historical chronicles written in Arabic which cover the period 1100-50 in Northern Syria and the Jazīra. The thirteenth and fourteenth centuries abound in histories which deal with this important time-span and so provide valuable information for Islamic and Crusader historians alike. But such well-known chronicles as those of Ibn al-Athīr and Ibn al-'Adīm, who wrote in the thirteenth century, relate and interpret the events which occurred a hundred years earlier from the vantage point of their own age. They inevitably distort or change their sources to accord with attitudes prevalent in their own society.[26]

It is because they provide a contemporary perspective on the period 1100-50 that the work of Ibn al-Qalānisī[27] and to a much lesser extent the fragmentary chronicle of al-'Aẓīmī[28] are so valuable. This does not imply, of course, that these two writers did not harbour their own

25. 'Awaḍ, *op.cit.,* 35; Ms.A, f. 7b.
26. Cf. Gibb's analysis of the way in which Ibn al-Athīr uses the work of Ibn al-Qalānisī (H.A.R. Gibb, "Notes on the Arabic Materials for the History of the Early Crusades", *Bulletin of the School of Oriental Studies* VII [1933-5], 739-54).
27. *Op.cit.*
28. C. Cahen, "La chronique abrégée d'al-'Aẓīmī", *Journal Asiatique* CCXXX (1938), 353-448.

prejudices and interpretations of events, but at least they reflect an aspect of contemporary opinion. It is of course crucial for an understanding of the period 1100-50 to be able to discern what their personal attitudes may have been.

Between the work of Ibn al-Qalānisī and al-'Aẓīmī, both of whom wrote in the first half of the twelfth century, and the great surge of historical works produced a hundred years or so later, there is a serious gap in published Arabic chronicles. It is a pity that the work of the Shī'ite historian of Aleppo, Ibn Abī Ṭayyi', is lost. Some of his accounts of the period 1100-50 are known from extensive acknowledged quotations found in the work of the fourteenth-century historian Ibn al-Furāt (died 807/1405) whose important history is gradually receiving the scholarly attention it deserves.[29]

The chronicle of Ibn al-Azraq, part of which forms the subject of this book, was written around the year 572/1176-7 and deals with the area of the Jazīra and Northern Syria. It thus provides a vital historiographical bridge between the chronicles of Ibn al-Qalānisī and al-'Aẓīmī on the one hand, and the great later historians of the thirteenth and fourteenth centuries on the other. In conjunction with the excerpts from Ibn Abī Ṭayyi' available in Ibn al-Furāt, the work of Ibn al-Azraq gives valuable new insights into the period 1100-50 in the Near East. The aftermath of the First Crusade, the initial stirrings of the Muslim counter-crusade, the gradual resurgence of the caliphate as a political force and the power struggles amongst the Saljuqs are only a few of the themes put in a fresh light by this hitherto under-exploited chronicle.

b) Relevant factors governing the selection of material from the Tārīkh Mayyāfāriqīn wa Āmid

The portion of the history of Ibn al-Azraq translated and discussed below is taken from those folios which deal with the years 1100-50. This selection is motivated by several considerations. It is well known that Muslim historians built upon the work of their predecessors whom they quoted and plagiarised as a matter of course. Whilst the early parts of the chronicle of Ibn al-Azraq are derivative, the author

29. Ibn al-Furāt, *Tārīkh al-Duwal wa'l-Mulūk*, Oesterreichische Nationalbibliothek, Vienna, Ms. A.F 118 (Flügel 814), II. Cf also the recent unpublished thesis of M.F. Elshayyal who edited the years 522-543 A.H. of Ibn al-Fūrat's history: *A critical edition of volume II of Tārīkh al-Duwal wa'l-Mulūk by Muḥammad b. 'Abd al-Raḥīm b. 'Alī Ibn al-Furāt*, (Edinburgh, 1986).

includes much that is new and original in his description of the period 500-572 A.H. For these years he must have had access to archives dealing with local administration, whilst at the same time drawing on his own personal experiences and on first-hand eye-witness accounts of important events.

Ibn al-Azraq treats the Marwānid dynasty in interesting detail in his chronicle. This part of the text is not included in the present book since it has been well edited by 'Awaḍ and analysed in some detail by Amedroz and more recently by me.[30] Instead, those folios which deal with the rule of the first two Artuqid rulers have been selected; these cover approximately the period 1100-50. The final part of the text, which describes the reign of Najm al-Dīn Alpï, the third Artuqid ruler, has been omitted from the present book. This is prompted partly by reasons of length but also by the fact that the material in the history of Ibn al-Azraq which has wider relevance to scholars of Islamic and Crusader history is found almost invariably in the period 1100-50. The folios of the *Tārīkh Mayyāfāriqīn wa Āmid* which describe the years 1150-70 are essentially local in their focus and chronicle a process familiar throughout medieval Islam, namely the attempt of a minor ruler to establish a dynasty. Moreover, Ibn al-Azraq shows in these folios an even greater preoccupation with minor administrative details and lists of officials.

Scholars have made little use of the section of Ibn al-Azraq's text which deals with the period 1100-50. In 1935 Cahen published a long article[31] on the early Artuqids in which he relied heavily on Ibn al-Azraq for his outline of the events preceding the establishment of Artuqid rule in the area of Mārdīn and Mayyāfāriqīn. Apart from Cahen's valuable but necessarily limited article, the only other serious attempt to exploit this section of the *Tārīkh Mayyāfāriqīn wa Āmid* is Minorsky's well-known analysis of the visit made by Ibn al-Azraq to Georgia. Finally, ff. 160b-200a of Ms. A and the corresponding section of Ms. B have been edited as separate texts, and given a brief introduction by A. Savran. This work, entitled *A critical edition of the Artuqid section in Tārīkh Mayyāfāriqīn wa Āmid*, was awarded a Ph.D. thesis by the University of St Andrews in 1975. It remains unpublished.

c) The historical value of the Tārīkh Mayyāfāriqīn wa Āmid

This chronicle presents a range of historical material from the

30. Amedroz, *op. cit.*, 785-812; "Marwānids", EI^2.
31. Cahen, " Le Diyār Bakr."

twelfth century. It contains a wealth of local detail - political, prosopographical and topographical - which is of great value to the historian of the Jazīra during a period when information is scanty. Indeed, Ibn al-Azraq's chronicle would appear to be the sole contemporary source for the history of the Artuqid dynasty in Mārdīn and Mayyāfāriqīn.[32] The chronicle also provides the first known genealogy of the Artuqids, and its information in this respect is uniquely full and detailed.

In its description of the careers of the first two Artuqids at Mayyāfāriqīn, the chronicle provides insights into the process whereby Turcoman power waxed in eastern Anatolia at the expense of the Saljuqs in Western Iran and Iraq. Specifically, there may be discerned in the careers of İl-Ghāzī and Temür-Tash the transition from the ambitious military leader, prepared to travel vast distances in search of new lands to conquer, to the more modest aspirations of a petty ruler concerned principally to retain what territory he has.

For the historian of the Crusades, Ibn al-Azraq gives important information not found elsewhere on the careers of two of the key military figures of the time, İl-Ghāzī and Zangī. He also provides fresh material on the early career of Nūr al-Dīn. The details on Zangī are especially informative besides providing a valuable foil to the pro-Zangid bias shown by Ibn al-Athīr in his *History of the Atābegs of Mosul.*

The social and economic import of the picturesque episodes of Georgian history contained in Ibn al-Azraq's work has already been emphasized by Minorsky. This unexpected excursus into Georgian affairs supplements the *Georgian Chronicle* used so extensively by Brosset in his monumental history of Georgia.

Of critical importance are the sections of Ibn al-Azraq's work which deal with three late 'Abbāsid caliphs - al-Mustarshid, al-Rāshid and al-Muqtafī - and their relationship with the Saljuq *sulṭān,* Mas'ūd. This part of his text, which consists of several very extended eye-witness accounts culled from Ibn al-Anbārī - one of the principal protagonists in the events themselves - does not appear to be in any other extant source contemporary with Ibn al-Azraq's work. These passages illuminate a crucial historical issue: the exact nature and extent of caliphal power in the twelfth century. In Ibn al-Azraq's pages are to be found, expressed with crystal clarity in the reported words of Sulṭān Mas'ūd, the attitudes of a late Saljuq *sulṭān* to the caliphal institution he was sworn to defend - attitudes which in nearly all other sources must be deduced from the course of the events

32. In his historical geography of these two cities Ibn Shaddād copied Ibn al-Azraq *verbatim.*

themselves. Ibn al-Azraq also shows how these three caliphs attempted to resist the blueprint of purely spiritual authority which Mas'ūd sought to impose on them. The well-known resurgence of the caliphate under al-Nāṣir later in the twelfth century[33] is thus seen in a new perspective.

The *Tārīkh Mayyāfāriqīn wa Āmid* also contains some material on Fāṭimid Egypt and on North Africa. The extracts from the text which deal with the Fāṭimids consist mostly of short unexceptionable obituaries of rulers, but there is one longer passage which is an interesting reflection of contemporary attitudes and stresses the orthodoxy of the 'Abbāsid caliphate whilst denouncing Fāṭimid claims. The long excursus on the history of the Maghrib, which deals with Ibn Tūmart and 'Abd al-Mu'min and the rise of the Almohad dynasty, is unexpected and inappropriate in a town chronicle of the Jazīra. Its equally incongruous presence in the local Syrian history of Ibn al-Qalānisī suggests that both historians lifted the material wholesale from another source where its exact context is a matter for speculation but where presumably it made much better sense. Although wildly inaccurate and garbled, this account by Ibn al-Azraq deserves some attention and comparison with other treatments of the same subject by Ibn al-Athīr[34] and Ibn al-Qalānisī.[35]

To summarize, then, it is clear that the *Tārīkh Mayyāfāriqīn wa Āmid*, despite its format of a city chronicle, has a surprisingly wide geographical and historical range. In addition to being the prime source for the history of the twelfth century in the Jazīra, and more especially of the Artuqid dynasty, Ibn al-Azraq's work sheds light on the major historical processes of the late Saljuq period, such as the growth of the atabegate, particularly under Zangī, the rise of minor Turcoman dynasties at the expense of Saljuq power and the revival of caliphal authority. Ibn al-Azraq is not a great historian; but the portion of his text translated and analysed below presents much new and wide-ranging material. This fact is underlined by the enthusiastic plagiarism of some parts of the work by later - and far better - Muslim historians, such as Ibn Wāṣil and Ibn al-Furāt.[36]

33. Cf. H. Mason, *Two Statesmen of Mediaeval Islam* (The Hague and Paris, 1972), 69-134; A. Hartmann, *An-Nāṣir li-Dīn Allāh (1180-1225). Politik, Religion, Kultur in der späten 'Abbāsidenzeit* (Berlin, 1975).
34. *Al-Kāmil fi'l-Tārīkh*, ed. C.J. Tornberg (Leiden and Uppsala, 1851-76), X, 400-14.
35. *Dhail*, 291-3.
36. Ilisch suggests that the lost history of Āmid written by the Artuqid vizier Sharaf al-Dīn Ismā'īl, known as Ibn Tītī (died 673/1274-5), may well have been a continuation of the chronicle of Ibn al-Azraq (*op.cit*, 11).

d) Ibn al-Azraq as a historian

Ibn al-Azraq set out to write an annalistic chronicle, in which events are related in roughly chronological sequence. In comparison with other medieval historians, however, and most relevantly his contemporary Ibn al-Qalānisī, Ibn al-Azraq's work is disordered and inaccurate. Major historical events are given wrong dates,[37] some episodes are treated twice under different[38] years with conflicting dates, and in general the work displays an inadequate grasp of genealogies and names.[39] These criticisms apply especially to the author's treatment of foreign material. Here it is evident that he understands only partially the information available to him. This is particularly true in his accounts of North African and Egyptian history. Even such well-known events as İl-Ghāzī's victory over Roger of Antioch at Balāṭ in 513/1119, or the murder of Maudūd at Damascus in 507, are treated briefly and elliptically, without care or comprehension.

The later section of the *Tārīkh Mayyāfāriqīn wa Āmid* is an account of Artuqid rule in Diyār Bakr. This is presented in the form of scraps of information with occasionally more detailed treatment of certain topics. Interspersed with this Artuqid material are isolated snippets of non-local subject-matter, usually about the Fāṭimids, and several extremely long anecdotes dealing with the author's own experiences, whether in Georgia or Baghdad. This uneasy juxtaposition of detailed anecdotes with successive gobbets of information is characteristic. It produces a very uneven, unco-ordinated narrative.

It is quickly apparent that the selection of historical material for inclusion in this chronicle has not been the result of a conscious, deliberate process of sifting. On the contrary, Ibn al-Azraq has used whatever material happened to be available to him.[40] It would of course be unrealistic to expect a medieval historian to interpret the

37. E.g. the death of al-Afḍal is recorded by Ibn al-Azraq as 517/1123-4 instead of 515/1121-2 (f. 162b). Similar examples abound in the text.
38. Ibn al-Azraq gives the date of the death of the Saljuq *malik,* Riḍwān, as 505/1111-2 ('Awaḍ, *op. cit.,* 278) and then later as 515/1121-2 (f. 162a). In fact, the usual date given is 507/1113-4 (Ibn al-Qalānisī, *Dhail,* 189; Ibn al-'Adīm, *Bughyat al-ṭalab fī tārīkh Ḥalab*, ed. A. Sevim [Ankara, 1976], 164).
39. E.g. the genealogy of the Saljuqs of Aleppo (f. 161a). Cf. also the confusion between Sukmān b. Artuq and Sukmān al-Quṭbī of Akhlāṭ.
40. Hence the extended treatment of the Tiflīs campaign of İl-Ghāzī in 515/1121-2 (ff. 161a-162b), details of which Ibn al-Azraq learned in Georgia.

events he records. It is rare to find a chronicler who is aware of the wider historical context of the events he sets down or of the implications of those events. Truly interpretative comments are rarer still. Ibn al-Azraq, however, compares unfavourably with many other medieval historians, even when judged by the standards of his own time. He lacks the perspicacity of Ibn al-ʻAdīm, Ibn al-Qalānisī or Ibn al-Athīr. Worse than this, Ibn al-Azraq repeatedly makes contradictory statements on important issues. In one part of his text he writes that the Ismāʻīlīs killed the caliphs al-Mustarshid and al-Rāshid. Later on, he lays the blame for these two murders at the door of Sulṭān Masʻūd. At no time does Ibn al-Azraq seem to see the need to adjudicate between these two mutually incompatible accounts.

Quite apart from his alarming chronological inaccuracies, Ibn al-Azraq biases his testimony heavily in favour of the Artuqids - especially Temür-Tash, in whose service he worked for a while. Even within the limited area of local rivalries, Ibn al-Azraq condemns the aggressive territorial ambitions of the Artuqid ruler of Ḥiṣn Kaifā, Dā'ūd, whilst similar actions on the part of Dā'ūd's cousin, the less bellicose Temür-Tash, are recorded without comment or on occasion with laudatory remarks.

Given his pronounced pro-Artuqid bias, Ibn al-Azraq's account of the humiliating defeat inflicted on İl-Ghāzī by the Georgian king, David the Restorer, is especially significant. Here the author's desire to make use of original information from eye-witness accounts prevails over his desire to please the Artuqid family and in this particular case he has produced a rare, valuable and probably reliable narrative.[41]

Ibn al-Azraq views history primarily from the vantage point of his home in Diyār Bakr. He therefore accords space and time to purely local matters. This is especially the case when he is dealing with the reign of Temür-Tash, a period when a more stable government existed and for which documentation was more copious. Within this category of historical information his narrative, which includes long lists of officials and descriptions of local events, such as the building of bridges, is probably quite accurate and may well be based on documentary material to which he would have had access as a bureaucrat.

The inclusion of the extended episodes dealing with the ʻAbbāsid caliphate is a break with the predominantly local focus of the *Tārīkh Mayyāfāriqīn wa Āmid*. As with some of the other idiosyncratic choices

41. Ibn al-Qalānisī, by contrast, who is far more aware of the wider issues involved, attempts to gloss over the extent of İl-Ghāzī's defeat (*op.cit.*, 204-5).

of material in this work, it is likely that the episodes set in Baghdad were not part of the original plan of the work. They seem rather to flow naturally from his pen because they spring from his own first-hand experiences.

These exceptional passages apart, it is clear that even in the main body of the text, which deals with those local events in Diyār Bakr which would have been most familiar to Ibn al-Azraq, there is a wide variation in the quality and insight of his historical writing. He is prepared to permit major disproportions to occur in the amount of detail he devotes to successive periods. An important decade may be glossed over in a few sentences, while ten uneventful years may have their trivia carefully chronicled. Thus the reign of İl-Ghāzī, which extended c. 500-516 A.H./1106-23, is covered only partially by Ibn al-Azraq. There are significant lacunae in his knowledge and he is particularly ignorant about the role played by İl-Ghāzī in the affairs of Aleppo. Ibn al-Azraq views İl-Ghāzī primarily as the ruler of Mayyāfāriqīn and barely alludes to the fact that for a time İl-Ghāzī was also lord of Mārdīn, most of Diyār Bakr and Aleppo too, and thus one of the great warlords of his time. By contrast, the reign of İl-Ghāzī's son, Temür-Tash - a virtual nonentity in comparison with his father - is treated by Ibn al-Azraq with greater confidence and detail.

It is important to refer to omissions on the part of Ibn al-Azraq. As mentioned elsewhere,[42] this chronicler of the Jazīra fails to make even passing allusions to important processes to which the area was subjected during his lifetime. For example, the impact of the nomadic presence is barely mentioned; nor are the preoccupations of the predominantly Christian population in the cities of Mayyāfāriqīn and Mārdīn discussed. These omissions are, of course, not unusual in the chronicle of a medieval Muslim historian; but in a border area such as eastern Anatolia, which forms much of the geographical setting of his chronicle, the absence of such material is all the more regrettable for the modern scholar.

However, despite his obvious short-comings as a historian and his marked inferiority in comparison with chroniclers roughly contemporary with himself, Ibn al-Azraq presents subject-matter with an intrinsic historical interest which overrides its unsatisfactory presentation.

42. Cf. C. Hillenbrand, "The History of the Jazīra, 1100-1250: A Short Introduction", in *The art of Syria and the Jazīra 1100-1250*, ed. J. Raby (Oxford, 1985), 16-17.

v) The title of Ibn al-Azraq's work

Both manuscripts of Ibn al-Azraq's chronicle lack folios at the beginning and end of the text, where the title of the work, the names of the author and scribes and the dates of composition and copying would probably be found. Fortunately, Ibn Shaddād in his historical geography of the Jazīra (Marsh 333) gives the full name of the author as Aḥmad b. Yūsuf b. 'Alī b. al-Azraq and the title of the work as the *Tārīkh Mayyāfāriqīn wa Āmid.*[43] Ibn Khallikān calls it the *Tārīkh Mayyāfāriqīn.*[44]

vi) Description of the manuscripts

There are two extant copies of the *Tārīkh Mayyāfāriqīn wa Āmid.* Both are in the British Library.

BL. Or. 5803 (hereafter referred to as Manuscript A)

This is the longer and larger of the two manuscripts. The pages edited below usually have 23 lines;[45] each measures about 17.5 cm x 12.5 cm. The manuscript is written in black ink on yellow paper. New sections of the text are marked by titles written in larger letters. The manuscript is written in a fine hand and is provided with vowels and diacritical points. There is ample evidence that alterations were made to the manuscript after it was copied. It contains a large number of marginal additions or corrections, deletions in the text and intercalations. In many places the text is illegible or difficult to decipher, as some words or even whole lines are now completely obliterated. A further problem is caused by the punctuation. The scribe often places the dots or vowel markings in the wrong place or where they are not needed at all. The manuscript contains two hundred folios. Its first few folios are missing. It is highly probable that some of the last folios are lost too, since it comes to an abrupt end.

43. Marsh 333, ff. 796 and 816.
44. Ibn Khallikān, *Kitāb Wafayāt al-A'yān*, tr. de Slane (Paris and London, 1843-7) I, 158.
45. Not 22, as stated by Amedroz (*op. cit.*, 785). Although the number of lines in the earlier part of the manuscript varies, from f. 120b onwards the pages contain 23 lines. The only exceptions are ff. 173a-b which have 22 lines.

In Ms.A, the material is presented within a chronological framework. The missing folios at the beginning probably contained a history of the early Islamic period, since the work actually begins with an account of 'Umar's caliphate. This is followed by a description of the founding of the city of Mayyāfāriqīn.[46] The next folios deal with the successive periods in the history of Diyār Bakr and of the caliphate and include a detailed account of the Ḥamdānid dynasty.[47] The history of 'Aḍud al-Daula and the subsequent rule in Diyār Bakr of Bādh the Kurd follows. Ibn al-Azraq then gives an account of the Marwānid dynasty and of the chaotic years between their downfall and the establishment of Artuqid power.[48] The remainder of the text consists of a detailed description of the history of the early Artuqids. The manuscript ends around the death of Najm al-Dīn Alpï in 572/1176-7. Folios 160b - 178b cover the reigns of İl-Ghāzī and Temür-Tash. It is these folios which are edited, translated and analysed in this book.

The subject-matter of Ms.A is more detailed than that of Ms.B and contains material which is restricted to the history of Diyār Bakr. This non-local subject-matter usually consists of obituary notices of Fāṭimid and other rulers and isolated snippets of information which are often inserted in the wrong place chronologically or in the middle of a totally unrelated episode. Sometimes such non-local material is repeated, without comment, under different dates. For the period of Temür-Tash's rule, Ibn al-Azraq frequently uses details from his own experience or has access to eye-witness accounts of historical events. Hence, no doubt, the more extended treatment which he accords to certain episodes in this period.[49]

Amedroz states that the date of the composition of this manuscript is 572 A.H.[50] without explaining how he arrived at this conclusion. 'Awaḍ, on the contrary, is unnecessarily indecisive, asserting that "no definite clues have been found which would lead to a correct

46. Ff. 7b-12b.
47. Ff. 12b-121b. The rise of the Ḥamdānids begins on f. 110a.
48. This is the section of Ibn al-Azraq's work which was edited by 'Awaḍ (ff. 121b-160b). Cf. also the article "Marwānids", *EI*[2].
49. The process can be noted at the end of the previous reign in the Tiflīs campaign of İl-Ghāzī which occupies ff. 161a-162b. Falling within the reign of Temür-Tash are the accounts of the 'Abbāsid caliphs, al-Mustarshid and al-Rāshid, which take up much of ff. 164b-167b. This is followed by a long excursus into the history of the Maghrib (ff. 168a-169a).
50. *Op.cit.*, 785.

answer."[51] In fact there are several clues in the text. On f.177a, Ibn al-Azraq mentions that Nūr al-Dīn Muḥammad "is now in power". This ruler succeeded his father Qara Arslan at Ḥiṣn Kaifā in 562/1166-7 and ruled until 581/1185-6. A little later, Ibn al-Azraq mentions the death of Shīrbārīk in 566/1170-1[52] and Balak b. Arslan Ṭoghmish b. Bektash who became an ascetic in (5)67/1171-2. On the evidence of these three references, it may be postulated that the manuscript was written in the reign of Nūr al-Dīn Muḥammad, some time between 567 and 581.

But the date of composition can be narrowed down further than this. The latest date mentioned by Ibn al-Azraq in the Artuqid section of Ms.A is found under the account of the reign of Najm al-Dīn Alpï, where the author states that he was at Akhlāṭ in 571/1175-6.[53] In another part of the text edited here Ibn al-Azraq, speaking of Arslan-Shāh b. Ṭoghrïl, states that "he is now *sulṭān* of the area from Iṣfahān ... up to the city of Ganja ... .[54] Arslan-Shāh died in Jumādā II 571/December-January 1175-6.[55] This evidence indicates that Ibn al-Azraq was well-advanced in the writing of the text by the early part of 571. The work was still unfinished in 572, however, since almost at the very beginning of his whole text he inserts the rulers of Mayyāfāriqīn up to his own time, which he gives here as 572/1176-7.[56] This last piece of evidence is presumably the basis of Amedroz' dating. From the evidence provided here it is probably safe to conclude that the final version of Ms.A was composed in the years 571/1175-6 and 572/1176-7.

It is not certain when and where the manuscript was copied. Amedroz, again without supporting evidence, states that it was probably copied at Damascus in the seventh century A.H.[57] 'Awaḍ, on the other hand, is justifiably unwilling to commit himself to a date for the copying but says that Mayyāfāriqīn would have been the most likely place.[58] Some version of Ibn al-Azraq's longer manuscript was certainly available to writers such as Ibn Khallikān, Sibṭ Ibn al-Jauzī and Ibn Wāṣil, all of whom wrote in the second half of the seventh

51. *Op.cit.*, 21.
52. F. 177b.
53. F.200a.
54. Ff. 163b-164a.
55. Rāwandī, *Rāḥat al-Ṣudūr wa Āyat al-Surūr*, ed. M. Iqbāl, (London, 1921), 301.
56. F. 7b.
57. *Op.cit.*, 785.
58. *Op.cit.*, 23.

century A.H.[59] Since none of these writers was based in Mayyāfāriqīn it seems a fair assumption that the manuscript was already extant in several copies by the early seventh/thirteenth century.

BL. Or. 6310 (hereafter referred to as Manuscript B)

This manuscript is shorter than Ms.A. It consists of 138 folios. Each page has 10 lines. The manuscript is written in black ink on yellow paper. It is to a great extent devoid of diacritical points or vowel markings. The pages of the manuscript are about half the size of those in Ms.A. Although deletions and corrections have been made to this manuscript, such features are not as frequent as in Ms.A. The first 31 folios are no longer legible. From the remainder of the text it is clear that the scribe had a better grasp of Arabic orthography than his counterpart for Ms.A. Whilst Ms.B displays a number of unusual grammatical and orthographical features, it is more carefully written than Ms.A.

Like Ms.A, this manuscript adheres to the format of an annalistic chronicle in which events are presented under a given year. Ms.B contains a limited amount of non-local material but its scope is less general than Ms.A. Like Ms.A, this manuscript lacks both a beginning and an end. It begins with material dating from the reign of the 'Abbāsid caliph al-Muhtadī (255/868-9) and ends with the first part of the description of the rule of Najm al-Dīn Alpï. There is no account of the years 549-60/1154-65.

Ms.B was probably composed in 560/1164-5,[60] since on folio 94b the author speaks of the year in which he was writing as 560. It is not possible to ascertain the date of the copying of this manuscript. One fact is certain: Ms.B was available in some form to Ibn Shaddād in the second half of the seventh/thirteenth century, since he copied long sections from it for his historical geography of the Jazīra. This latter work is found in the Bodleian manuscript entitled Marsh 333, which was composed in 679/1280-1 and copied in 789/1387-8.[61]

vii) Notes on the map of the Jazīra

It is only to be expected that a city chronicle should have a predominantly local focus. The *Tārīkh Mayyāfāriqīn wa Āmid* is no

59. Cf. Hillenbrand, "Approaches".
60. It was Amedroz who first mentioned this fact and cited f. 94b as proof (*op.cit.*, 785).
61. Amedroz, *op.cit.*, 801.

exception in this respect. As a result the text abounds in topographical detail: names of obscure towns, villages and castles follow each other in quick succession. In order to clarify the geographical framework of the text as much as possible, a detailed map of Syria and the Jazīra has been prepared; this map extends also to southern Iraq, westernmost Iran and the fringes of the Caucasus. The aim of the map is that all the places mentioned by Ibn al-Azraq in the text edited here (except a few like Marāgha, Tiflīs, Iṣfahān and Ḥulwān which are outside the area specified) should be located on it, provided that their identification can be regarded as established. There seems to be no point in larding the map with names for which only hypothetical locations can be proposed. Frequently the context indicates the general area in which these castles and settlements may be found.

In the preparation of the map the single most useful source was M. Canard's monumental *Histoire de la dynastie des H'amdanides de Jazîra et de Syrie* (Paris, 1953). This was supplemented where appropriate by E. Honigmann, *Die Ostgrenze des byzantinischen Reiches* (Brussels, 1935), J. Markwart, *Südarmenien und die Tigrisquellen* (Vienna, 1930) and by the numerous maps in *A History of the Crusades*, ed. K. Setton and M.W. Baldwin (Madison, Milwaukee and London, from 1969 onwards).

viii) Introduction to the translation of the text

Preliminary comments

The translation of the edited text of Ibn al-Azraq has been kept as literal as possible. On the other hand, a wider range of words and sentence structures has been introduced than is present in the original Arabic since the translation would have been virtually unreadable if the repetitiveness, the restricted vocabulary and the syntactical form of the Arabic original had been transferred wholesale into English. In spite of his protestations to the contrary and his profuse apologies for his "literal" translation, Gibb's achievement with *The Damascus Chronicle of the Crusades*[62] provides a polished model for any translator of an Arabic chronicle to try to emulate.

The shortcomings and limitations of Ibn al-Azraq's "literary" style are apparent from a reading of almost any page taken at random. To translate his work into readable English perhaps endows it with a

62. H.A.R. Gibb, *The Damascus Chronicle of the Crusades* (London, 1932), 13-14.

certain elegance which is quite undeserved. The alternative, however, would be to produce a text as confusing and unco-ordinated in English as it is in the Arabic original.

In the translation provided below, the simplistic style of the Arabic has mostly been retained. From time to time, however, subordinate clauses introduced by temporal conjunctions have been used to vary the constant succession of short main clauses. On occasion, pronouns have been replaced by proper names in order to impose some clarity on obscure parts of the text.[63] Similarly, words such as "then" have sometimes been added to render the sequence of events more understandable.

In view of the fact that the material contained in Ms.B is also included in Ms.A, a translation of Ms.B has not been given here.[64]

Points of detail

1. The division of the translation into separate chapters is, like the paragraphing, purely arbitrary, but both features are added to make the text more readable.
2. Brackets are used to indicate explanatory words or phrases which are not found in the Arabic original.
3. Question-marks in brackets denote doubtful translations or readings of names. The use of this device has been kept to a minimum but its limited appearance has proved inevitable.
4. Well-known words such as vizier and caliph appear in their westernised forms. This also applies to famous cities such as Baghdad, Jerusalem, Edessa and Constantinople.
5. The transliteration of Turkish names written in Arabic script presents a major problem. In face of a wide divergence of treatments for such names, it has seemed best in this work, as noted earlier, to opt for the versions found in *The Cambridge History of Iran, Vol. 5* as a general guide. For names which do not occur there, the works of Sauvaget[65] and Houtsma[66] have been

63. Above all, such a procedure is necessary for an understanding of the genealogical account (Ms.A, ff. 177b-178b) and the excursus into the history of the Maghrib (Ms.A, ff. 168a-169a).
64. This is to be found, however, in Appendix C of the original thesis.
65. J. Sauvaget, "Noms et Surnoms de Mamelouks", *Journal Asiatique* CCXXXVIII (1950), 31-58.
66. M.T. Houtsma, *Ein türkisch-arabisches Glossar* (Leiden, 1894).

consulted. Reservations may be expressed about some of the versions of Turkish names found in *The Cambridge History of Iran*, and the attentive reader may note a few minor divergences from this "canon"; but at least, in the face of continuing scholarly controversy, an attempt at consistency has been made here by the almost wholesale adoption of one system. Considerable doubt remains over the correct rendering of a number of the Turkish names mentioned in the text of Ibn al-Azraq. Many of these given in the translation are therefore tentative.

6. Although many personal and place-names occur in unusual forms in the edition of the text, which is based primarily on Ms.A, the more usual form of a name has been written in the translation.

   e.g. Ṭogh-Tegin *not* Ṭoghr-Tegin
   Ṭoghrïl-Beg *not* Ṭoghr-Beg
   Dhu'l-Qarnain *not* Bi'l-Qarnain
   Bahmard *not* Bahmūd

   Many versions of the modern Harput are found in medieval sources. In this text the unusual form *Khartabirt* predominates and it has therefore been retained in the translation.

7. The numbering in the chapters of the translation refers to the detailed notes in the commentary. Genealogical tables and a map are provided at the end of this work.

8. Ibn al-Azraq does not divide up his material formally into years but his narrative does follow a rough chronological order. The years covered in the translation have been given according to both the Muslim and Christian systems. When a year is mentioned for the first time the information is provided in full; for example, "in the year 520 (27 January 1126 - 16 January 1127)." Thereafter the year is cited simply as 520 (1126-7). Specific days and months are given according to both calendars.

9. Like many of his contemporaries Ibn al-Azraq prefaces many of his reports with the word *qīla* ("it was said") without explicitly identifying his sources of information. In view of the frequency and the imprecision of this term in the context of his work, the word *qīla* has not been translated; but it is indicated by the sign ¶ in the translation. Reports introduced by the word *qīla* have been presented in a fresh paragraph.

ix) The edition of the text

a) Preliminary comments

The most important decision for any editor of the *Tārīkh Mayyāfāriqīn wa Āmid* is whether to present the two manuscripts as one text or to edit them separately. 'Awaḍ adopted the former method. Minorsky, on the other hand, recommended that the two manuscripts should be edited separately, possibly in two parallel columns, since in his view the material they treat is so divergent.[67] A close examination of the material covered by both manuscripts for the period under discussion in this thesis reveals that the shorter manuscript, Ms.B, does not contain information which is not included in the longer text, Ms.A. The detailed indices which are provided below for both manuscripts confirm this. It is true that Ms.B sometimes presents episodes or individual facts in a different order from Ms.A and very occasionally adds the odd isolated detail, but with this very minor exception it remains true that all the information in Ms.B can be located somewhere in Ms.A. Ms.A, on the other hand, contains material which is not found in Ms.B.

Minorsky's suggestion of two separate editions in parallel columns would thus result in an unnecessarily cumbersome work and would make the text difficult to read. It is therefore not the method used here. The idea of editing the two manuscripts one after the other has also been rejected after some thought. This method would be justified only if Ms.B contained significant differences from Ms.A. A long, careful study and a separate translation of both manuscripts reveal that this is not the case. A complete translation of the relevant section of Ms.B can be found in my unpublished Ph.D thesis (II, 519-60).

The method adopted for this edition, therefore, is the one used by 'Awaḍ for his edition of the earlier part of Ibn al-Azraq's text. Ms.A is taken as the main text. For whole areas of the work it is the only version available. Where Ms.B covers the same material, it is used for comparison and for the clarification of difficulties. Significant variants in the two manuscripts are mentioned in the footnotes to the edition.

The edition of the *Tārīkh Mayyāfāriqīn wa Āmid* presented in this book covers Ms.A, ff.160b-178b and Ms.B, ff.100b-138b. The unpublished work of the historical geographer Ibn Shaddād on the Jazīra, entitled *al-A'laq al-Khaṭīra fī dhikr umarā' al-Shām wa'l-Jazīra,* is used in this edition to elucidate passages which are unclear in both Mss.A and B. The relevant part of this text is to be found in the

67. *Op.cit.*, 27.

Bodleian manuscript, Marsh 333.[68] It is a useful aid because a large portion of its contents are borrowed, often *verbatim*, from Ibn al-Azraq. Marsh 333 is based on Ms.B. It would have been of greater help in the preparation of this edition if it had taken material from Ms.A. Nevertheless, it is of value since it provides a third version of a limited number of incidents. Marsh 333 is cited in the edition only sparingly as it is so similar or even identical to Ms.B. Ibn Shaddād has a better grasp of geographical names than Ibn al-Azraq or his copyists and his work is of value in this respect too.

Transcriptions of both manuscripts and a detailed comparison between them has revealed a wealth of minor textual differences. Not all of these have been recorded, since the footnotes to the edition are already lengthy. Variant readings from Ms.B are given only if they help to clarify Ms.A, for example by providing better readings of proper names.

The orthography and many of the morphological idiosyncrasies of the manuscript have been standardised, except in certain specific situations mentioned below. As, however, the language of this chronicle is an important facet of its scholarly value, the syntactical peculiarities of the text have been left unchanged. The actual form used by the scribe is, however, indicated in the footnotes. The aim has been to ensure that every word of the original text can be reconstituted either from the edition or the footnotes.

b) Detailed comments on the edition

1. Ms.A contains numerous marginal comments. These are recorded in the footnotes.[69]
2. Ms.A has many instances of words or phrases intercalated in the text. Some of these are of no particular significance. Often they simply reveal the missing part of a name omitted in error by the scribe, who inserts it on re-reading his text. Intercalations are mentioned in the footnotes only when they are of importance to the edition. Instances where an alternative word or phrase is provided above the line of text in addition to the version written on the line are also recorded in the footnotes.

68. For a longer discussion of the relationship between Ibn al-Azraq and Ibn Shaddād cf. Hillenbrand, "Approaches", 213-25.
69. The marginal amendments in Ms.A are followed by *ṣaḥḥa* and their placing in the text is indicated by an arrow.

3. Punctuation has been added but is limited to the introduction of paragraphs.
4. In both mss., the definite article is usually omitted from dates which contain the elements of day and month, e.g.: *fī rābi' 'ashar Jumādā* (II) instead of *fi'l-rābi' 'ashara Jumādā* (II).[70] The examples of this practice have been left unchanged in the text.
5. Place-names have been recorded in the edition in the form in which they appear in Ms.A. The variants from Ms.B have been placed in the footnotes. Marsh 333 has been used for clarification. If a place-name occurs in the text in a strange form, it is given in its more usual version in the translation which accompanies the edition. For example, *Dhu'l-Qarnain* appears in the edition as *Bi'l-Qarnain*.
6. Personal names are given in the text in the form in which they appear in Ms.A. Any variants in Ms.B are placed in the footnotes. Often Ms.B contains the more usual form of a personal name but the unusual versions in Ms.A have been retained since they are of interest. Possibly they reflect the local pronunciation of such names. For example, the name Ṭoghrïl Beg is rendered in the usual way in Ms.B but it often appears in Ms.A as *Ṭ.gh.rb.k.* The more usual forms of personal names, have, however, been adopted for the translation.

   In the rendering of certain very common personal names such as Abu'l-Qāsim, Ibrāhīm, 'Uthmān, and above all Sulaimān, the manuscripts omit the notation of the length of the *alif* altogether.[71] They have been left unchanged in the text.

   A personal name is corrected in the edition only when there is a clear error either by the author or the scribes. For example, Zangī's son is called Quṭb al-Dīn *Mamdūd;* this has been changed to *Maudūd* in the text.[72]
7. If the reading of a word or phrase is doubtful, this is indicated in the footnotes with a question mark in brackets.
8. Illegible words or phrases and lacunae in the original text are mentioned in the footnotes.
9. Similarly, on the few occasions where a word has been added to the text, this is also noted.

70. Ms.A, f. 161a.
71. Such names as Sulaimān often occur in written Arabic with the *fatḥa* replaced by a vertical stroke.
72. Ms.A, f. 174b.

Abbreviations used in this edition

Ms. = Ms.A, i.e., B.L. Or. 5803
Ms.B = B.L. Or. 6310
Marsh 333 = Bodleian Ms. Marsh 333
'Awaḍ = B.A.L. 'Awaḍ, ed., *Tārīkh al-Fāriqī* (Cairo, 1959)
Amedroz = Ibn al-Qalānisī, *Dhail Tārīkh Dimashq*, ed. H.F. Amedroz (Leiden, 1908)
Ibn Wāṣil = Ibn Wāṣil, *Mufarrij al-Kurūb fī akhbār Banī Ayyūb*, ed. Jamāl al-Dīn al-Shayyāl (Cairo, 1953), I.

A TRANSLATION OF THE TĀRĪKH MAYYĀFĀRIQĪN WA ĀMID[1] *OF IBN AL-AZRAQ AL-FĀRIQĪ* *(B.L. Or. 5803)*

1. Ibn Shaddād names the author of the work from which he borrows his information on Mayyāfāriqīn as Aḥmad b. Yūsuf b. 'Alī b. al-Azraq. He gives the title of the work as the *Tārīkh Mayyāfāriqīn wa Āmid* (Ibn Shaddād, *Jazīra,* f.71b). Although Āmid is included in the title, Ibn al-Azraq's work concentrates for its local history almost exclusively on Mayyāfāriqīn. Information about Āmid occurs only occasionally. On the other hand, as Ibn Shaddād points out: "Most of the time, Āmid, Mayyāfāriqīn, Mārdīn and the fortresses attached to them were ruled as an entity from Mayyāfāriqīn and Āmid" *(ibid.)*. The history of these sites was inextricably linked. In the period treated below, it was Mārdīn which dominated Mayyāfāriqīn and Āmid. In his position as town chronicler of Mayyāfāriqīn, Ibn al-Azraq never explicitly states this important fact.

Chapter 2

The Reign of İl-Ghāzī

(f.160b) The account of the government and rule of Najm al-Dīn İl-Ghāzī[2] *in Mayyāfāriqīn*[3]

¶ When Ibn Jahīr[4] conquered Diyār Bakr, Amīr Artuq was with him. When Ibn Jahīr became established and no longer required the services of Artuq, Artuq broke away from him.[5] When Malik-Shāh

2. The initial letters of this name are *alif* and *lam* in MS.A and *alif, yā* and *lam* in Ms.B. A dotted *i* has been used in the transliteration of this name to remove any erroneous impression that the *alif* and *lam* have any connection with the Arabic definite article. The etymology of the word *İl* is discussed by Sir G.L.M.Clauson (*An Etymological Dictionary of pre-Thirteenth Century Turkish* [Oxford, 1972], 121).
3. The forms *Mayyāfāriqīn* and *Mīfarqīn* are both found in both manuscripts, although the latter is used more frequently. For a discussion of the form *Mīfarqīn*, cf. *EI*², "Mayyāfāriḳīn".
4. Fakhr al-Daula Abū Naṣr Muḥammad b. Jahīr held office with the Marwānid ruler of Mayyāfāriqīn until 453/1061-2. In the following year he became vizier to the caliph al-Qā'im. Niẓām al-Mulk intrigued for Ibn Jahīr's dismissal, which he achieved. Ibn Jahīr then went to Malik-Shāh in 467/1083-4 and pointed out to the *sulṭān* the advantages of taking Diyār Bakr. Malik-Shāh accordingly sent Ibn Jahīr to that area. The latter laid siege to Mayyāfāriqīn in 478/1085-6 and appropriated the treasures of the Marwānids. The *sulṭān* appointed Ibn Jahīr to rule Diyār Bakr in 482/1089-90. Ibn Jahīr died in the following year (cf. C.Cahen, articles "Diyār Bakr" and "Ibn Jahīr", *EI*²; Ibn Khallikān, *Wafayāt,* III, pt.1, 286-294; Ibn al-Athīr, *Kāmil,* X, 93-4).
5. Artuq was one of the military commanders of the Saljuq sulṭāns, Alp Arslān and Malik-Shāh. Malik-Shāh gave him Ḥulwān as an *iqṭā'* and employed him on military missions in Anatolia, Baḥrain and upper Mesopotamia. For his career in more detail, cf. A.Sevim, "Artukluların

came to Syria, Artuq went away[6] and took possession of Jerusalem and the surrounding area.[7] He remained in the Sāḥil[8] and died there. His sons, the *amīrs* Sukmān and Najm al-Dīn İl-Ghāzī, ruled Jerusalem after him for a time.[9]

Then Najm al-Dīn İl-Ghāzī went to Sulṭān Muḥammad[10] and remained in his service. Muḥammad granted him the *iqṭā'* of Ḥulwān[11] for a while. Then Sulṭān Muḥammad made him *shiḥna*[12] in

soyu ve Artuk Bey' in siyasî faaliyetleri", *Belleten,* cilt XXVI, sayı 101 (1962), 121-47; Ibn Khallikān, *Wafayāt,* III, 171-2.

6. Artuq had good reason to flee, since he had incurred Malik-Shāh's displeasure by intriguing in Diyār Bakr with Muslim, the Arab prince of Mosul and Aleppo, who was not on friendly terms with Malik-Shāh. For these events and for Malik-Shāh's Syrian campaign, cf. Ibn al-Athīr, *al-Kāmil,* X, 75-82, 89-91, 96-8; Ibn al-'Adīm, *Zubda,* II, 100-1.
7. Artuq re-entered the service of Tutush and governed Jerusalem on his behalf from 479/1086-7 until his own death (C. Cahen, "The Turkish Invasion", *A History of the Crusades* I, ed. M.W.Baldwin and K.M.Setton [Madison, Milwaukee and London, 1969], I, 158).
8. The term *Sāḥil* has not been translated. It is used by Arab historians of Egypt and Syria to denote that part of the Mediterranean coast which roughly corresponds to Phoenicia.
9. After Artuq's death, his two sons, Sukmān and İl-Ghāzī, ruled Jerusalem for a short time, until the Fāṭimids, under the leadership of al-Afḍal, took the city from them in 491/1098.
10. For a biography of Sulṭān Muḥammad, cf. Ibn Khallikān, *Wafayāt,* III, pt. 1, 236-9; al-Ḥusainī, *Akhbār,* 79-84. Sulṭān Muḥammad died in 511 (1117-18). Cf. also Ibn al-Athīr, *al-Kāmil,* X, 367-8.
11. Ḥulwān had been given to İl-Ghāzī's father Artuq (Ibn Khallikān, *Wafayāt,* III, 171). For a description of the town, cf. Le Strange, *Lands,* 191.
12. Ms.A: *thumma a'ṭāhu Sinjār al-'Irāq.*
Ms.B: *thumma a'ṭāhu shiḥnakiyya Baghdād.*

Whilst there is ample evidence from other sources that İl-Ghāzī was appointed *shiḥna* of Baghdad by Sulṭān Muḥammad in 495/1101-2, there would appear to be no corroboration for his being given Sinjār, as Ms.A would appear to suggest. What probably occurred was that the scribe of Ms.A was unfamiliar with the word *shiḥna,* which bears a certain superficial similarity to *Sinjār* when written in Arabic script. The form *shiḥnakiyya* is an Arabicisation of a Persian word (cf. M. E. Quatremère, *Histoire des Sultans Mamlouks, de l'Egypte* II, [Paris, 1845] pt. 1, 195, n.2; the work is a translation of al-Maqrīzī, *Al-Sulūk fī Ma'rifat Duwal al-Mulūk*).

The *shiḥna* was an important official of the Saljuq *sulṭān,* charged with the task of keeping him informed of events in Baghdad and with restraining the power of the caliph. According to Guseynov, the first *shiḥna* was appointed in the 1050's and the last one in 1135. The caliph could not prevent the existence of the *shiḥna* but he had the right to declare the candidature of a *shiḥna persona non grata,* whereupon the *sulṭān* would suggest someone else (R.A.Guseynov, "Sulṭān i Khalif (Iz

Iraq and İl-Ghāzī lived in Baghdad. After the Franks took the Sāḥil and Jerusalem,[13] Sukmān came to this country[14] and took possession of Ḥiṣn Kaifā.[15] Amīr al-Yāqūtī[16] had (already) taken possession of Mārdīn.[17] When Najm al-Dīn İl-Ghāzī came to this country al-

istorii syuzereniteta i vassaliteta na Blizhnem Vostoke XI-XII vv.)", *Palestinsky Sbornik* 19 [82, 1969], 133).

13. Ibn al-Azraq omits the whole interlude of Fāṭimid rule in Jerusalem and mentions only the subsequent passing of the city into the hands of the Crusaders. On other occasions, especially on the matter of the succession of Fāṭimid caliphs, he shows a greater interest in Egyptian affairs (cf. f.164a).

14. Ibn al-Azraq means Diyār Bakr.

15. Sukmān b.Artuq took Ḥiṣn Kaifā in 495/1101-2 from Amīr Mūsā ('Awaḍ, 269; Ibn al-Athīr, *al-Kāmil,* X, 235). For the activities of Sukmān after his departure from Jerusalem, cf. 'Awaḍ, 269, 271, 283.

16. There is a considerable divergence of opinion about the identity of (al)-Yāqūtī. Ibrāhīm Artuk calls him "the son of Artuk" (I.Artuk, *Mardin Artukloğulları Tarihi* [Istanbul, 1944], 34-6). Minorsky is uncertain if Yāqūtī was the son or grandson of Artuq ("Mārdīn", *EI*[1], 274). Dolapönü calls him the grandson of Artuq (H.Dolapönü, *Tarihte Mardin* [Istanbul, 1972], 41). Cahen says Yāqūtī is Sukmān's brother - i.e. the son of Artuq (*La Syrie du Nord,* 237). Ibn Shaddād, whose genealogical grasp is poor, describes Yāqūtī as "the son of the sister of Sukmān" (*Jazīra,* f.132b), "the son of Artuq" (*ibid.,* f.43a) and "the brother of Sukmān" (*ibid.*). Ibn al-Athīr writes "the son of Sukmān's brother, Yāqūtī b. Artuq" (*sic*) (*al-Kāmil,* X, 269).

It would appear likely from the genealogical information provided by Ibn al-Azraq (cf. Appendix B) that Yāqūtī was the son of Alp-Yaruq b. Artuq.

17. A detailed account of Yāqūtī's acquisition of Mārdīn is given by Ibn al-Athīr (*al-Kāmil,* X, 268-70) and is copied twice almost *verbatim* by Ibn Shaddād (*Jazīra,* ff.43a-b; ff.133a-b).

Yāqūtī was imprisoned in the citadel at Mārdīn which was governed by Berk-Yaruk's bard (*mughannī*). The town pleased Yāqūtī and he was determined to acquire it upon his release, which was effected through the intercession of Artuq's widow. He persuaded the governor of Mārdīn to hand over some soldiers to help him rid the countryside of Kurdish raiders. Yāqūtī eventually gained control of the citadel by threatening outside the gate to kill the soldiers one by one. Thus the town fell into his hands.

Yāqūtī died soon afterwards in a battle with Chökermïsh in 498/1104-5, whereupon his brother,'Alī, took the town under the suzerainty of Chökermïsh. 'Alī left a governor in Mārdīn who was also called 'Alī. This second 'Alī summoned Sukmān b. Artuq and asked him to come and take Mārdīn. The Artuqid 'Alī asked Sukmān to give him back Mārdīn but Sukmān only gave him the *iqṭā'* of Jabal Jūr.

Unfortunately, the dating of all this is very imprecise. Ibn Shaddād says that Yāqūtī took Mārdīn some time in 487 or 488/1094-5 (*Jazīra,* f.134a) but Ibn al-Athīr mentions no date at all for the whole episode.

Yāqūtī[18] had died. İl-Ghāzī had been there under the suzerainty of al-Yāqūtī. (Thereafter) he became subordinate to Sukmān of Ḥiṣn Kaifā. İl-Ghāzī remained in the area and took possession of it.[19]

¶ Amīr Sukmān died in 498[20] (23 September 1104 - 12 September 1105) and İl-Ghāzī remained there until Amīr Sukmān died.

Sukmān's son, Amīr Ibrāhīm b. Sukmān,[21] ruled after him. Ibrāhīm contacted[22] Shams[23] in Mārdīn[24] and took as a hostage a son of his who remained with him in Ḥiṣn Kaifā for a while. Then the news reached Shams that Ibrāhīm had harmed his son and imprisoned him. So when Najm al-Dīn İl-Ghāzī came (back again), Shams surrendered Mārdīn to Najm al-Dīn. After a while Amīr

18. Ms.A: *wa-māta al-bāqūna.*
The word *al-bāqūna* has been changed here to *al-Yāqūtī.* This emendation may be regarded as rather bold but these lines are the most obscure in the whole edited text and a certain temerity is needed to make any sense of them at all. The absence of dates and names is especially noticeable here. If Ms.A is translated literally as "the others died", an apparently insuperable problem of identification arises, for these "others" are not mentioned earlier in Ibn al-Azraq's text.

19. It is difficult to ascertain with any degree of precision the role of İl-Ghāzī in Diyār Bakr in the last decade of the fifth century A.H. It is clear that with two major citadels in the area - Ḥiṣn Kaifā and Mārdīn - in Artuqid hands, there was a concentration of other members of the Artuqid family in that area. It was inevitable that there should be conflict and shifting alliances between them. The date of Yāqūtī's acquisition of Mārdīn is known (487 or 488/1094/5) but the date when İl-Ghāzī took it is uncertain.
Ibn al-Azraq does not clarify the situation. He mentions few dates and makes no distinctions between the various separate occasions when İl-Ghāzī must have visited Diyār Bakr. He also omits any reference to the latter's absences on campaign. The only precise date is İl-Ghāzī's dismissal from the office of *shiḥna* in 498/1104-5 after which he returned to Diyār Bakr to participate in the power struggle amongst the members of his own family. From this struggle he ultimately emerged victorious.

20. For the death of Sukmān b. Artuq, cf. Ibn al-Athīr, *al-Kāmil,* X, 268; Ibn al-Qalānisī, *Dhail,* 147. It is generally agreed that he died in 498/1105. Ibn Khallikān says he died of quinsy (*op. cit.,* III, 171-2).

21. Cf. 'Awaḍ, 269, 279.

22. For a discussion of the verb *n.f.dh,* cf. Hillenbrand, "Approaches", 201.

23. Cahen reads the name of this *amīr* as Shamtar (?) ("Diyār Bakr", 232). He is right to be diffident about this reading. The name occurs three times in Ms.A and on only one occasion (f.161a, 1.21), can the name possibly be read as Shamtar. The three radicals seem to be *shīn, mīm* and *sīn.*

24. The form *Mīrdīn* is often used in Ms.B in place of the usual *Mārdīn.*

Ibrāhīm died in Ḥiṣn Kaifā. His brother, Amīr Dā'ūd, took over his position after him.[25] He remained for a while and Amīr Shams and Mārdīn were in his hand. Dā'ūd did not surrender the city to anyone. Then Najm al-Dīn İl-Ghāzī came and he surrendered it to him in the year 507 (18 June, 1113 - 6 June, 1114). So it came to İl-Ghāzī and his descendants from that day (f.161a) until now.[26] As for Amīr Shams, he was the father[27] of Amīr Sunqur who was the father of Yūsuf who himself was the father of Rasūl.

¶ Najm al-Dīn İl-Ghāzī took possession of Mārdīn in the years 507 or 508 (7 June, 1114 - 26 May, 1115), remaining there until the year 512[28] (24 April, 1118 - 13 April, 1119). Then he contacted the *sulṭān*[29] informing him that Mayyāfāriqīn was going to rack and ruin and was in decline, whilst (previously) it had been a city without peer.[30] The

25. Ms.A: *wa-walā mauḍa'ahu akhūhu al-amīr Dā'ūd ba'da akhīhi Sukmān.* This is a very confused genealogy. Ibrāhīm and Dā'ūd were brothers; so too were Sukmān and İl-Ghāzī. In order to make sense historically, the phrase *ba'da akhīhi Sukmān* has been translated simply as *ba'dahu.*
26. In his chapter on the Innsbruck dish, which he attributes to Dā'ūd b. Sukmān, van Berchem discusses some of the problems connected with the Artuqids at Mārdīn and Ḥiṣn Kaifā at the beginning of the sixth/twelfth century. He rightly pinpoints the difficulty of establishing the sequence of events at Mārdīn at a time when places constantly changed hands and he criticises Lane-Poole for linking İl-Ghāzī's acquisition of Mārdīn with the death of Ibrāhīm (M. van Berchem and J. Strzygowski, *Amida* [Heidelberg, 1910], 123-4).

    According to Ibn al-Furāt, İl-Ghāzī took Mārdīn in 502/1108-9 after using a trick to gain access to the citadel (I, f.21a *apud* Cahen, "Diyār Bakr", 232).

    Cahen erroneously cites the date given by Ibn al-Azraq on this folio (f.160b) as 509/1115-6 *(ibid.).*
27. Ms.A consistently uses the verb *aulada* where the form *walada* would be more usual.
28. The meaning of the phrase *'alā an baqiyā bi-hā ilā sanat...* is obscure. If *'alā an* denotes 'on condition that' a subjunctive verb would be correct grammatically.

    For a good description of Mārdīn, cf. Yāqūt, who writes: "(Mārdīn) is a citadel at the top of a mountain which overlooks Dunaisir, Dārā, Naṣībīn and that broad plain. In front of the citadel extends a large suburb with market places, Muslim and Christian inns... It is built like an amphitheatre... There is no doubt that there is no more beautiful, more solidly built and firm castle in the world than this" (*"Reisen"*, 436). Cf. also Ilisch, *Geschichte*, 208-10.
29. The *sulṭān* was now Sulṭān Maḥmūd. Sulṭān Muḥammad had died at the end of 511/1118 (Mustaufī, *Guzīda*, 278; Ibn Khallikān, *Wafayāt* [Cairo, 1310] II, 47; Ibn al-Qalānisī, *Dhail*, 198-9).
30. Lehmann-Haupt mentions Nāṣir-i Khusrau's visit to Mayyāfāriqīn in 438/1046-7. It was a very prosperous city before the advent of the Turks. The *rabaḍ* had caravanserais, bazaars, baths and a large mosque,

sulṭān got in touch with Ilduz Beg[31], ordering him to hand over Mayyāfāriqīn to Najm al-Dīn İl-Ghāzī. So when İl-Ghāzī arrived, Ilduz Beg handed it over to him. He entered the city on 14 Jumādā II, 512 (2 October, 1118),[32] and took possession of it. Ilduz Beg left and lodged at al-Rawābī[33] where he stayed for three days. On the fourth day, a messenger came in haste to him from the *sulṭān,* ordering him not to surrender the city,[34] but he found it was already too late. Najm al-Dīn became established in Mayyāfāriqīn and he showed justice and kindness to the inhabitants.[35] On their behalf he removed the *athqāl*[36] and the *aqsāṭ*[37] and the *anzāl*[38] from its (the city's) houses,

whilst the Friday mosque was abundantly supplied with water and other amenities (Lehmann-Haupt, *Armenien einst und jetzt. Reisen und Forschungen* [Berlin, 1910], 424).

For a scholarly and detailed study of the history of the city of Mayyāfāriqīn from Sasanian times onwards, cf. M. E. Quatremère, *Histoire des Mongols de la Perse écrite en persan par Rashid-eldin* (Paris, 1836) I, 360-5, n.160 (annotated edition of Rashīd al-Dīn Faḍlallāh, *Jāmiʿ al-Tawārīkh*). Cf. also Markwart, *Südarmenien,* 163-70 and *EI*², s.v.

Finally, Ibn Shaddād writes of Mayyāfāriqīn: "Until our own time it has never been taken by the sword forcibly. Beside it, Āmid is stronger and better fortified and (yet) it has been taken several times by the sword" (*Jazīra,* f.68b).

31. Ms.A: *alr.z.b.kī* and *alr.z.b.k* ʿAwaḍ: *alr.z.b.kī*
Ibn Shaddād: *Zangī.*
The reading of this name as Ilduz Beg is very uncertain. Cahen gives Ruzbakī ("Diyār Bakr", 234). A more likely reading is Ildız Bey (M. H. Yinanc, "Diyarbekir", *I.A.,* 614). Ibn Shaddād gives Zangī (*Jazīra,* f.101b). Whilst this is not totally impossible, Ibn Shaddād is, as noted elsewhere in this work, very inaccurate with names and genealogies.
Whatever the reading of this name, the *amīr* Ilduz Beg was appointed as *wālī* of Mayyāfāriqīn in 508/1114-5 by Qaracha, the governor of Mosul (ʿAwaḍ, 283).

32 According to Ibn al-Athīr, Sulṭān Maḥmūd gave Mayyāfāriqīn as an *iqṭāʿ* to İl-Ghāzī as late as 515/1121-2 (*al-Kāmil,* X, 418).

33. The *burj al-Rawābī* is mentioned by Ibn Shaddād in his description of the buildings of Mayyāfāriqīn (*Jazīra,* f.68b).

34. The reasons for this change of decision are not clear.

35. This is stock panegyric.

36. For *thaqal* (plural *athqāl),* cf. Dozy, *Supplément,* I, 161. Dozy defines this term as "ce dont on a besoin dans la guerre". This was one of the many kinds of extra tax which a ruler could levy.

37. For *qisṭ* (*aqsāṭ),* cf. Dozy, *Supplément,* II, 344. Dozy defines this term as "contribution, impôt, tribut". It would appear to imply the payment of a debt in instalments. A parallel account is found in Ibn Shaddād, who glosses *athqāl* and *aqsāṭ* by *kalaf* and *mu'an* (f.101b).
A similar list of taxes was abolished by Sukman al-Quṭbī at Mayyāfāriqīn in 502/1108-9 (ʿAwaḍ, 275).

38. Ms.A *anzāl.*
Two possibilities exist for this term:
i) *nuzl* (plural *anzāl)* "provisions que les sujets sont tenus de fournir

for the people were in great distress because of billeting in their homes. Most of the city was ruined because of constant changes of régime and overlord. Those who conquered them treated them unjustly and tyrannised them and mulcted[39] them, because they knew that they themselves would not endure and their rule would not last. From the time when[40] Najm al-Dīn İl-Ghāzī assumed power he became established, (so) their hearts became calm and the people became secure in their homes.

The soldiers who had no homes began living in it (the city) and setting up tents in the ruins of the city because most of the city was ruined and the roads were terrorised by robbers and highwaymen, to such an extent that the caravan could go to Āmid only if it was escorted by a *shiḥna*[41] and cavalry. It was the same to Arzan,[42] Ḥiṣn Kaifā, Ḥānī[43] and Mārdīn, for an escort was needed to guard the caravan even for a short distance because of the devastation of the towns and villages. From the moment Najm al-Dīn assumed power, the roads and the countryside became safe. The robbers fled and the

au souverain quand il est en voyage et à son armée" (Dozy, *Supplément,* II, 661).

ii) *nizāl* "l'obligation de loger des soldats" *(ibid.).*

Of these two suggestions, the second one, which means billeting, is more apposite to the context. Although Ms.A has the form *anzāl,* Ibn Shaddad reads *nizāl* (*Jazīra,* f.101b). The Arabic is clumsy, repetitive and unclear. A literal translation would read:

"he removed on their behalf the *athqāl, aqsāṭ* and *anzāl* from its (i.e. the city's) houses and the people were in great hardship because of the *nuzl* in their houses".

Ibn al-Athīr records that in 519/1125-6 the soldiers of Sulṭān Maḥmūd's army entered Baghdad and installed themselves in the houses of the inhabitants (*Atabegs,* 29).

39. Cf. the use of the term *muṣādārāt* by Bundārī (*Zubdat,* 132).
40. For a discussion of the conjunction *min ḥaith,* cf. Hillenbrand, *History,* 96. An alternative translation might be "Wherever İl-Ghāzī ruled, he became established".
41. This use of the term *shiḥna* probably implies some kind of military officer in charge of the garrison of a city. Minorsky translates the word in a similar context as "protector" ("Caucasica I", 32).
42. Arzan was situated at a distance of one day's journey from Mayyāfāriqīn. According to Ibn Ḥauqal, it was as important as Mayyāfāriqīn, Bitlīs, Manzikert and other cities in Armenia (Canard, *H'amdanides,* 84). According to Ibn Shaddād, Arzan had a round citadel on a high hill. The town had an abundance of vines (*Jazīra,* f.128b). It stands on a tributary of the Tigris called the Arzan-Su (Lehmann-Haupt, *op.cit.,* 385).
43. A small town 60 kms to the N.W. of Mayyāfāriqīn (Ilisch, *Geschichte,* 196).

villages flourished. Mayyāfāriqīn began to prosper and he ruled the people very well.[44]

He remained until the year 513 (14 April, 1119 - 1 April, 1120) when he took possession of Aleppo[45] and fought the Franks, inflicting a decisive defeat on them, plundering their possessions and taking a great number of them prisoner. This was the defeat at al-Balāṭ.[46] As for Aleppo, he took it from Sulṭān-Shāh b. al-Malik Riḍwān who had taken it from (another) son of Riḍwān.[47]

¶ In 513 (1119-20) the Friday mosque at Āmid was burned.[48] In

44. This apparently lavish praise should be treated with caution. Ibn al-Azraq was for a time in the service of İl-Ghāzī's son Temür-Tash and his sympathies are with the Artuqids. These are in any case conventional phrases applied indiscriminately by Ibn al-Azraq to other rulers of Mayyāfāriqīn.
   This description should be weighed against that of Ibn al-'Adīm who emphasises the rapacity of İl-Ghāzī and his soldiery when they entered Aleppo in 511/1117-8 (*Zubda,* II, 180).
45. Ms.A has 516/1122-3 which is the year İl-Ghāzī died. Ms.B has 513/1119-20. Neither of these two dates tally with the other chronicles, except for Michael the Syrian who also puts the date of the surrender of Aleppo to İl-Ghāzī in 513 (*Chronique,* 217). The other chronicles say that İl-Ghāzī took Aleppo in 511/1117-8 (Ibn al-'Adīm, *Zubda,* 180; Ibn al-Qalānisī, *Dhail,* 146; Ibn al-Athīr, *al-Kāmil,* X, 372).
46. For the location of al-Balāṭ cf. the discussion in Eddé, *Description,* 44, n.4. The victory at Balāṭ marked the apogee of İl-Ghāzī's military career. Ibn al-Qalānisī gives the most graphic account of the battle, which took place in Rabī' I 513/June 1119 (*Dhail,* 200-1). Michael the Syrian relates that in this battle Roger of Antioch was "hacked to pieces" (*Chronique,* 217). For a further discussion of Balāṭ, cf. Hillenbrand, "İl-Ghāzī", 276-8.
47. Ms.A: *wa-kāna akhadhahā min al-amīr ibn Malik (?).* Ibn al-Azraq is unsure of the name of one of the two young sons of Malik Riḍwān of Aleppo. When Riḍwān died in 507/1113-4, he was first succeeded by his son Alp Arslan al-Akhras, who ruled in collaboration with a *mamlūk,* Lu'lu'. Alp Arslan was murdered a year later by Lu'lu' and his associates and was replaced by his brother, Sulṭān-Shāh, whom Ibn al-Azraq identifies correctly. For these events at Aleppo, cf. Ibn al-'Adīm, *Zubda,* 167-172; *Bughyat,* 152-7.
48. Matthew of Edessa places this event in the years 508-9/1115-6 (*Chronique,* 291). As the local historian, Ibn al-Azraq would normally be the more trustworthy source, were it not for the fact that an inscription in the name of Sulṭān Muḥammad, datable c.510 and in any case before 511, the date of the *sulṭān's* death, is found on the west facade of this mosque, which was built at that time. The fire would provide the most natural motive for such a substantial rebuilding. For the text of this inscription, with commentary, see M. van Berchem and J. Strzygowski, *Amida* (Heidelberg, 1910), 55-9; see also M. van Berchem, "Arabische Inschriften", in Max Freiherr von Oppenheim, *Inschriften aus Syrien, Mesopotamien und Kleinasien* (Leipzig, 1909), 97.

514 (2 April, 1120 - 21 March, 1121) Najm al-Dīn took Naṣībīn.[49] Qāḍī 'Alam al-Dīn b. Nubāta[50] and a group of the inhabitants of Mayyāfāriqīn went and met him there and congratulated him on his conquest of the city. He put ceremonial garments on them and treated them well, and they returned to Mayyāfāriqīn.

¶ In 515[51] (22 March, 1121 - 11 March, 1122) the population of Tiflīs got in touch with Najm al-Dīn İl-Ghāzī,[52] asking him to come so that they might hand over Tiflīs to him. The city had been in the hands of its inhabitants for a period of forty years.[53] (Previously) its

49. Naṣībīn lay in Diyār Rabī'a, on the caravan route from Mosul to Syria, six days journey from Mosul and nine *farsakhs* from Sinjār (Yāqūt, "*Reisen*", 435). Already in the fourth century A.H. it had fallen from its former elevated status as the intellectual centre of the Nestorians (E. Honigman, "Naṣībīn", *EI*[1]). Cf. also Ilisch, *Geschichte*, 213-4.
Ibn Shaddād (*Jazīra*, f.37a) lists the rulers of this town as follows:

495/1101-2	Chökermish
500/1106-7	Qïlïch Arslan b. Sulaimān
500/1106-7	Chavlï Saqao
500/1106-7	İl-Ghāzī
502/1108-9	Maudūd
507/1113-4	Aq-Sonqur al-Bursuqī
512/1118-9	İl-Ghāzī
515/1121-2	Aq-Sonqur al-Bursuqī

It would appear that İl-Ghāzī had held Naṣībīn on an earlier occasion, during the years 500-2/1106-8. His rule in the town was ended by the appointment of Maudūd. After Maudūd's murder in 507/1113-4, another rival of İl-Ghāzī, Aq-Sonqur al-Bursuqī, who had ousted him as *shiḥna* of Baghdad, became governor of Mosul and ruled Naṣībīn.
Perhaps İl-Ghāzī's victory at Balāṭ in 513/1119-20 gave him the confidence to seize Naṣībīn the following year.

50. Elsewhere Ibn al-Azraq gives his full name as 'Alam al-Dīn Abu'l-Ḥasan 'Alī b. Yaḥyā b. Nubāta. He belonged to an illustrious family whose members had held the post of *qāḍī* in Mayyāfāriqīn. He was born in 464/1071-2 ('Awaḍ, 267).

51. The following passage about Georgia has been translated by Minorsky ("Caucasica I", 31-5). The Arabic text has been transcribed by Amedroz in a footnote to his edition of Ibn al-Qalānisī (*op.cit.*, 205). Part of this account and other subsequent passages in Ibn al-Azraq which refer to Georgia are also published in an Arabic reader for Georgian students (*Arabuli Krest'omathia*, ed. G.V. T'seret'heli [Tiflis, 1949], 68-72). T'seret'heli prefers to follow Ms.B, which is generally a more lucid account than Ms.A.

52. The reputation of İl-Ghāzī was never so high as after his resounding victory at the battle of Balāṭ. He was thus considered the most appropriate leader for this expedition to Georgia.

53. There is no textual justification for T'seret'heli's reading *wa-kāna ānifan bi-yad ahlihā* (*op.cit.*, 58).

rulers had been a group of its inhabitants, called the Banū Ja'far,[54] for about two hundred years. When their leaders finally died out, the administration of the city reverted (f.161b) to its citizens.[55] Every month one of them would govern them. This situation had prevailed for forty years.[56]

King Dā'ūd,[57] king of the Abkhāz[58] and the Gurj, had oppressed the city sorely and it had declined, (so) they had got in contact with Sulṭān Ṭoghrïl Beg[59] son of Sulṭān Muḥammad, who was ruler of Ganja[60] and Arrān,[61] and he sent a *shiḥna* to them. (But) the tyranny of the king of the Gurj towards them increased.[62] They carried on in this way for a while and agreed to pay him 10,000 *dīnārs* every year. (They also agreed) to have a *shiḥna* with (only) ten horsemen.[63] After continuing like that for a while, they approached Najm al-Dīn İl-Ghāzī and asked him to come. He set out[64] accompanied by a large

54. Lang says the Ja'farid *amīrs* struck silver *dirhams* in their own name, modelled on standard 'Abbāsid types (D.M. Lang, *The Georgians* [London, 1966], 104). It is not certain whether the Banū Ja'far were Arab or Georgian (Cf. "al-Kurdj", *EI*²).
55. This period must have been between the end of the rule of the Shaddādid, Faḍlūn (some time after 461-2/1068) and the occupation of King David the Restorer (515-6/1122).
56. M.F. Brosset, *Histoire de la Géorgie depuis l'antiquité jusqu'au commencement du XIXe siècle* (St. Petersburg, 1849) I/1, 334 and Minorsky, *Studies*, 64.
57. King David II Aghmashenebeli (the Restorer) ruled Georgia (K'art'li and Abkhazia) from 1089-1125. By the end of his reign he had extended the frontiers of Georgia substantially, taking in much of Armenia including Ānī, Shīrvān, and the foothills of Dāghistān as far as Darband (Lang, *op.cit.*, 112; Minorsky, *Studies*, 84). David had come to the throne after the death of his father, Giorgi, in 1089. After the death of Malik-Shāh, David dared to adopt a more aggressive policy. He stopped paying *kharāj* to the *sulṭān* and prevented the Turks from wintering in Georgia (Brosset, *op.cit.*, I, 352; "al-Kurdj", *EI*².)
58. Minorsky defines the territory of the Abkhāz as western Georgia. The energetic kings of Tiflīs were first of all kings of eastern Georgia (K'art'li) (V.F. Minorsky, review of H. Ḥasan, *Falakī-i Shīrwānī I* and *II*, *BSOS* V [1928-30], 907).
59. Ms.B: Ṭoghrïl. Cf. ff. 163b-164a.
60. The form used in this text is *Jnzā*.
61. cf. "Arran", *EI*².
62. Ms.A: *wa-zādat*
Ms.B: *mā-zālat*
In his transcription of this part of Ibn al-Azraq's text, Amedroz prefers the reading in Ms.A (Ibn al-Qalānisī, *Dhail*, 205). Minorsky, who translates the passage about Tiflīs, and T'seret'heli, who transcribes it, prefer to use the version in Ms.B.
63. Ms.B adds "and no more".
64. For a discussion of İl-Ghāzī's campaign into Georgia, cf. Hillenbrand, "İl-Ghāzī", 269-71, 279-80. Cf. also Brosset, *op.cit.*, 365-6.

number of troops and Dubais b. Ṣadaqa,[65] lord of the Arabs. This man was the son-in-law of Najm al-Dīn, being married to his daughter Guhar Khātūn, and he had joined him that year. Najm al-Dīn took troops with him, and having contacted Shams al-Daula Ṭoghan Arslan, lord of Arzan and Bitlīs,[66] to whom the city of Dvīn also belonged,[67] he ordered the latter to enter Tiflīs from the eastern side. When Najm al-Dīn left he (also) took with him Qāḍī 'Alam al-Dīn b. Nubāta and his son Qāḍī 'Alam al-Dīn Abu 'l-Fatḥ al-Kabīr, who is now *qāḍī* of Mārdīn; and the vizier Abū Tammām b. 'Abdūn also went with him. When they arrived in Erzerum the *qāḍī* and the vizier stayed behind there.[68]

Najm al-Dīn entered (Georgia) with his troops by way of the province of Kars[69] and T'rialet'.[70] They had agreed that all troops should assemble before Tiflīs. Sulṭān Ṭoghrïl Beg made his dispositions on the Ganja side and Ṭoghan Arslan al-Aḥdab marched

65. Ms.B calls him Dubais b. Ṣadaqa al-Mazyadī. For biographies of Dubais, cf. Ibn Khallikān, *Wafayāt*, I, 504-7; Ibn al-'Adīm, *Bughyat*, 224-250.
66. Ṭoghan Arslan is usually given the title *al-Aḥdab* ("the hunchback") (cf. Minorsky, *Studies*, 83, 85). For details on his descendants, cf. p. 128.
67. Minorsky states that Ṭoghān Arslan acquired Dvīn as a kind of "Transaraxian colony" (*ibid.*, 83). Here he clearly refers to the well-known Dvīn which lies north of the Araxes. In his earlier article, however, Minorsky very properly suggests that there is confusion between the well-known Dvīn and "the Duvin belonging to Arzan (i.e. to the valley situated between the river of Bitlis and that of Mayyafariqin)" ("Caucasica I", 32). The suggestion about the "Transaraxian colony" is made without any explanation and in complete contradiction to his earlier hypothesis, which he merely states "needs correction".
   In the Marwānid section of Ibn al-Azraq's text, Ibn al-Azraq appears to clarify the matter when he writes:
   wa-malaka Qïzïl Arslān al-Sab' al-Aḥmar Is'ird wa-Ṭanzī wa-Bāhmard wa-kāna malaka madīna Duwīn min balad Arzan ('Awaḍ, 269). It is certainly more logical to assume that a minor ruler like Ṭoghān Arslan held a small place in Diyār Bakr rather than an important city so far away from his other possessions.
68. *takhallafa* "to stay behind".
   Minorsky wrongly translates this sentence as: "They arrived in Arzan al-Rūm (Erzerum) where the *qāḍī* and the vazir quarrelled" ("Caucasica I", 32).
69. Ms.A: *al-Gh.rs.* Minorsky says Juvainī also spelt the name thus (*ibid.*). Amedroz is obviously wrong to read Fars (Ibn al-Qalānisī, *Dhail*, 205). T'seret'heli writes *Q.r.s* (*op.cit.*, 59).
70. Ms.A: *Trālīth.* T'rialet' is a district to the south of Kūr, upstream of Gori (cf. "al-Kurdj", *EI*²). Minorsky says that the route of the invaders must have been Kars-Ardahan Akhalkalaki ("Caucasica I", 32, n.10).

from Dvīn. Najm al-Dīn advanced until he reached the mountain which was a half day's journey from Tiflīs.[71] King Dā'ūd, accompanied by his son Dīmīṭrī,[72] sallied forth from the western side with a large number of troops.[73] He swooped down on them from the mountain while they were at the bottom of it. The troops of Sulṭān Ṭoghrïl Beg had not come, nor had Shams al-Daula al-Aḥdab with his men. They engaged in a mighty battle, and Najm al-Dīn was defeated.[74] The infidels killed a large number of his men and seized much plunder from them. (Only) Najm al-Dīn and Dubais escaped with (only) a small band of men,[75] with the result that the Georgians have retained prisoners right up to our own time.[76]

I saw the place of the battle when I entered Tiflīs in the year 548 (29 March, 1153 - 17 March, 1154). I stayed there, then I entered the service of the king of the Abkhāz with whom I remained (a while). I accompanied him on a visit round his territory for a period of over seventy days.[77] He crossed over to al-Lān[78] and the edge of Darband and the province of the Abkhāz. One day in the province of the Abkhāz we came to a broad meadow[79] in a forbidding citadel beneath

71. Presumably in the vicinity of Manglis. The syntax is odd: *ilā an baqiyā bainahu wa-baina Tiflīs al-jabal miqdar niṣf yaum*. Arab geographers comment generally on the mountainous environs of Tiflīs but are not very specific. Cf. *Ḥudūd*, 458. According to Matthew of Edessa, the mountain was called Tégor (or Didgor). Dulaurier adds in a note that this was to the south-west of Tiflīs (*op.cit.*, 304 and 460).

72. Dimitri I ruled 1125-54.

73. King David had brought into Georgia 40,000 Kipčaks and 5,000 slaves converted to Christianity. Although unruly, these troops had enabled him to rid himself of Saljuq domination. Cf. "al-Kurdj", *EI*².

74. Amedroz reads *kusira* (*op.cit.*, 205); Minorsky has *usira* (*op.cit.*, 33). Amedroz' reading makes better sense.

75. Ibn Shaddād writes that they escaped with twenty horsemen (*Jazīra*, f.102b). Cf. also Ms.B, f.103b.

76. Ibn al-Azraq refers to one such prisoner on f.161b.

77. Minorsky draws attention to an earlier passage in Ibn al-Azraq's text (Ms.A, f.64a) where the author describes a visit he made around the provinces with his master, King Dimitri. This may well be the same visit mentioned here. The details of the locality seem similar (V.F. Minorsky, *A History of Sharvān and Darband* [Cambridge, 1958], Annex V, 170-1).

78. Ms.A: *Alān*

Al-Lān were an Iranian people from the northern Caucasus (cf. V.F.Minorsky, "Alān", *EI*²).

79. Ms.A: *waṣalnā ilā marj wāsiʿ*.

There are several occasions in this text where it is difficult to distinguish between *marj* and *burj*. This is one such instance. A meadow inside the area of a citadel is attested at Ḥiṣn Kaifā where crops were grown inside the citadel (Ibn Shaddād, *Jazīra*, f.127a). On the other hand, the translation of *burj wāsiʿ* ("broad tower") is also possible.

a mountain. The *malik* (of Darband) was encamped here.[80] The king of the Abkhāz said to me: "O so and so! In this citadel there is an Arabic-speaking[81] prisoner from İl-Ghāzī's troop.[82] When morning comes, go up and see him and ask him where he comes from". So I decided to do so and I said (to myself): "I will ask the king to let him go." After I had slept that night and daybreak had come, the bugle (f.162a) for departure was sounded because the king had received the news that some of his territory had rebelled against him. When he heard the news, he and his entourage left and God did not decree that I should meet that man.

¶ In 515 (1121-2) Malik Riḍwān died in Aleppo, but the first date is more accurate.[83]

When Najm al-Dīn had been defeated and retreated with the men remaining, the king of the Abkhāz withdrew with the plunder and the prisoners. He camped before Tiflīs and besieged it for a while. Then he tore down its walls from the west and entered it by the sword, burning and plundering it. After three days he gave its inhabitants security, soothed their hearts and made them fair promises.[84]

80. Ms.A: *fa-nazala al-malik hunāka wa-qāla lī malik al-Abkhāz.*
This rather strange repetition of the word *malik* is possibly prompted by the fact that two separate rulers are involved. In the earlier description of this visit (Ms.A, f.64a), the *malik* of Darband, Amīr Abu'l-Muẓaffar, came to pay his respects to Dimitri, the king of the Abkhāz (Minorsky, *A History of Sharvān*, 170).

81. Two readings are possible here:-
i) *musta'rib:* an Arabic speaker
ii) *mustaghrib:* a foreigner
'Awaḍ, who describes this anecdote in his introduction, opts for *musta'rib* (*op.cit.,* 2). The other hypothesis of *mustaghrib* is also perfectly possible. If the prisoner were an Arabic speaker, he would probably have been one of Dubais' men. On the other hand, had he been a foreigner he could just as well have been a Turcoman from İl-Ghāzī's contingent.

82. *nauba:* group of people (*Lisān,* III, 737).

83. Ms.A: *māta wa'l-awwal aṣaḥḥ al-malik Riḍwān bi-Ḥalab.*
In an earlier passage, Ibn al-Azraq states that Malik Riḍwān died in 505/1111-2 ('Awaḍ, 278). Here he gives the date as 515/1121-2. Unusually for him, he expresses an opinion on their relative accuracy, opting for the earlier date. In fact, both the dates he gives are wrong, since Malik Riḍwān died in 507/1113-4 (Ibn al-'Adīm, *Zubda,* 164; Ibn al-Qalānisī, *Dhail,* 189). For the career of the Saljuq Riḍwān, who succeeded his father at Aleppo in 488/1095, cf. "Riḍwān", *EI*[1].

84. Ms.A: *wa-wa'adahum bi'l-jamīl.*
Minorsky has made an error here by confusing *wada'a* and *wa'ada.* He translates this phrase as "he left them alone in all goodness" ("Caucasica I", 33).

That year, he removed from them the *athqāl*, the *mu'an*,[85] the *aqsāṭ* and the *kharāj*.[86] He laid down for the Muslims all the conditions they wanted; these are still valid in Tiflīs today. (He stipulated) that no pigs should be brought over to the area where the Muslims lived or to the city and that these animals should not be slaughtered there or in the market. He struck *dirhams* for them on one side of which was the name of the *sulṭān* and the caliph, and on the (other) side was the name of God and the name of the Prophet (on him be peace), while the king's name was on the margin of the *dirham*.[87] He proclaimed in the town that the blood of anyone who harmed a Muslim might be shed with impunity. He granted them the call to prayer, the prayer, and the reading (of the Qur'ān) in public. He also guaranteed that on Fridays sermons and public prayers should take place, and that prayers should be said from the *minbar* for the caliph and the *sulṭān* but for no-one else. He also guaranteed that no Georgian, Armenian or Jew should enter the bath of Ismā'īl in Tiflīs. He assessed the *khidma* of a Georgian[88] at a rate of five *dīnārs per annum*, that of a Jew at four *dīnārs* and that of a Muslim at three *dīnārs*. He treated the Muslims extremely kindly, whilst to the people of *'ilm* and religion and the *Ṣūfīs* he accorded a level of respect which they did not receive (even) amongst the Muslims.[89]

85. *mu'an* probably means "maintenance costs". It came under the category of illegal taxes (Horst, *Staatsverwaltung*, 80). Cf. also Dozy, *Supplément* II, 566.
86. Cf. "Kharāj", *EI*²; Horst, *Staatsverwaltung*, 78-9.
87. According to Minorsky, coins dating from the reign of David the Restorer bear the image of the Virgin ("Kurdj", *EI*²). Copper coins which correspond to this description and which have the Georgian king's name or monogram on the obverse and the caliph's name on the reverse were, however, minted in large numbers under King Dimitri (D.M.Lang, *Studies in the Numismatic History of Georgia in Transcaucasia* [New York, 1955], 17). Ibn al-Azraq may well have confused the coins of David with those of his employer, Dimitri. Lang interprets the presence of the caliph's name on the coin not as a sign of political dependence on the part of the Georgian king, but as a conciliatory gesture towards the Muslim inhabitants of the Georgian capital (*ibid.*). It was certainly important to treat the Muslims of Tiflīs with great care because, as the Georgian chronicle indicates, fighting between Muslims and Christians was still very bitter (cf. Brosset, I, 380).
88. The exact meaning of *khidma* is unclear. It is difficult to assess the balance at this time between the Muslims and Christians within the city of Tiflīs but it would appear that Ibn al-Azraq cites these details as instances of David's good treatment of the Muslims. *Khidma* can mean 'pay for service' (Lane, I, 711).
89. King David is praised here for his kind treatment of his Muslim subjects, just as Malik-Shāh is mentioned in laudatory terms by Georgian sources. Giorgi, the father of King David, went in person to Malik-Shāh in Iṣfahān to complain about the ravages of the Turks into

I witnessed all these privileges when I entered Tiflīs in 548 (1153-4). I saw the king of the Abkhāz, Dīmīṭrī, in whose service I was and who had come to Tiflīs. After he had stayed there a few days, he went down one Friday to the mosque and sat down on a *dikka*[90] opposite the preacher. He stayed in his place until the preacher had preached....[91] (and) he listened to the entire *khuṭba*. Then he went out and donated two hundred gold *dīnārs* to the mosque. I used to see him honour, reward and respect the *'ulamā'*, preachers, and *sharīfs* who sought him out, *Ṣūfīs* and others[92] who came to him[93]; and (he would) show unparalleled reliance on them. And from him I saw such esteem for the Muslims as they would not have enjoyed even if they had been in Baghdad.

¶ In the year 515 (1121-2) there was an earthquake in the city of Janza, which is Ganja.[94] Part of it fell to pieces and its walls collapsed. King Dā'ūd went with his retinue, horsemen and infantry and attacked the city.[95] He plundered their possessions and everything he found there, killing a large number of people and imprisoning innumerable crowds of them, so many of them that the prisoners entered Tiflīs on carts,[96] there being so many of them. (f.162b) The

his territory. Malik-Shāh stopped these incursions into Georgia, on condition that Giorgi paid *kharāj* (Brosset, *Géorgie* I, 349).

90. For the *dikka,* cf. J. Pedersen, "Masdjid", *EI*[1].
91. Ms.A has a lacuna here.
92. Literally: "those who came to him".
93. Sibṭ b. al-Jauzī interprets this passage more literally (cf. Hillenbrand, "Approaches", 202-3).
94. Cf. Yāqūt, *"Reisen"*, 17.
95. Sibṭ b. al-Jauzī, *Mir'āt,* 102. An earlier attack on Ganja by the Georgians in 503/1109-10 had been repelled (Ibn al-Qalānisī, *Dhail,* 167; al-Ḥusainī, *Akhbār,* 81). King David obviously saw the devastated city as a prime source of plunder.
96. Ms.A *dakhalat al-asārā ilā Tiflīs 'alā al-'ajl min kathratihim.*

Three possible meanings may be adduced for the phrase *'alā al-'ajl.* The first would appear to be the most satisfactory.

i) "on carts"

The meaning "cart" is attested by Sauvaget (J. Sauvaget, *Les Trésors d'Or de Sibṭ b. al-'Ajamī* [Beirut, 1950], II, 76). King David would use carts in order to prevent the enormous number of prisoners mentioned from escaping and to speed up his departure from Ganja where he was vulnerable to attack.

ii) "hurriedly"

King David would be anxious to get back to Tiflīs with the greatest possible haste.

iii) "sheep-fold"

This is a rather unlikely possibility. *'.j.l* might be an Arabicisation of the Turkish word *agil,* "enclosure for livestock, sheep-fold" (Clauson, *op.cit.,* 83a).

Muslim prisoners were driven along like herds of sheep. When Dā'ūd brought them into Tiflīs, the citizens of Tiflīs bought most of them and set them free. Some of the citizens of Tiflīs said to me, "We were only in straitened circumstances from that year onwards."

¶ In the year 515 (1121-2) Maudūd was killed in the Friday mosque of Damascus and was buried in the *burj*.[97]

¶ In the year 515 (1121-2) Najm al-Dīn returned to Mārdīn where he remained until 516 (12 March, 1122 - 28 February, 1123).[98] He went to Aushal al-Haina[99] in the district of Mayyāfāriqīn and stayed there with his wife the *khātūn*, the daughter of Ṭogh-Tegin, the lord of Damascus. He became ill and died on Thursday, 27 Ramaḍān (30 November, 1122).[100] He was carried by night. His son, Amīr Shams

97. Ibn al-Azraq has already given the date of Maudūd's death as 508/1114-5, ('Awaḍ, 280). There he writes that Maudūd was buried in the "Green Tower" (*ibid.*). It is generally accepted that Maudūd, the famous governor of Mosul and early opponent of the Crusaders, was assassinated in 507/1113-4. Ibn Khallikān gives the date as Friday, 12 Rabī' II, 507/ 26 September, 1113 (*Wafayāt*, I, 227). Cf. also H.S.Fink, "Mawdūd of Mosul, Precursor of Saladin", *The Muslim World*, XLIII (1953), 18-27. According to Ibn al-Qalānisī, he was buried in the *mashhad* inside the Bāb al-Farādīs (*Dhail*, 187-8).

98. Mārdīn was clearly the centre of İl-Ghāzī's power, the place to which he always returned for rest and reinforcements. Ibn Shaddād gives a long description of the town. He mentions a *madrasa* which was founded by İl-Ghāzī. Outside the town to the east was an open square around which the Artuqids built a wall (*Jazīra*, ff.130a-b).

    Ms.B points out that Temür-Tash had stayed behind in Mārdīn, while the Khātūn and Sulaimān accompanied İl-Ghāzī to Mayyāfāriqīn (f.105a).

99. The exact locality of this place remains obscure. Honigman mentions a place called Ausal/Ōsl "before the gates of Āmid" (*Ostgrenze*, 98). Matthew of Edessa writes about a place called "Aucal, à deux portées de flèche d'Amid" (*Chronique*, 13).

    Ibn al-Qalānisī states that İl-Ghāzī died at a village called al-Fuhūl in Diyār Bakr (*Dhail*, 208). For this kind of information, however, Ibn al-Azraq is more likely to be correct.

100. The dates given by the chroniclers for the death of İl-Ghāzī may be tabulated as follows:

Ibn al-Azraq, Ms.A:	27 Ramaḍān, 516
Ibn al-Azraq, Ms.B:	17 Ramaḍān, 516
Sibṭ b. al-Jauzī :	(*Mir'āt*, 103)
Ibn al-Qalānisī :	6 Ramaḍān, 516
	(*Dhail*, 208)
Ibn al-'Adīm	1 Ramaḍān, 516
	(*Zubda*, 206)

Again, in spite of Ibn al-Azraq's unreliable chronology, one of the dates in his history is more likely to be correct here. He should know best

al-Daula Sulaimān, and the *khātūn* rode and came to Mayyāfāriqīn by night, arriving at the Huwa gate.[101] They sat the *amīr* on his horse, held upright by a man behind him, moved forward and shouted. The *wālī*,[102] whose name was Oghuzoghlu,[103] came down. A *shaikh* who had been a companion of Najm al-Dīn since his early days, and to whom Shams al-Daula and the *khātūn* had given instructions, went inside.[104] Then he (the *wālī*) opened the gate and they said that the *amīr* was ill. When they reached the grounds of the citadel, they shouted and yelled that the *amīr* had just died.[105]

In the morning the population of the town and those soldiers who were there went up to the citadel. The *amīr* was washed, prayers were said over him and he was buried in the *sidillī*[106] for a while. Then he

when a major political figure from his own area died. However, it must be admitted that neither 17 nor 27 Ramaḍān fell on a Thursday.

101. The Huwa gate is mentioned by Ibn Shaddād, who recounts an anecdote to explain how it acquired its name (*Jazīra,* f.69b).

102. The term *wālī* presents problems of precise definition. Its meaning under the Saljuqs is well known. The *wālī* was the representative of the ruler, responsible for all aspects of the administration of a province (Horst, *Staatsverwaltung,* 46). In outlying districts such as Diyār Bakr in the early sixth/twelfth century a new overlord of a town would leave behind a *wālī* to ensure his master's continued tenure there.

103. *K.z.gh.ly:* This name presents great problems. Ibn Shaddād renders it in three different ways:

K.z.gh.ly (*Jazīra,* f.102b), *Q.zāghly* (*ibid.,* f.104b) and *Gh.zā'ly* (*ibid.,* f.58b). The vocalisation of all three versions is of course uncertain.

Koprülü rightly criticises Cahen for his reading of this name as Kuzugli (see his review of "Diyār Bakr" in *Belleten,* Cilt 1, Sayı 1 [1937], 287). Similarly, Artuk's version of Küngli is very unsatisfactory (*op.cit.,* 60). Turan's reading would appear to be the most sensible: Oğuzoğlu (*Doğu Anadolu,* 89).

There is a possibility that the name might be Kızoğlu but it is less satisfactory.

Whatever the reading of the name, this man was the *mamlūk* of Sukmān al-Quṭbī who appointed him *wālī* of Mayyāfāriqīn in 502/1108-9, where he remained until 506/1112-3 (Ibn Shaddād, *Jazīra,* f.101a; 'Awaḍ, 274-5, 279).

104. Ms.A: *wa-kallamahu Shams al-Daula wa'l-Khātūn fa-fataḥa al-bāb.*

This passage is very obscure. The sequence of events is not clear, nor is it certain who opened the gate of the city. It might well have been the *shaikh* rather than the *wālī.*

105. This subterfuge was necessitated by their desire to enter Mayyāfāriqīn at all costs and gain possession of the citadel before news of İl-Ghāzī's death leaked out. Hence they travelled by night. Once in control of the citadel, they could announce officially that İl-Ghāzī was dead and thus secure the city for Sulaimān.

106. Ibn Khallikān, in his biography of Naṣr al-Daula b.Marwān al-Kurdī, quotes Ibn al-Azraq to the effect that this ruler was buried in the castle

was removed and buried in the *masjid al-amīr* to the east of the *qubbat al-sulṭān*.[107] He was buried there (*sic*).

Najm al-Dīn İl-Ghāzī had married Farkhunda Khātūn, the daughter of Malik Riḍwān, when he had taken possession of Aleppo.[108] He had contracted a marriage with her but did not consummate the union with her nor did he see her; and he died without having met her.[109] Amīr Balak b. Bahrām b. Artuq married her after him.

Shams al-Daula Sulaimān became established in Mayyāfāriqīn, and he appointed as vizier 'Abd al-Malik b. Thābit and turned affairs over to him. He took Khartabirt[110] from Amīr Balak[111] and it remained in his possession until he died, whereupon Amīr Dā'ūd took it. Sulaimān (also) took the town of Ḥaza[112] from Amīr Dā'ūd and the villages in the district of Mayyāfāriqīn which Ḥusām al-Daula,[113] lord of Arzan, had taken.

In the year (5)17 (1 March, 1123 - 18 February, 1124), al-Afḍal, *amīr al-juyūsh* in Egypt, was killed, murdered by the Bāṭiniyya.[114]

of al-Sidillī, whence his body was afterwards removed to the vault of the Banū Marwān adjoining the Muḥaddatha mosque. Ibn Khallikān notes that al-Sidillī is the name of a dome situated in the castle of Mayyāfāriqīn, that this dome is built upon three pillars and that *sidillī* is a Persian word, signifying "three props" (*Wafayāt,* I, 157-9).

107. The Qubbat al-Sulṭān was built by Khumar-Tash, the *mamlūk* of Qïlïch Arslan b. Sulaimān b. Qutlumush. Qïlïch Arslān was buried there after his body had been retrieved from the Khābūr and brought to Mayyāfāriqīn ('Awaḍ, 273).

108. İl-Ghāzī settled Sulṭān-Shāh b. Riḍwān and the daughters of Riḍwān in a house at Aleppo after he had taken the city (Ibn al-'Adīm, *Zubda,* 185). He later married one of Riḍwān's daughters to consolidate his position in Aleppo, after his son, Sulaimān, had rebelled there in 515/1121-2 (*ibid.,* 202-3).

109. This assertion is contradicted by Ibn al-'Adīm who writes that the union was consummated in Aleppo (*ibid.,* 203).

110. For Khartabirt, cf. M. Canard, *H'amdanides,* 260; J.Markwart, *Südarmenien,* 69, 95; "Khartpert", *EI*².

111. For the career of Balak, cf. C. Cahen, "Balak", *EI*²; O. Turan, *Doğu Anadolu,* 151-5.

112. For an analysis of Dā'ūd b. Sukmān of Ḥiṣn Kaifā, cf. Hillenbrand, "Establishment", 142-5.
Sulaimān was attempting to restore to the territory of Mayyāfāriqīn its old boundaries by taking Ḥaza from his cousin, Dā'ūd of Ḥiṣn Kaifā, and by reconquering the lands taken by Ḥusām al-Daula of Arzan.

113. Cahen rightly amends the name Ḥusām al-Dīn to Ḥusām al-Daula ("Diyār Bakr", 241). This ruler is in fact Qurtï, the son of Ṭoghān Arslan al-Aḥdab, who inherited the family territories of Bitlīs and Arzan (Minorsky, *Studies,* 85).

114. Al-Afḍal b. Badr al-Jamālī, the famous Fāṭimid vizier, was assassinated

Sulaimān left as governor of Mayyāfāriqīn in the *burj al-mulk*[115] his *mamlūk*, Khutlugh-Shāh,[116] and he made overtures for the hand in marriage of Sayyida Khātūn, daughter of Sulṭān Qïlïch Arslan b. Sulaimān b. Quṭulmush. The *qāḍī* Tāj al-Dīn Abū Sālim b. Nubāta went to bring her from Malaṭya to him. He consummated the marriage with her and he made Mayyāfāriqīn[117] his place of residence.

It turned out that when Najm al-Dīn died, al-Sa'īd Ḥusām al-Dīn Temür-Tash[118] was in Mārdīn.[119] He therefore took over Mārdīn and assumed sole control there.[120] He had with him al-Ṣāḥib, the

in 515/1121. Ibn al-Qalānisī strongly refutes the suggestion that the Bāṭinīs were responsible for his death. He claims that the real cause was an estrangement between al-Afḍal and the caliph (*Dhail*, 203). For the death of al-Afḍal, cf. also Ibn al-Athīr, *al-Kāmil*, X, 416; Ibn Khallikān, *Wafayāt*, I, 614; F.Wüstenfeld, *Geschichte der Faṭimiden-Chalifen* [Göttingen, 1881], 289-90.

115. Ibn Shaddād describes the building of this tower at Mayyāfāriqīn (*Jazīra*, f.68a).

116. Ms.A: *Khtlḥshāh*. This name has been read as Khutlugh-Shāh.

117. For the career of Qïlïch Arslan I, the second Saljuq ruler in Rūm, cf. EI^2, s.v.
This marriage of Sulaimān b. İl-Ghāzī with the daughter of Sulṭān Qïlïch Arslan of Malaṭya may well represent an attempt by Sulaimān to emulate his successful cousin Balak, who had allied himself to the Saljuqs of Rūm and wielded power thereby. For a detailed account of the history of Malaṭya, cf. Eddé, *Description*, 110-4; Le Strange, *Palestine*, 499-500; "Malaṭya", EI^2.
Little is known of the short rule of Sulaimān (516-518/1122-4). For a brief analysis, cf. Hillenbrand, "Establishment", 136-7 and Cahen, "Diyār Bakr", 241.

118. The name of Temür-Tash only rarely occurs in Ibn al-Azraq's text. Usually this ruler is known under the title al-Sa'īd Ḥusām al-Dīn. When the name Temür-Tash appears, it has the form *T.mrdāsh*. For the etymology of this name, cf. J. Sauvaget, "Noms et Surnoms de Mamelouks", *Journal Asiatique* CCXXXVIII (1950), 47.

119. Ms.A: *wa-kāna lammā māta Najm al-Dīn anna al-Sa'īd Ḥusām al-Dīn Tmrdāsh wa-waladahu bi-Mārdīn.*
In the edition, the underlined *wa* has been removed. Whilst it is possible that "Ḥusām al-Dīn and his son were in Mārdīn", the most likely reading is "When Najm al-Dīn died, it happened that his son Ḥusām al-Dīn Temür-Tash was in Mārdīn." On f.163a Ibn al-Azraq lists the children of Temür-Tash. The only one of them born before 520/1126-7 was Ṣafiyya Khātūn whom he describes as the eldest of Temür-Tash's children. His sons whose names are known were born in 520 and thereafter.

120. There is general agreement in the sources that Temür-Tash succeeded his father at Mārdīn (cf. Anon. Syr. Chron., 89; Ibn al-Qalānisī, *Dhail*, 208; Ibn al-Athīr, *al-Kāmil* X, 426; Ibn al-'Adīm, *Zubda*, 209).

chamberlain, Shams al-Ḥujjāb Muḥammad Igdish,[121] whom Najm al-Dīn İl-Ghāzī had married to the mother of Ḥusām al-Dīn.[122]

¶ On 26 Rabīʿ II (11 June 1124) the *qāḍī* ʿAlam al-Dīn Abu'l-Ḥasan ʿAlī b. Yaḥyā b. Nubāta died in Mayyāfāriqīn.[123] His son, the *qāḍī* Tāj al-Dīn, took over the office of *qāḍī*. He was (also called) Abū Sālim, may God have mercy on him. Shams al-Daula laid ceremonial garments on him, honoured him by giving him his father's post, and he became established in the office of *qāḍī*. Shams al-Daula had a son (f.163a) whose name was Maḥmūd.[124] I saw him in Mārdīn. He was in the worst possible condition because of the evil life he led, his own shameful conduct in his personal life, his disobedience to his family and his depravity. I do not know what became of him. Shams al-Daula was an *amīr* who was just, virtuous, daring and courageous. He lived until the afternoon of Thursday, 6 Ramaḍān 518 (17 October, 1124)[125] and was buried with his father in the *masjid al-amīr*.[126] The *wālī* Khutlugh-Shāh[127] assumed sole control in Mayyāfāriqīn and it came into his possession and under his sway.

121. Ikdīsh: Cahen gives this name as Akdīš ("Diyār Bakr", 240). One possible reading of this word might be Ighdish ("eunuch") (cf. Uzunçarşili, *Osmanli devleti*, 115).

A more attractive alternative is Houtsma's reading of "ägdish", which he translates as "Pferd von gemischter Rasse" (M.T. Houtsma, *Ein Türkisch-Arabisches Glossar* [Leiden, 1894], 51). In a later work, Cahen defines the word *ikdīsh* as a "gelding or cross-bred animal". From this meaning it came to mean a human being of mixed race. In Asia Minor, it referred mainly to the offspring of unions between Turks and the indigenous inhabitants (C. Cahen, *Pre-Ottoman Turkey*, tr. J. Jones-Williams, [London, 1968], 192).

122. It was the common practice at this time amongst the Saljuqs and other Turkish rulers for an *atābeg* to marry the mother of his young ward.

123. ʿAlam al-Dīn Abu'l-Ḥasan ʿAlī b. Yaḥyā b. Nubāta was born in 464/1071-2 (ʿAwaḍ, 267). He became *qāḍī* in 507/1113-4 and remained in the post until he died (*ibid.*, 279 and 282).

124. Cahen mentions in a footnote to his genealogical table of the Artuqids that Maḥmūd was a governor of Mārdīn and then exiled ("Diyār Bakr", 168) but he does not cite his source.

125. For the death of Sulaimān, cf. also Sibṭ b. al-Jauzī (*Mir'āt*, 117); Michael the Syrian (*Chronique*, 220).

126. The bodies of İl-Ghāzī and his son, Sulaimān, were later transferred to Mārdīn by Temür-Tash (cf. f.171a).

127. *Kh.tlshāh*. This is probably another attempt to reproduce the name Khutlugh-Shāh.

Chapter 3

The early reign of Temür-Tash

When Shams al-Daula died, Khutlugh-Shāh assumed sole control in Mayyāfāriqīn with the vizier ʻAbd al-Malik. Ḥusām al-Dīn came, approached the gate of the city, encamped outside the town and sent a message to Khutlugh-Shāh.[1] The *amīr* Dā'ūd b. Sukmān,[2] lord of Ḥiṣn Kaifā,[3] was about to leave (for Mayyāfāriqīn) but al-Sa'īd

1. The acquisition of the citadels of Mayyāfāriqīn and Mārdīn presented great difficulties to any would-be conqueror. They could be taken either by negotiation, usually after a protracted siege (e.g. the conquest of Mayyāfāriqīn by Ibn Jahīr in 478/1085-6) or by subterfuge (e.g. Yāqūtī's acquisition of Mārdīn, cf. *supra,* n.17). Typically Temür-Tash preferred to negotiate with the *wālī* of his late brother. Sulaimān, of course, had opted for a trick to enter the citadel. Temür-Tash was not the only ruler interested in Mayyāfāriqīn and his succession there after his brother's death was by no means a foregone conclusion
2. The death of the senior member of the family, Īl-Ghāzī, shortly followed by that of his son Sulaimān, left a power vacuum in Diyār Bakr. Both Dā'ūd and Temür-Tash possessed a strong base in the area, at Ḥiṣn Kaifā and Mārdīn respectively, but Mayyāfāriqīn lay without a protector.

   The history of the period 518-538/1124-44 in Diyār Bakr is dominated by the rivalry of these two cousins and by their relationship with Zangī.
3. Ibn Shaddād gives a detailed description of Ḥiṣn Kaifā. He stresses the impregnability of its citadel and lists the town's monuments. The citadel had within its enclosure a green *maidān* and fields where enough wheat, barley and grains were grown to feed its inhabitants from year to year. In the *rabaḍ* to the north were bazaars, *khāns, madrasas, hammāms,* tombs and the *turbas* of the Banū Marwān and the Banū Artuq (*Jazīra,* f. 127a).

Ḥusām al-Dīn arrived (there) first.[4] He contacted Khutlugh-Shāh and he swore to meet his demands, swearing to him that he would make no changes which would put the people of the town at a disadvantage and that he would appoint ʻAbd al-Malik as vizier. He took an oath agreeing to their demands and entered the town in Shawwāl 518[5] (11 November - 10 December 1124). He appointed ʻAbd al-Malik as vizier. His position became established and he acquired everything that had belonged to his father Najm al-Dīn. He treated the people kindly and they liked him. He assumed sole control.

He married the wife of his brother, the *amīr* Ayāz[6] b. Najm al-Dīn, who had had by her Shihāb al-Dīn Muḥammad b. Ayāz. Temür-Tash had by her a daughter, Ṣafiyya Khātūn, who was the eldest of his children. After a while he married the *khātūn*, daughter of the *amīr* Ghāzī[7] from Erzerum. She came to Mayyāfāriqīn and he had by her the lord Najm al-Dīn Alpï in 520 (27 January 1126 - 16 January 1127). Then he had (by her) the *amīr* Jamāl al-Dīn Qurtï (?)[8] in 521 (17 January 1127 - 5 January 1128). After Ḥusām al-Dīn took possession of the country, he begat Hadiyya Khātūn, and then Amīr Ṣamṣām al-Dīn Bahrām in 5??.

Ḥusām al-Dīn took possession of Aleppo which remained in his

4. Temür-Tash had hurried to Mārdīn from Aleppo on 25 Rajab 518 to ask for help from his brother against the Franks at Aleppo and to collect troops (Ibn al-ʻAdīm, *Zubda,* 223). While Temür-Tash was at Mārdīn, Sulaimān died and Temür-Tash went quickly to Mayyāfāriqīn. He was preoccupied with the acquisition of his brother's territories to the exclusion of thinking about Aleppo (*ibid.,* 225).
5. The negotiations must have lasted several weeks since Sulaimān had died at the beginning of the previous month, Ramaḍān, and it is to be assumed that Temür-Tash acted quickly.
6. According to Sauvaget, there were two versions of this name: Ayāz (or Iyāz) and Ayās (or Iyās) (*op.cit.,* 39). Ms.A has the form Ayās (or Iyās) whilst Ms.B prefers Alyās (or Ilyās).
7. This is a reference to the third Saltuqid ruler of Erzerum (cf. O. Turan, *Doğu Anadolu,* 8 and 241). His full title was Alp Ṭoghrïl Beg Abu'l-Muẓaffar Ghāzī (cf. R.H. Ünal, *Les Monuments Islamiques Anciens de la Ville d'Erzurum et de sa Région* [Paris, 1968], 26).
8. This name is unclear in the manuscripts. The word probably contains four letters, of which the second is an r (or z) and the fourth is a y. Cahen read Tafratī ("Diyār Bakr", 268). Artuk prefers Ṭughrati: I. Artuk, *Mardin Artukoğullari Tarihi* (Istanbul, 1944) - Artuk's genealogical table is on the last unnumbered page of his book. Neither of these options are very satisfactory. Perhaps it should read Qurtï.

hands for a while.[9] Then he exchanged it for (ʻAzāz (?)) or he handed it over and it left his possession.[10]

¶ Sulṭān Maḥmūd set out for Iraq and wanted to enter (the country), but the caliph al-Mustarshid prevented him from doing so. Much fighting took place between them. Al-Mustarshid was defeated, his possessions were plundered, and Sulṭān Maḥmūd entered Iraq without his permission. After a while they became well reconciled.[11]

¶ In 519 (7 February 1125 - 26 January 1126) or at the beginning of 520 (January 1126) al-Bursuqī was killed in the Friday mosque in

9. The order of events is confused here. According to Ibn al-ʻAdīm, Temür-Tash took possession of Aleppo on Wednesday, 20 Rabīʻ I, 518 after the death of Balak two days before. He then left for Mārdīn on 25 Rajab, 518 and acquired Mayyāfāriqīn after the death of his brother Sulaimān (*Zubda,* 220-5).

A striking characteristic of Ibn al-Azraq's history is his lack of interest and information about Aleppan affairs. This elliptical reference to Temür-Tash's acquisition and loss of Aleppo may be the result of a genuine lack of information about these events. A more probable motive, however - in this instance at least - is a desire on the part of Ibn al-Azraq to suppress those facts about Temür-Tash's role in Aleppan affairs which did not redound to his credit.

10. Once in power at Aleppo, Temür-Tash's first important step was to release Baldwin; this was on Friday 17 Rajab 518. Baldwin had agreed to hand over a number of citadels and a large ransom, but immediately after his release he violated his agreement with Temür-Tash. Baldwin allied himself with Dubais and other parties interested in Aleppo while Temür-Tash went to Mārdīn to seek help from his brother. Messengers were sent to Temür-Tash from the people of Aleppo. He ignored their entreaties, temporised with them and finally imprisoned them. The messengers, one of whom was an ancestor of Ibn al-ʻAdīm, escaped and sought help instead from Aq-Sonqur al-Bursuqī, who took Aleppo in Dhu'l-Ḥijja 518/January 1125 (Ibn al-ʻAdīm, *Zubda,* 223-30; *Bughyat,* 204-7).

The illegible part of this passage in Ms.A is not found in Ms.B. The text seems to read: *ʻwaḍa bi-hā Kh.dh.k au sallama Ḥalab.*

11. This incident is recorded in detail by Ibn al-Athīr. The *shiḥna* of Baghdad came into conflict with the caliph, al-Mustarshid, in 519/1125-6. The *shiḥna* left Baghdad that same year and complained to the *sulṭān* of his treatment at the hands of the caliph. He informed the *sulṭān* that the caliph was raising troops to prevent him from entering Iraq. Sulṭān Maḥmūd left for Iraq and although the caliph asked him not to come to Baghdad, the *sulṭān* persisted. He arrived in Baghdad on 20 Dhu'l-Ḥijja, 519 and stayed until 10 Rabīʻ II, 520. There were skirmishes between the troops of the *sulṭān* and caliph and finally the caliph sought peace. Maḥmūd appointed a new *shiḥna* of Baghdad, Zangī (*Atabegs,* 28-31; *al-Kāmil,* X, 447-450). Cf. also Mustaufī, *Guzīda,* 345; al-Ḥusainī, *Akhbār,* 97.

Mosul by the Bāṭiniyya.[12] His son Mas'ūd[13] took over the land of Diyār Rabī'a and other places. The *qāḍī* Bahā' al-Dīn al-Shahrazūrī,[14] Naṣīr al-Dīn Jaqar[15] and Ṣalāḥ al-Dīn Muḥammad Yaghi-Siyanī[16] met together, collected money and taxes[17] and went down to Baghdad to pay their respects[18] to Sulṭān Maḥmūd and to establish Amīr Mas'ūd b. al-Bursuqī in the land.[19] When they arrived, they reconsidered (the matter) and said: "He is a young boy, who won't concern himself (f.163b) with governing and who may well not administer the country wisely. We will be blamed for the wrong he

12. For the death of Aq-Sonqur al-Bursuqī, the ruler of Mosul, cf. Ibn al-Qalānisī, *Dhail*, 214; al-'Aẓīmī, *"Chronique"*, 397; Ibn al-'Adīm, *Bughyat*, 213; Ibn Khallikān, *Wafayāt*, I, 227; Ibn al-Athīr, *Atabegs*, 31; *al-Kāmil*, X, 446-7; Bar Hebraeus, *Chronography*, 252. Ibn al-Azraq's dates are wrong, since the sources seem agreed that the murder of Aq-Sonqur al-Bursuqī took place at the end of 520 in Dhu'l-Qa'da. Ibn al-'Adīm and Ibn Khallikān agree that the exact date was Friday 9 Dhu'l-Qa'da,520. Ibn al-Athīr has 8 Dhu'l-Qa'da.
13. 'Izz al-Dīn Mas'ūd succeeded his father at Mosul and was confirmed in his post by Sulṭān Maḥmūd. Mas'ūd took as main adviser, Chavli, who had been one of his father's *mamlūks*. The following year, however - 521/1127 - Mas'ūd died (Ibn al-Athīr, *Atabegs*, 32). Cf. also Bar Hebraeus, *Chronography*, 252-3.
14. Bahā' al-Dīn al-Shahrazūrī belonged to the eminent Shahrazūrī family which furnished the Zangid dynasty with many of its *qāḍīs* (cf. Chapter 6, n. 100).
15. Naṣīr al-Dīn Jaqar was an important adviser and associate of Zangī. Indeed, he served as Zangī's deputy in Mosul. Cf. Ibn al-Furāt (Shayyāl), 129-30.
16. Ms.B writes the name *al-Yaghisiyanī* as *al-Aghisiyanī*. According to Usāma, Salāḥ al-Dīn possessed unusual ferocity and cruelty. This man, who had held the office of *ḥājib* in the time of Aq-Sonqur al-Bursuqī, is mentioned frequently by Usāma (*Memoirs*, 187-9).
17. Ibn al-Athīr also mentions that Chavli's envoys took a large sum of money with them (*Atabegs*, 32).
18. *Khadama* is used here in accordance with Dozy's definition: "témoigner son respect à quelqu'un, en lui offrant quelque chose" (*Supplément* I, 354).
19. Ibn al-Azraq's account differs from that of Ibn al-Athīr in a number of important details. Ibn al-Athīr puts the date of the visit to Baghdad of officials from Mosul in 521/1127-8. Jaqar was not in Mosul, as Ibn al-Azraq suggests, but in Baghdad with Zangī. Chavli, who had taken control in Mosul, sent Bahā' al-Dīn al-Shahrazūrī and Ṣalāḥ al-Dīn al-Yaghi-Siyanī to Baghdad to ask the *sulṭān* to confirm the young brother of 'Izz al-Dīn Mas'ūd as ruler of Mosul. According to Ibn al-Athīr, Mas'ūd himself had died in 521/1127 (*Atabegs*, 32). This date is confirmed by Ibn al-Qalānisī (*Dhail*, 217) and Ibn Khallikān, who gives the exact day as 22 Jumādā II, 521 (*Wafayāt*, I, 228).

does."[20] So they agreed to meet Zangī b. Qasīm al-Daula Āq Sonqur,[21] who was the *shiḥna* of Baghdad that year. They established with him what offices they wanted[22] and they exacted an oath from him promising that Bahā' al-Dīn should become *qāḍī* of Mosul and should exercise control over the posts of *qāḍī* in the whole country and over religious affairs.[23] He (also) swore that the offices of *ḥājib*[24] and of *amīr al-ʿaskar*[25] should go to Ṣalāḥ al-Dīn[26] and that Naṣīr al-Dīn should govern Mosul and the whole country and appoint as his *wālīs* whom he thought fit.[27] So Zangī swore to them that he would do this and the matter was settled to their mutual satisfaction. Then they paid their respects to the *sulṭān* and his retinue and to the caliph and his retinue, handing over the money which they had brought with

20. *al-ḥaif ʿalainā*. Two other translations are possible for this phrase:-
 i) what a pity for us!
 ii) there will be injustice on us (i.e. injustice will fall on us).
 According to Ibn al-Athīr, Bahā' al-Dīn and Ṣalāḥ al-Dīn were worried by Chavlī's power at Mosul. When they arrived in Baghdad, therefore, Ṣalāḥ al-Dīn consulted Naṣīr al-Dīn Jaqar who was a relation of his by marriage. Jaqar suggested that Zangī should assume power at Mosul. Jaqar and Ṣalāḥ al-Dīn then returned to Bahā' al-Dīn and tried to persuade him to give Zangī his support. After the promise of *iqṭāʿs*, Bahā' al-Dīn agreed to the plan. The two envoys from Mosul then had a meeting with the *sulṭān's* vizier, Anūshīrvān b. Khālid. They said that the son of al-Bursuqī was a mere child and that Mosul needed a determined, courageous man to defend it (*Atabegs*, 34-5). Cf. also Bar Hebraeus' account (*Chronography*, 253).

21. Ms.A has the name Qasīm al-Daula Zangī b. Aq-Sonqur (*sic*). This has been corrected in the translation to read "Zangī b. Qasīm al-Daula Aq-Sonqur".
 The father of Zangī was called Qasīm al-Daula Aq-Sonqur, whilst Zangī himself was known as "Atābeg b. Qasīm al-Daula" (Ibn al-ʿAdīm, *Bughyat*, 97 and 251).

22. *mā arādū min maṣāliḥihim*: literally "what they wanted in the way of things to their advantage". Ibn al-Athīr mentions no meeting with Zangī to discuss the distribution of offices.

23. According to Ibn al-Athīr, Bahā' al-Dīn was made chief *qāḍī* of all Zangī's existing territories and any other places which might be conquered subsequently. Of all the officials, he was the closest to Zangī and the most powerful (*Atabegs*, 35).

24. For a description of the office of *ḥājib* in Saljuq times, cf. Uzunçarşīlī, *op.cit.*, 35-6. The *ḥājib* acted as an intermediary between the ruler and his government (cf. also *EI*², s.v. *ḥājib;* Horst, *Staatsverwaltung*, 18-9).

25. The head of the ruler's own personal troops.

26. According to Ibn al-Athīr, Ṣalāḥ al-Dīn received the office of *amīr ḥājib* (*Atabegs*, 35).

27. Naṣīr al-Dīn Jaqar was made governor of Mosul and was given overall responsibility for the administration of the province and its citadels (*ibid.*).

them.[28] They sought out Zangī and the *sulṭān* handed over to him his two sons Alp Arslan and al-Khafājī.[29] Zangī became *atābeg* to them both[30] and gained control of the country.[31] He went and took possession of Mosul and the country at the beginning of 522 (January 1128).[32]

¶ In 522 (6 January - 24 December 1128) Nūr al-Daula (Balak) was killed. While he was attempting to seize Manbij[33] in Syria and was besieging it, he was struck by an arrow which killed him.[34] Amīr

28. The account given by Ibn al-Azraq broadly agrees with that of Michael the Syrian (*Chronique,* 229).
    Ibn al-Athīr has another account of Zangī's acquisition of Mosul (*al-Kāmil,* X, 453-4). Cf. also Bar Hebraeus, *Chronography,* 253-4; Ibn Khallikān, *Wafayāt,* I, 540.
29. Maḥmūd had two small sons, Alp Arslan and Farrukh-Shāh. There is, however, confusion in the sources on the question of which of them had the title al-Khafājī. Ibn al-Azraq clearly does not give the title to Alp Arslan but he does not know the names of Maḥmūd's other son. Ibn al-Athīr speaks of Alp Arslan al-Khafājī (*Atabegs,* 71), whilst Bundārī mentions Farrukh-Shāh al-Khafājī (*Zubdat,* 205).
30. For a definition of the term *atābeg,* cf. M.F. Sanaullah, *The Decline of the Saljūqid Empire* (Calcutta, 1938), 5-7.
31. Ms.B has: "They asked for one of his sons and that Zangī should be his atābeg".
    It is significant to note that it was regarded as necessary to preserve the fiction that by the use of the two *maliks* the sulṭān's line was still in power. By the same token, Chavlï had wanted the stamp of the sulṭān's official approval for the government at Mosul to be invested in the son of Aq-Sonqur al-Bursuqī. The *de facto* ruler would of course have been Chavlï, if his plan had succeeded.
32. The sources are generally agreed that Zangī took possession of Mosul in 521/1127. This year is given by Ibn al-Athīr (*Atabegs,* 34; *al-Kāmil,* X, 454) and Ibn Shaddād (*Jazīra,* f. 45a). Ibn Khallikān records the exact date as 10 Muḥarram,521/27 January,1127 (*Wafayāt,*I, 540).
33. For a lengthy account of this town in northern Syria, cf. Eddé, *Description,* 281-97. Cf. also *EI²*, s.v.
34. Once again, Ibn al-Azraq's chronology is inaccurate. The date of Balak's death is discussed by J. Sauvaget ("La tombe de l'Ortoḳide Balak", *Ars Islamica* V [1938], 207-15). The inscription on his tomb records the date of Balak's death as Rabī' I,518 (April-May 1124.)
    Amongst the chroniclers, Ibn al-'Adīm gives the most detailed account of Balak's death. He notes the date as 19 Rabī' I,518 (*Zubda,* 219). Cf. also Ibn al-Athīr, *al-Kāmil,* X, 436; al-'Aẓīmī, "Chronique", 394; Ibn al-Furāt, *Duwal,* I, f. 196a (*apud* Cahen, notes to al-'Aẓīmī, "Chronique", 440).
    For an account of Balak's career, cf. O. Turan, *Doğu Anadolu,* 151-5.

Dā'ūd took possession of his territories: Khartabirt, Bālū,[35] Mīzgard[36] and its neighbourhood. Amīr Balak had taken this province from the sons of Jubuq.[37] When Balak died, he left no successors other than a daughter whom Fakhr al-Dīn Qara Arslan b. Dā'ūd married.[38]

¶ In 523 (25 December 1128 - 14 December 1129) Atābeg Ṭogh-Tegin died[39] in Damascus and his son Tāj al-Mulūk Būrī assumed control over Damascus and its environs.

¶ On 5 Shawwāl 524 (11 September 1130) Sulṭān Maḥmūd, lord of Iṣfahān, died.[40] Also in that year the vizier al-Mazdaqānī, Bahrām and all the Ismā'īlīs in Damascus were killed.[41] Sulṭān Maḥmūd was

35. Ms.A *kālwā (sic)*. Bālū was also called Palu (cf. Honigmann, *Ostgrenze,* 30-2; Markwart describes Bālū as lying west of Khartabirt (*kh.t.b.rt)* and east of Sumaisāṭ (*Südarmenien,* 242).

36. Cf. Abū Bakr Tihrānī, *Kitāb Diyārbakriyya,* ed. N. Lugal and F. Sümer (Ankara, 1962) II, 222.

37. Jubuq was in the service of Ibn Jahīr when the latter took Mayyāfāriqīn. Ibn Jahīr gave him Khartabirt which remained in the possession of Jubuq and his descendants until Balak took it from them. After losing Khartabirt, Jubuq's descendants served the Artuqids at Ḥiṣn Kaifā ('Awaḍ, 212-3). Ibn Shaddād relates that after Ibn Jahīr had taken Diyār Bakr, Amīr Jubuq stayed behind with 300 horsemen. After he died, his sons took his territory (*Jazīra,* f. 94a).

38. Whilst Temür-Tash managed to forestall him at Mayyāfāriqīn, Dā'ūd moved quickly to seize Balak's territories, thus arriving before the Danishmendid Gümüsh-Tegin Ghāzī from Malaṭya. For Dā'ūd's attack on Bālū, cf. Ibn al-Furāt, *Duwal,* f. 196b (*apud* Cahen, "Diyār Bakr", 242).

Michael the Syrian relates that since Dā'ūd had stolen a march on Gümüsh-tegin Ghāzī at Khartabirt, the latter pillaged the area of Khanzīt and took Mazara (*Chronique,* 220).

39. Ṭogh-Tegin died on Saturday 8 Ṣafar,522 (Ibn al-Qalānisī, *Dhail,* 219; Ibn Khallikān, *Wafayāt,* I, 274. Būrī died on 21 Rajab,526 (June 1132) (*ibid).*

40. Ibn al-Furāt gives the date of Sulṭān Maḥmūd's death as Thursday 5 Shawwāl,525. He then adds without comment that "Ibn al-Azraq al-Fāriqī gave the date as 15 (*sic)* Shawwāl,524 and mentioned that he died outside Iṣfahān, where he was buried" (*Duwal,* f. 29b).

Ibn Khallikān gives the date as Thursday 15 Shawwāl,525. He also cites the date given by Ibn al-Azraq but he too makes no comment on its accuracy (*Wafayāt,* III, pt. 1, 346). For other accounts of Sulṭān Maḥmūd's death, cf. *Akhbār* 99, Rawandī, *Rāḥat,* 204; Ibn al-Athīr, *al-Kāmil,* X, 470; Bundārī, *Zubdat,* 154-5.

41. Ms.A: *wa-fīhā q.t.la al-wazīr al-Mazdaqānī wa-Bahrām al-Bāṭiniyya ajma'*.

This has been translated as "Also in that year the vizier al-Mazdaqānī, Bahrām and all the Ismā'īlīs were killed".

This passage reveals a complete confusion on the part of Ibn al-Azraq or his scribe or both. In order to make sense of the historical facts, *wa* has been added between "Bahrām" and "all the Bāṭinīs".

This incident is covered in detail by Ibn al-Qalānisī (*Dhail,* 220-5).

buried in Iṣfahān. His brother, Sulṭān Ṭoghrïl Beg, became *sulṭān* for a period of two years and he died early in 527 (November 1132), whereupon his brother, Sulṭān Mas'ūd, became *sulṭān*.[42]

¶ Sulṭān (Muḥammad)[43] left a number of sons, amongst whom was Sulṭān Maḥmūd, who wielded exclusive power, Ṭoghrïl Beg, Sulṭān Sulaimān-Shāh, Mas'ūd, Saljuq-Shāh, and Bahrām-Shāh.[44] He took

Bahrām, the propagandist of the Bāṭinīs at Damascus, was aided in the advancement of his aims by the vizier Abu'l-Ṭāhir al-Mazdaqānī. The latter was killed at Damascus at the instigation of Būrī b. Ṭogh-Tegin on 17 Ramaḍān, 523 (1129). Thereafter the townspeople seized known Ismā'īlīs and killed them.

Bahrām was not killed at Damascus but in the valley of Tayyim during the previous year. He had been given the frontier fortress of Bāniyās by Ṭogh-Tegin to hold against the Franks. Whilst Īl-Ghāzī was in charge of Aleppo, Bahrām had persuaded him to recommend him to Ṭogh-Tegin. At Damascus he had preached openly (M.G.S. Hodgson, *The Order of Assassins* [The Hague, 1955], 104-5).

For other accounts of the Ismā'īlīs' massacre at Damascus, cf. Michael the Syrian, *Chronique*, 239-40; al-'Aẓīmī, "Chronique", 400-1; Ibn al-Furāt (Shayyāl), 15-6. Ibn al-Azraq wrongly inserts this incident in the middle of Sulṭān Maḥmūd's death notice.

42. Ibn al-Azraq is probably unaware of the complicated power-struggle which followed the death of Sulṭān Maḥmūd. Ṭoghrïl was Sanjar's candidate. He acceded to the throne after Sanjar had defeated Mas'ūd and Dā'ūd, who also aspired to the sultanate in the western part of the Saljuq empire.

For the short reign of Ṭoghrïl and the troubled events of the years 525/1131 - 529/1135, cf. Bundārī, *Zubdat*, 160-172; al-Ḥusainī, *Akhbār*, 101-3; Mustaufī, *Guzīda*, 335-346; Ibn al-Athīr, *al-Kāmil*, X, 474-7, 480).

Ṭoghrïl finally came to the throne in Jumādā II, 526 (Bundārī, *Zubdat*, 160). As for his death, whilst Ibn al-Qalānisī puts it in 528, most sources give Muḥarram 529 (e.g. *al-Kāmil*, XI, 11; *Atabegs*, 49; Rāwandī, *Rāḥat*, 208; Mustaufī, *Guzīda*, 346). Ibn al-Jauzī gives an exact date of Wednesday 3 Muḥarram 529 (*Muntaẓam*, X, 53). Once again Ibn al-Azraq's dates are chaotic.

43. The text of Ms.A mentions no name for this *sulṭān* but the context makes it clear that Sulṭān Muḥammad is meant. For a genealogical table of the late Saljuqs and especially of those mentioned by Ibn al-Azraq on these pages, cf. Appendix B.

44. Justi's genealogical table, which is very detailed, has no mention of a son of Muḥammad called Bahrām-Shāh (F. Justi, *Iranisches Namenbuch* [Marburg, 1895], 452). Ibn al-Azraq is probably making a garbled reference to Bahrām-Shāh b. Ṭoghrïl b. Muḥammad who wielded power in Jīruft from 565/1169-70 - 570/1174-5 (cf. Bosworth, 'Iranian World', 173).

(Jīruft) (?).[45] Sulṭān Maḥmūd left Sulṭān Dā'ūd, who was the eldest of his children, and took possession of Āzarbāījān. He was killed in Tabrīz in 539 (4 July 1144 - 23 June 1145) by the Bāṭiniyya in the centre of the bazaar and was buried in Tabrīz.[46] Sulṭān Maḥmūd also left Muḥammad-Shāh who became *sulṭān* after his uncle Mas'ūd, whose daughter he married.[47] Maḥmūd (also) left Malik-Shāh, who during the lifetime of his uncle Mas'ūd was in the *'askar* with him. (Thereafter) he took Khūzistān.[48] Maḥmūd (also) left Alp Arslan and al-Khafājī with Atābeg Zangī in Mosul where they were both killed.[49] He also had a daughter, Guhar, by the daughter of Sulṭān Sanjar. Guhar lived until around the year 557 (21 December 1161 - 9 December 1162).

As for Sulaimān-Shāh, he died and left no heirs.[50] As for Saljuq,[51] he

45. Ms.A *wa-Bahrām Shāh qīla wa-akhadha/ukhidha*

This part of the text is almost certainly incomplete. Ms.B offers no help. Either a place-name such as Jīruft should be inserted, or - if translated as it stands - *ukhidha* might mean the same as *tuwuffiyā*. This latter suggestion is far from satisfactory. Later on in the text Ibn al-Azraq lists in turn the offspring of Sulṭān Muḥammad's sons and omits Bahrām Shāh, thereby confirming that this piece of the text is corrupt.

46. There is general agreement in the sources that Dā'ūd died in 538/1143-4, not in 539/1144-5 as Ibn al-Azraq suggests..Bundārī says that Dā'ūd married a daughter of Sulṭān Mas'ūd and that he died in Tabrīz in 538. Bundārī also hints that Zangī had instigated his murder (*Zubdat*, 195). Al-'Aẓīmī gives a more precise date, Rabī' I, 538, and states that he was killed in Tabrīz by three men ("Chronique", 423). Cf. also Ibn al-Qalānisī, *Dhail*, 277; al-Ḥusainī, *Akhbār*, 114.

Dā'ūd was a claimant to the sultanate after the death of Maḥmūd, his father, but Sanjar opted for Ṭoghril. Dā'ūd's power base was Ādharbāījān. After Mas'ūd's accession, Dā'ūd was finally mollified by Mas'ūd's appointing him his heir (cf. Bosworth, "Iranian World", 124-5).

47. Muḥammad b. Maḥmūd is discussed in greater detail by Ibn al-Azraq on f. 175b.

48. Malik-Shah b. Maḥmūd is also discussed by Ibn al-Azraq on f. 175b.

49. According to Ibn al-Athīr, Alp Arslan was still alive in 539/1144-5 and it was he who was responsible for the death of Naṣīr al-Dīn Jaqar in that year. Zangī was waiting for Mas'ūd to die so that he could make Alp Arslan *sulṭān* in his place (*Atabegs*, 71-2).

Alp Arslan was a significant protagonist in the events which followed the assassination of Zangī in 541/1146. He was misled into the belief that he would rule at Mosul but was in fact taken prisoner (Ibn al-Azraq, f. 172a).

50. Whilst Justi's genealogical table gives no heirs to Sulaimān-Shāh b. Muḥammad b. Malik-Shāh (*op.cit.*, 452-3), Luther says that he had a son called Sanjar (K.A. Luther, *The Political Transformation of the Seljuq Sultanate of Iraq and Western Iran: 1152-78*, unpublished Ph.D. thesis, [Princeton, 1964], 291).

For a detailed analysis of the short reign of Sulaimān-Shāh, cf. *ibid.*,

had a son who lived in Mosul, having been with Mas'ūd Bilāl in the citadel of Takrīt.[52] When it was taken, he was brought to Mosul where he is now. He has some children. As for Sulṭān Ṭoghrïl Beg, he sired Arslan-Shāh whose mother was the wife of the *amīr* Eldigüz.[53] He is now *sulṭān* (f.164a) (of the area) from Iṣfahān, Hamadhān, Āzarbāījān and Arrān up to the city of Ganja and Shamkūr (?).[54]

In 524 (15 December 1129 - 3 December 1130), Ḥusām al-Dīn and Dā'ūd were defeated at Sarja[55] below Dārā.[56] They were defeated by Atābeg Zangī.[57]

114-128. The important events in the career of Sulaimān-Shāh before he became *sulṭān* are discussed by Bosworth, "Iranian World", especially 144, 155 and 169. He ruled 555-6/1160-1 and was murdered in 556/1161 (Rāwandī, *Rāḥat,* 279; Ibn al-Athīr, *al-Kāmil,* XI, 175; Bundārī, *Zubdat,* 296; al-Ḥusainī, *Akhbār,* 144).

51. Saljuq-Shāh was the only one of Muḥammad's five sons who did not eventually rule as sulṭān (Bosworth, "Iranian World", 119). On the death of Maḥmūd, he had made a bid for authority from his power base in Fārs and Khūzistān, supported by his *atābeg,* Qaracha. He was also involved in the events of the caliphal crisis of 529-30/1134-6 and thereafter (*ibid.,* 128-9). In 532/1137-8 Saljuq-Shāh made peace with his brother Mas'ūd. The latter gave him the territories which had belonged to the Shāh-i Arman, whose centre of power was Akhlāṭ (Bundārī, *Zubdat,* 185; al-Ḥusainī, *Akhbār,* 111). It is significant to note Ibn al-Azraq's isolated comment in Ms.A, f.167b where he notes that Saljuq-Shāh laid siege to Akhlāṭ in 532 but then withdrew.

Qara-Sonqur put Saljuq-Shāh in power in Fārs in 533/1138-9 but the following year he was deposed by Boz-Aba. He probably died in captivity (Bosworth, "Iranian World", 129-30).

52. Mas'ūd Bilāl was *shiḥna* of Baghdad until al-Muqtafī drove him out on the death of Sultan Mas'ūd. Cf. f. 175b.

53. Arslan-Shāh's mother married Eldigüz after the death of Ṭoghrïl (Mustaufī, *Guzīda,* 352 and 358). Arslan Shāh came to the throne in Dhu'l-Qa'da 555/1160 at Hamadhān (Ḥusainī, *Akhbār,* 145). Eldigüz was proclaimed *atābeg al-a'ẓam* and was to play the key role in the new régime (*ibid.;* Bundārī, *Zubdat,* 297). Arslan-Shāh died in Jumādā II 571/December-January 1175-6 (Rāwandī, *Rāḥat,* 301).

54. Ms.A *Sh.m.l.lwā*

Under Arslan-Shāh and the *de facto* ruler, his step-father Eldigüz, Arrān and Ādharbāījān were again closely united with al-Jibāl (Luther, *op.cit.,* 141).

According to Le Strange, Shamkūr was one of the major cities of Arrān; it lay to the north-west of Bardhā'a, on the road to Tiflīs (*Lands,* 178-9).

55. Sarja was a fortress some fifteen kilometres west of Naṣībīn (cf. Canard, *H'amdanides,* 100, n.54; Honigmann, *Ostgrenze,* 20). According to Yāqūt, the fortress lay between Naṣībīn, Dunaisir and Dārā ("Reisen", 436). For another version of these events, cf. Ibn al-Furāt (Shayyāl), 30. Ibn al-Furāt does not state his source.

56. Dārā lay to the south-east of Mārdīn, five *farsakhs* from Naṣībīn

¶ In 524 (1129-30), Sayyida Khātūn,[58] the daughter of Qïlïch Arslan, died in Mayyāfāriqīn and was buried beside her father in the *qubba*.[59] Her mother was the wife of the *amīr* Rukn al-Daula Dā'ūd.[60] After a few days her brother, Sulṭān Ṭoghrïl Beg,[61] came from Ḥiṣn Kaifā to Mayyāfāriqīn. He was the son-in-law of Rukn al-Daula Dā'ūd, being married to his daughter. He stayed in the *qubba* and took all her income.

¶ In 525 (4 December 1130 - 22 November 1131) al-Āmīr bi Aḥkām Allāh, caliph of Egypt, died. He left behind him a pregnant wife, but no son.[62]

¶ In this year Sulṭān Sanjar contacted Zangī, ordering him to

(Honigmann, *Ostgrenze*, 20-4). It received its name from Darius (Yāqūt, "Reisen", 436). In Byzantine times Dārā was made into a strong fortress against the Sasanians but it ceded its importance during the Middle Ages to nearby Naṣībīn (Ilisch, *Geschichte*, 201). When Ibn Baṭṭūṭa visited Dārā he saw only impressive ruins and a village which lay outside the town (trans. Gibb, II, 352).

Sibṭ b. al-Jauzī says that Zangī took Dārā in 524 (*Mir'āt*, 189).

57. This incident is repeated on f. 164b.

Here, as on several other occasions, Ibn al-Azraq is apparently unaware that he repeats his material. Such lack of care adds confusion to his already generally inaccurate dates.

58. Sayyida Khātūn had married Sulaimān b. İl-Ghāzī when he had assumed power at Mayyāfāriqīn in 516/1122. Cf. also Ibn Shaddād, *Jazīra*, f. 103a.

59. For an account of the *qubbat al-sulṭān*, cf. Ch. 2, n.1.

60. Ms.B: "Amir Dā'ūd had married her mother, 'Ā'isha Khātūn".

61. Ms.B calls him Malik Ṭoghrïl. This must be a reference to the son of Qïlïch Arslan whom Justi call Ṭoghrïl Arslan. Justi says he was driven out in 1109 and died around 1128 (*op.cit.*, 453). He gives no source for this information.

After Qïlïch Arslan died in 500/1106-7, his widow sought out Balak, who married her and gave her his protection (Michael the Syrian, *Chronique*, 200). Amongst the sons whom Qïlïch Arslan left were Mas'ūd, Malik-Shāh, 'Arab and Ṭoghrïl Arslan (Bar Hebraeus, *Chronography*, 298-9).

Chabot (*Chronique de Michel le Syrien*, 294, n.4) and Turan are in no doubt that the sulṭān of Malaṭya was Ṭoghrïl Arslan (O. Turan, *Selcuklular Zaminda Türkiye* [Istanbul, 1971], 153). Dulaurier, on the other hand, is more tentative but nevertheless opts for Ṭoghrïl Arslan as the most likely person (Matthew of Edessa, 466 n. 3).

62. Al-Āmir was caliph of the Fāṭimids from 495/1101 - 524/1130. Ibn al-Qalānisī records the date of his death as Tuesday 2 Dhu'l-Qa'da 524/ November 1130 (*Dhail*, 228). The year 524 is also attested by al-'Aẓīmī ("Chronique", 403), whilst Ibn al-Jauzī confirms the exact date given by Ibn al-Qalānisī (*Muntaẓam*, X, 16). Ibn al-Furāt, quoting Ibn Abī Ṭayyi', gives the date as 13 Dhu'l-Qa'da 524 (*Shayyāl*).

release Dubais.[63] So Zangī released Dubais who went to Sulṭān Mas'ūd. In 526 (23 November 1131 - 11 November 1132), the Akhlāṭī ships were sunk in the sea at Constantinople and a group of people from Akhlāṭ[64] perished in them.[65] In that year Nūr al-Daula, lord of Finik, died.[66] His son, the *amīr* Abū Naṣr, succeeded him. In that year Amīr Dā'ūd seized the citadel of Qaṭalbas[67] and Bātāsā.[68]

¶ [69] The people of Egypt were in disagreement and disarray, saying: "Before he dies, the *imām* of this family always leaves a male son nominated to succeed him in the imāmate.[70] This man has left no son

63. For various explanations of how and why Zangī came to have Dubais with him, cf. Ibn al-'Adīm, *Zubda*, 248-9; *Bughyat*, 231-2; Ibn al-Athīr, *Atabegs*, 46-7; *al-Kāmil*, X, 470-1; Michael the Syrian, *Chronique*, 241; Ibn al-Qalānisī, *Dhail*, 230-1. Ibn al-'Adīm stresses that Dubais was surprised to be well treated by Zangī. After the caliph al-Mustarshid had tried unsuccessfully to persuade Zangī to surrender Dubais, the caliph defeated the joint forces of Zangī and Dubais in Sha'bān 526. Zangī returned to Mosul, whilst Dubais fled to Sanjar (*Zubda*, 251).
64. Cf. *EI*², s.v. Akhlāṭ.
65. Turan reads this passage as: "Gurikat Merâkib al-ahlatiyye bi'l - bahr Konstantiniyye fe-tagarrakta fihâ cema'atun min el-Ahlatiyye" (*sic*) (*Doğu Anadolu*, 90, n.21). Ms. A clearly has *bi'l baḥr bi'l Quṣṭanṭiniyya* whilst the word transcribed by Turan as "fe-tagarrakta" is illegible in the manuscript. The letters seem to include *qḍt* (*inqaḍat* [?]). The translation given is only tentative but is derived from the context. It has proved impossible to locate this event from other sources.

    Turan accepts the date 506 given by Ibn al-Azraq as correct, although this piece of information is placed in a group of events which occurred in 525 and 526. Even Ibn al-Azraq keeps to a rough chronological framework, although many individual dates are inaccurate.

    One perplexing aspect of Turan's book is the way in which he cites references from Ibn al-Azraq. He states in his bibliography that he has used B.M. Or. 5803 (*ibid.*, 249), yet his individual folio references to that manuscript (Ms.A) do not tally remotely with the information he cites. The above passage which has been quoted in full from Turan is found on f. 163a. Turan says it comes from f. 172a. His book abounds with similar instances.
66. Finik was formerly called Phoenica and Fanak. It was situated twelve kilometres from Jazīra b. 'Umar (V.F. Minorsky, "Kurds", *EI*¹).
67. The exact location of Qaṭalbas is not clear. Cahen places it between Is'ird and Khīzān ("Diyār Bakr", 223). The place is mentioned without details by Ibn Shaddād (*Jazīra*, f. 65b).
68. Bātāsā is listed by Ibn Shaddād amongst the fortresses of Diyār Bakr (*ibid.)* The name is spelt in Marsh 333 as *Bātāsāh*. Cahen places it in the region of Is'ird ("Diyār Bakr", 221).
69. This is a continuation of the discussion of Fāṭimid history which was cut short above.
70. In the earlier part of Ibn al-Azraq's history which deals with the Marwānids, the author discusses in some detail the question of the *naṣṣ*

and has nominated no successor other than an unborn child." Before his death he had named the unborn child as his successor. The people said: "The nomination (*naṣṣ*) of an unborn child is permissible and it may be that a male child is born." So they went on waiting for the unborn child to be born; but a girl was born.[71] The people were (again) in disagreement and agitation. At the end of 525 (November 1131) they brought out from the castle a man who was one of the sons of al-Mustanṣir. His *ism* was 'Abd al-Majīd, his *kunya* was Abu 'l-Maimūn, and his *laqab* was al-Ḥāfiẓ li-Dīn Allāh. One report says that he was 'Abd al-Majīd b. al-Mustanṣir. Another report says that he was 'Abd al-Majīd b. Abi'l-Qāsim al-Musta'lī b. al-Mustanṣir. Yet another report says that he was the son of another son of al-Mustanṣir - other than al-Musta'lī.[72] Al-Ḥāfiẓ took over the caliphate.[73] The

and the circumstances of the Nizārī schism ('Awaḍ, *op.cit.*, 276). There the phraseology is virtually identical.

71. Literally:"she brought forth a daughter". For the confused events surrounding the succession of al-Āmir see S.M. Stern, "The succession to the Fatimid caliph al-Āmir", *Oriens* 4 (1951), 193-255. According to some sources, an heir, al-Ṭayyib, was born to al-Āmir in 524/1130 but his fate was shrouded in mystery (*ibid.*, 195-202).

On the other hand, Wüstenfeld, who follows a similar account to that of Ibn al-Azraq's source, relates that as al-Āmir left no male successor, his cousin, 'Abd al-Majīd, was next in line of succession. The populace, however, demanded a delay until the pregnancy of al-Āmir's wife reached its term. If a son should be born, 'Abd al-Majīd was only to act as regent. The wife had a daughter, however (F. Wüstenfeld, *Geschichte der Faṭimiden- Chalifen* [Göttingen, 1881], 300).

In his biography of al-Ḥāfiẓ, Ibn Khallikān adheres to a narrative similar to that of Ibn al-Azraq (*Wafayāt,* II, 179-181).

What is more certain is that 'Abd al-Majīd at first acted only as regent temporarily but he later proclaimed himself caliph (*ibid.*, 202-7).

72. The following genealogy of the Fāṭimids is relevant here:-

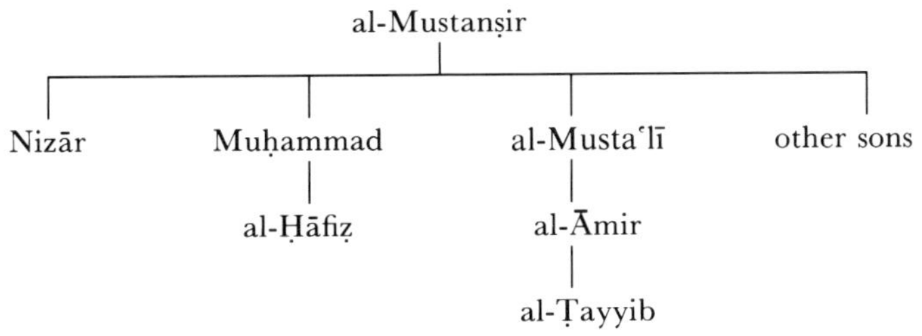

(Hodgson, *op.cit.*, 160-1).

From the above table, it is clear that neither of the first two reports of al-Ḥāfiẓ's genealogy are correct, since al-Ḥāfiẓ was neither the son of

people agreed on him and the line of legitimate succession (*naṣṣ*) on behalf of al-Musta'lī and his descendants was quashed. The Ismā'īlīs believe the following: that the line of succession (*naṣṣ*) in their (own) time is a continuous one from al-Mustanṣir through Nizār until now. This is their way (*madhhab*) but they are all wrong.[74] Al-Ḥāfiẓ remained in the caliphate and became established and his power became strong. There is no caliphate except within the 'Abbāsid family because the Prophet (prayers and blessings be upon him) said concerning al-'Abbās:[75] "You are the ancestor of the kings[76] of my *umma* until the Day of the Resurrection." The people of Egypt and the

al-Mustanṣir nor of al-Musta'lī. If the phrase *qīla w.l.d ghayr al-Musta'lī li'l-Mustanṣir* is translated as: "Another report says that he was the son of another son of al-Mustanṣir other than al-Musta'lī" it would make correct sense historically. The Arabic sentence might, however, also be translated simply as "Another report says that sons other than al-Musta'lī were born to al-Mustanṣir". For the accession of al-Ḥāfiẓ, cf. Ibn al-Athīr, *al-Kāmil,* X, 468; Ibn al-Furāt (quoting Ibn Abī Ṭayyi') (Shayyāl), 43.

73. 'Abd al-Majīd was proclaimed *imām* under the title al-Ḥāfiẓ li-Dīn Allāh on 3 Rabī' II 525 (Stern, *op.cit.,* 207).

74. Ibn al-Azraq is interested in Fāṭimid history. This unusually long excursus is a continuation of a series of discussions on the Fāṭimids and Ismā'īlīs which occur at intervals in Ms.A.

In an earlier passage, Ibn al-Azraq relates how, at al-Mustanṣir's death, Fāṭimid Egypt was divided; one faction supported an elder son of al-Mustanṣir, Nizār, whilst the other gave allegiance to al-Musta'lī, a younger son of al-Mustanṣir. Al-Musta'lī's mother was the sister of the powerful vizier al-Afḍal who was responsible for by-passing Nizār in favour of his nephew ('Awaḍ, 267).

Ibn al-Azraq then relates how Nizār went away, thus creating the rift between the Fāṭimids in Cairo and the supporters of Nizār which is mentioned in this passage. Viewing events from his own time (572/1176-7) Ibn al-Azraq says that Nizār's grandson, Nizār b. Muḥammad b. Nizār, "is now caliph of the Ismā'īlīs ... and is now in Egypt" (*ibid.,* 276-7).

75. For the development of pro-'Abbāsid *ḥadīths* cf. I. Goldziher, *Muslim Studies,* ed. S.M. Stern, tr. C.M. Barber and S.M. Stern (London, 1971), II, 97-101. Goldziher cites the example of a court poet of al-Mahdī who quoted the Qur'ān to prove that 'Abbās was the rightful heir to the Prophet (*op.cit.,* 100). Here the legitimacy of 'Abbās and his line is put into the mouth of Muḥammad himself. The pronouncement is very reminiscent of the caliph al-Qā'im's statement, quoted by Bundārī, on the occasion of Ṭoghrïl's request to marry his daughter: *naḥnu Banu'l-'Abbās khayr al-nās fīnā al-imāma wa'l-za'āma ilā yaum al-qiyāma* (*Zubdat,* 20).

76. *anta abū al-amlāk min ummatī ilā yaum al-qiyāma.*

This is probably a spurious *ḥadīth,* given the use of the term *amlāk.* The word *amlāk,* which is most commonly the plural of *milk* ("property, possession"), is occasionally found as the plural of *malik* ("king").

Ismā'īlīs are in error. Only prejudiced and biased people think those beliefs are right. There is no *imām* and no caliph except one from the 'Abbāsid family in Baghdad.[77]

¶ In 525 (1130-31) Amīr Dā'ūd took possession of Is'ird,[78] Bahmard[79] and Bātāsā.[80] In (f.164b) 524 (1129-1130) Atābeg Zangī joined battle against Ḥusām al-Dīn and Amīr Dā'ūd.[81] After they had been defeated outside Sarja they fled for safety to Dārā. Zangī[82] went to Syria and took Ḥamā[83] and its environs as well as Ḥimṣ.[84] He made

77. At the time of the Saljuq conquests, the religious authority of the 'Abbāsid caliphate had been deliberately strengthened by the Saljuqs. Saljuq power had persuaded independent rulers to reject Fāṭimid authority in favour of recognition of the 'Abbāsids (cf. Ibn al-Athīr, *al-Kāmil*, X, 42-3).
78. Yāqūt places Is'ird in the Jazīra, whilst other authors put it in Armenia (Canard, *H'amdanides*, 85). Is'ird (Si'ird, Siirt) lies some 75 kms north of Jazīrat b. 'Umar. It flourished from the early eleventh century until the Mongol period. For a detailed description of the town, cf. Ilisch, *Geschichte*, 205.
79. *Bāhmūd*. Bahmard is also referred to as Bahmūd in Ms.A.
80. These acquisitions were made by Dā'ūd after his defeat at Zangī's hands in the previous year. Other sources say that it was Zangī who took Bahmard in 525/1131-2 (al-'Aẓīmī, "Chronique", 405; Ibn al-Furāt, *Duwal*, f. 29b). At any rate, Dā'ūd was not destined to hold Bahmard for long, if he held it at all. Ibn al-Athīr says that Zangī took the citadel in 526/1131-2 (*Atabegs*, 47).
81. This incident has already been mentioned on f. 164a.
82. According to Ibn al-Athīr, the two Artuqid cousins had already joined forces in 521/1127-8 against Zangī, who had marched against Naṣībīn, a possession of Temür-Tash. Zangī had intercepted a pigeon carrying a message to the garrison at Naṣībīn. The message which came from the Artuqids promised to bring help and urged them to hold out for three more days. Zangī changed the message to a period of twenty days and thereby caused the people of Naṣībīn to hand over the citadel to him (*Atabegs*, 36-7).

    On his campaign into Artuqid territory in 524/1129-30, Zangī met Dā'ūd and Temür-Tash outside Dārā, defeating them and taking Sarja and Dārā. He was reluctant, however, to pursue Dā'ūd further into Diyār Bakr because of the difficulty of the terrain (*ibid.*, 38-9; *al-Kāmil*, X, 497).

    This incident is also described by Michael the Syrian, who says that Zangī knew he would be defeated but that he managed to hold out for one day. Then the two Artuqid cousins quarrelled and Dā'ūd withdrew. Zangī pursued Temür-Tash and then made peace with him (*Chronique*, 240-1).
83. For Zangī's capture of Ḥamā, cf. Ibn al-Qalānisī, *Dhail*, 228; Ibn al-'Adīm, *Zubda*, 246. Ibn al-Athīr gives the date as 523/1129 (*Atabegs*, 35; *al-Kāmil*, X, 463-4).
84. Other sources state that Zangī did not succeed in his attempt to capture

for Damascus from where he took Dubais and returned to Mosul, taking with him Dubais in fetters.

¶ In Ramaḍān 526[85] (16 July - 14 August 1132), the caliph al-Mustarshid went to Mosul. He encamped before it and laid siege to it for a while. In command of the city was Naṣīr al-Dīn Jaqar.[86] The caliph engaged in fighting the inhabitants but Naṣīr had fortified the city and had strengthened the ditch.[87] Although the caliph pressed on hard with the siege, he was unsuccessful and he returned to Baghdad, entering the city on 29 Dhu'l-Qa'da (11 October 1132).[88]

¶ In 527 (12 November 1132 - 31 October 1133) the vizier 'Abd al-Malik died in Mayyāfāriqīn and al-Nāṣiḥ 'Alī b. Aḥmad al-Āmidī took over the supervision of the *dīwān*. When he was *mutawallī*[89] in Āmid, Mu'ayyid al-Dīn b. Nīsān[90] had seized him, mulcted him for 30,000 *dīnārs* and taken over his position. Al-Nāṣiḥ came to Mayyāfāriqīn and his son Abū Naṣr collected (the revenue from) the harvest[91] while al-Nāṣiḥ was given the post of administering the *waqfs*. After the vizier died he took control of the *dīwān*.[92]

Ḥimṣ that year (Ibn al-'Adīm, *Zubda*, 246; Ibn al-Athīr, *al-Kāmil*, X, 464; Ibn al-Qalānisī, *Dhail*, 228).

Ibn al-Azraq does not mention Zangī's capture of Aleppo but he is generally ill-informed about Aleppan affairs. For Zangī's conquest of Aleppo in 522/1128 cf. Ibn al-'Adīm, *Zubda*, 242. Ibn al-Furāt, citing Ibn Abī Ṭayyi', says that Zangī took the citadel of Aleppo on 10 Muḥarram 522/15 January 1128 (f. 2a).

85. Once again, Ibn al-Azraq has a different date from other sources. Ibn al-Athīr and Ibn Khallikān put this event in 527/1133 (Ibn al-Athīr, *Atabegs*, 47 and *al-Kāmil*, XI, 2-3; Ibn Khallikān, *Wafayāt*, I, 330).
86. His full name was Abū Sa'īd Jaqar b. Ya'qūb al-Hamadhānī; his *laqab* was Naṣīr al-Dīn. He had been made governor of Mosul by Zangī and was "tyrannical, unjust, a shedder of blood and a violator of property" (Ibn Khallikān, *Wafayāt*, I, 329).
87. Literally: "dug the ditch". It is unlikely that he dug it for the first time.
88. When Zangī heard that the caliph al-Mustarshid was approaching Mosul with 30,000 men, he left the city at once with some of his troops. Whilst Jaqar defended Mosul vigorously against the caliph, Zangī cut off al-Mustarshid's food supplies. After three months, the caliph returned to Baghdad (Ibn al-Athīr, *Atabegs*, 47).

    According to Ibn Khallikān, Jaqar had already fortified and entrenched the city and he resisted the attacks of the caliph, forcing him to retire. This episode occurred in Ramaḍān 527/July 1133 (*Wafayāt*, I, 330).
89. For a description of the duties of the *mutawallī*, cf. Horst, *Staatsverwaltung*, 70.
90. The influence of the powerful Nīsānid family in Āmid is discussed in some detail by Van Berchem (M. van Berchem and J. Strzygowski, *Amida* [Heidelberg, 1910], 55).
91. *thamara* "rapport de la terre" (Dozy, *Supplément* I, 164).
92. Cahen suggests that al-Nāṣiḥ 'Alī b. Aḥmad incited his new master,

¶ In 528 (1 November 1133 – 22 October 1134) al-Mu'ayyid Abu'l-Ḥasan b. Mukhtar arrived in Mayyāfāriqīn from the Jazīra. He had been muleted by the vizier ʿAbd al-Malik who had tortured him and taken a lot of money from him. He had gone off to the Jazīra until the vizier ʿAbd al-Malik died and had then returned to Mayyāfāriqīn and taken over the *dīwān al-istīfā'*[93] with al-Nāṣiḥ[94].

(In) 528 (1133-4) Sharaf al-Dīn Ḥabashī Abū Ṭālib b. Ḥabashī left the people of Iraq for the service of al-Saʿīd Ḥusām al-Dīn. He remained with him, receiving most generous hospitality. He had worked in Ḥamā for Ṣalāḥ al-Dīn Muḥammad al-Yaghī-Sīyanī, who had seized him and tortured him by tying a dog to him inside a sack. While the dog struck and bit his body, he rolled around in the sack until the dog's head positioned itself between his thighs, whereupon he wrung its neck until it died in the sack and he was released. Then Ḥabashī fled to Qalʿat Jaʿbar[95] where he stayed with Najm al-Daula Mālik b. Sālim b. Mālik.[96] Thereafter he went to Mārdīn and stayed with Ḥusām al-Dīn for a while, taking over as the vizier of al-Saʿīd Ḥusām al-Dīn. He acquired a degree of authority so comprehensive as to be without precedent,[97] ruling with full powers.[98]

Temür-Tash, against his old lord, the ruler of Āmid ("Diyār Bakr", 244-5).

93. For a discussion of the functions of a provincial department of finance in Saljuq times, cf. Horst, *Staatsverwaltung*, 51. For a description of the office under the Saljuqs of Rūm, cf. Uzunçarşili, *Osmanli devleti*, 103.
94. Ibn Shaddād says that Ibn Mukhtār and al-Nāṣiḥ were brothers (*Jazīra*, f. 103a).
95. For Qalʿat Jaʿbar, a fortress on the left bank of the Euphrates between Bālis and al-Raqqa, cf. *EI*², "Djaʿbar".
96. This ʿUqailid ruler of Qalʿat Jaʿbar was the son of Shams al-Daula Sālim b. Mālik who died in 519/1125 (cf. Zambaur, *op.cit.*, 135). Sālim b. Mālik had received this citadel and al-Raqqa from Malik-Shāh when the latter had removed him from Aleppo. When Sālim grew old, he entrusted these two citadels to his son, Mālik (Ibn Shaddād, *Jazīra*, f. 24a).

    There is, however, doubt about the *laqab* of Mālik b. Sālim. Ms.A and Ibn Shaddād refer to him as Najm al-Daula, whilst Ms.B, al-ʿAẓīmī and Ibn al-Furāt write Shihāb al-Dīn (Ms.B., f. 109b; al-ʿAẓīmī, "Chronique", 396; Ibn al-Furāt, *Duwal*, f. 2b). Zambaur writes Shihāb al-Daula (*op.cit.*, 135).
97. The post of vizier at Mārdīn was clearly more important than that at Mayyāfāriqīn. Ibn al-Azraq never explicitly states that Temür-Tash's main residence was at Mārdīn, although other sources refer to him as the "lord of Mārdīn". Ḥabashī was empowered the following year (529/1134-5) to conduct an inspection of the officials at Mayyāfāriqīn. This rapidly degenerated into a purge.
98. These anecdotes about the fluctuating fortunes of officials in these chaotic times reveal the frequency with which posts changed hands and

In this year al-Makīn Abu'l-Barakāt b. Abi'l-Fahm al-Ḥarrānī[99] arrived in Mārdīn, having fled his uncle's family in Ḥarrān.[100] He stayed with al-Sa'īd Ḥusām al-Dīn as his guest.

One report states that al-Mustarshid left Baghdad in Sha'bān 529 (17 May - 14 June 1135). Another report says it was in 528 (1133-4). He joined battle against Sulṭān Mas'ūd outside Hamadhān at a place called Day Marg near the mountain Bihistūn and the camp (?)[101] was plundered. The *sulṭān* had assembled a large number of men, (f.165a) together with the lord of Khartabirt with his army and troops. Moreover, Mas'ūd's uncle, Sulṭān Sanjar, had sent him a large force. They joined battle and, having defeated the caliph, they took him and all his state officials[102] prisoner.

I asked al-Sa'īd Mu'ayyid al-Dīn Abū 'Abdallāh Muḥammad b. 'Abd al-Karīm al-Anbārī[103] (may God have mercy on him) in 534

the ease with which officials could move around seeking positions with different rulers within a limited geographical area. It was clearly a regular practice for officials to be tortured so that they would divulge the whereabouts of their ill-gotten gains. Such money was often hidden in the citadel.

It is interesting to note that Zangī never kept all his money in one place, preferring to spread it over several citadels in case he should lose all his wealth at once (*Atabegs*, 80).

99. Ms.A appears to have this name as al-*Malikīn* Abu'l-Barakāt b. Abi'l-*Fahr* al-Ḥarrānī. Ms.B and Ibn Shaddād make much better sense with al-*Makīn* ... *Abu'l-Fahm* (Ms.B., f. 109a; Ibn Shaddād, *Jazīra,* f. 103a).

100. The reading of Ms.B is confirmed by Ibn al-Qalānisī (*Dhail,* 275) and by al-'Aẓīmī who writes that this man was arrested in Aleppo in 535/1140-1 ("Chronique", 419). On this town in Diyār Muḍar, cf. *EI²*, "Ḥarrān"; D.S. Rice, "Medieval Ḥarrān" in *Anatolian Studies*, II, (1952), 36-83; Ilisch, *Geschichte,* 196-9.

101. Ms.A *wa-nuhiba al-'askar*. This is probably a scribal error. The sentence is misplaced here. It is repeated later on f. 165a, where it is more appropriate to the context. Here it would read better as *wa-nuhiba al-ma'skar*.

102. For other accounts of the conflict between al-Mustarshid and Mas'ūd , the battle of Day Marg and the subsequent death of the caliph, cf. Ibn al-Jauzī, *Muntaẓam,* X, 41-50; Ibn al-Ṭiqṭaqā, *al-Fakhrī,* 521-3; Sibṭ b. al-Jauzī, *Mir'āt,* 156-7; Bundārī, *Zubdat,* 176-8; al-Ḥusainī, *Akhbār,* 108; al-'Aẓīmī, "Chronique", 410; Ibn Khallikān, *Wafayāt,* I, 506; Ibn al-Athīr, *al-Kāmil,* XI, 14-17; *idem, Atabegs,* 48-50; Ibn al-Qalānisī, *Dhail,* 248-50.

Ibn Wāṣil has taken this passage and uses it with certain changes in his work *Mufarrij al-Kurūb fī Akhbār Banī Ayyūb*, 58-68. Comparisons will be made from time to time between his text and that of Ibn al-Azraq.

103. For a biography of this important official, cf. Ibn al-Jauzī, *Muntaẓam,* X, 206. There his name is given as Muḥammad b. 'Abd al-Karīm ... Abū 'Abdallāh b. al-Anbārī, and his *laqab* as Sadīd al-Daula. Ms.B also has Sadīd al-Daula.

Ibn al-Anbārī held the office of *kātib al-inshā'* for a long time, went as

(1139-40) in Baghdad, when I stayed with him that year, about the affair of al-Mustarshid, about the battle and its outcome. He said: "May God be pleased with him. Hostilities had flared up between the *sulṭān* and the caliph in the time of Sulṭān Maḥmūd who went out and defeated the caliph twice.[104] When Mas'ūd succeeded him, his deputies became high-handed in Iraq and they opposed the caliph in his own lands.[105] Relations (between the *sulṭān* and caliph) became strained and al-Mustarshid collected troops, having seriously resolved to rebel. It happened that one day the vizier Sharaf al-Dīn al-Zainabī 'Alī b. Ṭirād[106] called on the caliph, and the treasurer Jamāl al-Dīn Ṭalḥa[107] and I were with him. The caliph had driven the *sulṭān's* representatives out of Iraq[108] and he had appointed the treasurer to take charge of the town and the *sulṭān's maẓālim* office.[109] When we went on that day, the vizier Sharaf al-Dīn said to him: 'O master! Your slave has something on his mind. May he speak?' He said: 'Go ahead.' The vizier said: 'O master! Where are you going, and with

ambassador to Sanjar and held a correspondence with al-Ḥarīrī (*ibid.*). He lived from 469-558/1076-1163.

104. In his transcription of this passage, Amedroz misreads *kasarahu* and writes *asarahu* (Ibn al-Qalānisī, *Dhail*, 250, n. 1).

105. Ms.A: *wa-'āraḍū al-khalīfa fī amlākihi.* These words are copied *verbatim* by Ibn Khallikān in his biography of Sultan Mas'ūd (*Wafayāt*, II, 93). Ibn Wāṣil changes this phrase to read *wa-'araḍa al-khalīfa fī iqṭā'ihi* "the caliph resisted in his territory" (*op.cit.*, 58).

106. According to the biography given by Ibn al-Jauzī, 'Alī b. Ṭirād al-Zainabī was born in 462/1069-70 and died in 538/1143-4 (*Muntaẓam*, X, 109). He is often mentioned by Ibn Khallikān (*Wafayāt*, III, pt. 1, 156-7, 239, 287). He served as vizier both to al-Mustarshid and to al-Muqtafī, in whose appointment he played a key role (Ibn al-Jauzī, *Muntaẓam*, X, 106; Ibn al-Ṭiqṭaqā, *al-Fakhrī*, 525-6).

107. Ibn Wāṣil changes the name Jamāl al-Dīn to Kamāl al-Dīn Muḥammad al-Khāzin who held office as vizier to Mas'ūd for a short time in 533/1138-9 (Klausner, *op.cit.*, 39-40).

Ibn al-Athīr calls him Ibn Ṭalḥa (*al-Kāmil*, XI, 15). Ibn al-Furāt speaks of a *madrasa* built by Ibn Ṭalḥa the treasurer (*Duwal*, f. 129b).

108. Baghdad and its surrounding area proved to be the region where the *sulṭān's* authority was most vulnerable and where his representative, the *shiḥna*, was often at loggerheads with the caliph. For a detailed analysis of this question, cf. A.H. Siddiqi, *Caliphate and Kingship in Medieval Persia* (Lahore, 1942).

109. Ms.A *wa-rataba ṣāḥib al-makhzan 'alā dār al-sulṭān li'l-maẓālim wa'l-balad.*

This phrasing is rather obscure. Ibn Wāṣil solves the problem by removing the words *wa'l-balad* and writes:- *wa-rataba ṣāḥib al-makhzan li'l-naẓar fi'l-maẓālim*

"He appointed the treasurer to administer the *maẓālim* (court)" (*op.cit.*, 59).

For a description of the *maẓālim* court, cf. A.K.S. Lambton, "The Internal Structure of the Saljuq Empire", *CHI*, 5, 227-8. Cf. also Uzunçarşili̇, *Osmanli̇ devleti*, 9-10.

whom do you seek help, refuge and support?[110] We are strongest if we stay in Baghdad. No-one can attack us and Iraq will be sufficient protection for us. When al-Ḥusain b. ʿAlī (peace be upon him) left for Iraq, he met his fate. If he had stayed in Mecca no-one would have clashed with him.'[111] The caliph said to me: 'What do you advise, O scribe?' So I said: 'O master, the right course of action is to stay put. What the vizier has suggested is right. No-one will attack us. Would to God that Iraq remains ours!' So he said to the treasurer: 'O *wakīl*, what do you say?' He replied: 'I think the same way as my master.'[112] He was the one who egged the caliph on to rebel. Al-Mustarshid said:[113] 'If death is inevitable, it is despicable[114] to die a coward.'

Then he got ready and mobilised troops. A group of Turkish *amīrs*[115] had joined his service and he had given them a large amount of money. Then he set out and we accompanied him. When we came near to Hamadhān, Sulṭān Masʿūd sallied forth and they joined battle at a place called Day Marg in the vicinity of the mountain of Bihistūn near Hamadhān.[116] When the troops had lined up and were about to fight, all the *amīrs* and Turks deserted from our camp to the *sulṭān's* side, whereupon the caliph and his remaining followers fled. The troops were seized[117] and the caliph and his officials of state were taken (prisoner). The vizier, the treasurer, the *naqīb* of the ʿAlids[118] and I were taken to the castle of Sar-i Jahān[119] near Qazwīn and Rayy."

110. An equally acceptable reading of Ms.A would be *ilā ain namḍī wa-biman naʿtaḍidu wa-ilā man naltajī'*. Cf. Ibn Wāṣil, *op.cit.*, 59.
111. Ms.B, f. 110b: "No two people would have disagreed with him" (i.e. nobody at all).
112. "I think the same way as my master". The treasurer has divined the intention of the caliph and complied with it.
113. Here Ibn Wāṣil adds the explanatory comment that the caliph was quoting from al-Mutanabbī (*op.cit.*, 59).
114. Ms.A *min al-ʿajz*; Ms.B *min al-ghaban*. As is usually the case, the wording of Ms.B is correct.
115. Ibn al-Qalānisī attributes the blame for al-Mustarshid's rebellion and subsequent defeat to these Turkish *amīrs* (*Dhail*, 249).
116. Cf. n. 102. The battle took place on 10 Ramadān, 529/24 June 1135 (Ibn al-Athīr, *al-Kāmil*, XI, 14).
117. Cf. n. 101. In this case, in view of the proximity of the word *muʿaskar*, the word *ʿaskar* has been translated as troops.
118. The office of *naqīb al-nuqabā'* was also known as *naqīb al-ʿalawiyyīn*.

    Klausner cites this office as an instance of the combination of religious and administrative functions in Saljuq times. ʿAlī b. Ṭirād, who had previously been *naqīb al-nuqabā'* (chief of the ʿAlids), served as vizier to two caliphs (*op.cit.*, 26-7). For a description of how the office of *naqīb* came into being, cf. R. Levy, *A Baghdad Chronicle* (Cambridge, 1929), 161-2.
119. "Serdjihan est un château dans les montagnes du côté du Deilem; il

When I (the author) went to Rayy in 549 (18 March 1154 - 6 March 1155), I saw the citadel looming into view at the top of a high hill. The *sulṭān* took al-Mustarshid with him and went round Āzarbāījān with him until he brought him to Marāgha, where he made camp.[120] Three heretics[121] went in to him (the caliph) and killed him (may God be pleased with him). A man (f.165b) called Ibn Sakīna,[122] who was leading him in prayer, was killed with him. It was Thursday, 16 Dhu'l-Qa'da 529 (28 August 1135).[123] The caliphate of al-Mustarshid lasted seventeen years, seven months and two days.

He had appointed as heir his son, Abū Ja'far al-Manṣūr al-Rāshid bi'llāh, who had stayed behind in Baghdad. When the news that al-Mustarshid had been murdered reached Baghdad, the people pledged allegiance to al-Rāshid as caliph.[124] One report said that Sulṭān

domine la plaine de Qazwin ainsi que Zendjan et Abhar ... C'est une des citadelles les plus belles et les mieux fortifiées que j'aie vues" (C.A.C. Barbier de Meynard, *Dictionnaire géographique de la Perse, extrait du Moudjem oul bouldan* [Paris, 1861], 307).

Rāwandī also mentions this citadel (*Rāḥat,* 338 and 366). Mustaufī says it was five *farsakhs* from Sulṭāniyya and was destroyed by the Mongols (Barbier de Meynard, *op.cit.,* 307, n. 1).

120. An even more humiliating fate awaited Sulṭān Sanjar after his capture by the Ghuzz.

121. Ibn Wāṣil: *thalātha nafar min al-mulāḥida al-Bāṭiniyya* (*op.cit.,* 60). Cf. also Ibn al-Furāt (*Duwal,* f. 133b).

122. Both Ibn al-Jauzī and Sibṭ b. al-Jauzī mention that Ibn Sakīna was killed too (Ibn al-Jauzī, *Muntaẓam,* X, 49; Sibṭ b. al-Jauzī, 156). According to al-Ḥusainī, *Akhbār,* 107, the person with al-Mustarshid was the *ḥakīm* Abu'l-Barakāt b. Malkā.

123. The dates given by the sources for al-Mustarshid's death may be tabulated as follows:

Ibn al-Azraq, Ms.A:	Thursday, 16 Dhu'l-Qa'da, 529
Ibn al-Azraq, Ms.B:	Thursday, 26 Dhu'l-Qa'da, 529
Ibn Khallikān:	14 or 28 Dhu'l-Qa'da, 529 (*Wafayāt,* I, 506)
Ibn al-Jauzī:	Thursday, 17 Dhu'l-Qa'da, 529 (*Muntaẓam,* X, 49 and 53) (Sunday 29 August 1135)
Ibn al-Athīr:	Sunday, 17 Dhu'l-Qa'da, 529 (*al-Kāmil,* X, 17)
Ibn al-Qalānisī:	Thursday, 28 Dhu'l-Qa'da, 529 (*Dhail,* 250)
Bundārī:	Thursday 28 Dhu'l-Qa'da, 529 (*Zubdat,* 178)

The only version which fits the day of the week with the correct date of the month is given by Ibn al-Jauzī.

124. For the brief caliphate of al-Rāshid, cf. Ibn al-Ṭiqṭaqā, *al-Fakhrī,* 529-

Sanjar sent the people who killed al-Mustarshid.[125] But according to another report Sulṭān Mas'ūd applied to his uncle Sanjar for permission to kill him and Sanjar concurred.[126] Mas'ūd therefore commissioned those (men) who accordingly went in to him and killed him.[127] He was buried in the city of Marāgha.

31; Ibn al-Jauzī, *Muntaẓam,* X, 54-62; Ibn al-Athīr, *al-Kāmil,* XI, 22-4, 26-7; Ibn al-Qalānisī, *Dhail,* 256-7; Ibn al-'Adīm, *Zubda,* 259-60; al-Ḥusainī, *Akhbār,* 108-9; Rāwandī, *Rāḥat,* 228-9; Abu'l-Fiḍā', *Mukhtaṣar,* III, 10-13; al-'Aẓīmī, "Chronique", 410-11.

The dates for the beginning of his caliphate may be tabulated as follows:

Abu'l-Fiḍā':	Monday, 27 Dhu'l-Qa'da, 529 (*Mukhtaṣar,* III, 10).
Sibṭ b. al-Jauzī:	Monday, 17 Dhu'l-Qa'da, 529 (*Mir'āt,* 158).
Ibn al-Athīr:	Monday, 26 Dhu'l-Qa'da, 529 (*Atabegs,* 50).

125. Ibn Wāṣil implicates both Sanjar and Mas'ūd in the caliph's death. He describes how, on the day that the caliph was killed, a messenger brought a letter to Mas'ūd from Sanjar. Its overt contents were an order that Mas'ūd should honour the caliph and restore him to his throne. Its hidden message was that he should get rid of him. When the caliph had been murdered, Sulṭān Mas'ūd made an elaborate show of grief (*op.cit.,* 61.)

A similar account is given by Bar Hebraeus who says that two letters were sent; in the secret one, Sanjar rebuked Mas'ūd, saying: "Why didst thou not kill the khalîfah during the confusion of war?" (*Chronography,* 259).

126. By virtue of his long tenure of office and the support which he enjoyed in Iraq, al-Mustarshid was a difficult opponent to eliminate or to mollify. Perhaps this was the reason that Mas'ūd felt the need to apply to Sanjar for permission to kill al-Mustarshid. Since Sanjar was based at Merv, a courier would need time to make the return journey to Mas'ūd. Perhaps this was why he delayed the killing of al-Mustarshid until they reached Marāgha.

127. Here Ibn al-Azraq does not lay the blame for al-Mustarshid's murder either on Sanjar or Mas'ūd but simply presents the evidence before him. He is apparently unaware of this when he later describes Mas'ūd as the murderer of both al-Mustarshid and al-Rāshid (Ms.A, f. 175b).

Chapter 4

Events following the murder of al-Mustarshid

Dubais b. Ṣadaqa b. Mazyad was with the *sulṭān* in his camp. After a while the *sulṭān* set out for Tabrīz. He rode for some days and made camp. Saif al-Daula Dubais went in to see him and he executed him.[1] After a few days, the *sulṭān* married the daughter of Dubais. Her mother was Sharaf Khātūn, daughter of 'Amīd al-Daula b. Jahīr[2] b. Zubaida,[3] daughter of Niẓām al-Mulk.[4] Dubais was taken to Mārdīn to his wife Guhar Khātūn[5] and was buried in the *mashhad* beside Najm

1. Dubais was killed at a judicious moment (Ibn Khallikān, *Wafayāt,* I, 506; al-'Aẓīmī, "Chronique", 410; Ibn al-Qalānisī, *Dhail,* 251). According to Ibn Khallikān, Dubais died exactly one month after al-Mustarshid, on 14 Dhu'l-Ḥijja,529 (*Wafayāt,* I, 506). Cf. also Ibn al-'Adīm, *Bughyat,* 250; Ibn al-Athīr, *al-Kāmil,* XI, 18-9; Sibṭ b. al-Jauzī, *Mir'āt,* 154; al-Ḥusainī, *Akhbār,* 108; Bundārī, *Zubdat,* 178-9.
2. The son of Ibn Jahīr and the son-in-law of Niẓām al-Mulk.
3. The daughter of Niẓām al-Mulk who married 'Amīd al-Daula b. Jahīr was called Ṣafiyya, not Zubaida (Bosworth, "Iranian World", 60). The marriage is recorded by Ibn al-Athīr, *al-Kāmil,* X, 41. Cf. also Sibṭ b. al-Jauzī, *Mir'āt,* 155.
4. Ms.B gives this name as Niẓām al-Mulk al-Ḥasan b. Isḥāq (f.111b). This title is the wrong way round and is incomplete. It should read Abū 'Alī al-Ḥasan b. 'Alī b. Isḥāq (E. E. Herzfeld, "Eine Bauinschrift von Niẓâm al-mulk", *Der Islam* XII (1921), 98).
5. Guhar Khātūn, the daughter of Īl-Ghāzī, had escaped falling into the hands of al-Bursuqī in 517/1123-4 when all the wives and concubines of Dubais, except herself and one other, had been taken prisoner (Ibn al-Athīr, *Atabegs,* 26).

al-Dīn İl-Ghāzī, may God have mercy on them both.[6] There had been a report that Dubais had incited the *sulṭān* to kill al-Mustarshid.[7]

The narrative of Mu'ayyid al-Dīn continued thus: "When al-Mustarshid was killed, Sulṭān Mas'ūd summoned us to his presence, so the vizier Sharaf al-Dīn, the treasurer Jamāl al-Dīn and I went to see him. The *naqīb* of the 'Alids had died in the citadel of Sar-i Jahān where he had been buried.[8] When we went to see the *sulṭān*, he said: 'What is your opinion? What should be done about the caliphate? Whom do you think suitable?' The vizier said: 'O master, the caliphate belongs to the heir apparent, for the people have already pledged allegiance to him; he has come to the throne and become established. Allegiance was pledged to him when he was made heir-apparent and now (yet again) after the murder of his father.'

The *sulṭān* said: 'That is completely impossible. I will not confirm him in the caliphate for he is thinking of rebellion just as his father did.[9] Al-Mustarshid constantly rebelled against us from the moment he assumed power;[10] he rebelled against my brother Maḥmūd twice, against me once (before) and now yet again this time. Then he met his fate,[11] but it is we who will be saddled with great disgrace and ignominy until the end of time. People are saying, «They (the Saljuqs) killed the caliph, even though it was they who caused (the dignity of)

6. For the burial of Dubais at Mārdīn, cf. Ibn Khallikān, *Wafayāt*, I, 504; Sibṭ b. al-Jauzī, *Mir'āt*, 155.
7. According to Ibn Khallikān, the *sulṭān* was afraid of the odium which the murder of al-Mustarshid would arouse. He therefore decided to kill Dubais and to try to persuade the world that Dubais had instigated the caliph's death (*Wafayāt*, I, 506).
8. According to Ibn al-Jauzī, the name of the *naqīb al-nuqabā'* was Abu'l-Ḥasan b. al-Mu'ammar. Ibn al-Jauzī confirms that he died when he was brought down from the citadel (*Muntaẓam*, X, 55). No doubt the sulṭān asked to see his eminent prisoners upon ordering their release from the citadel.
9. Ibn al-Azraq does not relate the events which preceded Sulṭān Mas'ūd's visit to Baghdad in 530/1135-6 when he subjected the city to a protracted siege. Al-Rāshid received a delegation of *amīrs*, including Zangī, who were clad in mourning clothes, at the beginning of Ṣafar 530/1135-6. These *amīrs* succeeded in persuading al-Rāshid to rebel and on Friday 14 Ṣafar, 530 (23 November 1135) he had the *khuṭba* said in the name of Dā'ūd, not Mas'ūd (Ibn al-Jauzī, *Muntaẓam*, X, 55).
10. Ms.A: *kull yaum min ḥaith walā al-Mustarshid*
"From the moment al-Mustarshid assumed power".
Ibn Wāṣil has: *min ḥīna tawallā abīhi lam yatruk al-khurūj 'alainā* (*op.cit.*, 61).
11. *thumma tamma 'alaihi mā tamma.* It is conceivable that *tamma* might mean "to persist" or "persevere" (i.e. in his rebellious course of action)

the caliphate to be restored to this family.»[12] I want someone on the throne who will meddle in nothing but religious matters, who will not raise an army, take up (arms) or assemble (men) and who will rebel neither against me nor the members of my family.[13] There are a number (of 'Abbāsids) in the palace, so place your reliance in a *shaikh* from amongst their number who possesses a good intellect, judgement and resourcefulness,[14] who adheres constantly to the obligation of obedience to us and who does not leave his house. Do not overlook Hārūn b. al-Muqtadī, for he is an old man; he will not contemplate religious dissension and he was recommended by my uncle Sanjar.'"

There were at that time[15] in the palace seven brothers from amongst the sons of al-Muqtadī;[16] they too had sons and grandsons. Some of these seven lived until the 550's.[17] There were (also) in the palace seven brothers from amongst the sons of al-Mustaẓhir,[18] amongst whom were the *amīr* Abū 'Abdallāh, Abū Ṭālib, Abū Naṣr, Abu'l-Qāsim, Abū 'Alī, Ismā'īl and Yaḥyā. They (too) had a number of sons. Al-Mustarshid also had a number of sons. And then there was al-Rāshid, who had some twenty sons, the eldest of whom was the *amīr al-jaish* who had been born to his father when he was nine years old.[19] This is an unprecedented phenomenon.

The following story was told to me by someone in Baghdad whom I trust, who heard it from a person who used to visit (f.166a) the

12. This no doubt refers to the way in which the early Saljuq rulers had generally raised the status of the 'Abbāsid caliphate and more particularly to the support given by Ṭoghrïl to al-Qā'im.
13. This speech by Mas'ūd is an admirable summary of the later Saljuq *sulṭāns'* attitude towards the caliph. As Guseynov expresses it: "The *sulṭāns* were attentive to the caliphs in everything that did not touch on their own sovereignty" (Guseynov, "Sulṭān i Khalif," 128).
14. *tadbīr* is a difficult word to translate. It implies a skill in arranging matters.
15. This passage is found almost *verbatim* in Ibn al-Furāt who copies it from Ibn Wāṣil (*Duwal,* f.133b).
16. 'Abbāsid caliph 467-487/1075-94.
17. This is scarcely surprising.
18. 'Abbāsid caliph 487-512/1094-1118.
19. Ibn al-Athīr confirms that there were a large number of princes of the 'Abbāsid house at this time. Twenty of them were present at the ceremony of allegiance to al-Rāshid (*Atabegs,* 50).

    Sibṭ b. al-Jauzī borrows details from Ibn al-Azraq here. He states that al-Rāshid had some twenty children when he became caliph and that his first child had been born to him when he was nine years old (*Mir'āt,* 158).

    Presumably this lengthy list of 'Abbāsids is included to indicate that there was a wide choice for a suitable caliph to be found.

caliph's palace regularly and knew what was going on.[20] Al-Mustarshid bought five concubines for al-Rāshid when he was seven years old. He ordered them to dally with him, to put themselves at his disposal and to bring him on (sexually). The concubines remained thus engaged with him until he was nine years old and had reached puberty. Amongst the girls was a yellow-skinned Abyssinian slave-girl. One day he had sexual relations with her and she became pregnant by him. This information reached al-Mustarshid, who refused to believe it. He summoned the girl and threatened her. She said, "By God, he is the only person who has been near me. He is mature like all men." The other slave-girls were questioned and they told the same story. So the caliph gave orders that the slave-girl should bring a piece of cloth. Then he had intercourse with her. When he rose from her she removed the piece of cloth and there was semen on it.[21] He did the same with the other slave-girls and semen came forth too. Al-Mustarshid rejoiced at that. When her confinement came to an end, the slave-girl gave birth to a son whom al-Mustarshid called *amīr al-jaish*, and he was extremely happy about his birth. This is an unheard-of occurence, except in the Ḥijāz. It is said that girls from Tihāma menstruate at nine and that their boys reach puberty at nine. The nearest (age) gap known between father and son is the case of 'Amr b. al-'Āṣ and his son 'Abdallāh who was born when he ('Amr) was twelve years old. There has been no similar case except that of al-Rāshid which we have already mentioned.

Al-Rāshid followed in his father's footsteps and the people pledged allegiance to him at the end of 529 (October 1135). Al-Rāshid was an astute and noble-minded man who possessed judgement and ambition. That is why the *sulṭān* was reluctant to appoint him as caliph.

¶ In Dhu'l-Ḥijja 529 (12 September - 10 October 1135) Sulṭān Mas'ūd had Ṣadaqa b. Dubais (*sic*) killed in his presence while he was his prisoner.[22] I think this report is inaccurate because the people he killed were Qaracha (and) Mengü-Bars.

20. The phrase *yaṭlu'u 'alaihim* is rendered by Ibn Wāṣil as *yaṭl'u 'alā asrārihim* (*op.cit.*, 62). Ibn Wāṣil's phrase may be translated as "was privy to their secrets." This is one occasion where Ibn al-Azraq relies on an eye-witness account but does not divulge his source.
21. Ibn Wāṣil omits parts of this account, probably out of propriety. Presumably the caliph wished to verify for himself his son's precocious sexual prowess, though a certain ambiguity remains because of the lack of a specified subject for the verb.
22. *qatala al-sulṭān Mas'ūd Ṣadaqa b. Dubais*
This passage is extremely garbled. It is well known that Sulṭān Mas'ūd killed Dubais b. Ṣadaqa one month after the death of the

¶ Sulṭān Mas'ūd approached his uncle Sanjar seeking his advice on whom he should appoint.[23] Sanjar sent back the following reply: "Appoint only someone vouched for by the vizier, the treasurer and Ibn al-Anbārī". So the *sulṭān* had a meeting with them. He consulted them, referred to Hārūn and told them what Sulṭān Sanjar had ordered them to do. The vizier said: "If we are bound by this order (from Sanjar) then we will appoint someone we think suitable; the person (we have in mind) is ascetic and religious; there is none like him in the palace." The *sulṭān* asked, "Who is he?" The vizier replied: "He is the *amīr* (Abū) 'Abdallāh b. al-Mustaẓhir." The *sulṭān* said: "Do you vouch for his good conduct?" The vizier said "Yes".[24] The *amīr* Abū 'Abdallāh was the son-in-law of the vizier Sharaf al-Dīn, being married to his daughter. When she went into the palace one day, in the reign of al-Mustaẓhir, the *amīr* Abū 'Abdallāh saw her and asked for her hand in marriage from his father, who married him to her. At that time Sharaf al-Dīn was the *naqīb al-nuqabā'*.[25] Abū

caliph al-Mustarshid. Dubais's murder occurred on 14 Dhu'l-Ḥijja, 529 (15 September 1135) (Ibn al-'Adīm, *Bughyat,* 249).

Ibn al-Azraq has already described the killing of Dubais in its right place, after the murder of al-Mustarshid (Ms.A, f.165b). Here, the author cites the month and year of Dubais' murder but gives the name as Ṣadaqa b. Dubais.

Ibn al-Azraq then makes a rare personal comment, casting doubts on the reliability of his source (*wa- aẓannahu wahman*). His own suggestions to clarify the report, however, are disastrously inaccurate.

Qaracha al-Sāqī was the *atābeg* of Saljuq-Shāh b. Muḥammad. He was not killed by Mas'ūd but by Sanjar, in 526/1132 (al-Ḥusainī, *Akhbār,* 101).

As for the name *Mnkwrs,* this is probably a reference to Mengü-Bars who was appointed governor of Fārs in 526/1132 by Sulṭān Ṭoghrïl, who made him *atābeg* to his son, Alp Arslan (*ibid.*). Mengü-Bars was not killed until 532/1138 (Ibn al-Athīr, *al-Kāmil,* XI, 39). For the record, Ṣadaqa b. Dubais had been killed by Sulṭān Muḥammad in 501/1108 (*Akhbār,* 80).

23. *nafadha al-sulṭān ... ya'khudhu idhnahu fī man yuwallī...* Ibn Wāṣil interprets this sentence as follows: *arsala al-sulṭān Mas'ūd ilā 'ammihi al-sulṭān Sanjar yastashīruhu fī man yuwallī al-khilāfata*

"Sulṭān Mas'ūd sent to his uncle, Sulṭān Sanjar, asking his advice as to whom he should appoint" (*op.cit.,* 63).

24. The account by Ibn al-Athīr given in his *History of the Atabegs of Mosul* resembles that of Ibn al-Azraq in certain important details, although the order of events differs. In Ibn al-Athīr's version, al-Rāshid was first deposed. Then Mas'ūd took advice on a suitable person to succeed as caliph. The vizier, Sharaf al-Dīn al-Zainabī, recommended Abū 'Abdallāh b. al-Mustaẓhir. Although someone else spoke against this nomination, Abū 'Abdallāh was chosen (*Atabegs,* 53).

25. Ms.B explains more clearly: "At that time Sharaf al-Dīn (al-Zainabī) was *naqīb al-nuqabā'*; then he was transferred to the vizierate."

'Abdallāh consummated the marriage with her and she remained with him for a while and (then) she died. The *sulṭān* said: "The decision is yours. Keep the matter hidden lest the affair be noised abroad and al-Muqtafī be killed in Baghdad."[26] Then the *sulṭān* and his retinue set off for Baghdad (f.166b) accompanied by the vizier and all of us.

After the murder of his father, the people pledged allegiance to al-Rāshid. He took sole control and became established. He sent a message to the Atābeg Zangī in Mosul,[27] asking him to come and giving him a guarantee that al-Malik Alp Arslan b. Maḥmūd who was with the *atābeg* should become *sulṭān* and that Zangī would be in charge of the atabegate and the caliphate. Zangī therefore went down to Baghdad and took up residence on its eastern side in one of the houses belonging to the *sulṭān*. He stayed there until the news reached him that the *sulṭān* had set out for Baghdad, whereupon he encamped on the western side of Baghdad.[28]

When the *sulṭān* approached Baghdad and camped near al-Nahrawān,[29] al-Rāshid found out what was happening and (realised) that it was inevitable that someone other than himself would be appointed (as caliph). He assembled in a cellar all the *amīrs* of the caliphal family who were living in the palace and he gave orders that the cellar should be closed up. I heard this story from Zain al-Daula Abu 'l-Qāsim 'Alī b. al-Ṣāḥib who was the *ḥājib al-bāb*[30] like his father

26. Ibn Wāṣil is more explicit: "Keep the matter hidden lest the affair be noised abroad and al-Rāshid bi'llāh should kill his uncle, Amīr Abū 'Abdallāh" (*op.cit.*, 63). Al-Muqtafī was to be the title of the new caliph.
27. Zangī was besieging Damascus when he received al-Rāshid's request for help in Baghdad. He made peace terms with Shihāb al-Dīn Maḥmūd b. Būrī and moved on to Ḥamā before going to Baghdad (Ibn Wāṣil, *op.cit.*, 63-4).
28. Ibn al-Azraq's informant greatly simplifies the complicated events in Baghdad at the time of the deposition of al-Rāshid. His account implies that Zangī alone was involved in the resistance to Mas'ūd. Other sources, however, make it clear that many more *amīrs* joined in the uprising against Mas'ūd; their number included Dā'ūd b. Maḥmūd b. Malik Shāh, lord of Ādharbāījān, Ṣadaqa b. Dubais, lord of Ḥilla, and Ibn al-Aḥmadīlī.

    The caliph had Dā'ūd's name mentioned in the *khuṭba* at Baghdad and he paid Zangī 30,000 *dīnārs* (Ibn Wāṣil, *op.cit.*, 64; Ibn al-Athīr, *al-Kāmil*, XI, 22-4).
29. According to Yāqūt, this fertile area on the eastern side of Baghdad was greatly devastated under the Saljuqs ("Reisen", 406).
30. For the office of *ḥājib*, cf. Uzunçarşīlī, *Osmanlï devleti*, 35-6; Horst, *Staatsverwaltung*, 18; Lambton, *op.cit.*, 226.

    According to Lambton, there was a certain blurring of functions

and grandfather before him and who was with al-Rāshid. He said: "When al-Rāshid had assembled the *amīrs* in the cellar, he called me in and said, 'O 'Alī, take this sword.' He had a sword in his hand (and then) he said: 'I will take care that my sword outstrips yours,[31] for I want to fetch out everyone in the cellar and kill them all so that no-one remains who is fitting to become caliph. For these men may well come, change (things) and appoint somebody other than me.' Then he ordered the cellar to be opened. (Just then) the messenger[32] came to al-Rāshid, who said, 'What is the news?' He replied, 'The Atābeg Zangī plundered the Ṭāhirid *ḥarīm*[33] and intended to leave for Mosul in Dhu'l-Qa'da (530/ 1-30 August 1136). As for the *sulṭān*, he arrived and crossed to al-Nahrawān. When the *atābeg* learned that the *sulṭān* had camped at al-Nahrawān he fled.' Thereupon al-Rāshid threw away the sword from his hand and went into the palace. He grabbed for himself jewels of inestimable value, giving me some of them too, and then went away, taking with him the chief *qāḍī* al-Zainabī[34] and having left as vizier Jalāl al-Dīn Abu'l-Riḍā (b.) Ṣadaqa.[35] We left with him and he joined Zangī on the way to Mosul."

Al-Sa'īd Mu'ayyid al-Dīn, may God have mercy on him, said: "The following morning the *sulṭān* entered Baghdad and we were with him. He took up residence in his palace and we did the same in our houses. The day of our arrival was 10 Dhu'l-Qa'da 530 (10 August 1136).

between the *wakīldār* and the *amīr ḥājib* towards the end of Sulṭān Muḥammad's reign (*ibid.*). The term *ḥājib al-bāb* may well be a calque of *wakīldar*.

31. It is possible to read the Arabic differently here to yield the translation: "Take care that your sword outstrips mine". The difficulty here is that only one sword is mentioned as being in the caliph's hand.

32. *al-ṣā'iḥ* "crieur public" (Dozy, *Supplément* I, 856).

33. Once again, Ms.B is more accurate with its version of the text (*al-ḥarīm al-ṭāhirī*). For a description of the Ṭāḥirid Ḥarīm in Baghdad, cf. G. Le Strange, *Baghdad during the Abbasid Caliphate* (Oxford, 1900), 119-21. This palace had the rights of sanctuary granted to it.

According to the sources cited by Le Strange (*ibid.*, 121), it was the populace of Baghdad who plundered the Ṭāhirid Ḥarīm in 530/1136 after the siege of the city by Sulṭān Mas'ūd. At this point, much wealth was removed from the palace (*ibid.*, 120-1).

34. The family of al-Zainabī was conspicuous in the office of *naqīb al-nuqabā'* and also as viziers and *qāḍīs*. The chief *qāḍī* mentioned here is the cousin of the vizier, Sharaf al-Dīn al-Zainabī. This cousin was called 'Alī b. al-Ḥusain and is mentioned by Ibn al-Jauzī (*Muntaẓam*, X, 109).

35. Jalāl al-Dīn Abu'l-Riḍā b. Ṣadaqa was appointed vizier by al-Rāshid in 529/1134-5 (al-'Aẓīmī, "Chronique", 410; Ibn al-Ṭiqṭaqā, *al-Fakhrī*, 531).

The next day we and the vizier went to the *sulṭān's* palace, and the vizier asked the *sulṭān's* permission for what he was going to do. The *sulṭān* secured the vizier's signature and ours on the guaranty and we then returned to our houses. On the morning of Monday 12 Dhu'l-Qa'da[36] 530 (12 August 1136) we went to see the *amīr* Abū 'Abdallāh and we and the vizier had a talk with him. The vizier fixed the conditions on which he was to become caliph and stipulated that he should obey the *sulṭān*. We informed him that we had vouched to the *sulṭān* for all the conditions which the *sulṭān* had laid down for him. He was content with that and we left him, went to the *sulṭān* and told him what had happened and that Abū 'Abdallāh had agreed to the conditions imposed on him. (f.167a) So the *sulṭān* said: 'Tomorrow let the people pay allegiance to him.' In the morning, we went up to the palace and removed from it musical instruments and improper things.[37] Some of the people in the palace testified that al-Rāshid had drunk wine. The *'ulamā'* duly gave a *fatwā* deposing him and the *qāḍī* 'Imād al-Dīn Sharaf al-Quḍāt Abū Aḥmad b. al-Karkhī,[38] the *muḥtasib*, who was the *qāḍī* of the Shāfi'ites, may God have mercy on him, pronounced judgement on that.[39] The *'ulamā'* and notables met together and deposed al-Rāshid.[40]

The vizier, the treasurer and I went in to see Abū 'Abdallāh. We talked together and I handed him a piece of paper on which were some suitable *laqabs:* on it were (the names) al-Muqtafī li-Amr Allāh and al-Mustaḍī bi-Amr Allāh[41] and al-Mustanjid bi'llāh. The vizier said, 'It is up to you to choose', so the caliph asked me, 'What do you think?' So I said, 'Al-Muqtafī li-Amr Allāh', whereupon he said, 'Blessed (be that name).' Then the caliph stretched out his hand and

36. Ms.A writes 17 Dhu'l-Qa'da 530. This date has been changed in the translation to 12 Dhu'l-Qa'da. Given the day-by-day sequence of events described here, beginning on 10 Dhu'l-Qa'da, the date required here should be 12 Dhu'l-Qa'da. The day after, which is the day suggested by Mas'ūd for the pledging of allegiance to al-Muqtafī, should logically be 13 Dhu'l-Qa'da. Fortunately, this hypothesis is supported by Ms.B which has: "The following day, which was Tuesday 13 Dhu'l-Qa'da...."
37. Literally: "items consisting of instruments which are suitable for singing and improper things".
38. Ibn al-Athīr also mentions Ibn al-Karkhī's role in the deposition of al-Rāshid (*Atabegs,* 53). Ibn al-Karkhī was consulted because the chief *qāḍī* was no longer in Baghdad but was with Zangī in Mosul (*al-Kāmil,* XI, 27).
39. Ibn Wāṣil changes *i'tanaqa* to *ḥakama* (*op.cit.,* 67).
40. This account is also found in Ibn al-Furāt (*Duwal,* f.144b).
41. Ms.B has al-Mustaḍī bi-Nūr Allāh.

the vizier took it, kissed it and said, 'I have pledged allegiance to our lord and master, al-Muqtafī li-Amr Allāh, Commander of the Faithful, on God's book and on the *sunna* of the Prophet of God and his *ijtihād*.' Then the treasurer took his hand, kissed it and pledged allegiance in the same way. Then I took his hand and having kissed it, I said: 'I have pledged allegiance to our lord and master, the *imām* al-Muqtafī li-Amr Allāh, Commander of the Faithful, on the same conditions as I pledged allegiance to his father, his brother, and his nephew at his heir-apparent ceremony.' I had pledged allegiance to the *imām* al-Mustaẓhir bi'llāh when I served as his *wakīl al-dār*[42] in the year (4)92 (28 November 1098 - 16 November 1099).[43] I had remained (in that post) until the year 507 (18 June 1113 - 6 June 1114) when I was given charge of the *dīwān al-inshā'*.[44] I had (also) pledged allegiance to al-Mustarshid and al-Rāshid. Then we stood up and left him and he went into the palace. After the people had pledged allegiance to him, all the *'ulamā'*, *fuqahā'*, *qāḍīs* and notables went in and did likewise. Three days later, Sulṭān Mas'ūd arrived and pledged allegiance to him. Then all the *khwājas* in his retinue and al-Amīr Ḥājib (Tatār)[45] and all his state officials pledged allegiance to al-Muqtafī, who assumed sole command and became established in the caliphate."

¶ In 529 (1134-5) Najm al-Daula b. Mālik[46] died in Qal'at (Ja'bar) and was succeeded by his son.[47] Also in that year the Atābeg Zangī took al-Raqqa[48] from Musayyib b. Mālik.[49]

42. The position of *wakīldār* was that of a "middle-man" between the ruler and his subjects. He was also responsible for the checking of the sulṭān's *farmāns* (Horst, *Staatsverwaltung*, 17). The *wakīldār*, the "keeper of the household, was supposed to be eloquent and knowledgeable, as well as tactful and understanding concerning the moods and temper of the sulṭān" (Klausner, *op.cit.*, 18, citing Bundārī, *Zubdat*, 93-4).
43. The Ms. has a lacuna here. Ibn Wāṣil, who copies this passage, has 492 (*op.cit.*, 68).
44. The *dīwān al-inshā'*, the "state chancery", was the department responsible for conducting correspondence at home and abroad, as well as for drawing up deeds (Horst, *Staatsverwaltung*, 31).
45. Ms.A: al-Amīr Ḥājib; Ms.B: al-Amīr Ḥājib Tatār.
46. Ms.A has Najm al-Daula b. Mālik. For a discussion of this name, cf. n.96. The correct reading should probably be Shihāb al-Dīn Mālik.
47. This unnamed son of Mālik b. Sālim is Badrān.
48. Ibn Shaddād gives a brief description and history of al-Raqqa and lists its rulers with his customary inaccuracy over names (*Jazīra*, f.24). For further details on "al-Raqqa", cf. E. Honigmann, "al-Raḳḳa", *EI*[1].
49. Ibn al-Azraq calls Musayyib the son of Mālik. Ibn Shaddād says he is Mālik's brother, appointed by Mālik to govern al-Raqqa (*ibid.*). Musayyib is mentioned by Ibn Khallikān, who does not, however,

A number of people had held office as vizier to al-Mustarshid in his time. Amongst them were Amīn al-Dīn Khwāja Aḥmad b. Niẓām al-Mulk[50] and Sharaf al-Dīn Anūshīrwān,[51] each of whom held office twice: then Jalāl al-Dīn Abū ʿAlī b. Ṣadaqa was vizier until he died.[52] Then Sharaf al-Dīn al-Zainabī held office as vizier until the caliph was killed. Al-Zainabī had been taken prisoner with him as we have already mentioned.

To go back to what happened to al-Rāshid: he left for Mosul with the Atābeg Zangī in Ṣafar 531 (29 October - 26 November 1136) accompanied by the chief *qāḍī* al-Zainabī and Jalāl al-Dīn Abu'l-Riḍā b. Ṣadaqa, the nephew of the vizier Abū ʿAlī. Having stayed with Zangī for a while, al-Rāshid went with him as far as Naṣībīn, where he stayed a few days. Thereafter he left the *atābeg* and went to Sulṭān Masʿūd to ask if he might enter his territory and proceed to Sulṭān Sanjar.[53]

specify who he is (*Wafayāt,* I, 505). De Slane is not sure, either. He calls Musayyib "probably a near relative to Badrān" (*ibid.,* 507, n.6). Ibn al-ʿAdīm agrees with Ibn al-Azraq, calling him Musayyib b. Mālik (*Zubda,* 257).

Zangī took al-Raqqa from Musayyib on 20 Rabīʿ II 529 (7 February, 1135) by means of a ruse, in which he asked merely for a bath for himself and his men. Once inside the citadel, he gained possession of it (*ibid.).*

50. Ms.B calls this person Niẓām al-Dīn Abū Naṣr Aḥmad b. Niẓām al-Mulk. This man served as vizier to Sulṭān Muḥammad (Klausner, *op.cit.,* 106) and then to the caliph al-Mustarshid (Ibn al-Athīr, *al-Kāmil,* X, 428). Ibn al-Athīr calls him Niẓām al-Dīn too, whilst Klausner uses the *laqab* Ḍiyāʾ al-Mulk (*op.cit.,* 137). This son was but one of the many descendants of Niẓām al-Mulk who held high office. He died in 544/1149 (cf. Ibn al-Ṭiqṭaqā, *al-Fakhrī,* 526-7).

51. For a description of Anūshīrwān b. Khālid, cf. Ibn al-Ṭiqṭaqā, *al-Fakhrī,* 527-9; Ibn al-Jauzī, *Muntaẓam,* X, 77-8; Ibn al-Furāt (Shayyāl), 350-2.

There was great professional rivalry between Anūshīrwān and Sharaf al-Dīn al-Zainabī (*al-Fakhrī,* 528). Anūshīrwān was appointed vizier to the caliph al-Mustarshid in 526/1131-2 (Ibn al-Athīr, *al-Kāmil,* X, 480).

52. This man also held the office of vizier twice. He died in 522/1128. Cf. Ibn al-Ṭiqṭaqā, *al-Fakhrī,* 523-5.

53. According to al-Ḥusainī, al-Rāshid was afraid that Zangī would come to an arrangement with Masʿūd to hand him over. He therefore left Mosul with the intention of going to Sulṭān Sanjar in Khurāsān. Al-Rāshid, hearing that al-Muqtafī had been appointed caliph, wrote to Sulṭān Sanjar at the beginning of Ramaḍān 531, complaining bitterly about Sulṭān Masʿūd and asking for military help. When he received a negative response from Sanjar, al-Rāshid made for Iraq but was killed whilst at Iṣfahān (*Akhbār,* 108-9).

¶ He sought out Sulṭān Dā'ūd and went to see him (to seek) his own reinstatement (f.167b) as caliph.[54] When he was near Iṣfahān, a group of heretics (*mulāḥida*) rose against him, went into him and killed him in Ramaḍān 532 (13 May - 11 June 1138).[55] He was taken to Iṣfahān and was buried there in the city of Shahristān,[56] which is one *farsakh* from Iṣfahān. It is said that it was one of the buildings of Alexander on the bridge over a river known as the Zāyanda Rūd.[57] The caliphate of al-Rāshid, from the time allegiance was pledged to him after the murder of his father until the ceremony of allegiance to al-Muqtafī, was more or less 11 months.

According to another report, the *sulṭān* sent those who went in and killed al-Rāshid.[58] He left in the palace some twenty sons of his, amongst whom the eldest was *amīr al-jaish*, and it is said that he appointed him as his heir apparent before he left Baghdad. As for the chief *qāḍī*, al-Zainabī, may God have mercy on him, he returned (from Mosul), went down to Baghdad and returned to his post. As for Jalāl al-Dīn Abu'l-Riḍā b. Ṣadaqa, he became vizier to Atābeg Zangī for a while,[59] before being dismissed and returning to Baghdad. He had become vizier to Zangī after the death of Ḍiyā' al-Dīn Abū Sa'īd al-Kafartūthī.[60] Al-Muqtafī became established in the caliphate and his rule was secure.

54. According to Abu'l-Fiḍā', al-Rāshid went to Dā'ūd in Āzarbāījān and Dā'ūd and other border lords agreed to help to restore him to the caliphate. After Mas'ūd had routed Dā'ūd, the latter fled to Fārs, whilst al-Rāshid went to Iṣfahān (*Mukhtaṣar* III, 13). Cf. also Ibn al-Athīr, *al-Kāmil,* XI, 39-40.
55. Sibṭ b. al-Jauzī gives the exact date of al-Rāshid's death as 27 Ramaḍān,532 (9 June 1138) (*Mir'āt,* 167), whilst Ibn al-Athīr has 25 Ramaḍān,532 (7 June 1138) (*al-Kāmil,* XI, 41).
56. According to Yāqūt, Shahristān was situated beside the Zāyanda Rūd. The tomb of al-Rāshid was situated there (Barbier de Meynard, *op.cit.,* 520).
57. The scribe has more difficulty than usual with these Persian words. The usual forms are *Zandrūdh* and *Zandrūd.*
58. Sibṭ b. al-Jauzī analyses the murder of al-Rāshid in more detail than the other chroniclers. He says that there are differing reports on this event. Al-Rāshid was either poisoned; or killed by some Persians in his service; or murdered by the Ismā'īlīs, who were sent by Sanjar and Mas'ūd (*Mir'āt,* 167). Ms.B adds here: *wa-ja'ala al-ism al-mulāḥida* ("and he named the *mulāḥida*" - i.e. blamed them).
59. Jalāl al-Dīn Abu'l-Riḍā b. Ṣadaqa was appointed vizier to Zangī on the death of Ḍiyā' al-Dīn b. al-Kafartūthī in 536/1141-2. He was dismissed two years later (Ibn al-'Adīm, *Zubda,* 276; Ibn al-Qalānisī, *Dhail,* 277; al-'Aẓīmī, "Chronique", 422).
60. Al-Kafartūthī was appointed by Zangī as his vizier in 528 (1133-4) (Ibn al-Furāt [Shayyāl], 142).

In (5)32 (19 September 1137 - 7 September 1138) Sulṭān Saljūq-Shāh besieged Akhlāṭ for a while and then withdrew.[61] In (5)33 (8 September 1138 - 27 August 1139) Amīr Dā'ūd had the *khuṭba* said in the name of al-Muqtafī on Friday 23 Muḥarram (30 September 1138).

In the year (5)3(3?) (1138-9) the Sanāsuna[62] imprisoned the lord of Akhlāṭ;[63] they were given Khūwīth[64] and he was released through the mediation of Ḥusām al-Dīn in Jumādā I (5)33 (4 January 1139 - 2 February 1139).

¶ In 529 (1134-5) Malik Ṭoghrïl Beg died outside Damascus and was taken to Iraq.[65]

In 529 (1134-5) I travelled from Mayyāfāriqīn to Mārdīn, having not previously left Mayyāfāriqīn, and I stayed in Mārdīn for a while. While I was in Mārdīn, Dubais' bier arrived and he was buried in the *mashhad*. In this year the wife of the *amīr* Shihāb al-Dīn Muḥammad b. Ilyās died. She had also been married to the *amīr* Ḥusām al-Dīn and she had Ṣafiyya Khātūn by him.[66] I was in Mārdīn this year when al-Sa'īd Ḥusām al-Dīn married the princess, Khātūn, daughter of al-Malik Riḍwān. She had come that year from Aleppo. She had been the wife of Badr al-Daula Sulaimān[67] b. 'Abd al-Jabbār b. Artuq and

61. For a discussion of Saljuq-Shāh, cf. f. 163b.
62. The Sanāsuna (Armenian *Sanasnaik;* Greek *Sanasounitai)* were the inhabitants of the region of Sasun to the west of Bitlīs (Canard, *H'amdanides,* 185). They pillaged armies and caravans. Cf. also Honigmann, *Ostgrenze,* 184.
63. The lord of Akhlāṭ in 533/1138-9 was Sukmān b. Ibrāhīm (cf. Appendix A).
64. Khūwīth (also known as Khoit) lay in a mountainous district to the east of Sasun. It was inhabited by the Khuwaithiyya (cf. Honigmann, *Ostgrenze,* 206; Canard, *H'amdanides,* 185).
65. On f.163b Ibn al-Azraq mentions the death of Sulṭān Ṭoghrïl who according to him was murdered in 527, whilst the majority of sources agree on Muḥarram 529/October-November 1134 (cf. n.42). Here "Malik Ṭoghrïl" is said to have died in 529 outside Damascus.

    This report is therefore most confused. Either this is a second reference to Sulṭān Ṭoghrïl's death with the correct date but the wrong place (Sulṭān Ṭoghrïl died outside Hamadhān) or the reference concerns Malik Ṭoghrïl Arslan b. Qïlïch Arslan of Malaṭya. There is a superfluous *qīla* which makes no sense either with the preceding or following narrative.
66. Cf. f.163a.
67. Badr al-Daula Sulaimān had been made governor of Aleppo in 516/1122 by Īl-Ghāzī after the latter's own son, Shams al-Daula Sulaimān, had rebelled against him. Badr al-Daula Sulaimān held Aleppo for only a short time since Balak took it from him in Jumādā I 517/June 1123 (Ibn al-'Adīm, *Bughyat,* 198).

she died in Mārdīn. She came from Aleppo, accompanied by a son whose *ism* was Köpek[68] and whose *laqab* was Majd al-Mulūk. She remained for a while and al-Sa'īd Ḥusām al-Dīn married her. In this year Tāj al-Dīn Abū Sālim b. Nubāta, may God be pleased with him, had come to Mārdīn.

¶ In 528 (1133-4) Atābeg Zangī and Ḥusām al-Dīn had attacked the citadel of al-Ṣūr.[69] After Zangī had taken it on 21 Rajab (17 May 1134),[70] he handed it over to al-Sa'īd Ḥusām al-Dīn.[71] Ḥamdān[72] b. Aslam was killed. He was a courageous *amīr* in the retinue of Amīr Dā'ūd and had been governor of al-Ṣūr on his behalf. In this year, (f.168a) Atābeg Zangī came to Tall Shaikh[73] and joined up with Ḥusām al-Dīn. They (then) encountered Dā'ūd outside Āmid and

During his tenure of Aleppo he had begun building a *madrasa* there in 517/1123. After Zangī conquered Aleppo, he transferred the body of his father to the *madrasa* and finished building it (*ibid.*, 106-7).

Badr al-Daula Sulaimān married one of the daughters of Malik Riḍwān (*ibid.*, 216-7). It is not clear if the daughter in question was Farkhundā Khātūn or another one. Farkhundā Khātūn had married Īl-Ghāzī when he took Aleppo (cf. f.162b) but the union was unconsummated. She then married Balak (*ibid.*). Zangī had also married a daughter of Malik Riḍwān (Ibn al-'Adīm, *Zubda*, 244).

68. *k.b.k.* Sauvaget attests the name Köpek as a proper name (*op.cit.*, 54). Cf. the Rūm Saljuq official Sa'd al-Dīn Köpek or the early 14th-century Transoxanian ruler of the same name.

69. Al-Ṣūr is listed by Ibn Shaddād amongst the citadels of Diyār Bakr (*Jazīra*, f.65b). Michael the Syrian places it near Mārdīn (*Chronique*, 250).

70. Ibn al-Azraq's chronology is probably erratic here. It would appear from other accounts that Zangī attacked Āmid first and then made for the citadel of al-Ṣūr. According to Ibn al-Athīr, Zangī took al-Ṣūr because he failed to take Āmid. The battle outside Āmid took place in Jumādā II, 528 (29 March - 26 April 1134); the conquest of al-Ṣūr occurred in Rajab, 528 (27 April - 26 May 1134) (*al-Kāmil*, XI, 6-7). The account of Ibn al-Qalānisī is similar to that of Ibn al-Athīr (*Dhail*, 243). Cf. also Usāma, *Memoirs*, 185.

71. Probably because of his undeniably pro-Artuqid bias, Ibn al-Azraq never explicitly states that Temür-Tash became the vassal of Zangī. Al-'Aẓīmī has no such deference for the Artuqids. He specifically says that in 528/1133-4 Ḥusām al-Dīn became the vassal of Atābeg Zangī and went with him to fight Dā'ūd b. Artuq ("Chronique", 408). No doubt as a reward for his services, Zangī gave Temür-Tash al-Ṣūr.

72. Ms.A: Jandāl b. Aslam; Ms.B and Ibn Shaddād (*Jazīra*, f.103a): Ḥamdān b. Aslam.

73. Tall Shaikh was situated below Mārdīn and Ḥiṣn Kaifā. It was a frequent meeting place for troops in the twelfth century (Cahen, *Syrie*, 215, n.35).

defeated him.[74] Zangī entered al-Ṣūr and took it. In this year Atābeg Zangī took possession of Ṭanzī[75] and Tall Shaikh. Ḍiyā' al-Dīn Abū Sa'īd b. al-Kafartūthī became vizier to Atābeg Zangī and entered his service.[76] In that year Shams al-Daula al-Aḥdab died.[77]

¶ In the year (5)30 (1135-6), Ḥusām al-Dīn ordered the destruction of the *rabaḍ*[78] and the *Muḥaddatha*[79] and they were (duly) destroyed.[80] Disagreement had arisen between al-Sa'īd Ḥusām al-Dīn and Amīr Dā'ūd, with Zangī siding with Amīr Ḥusām al-Dīn. After they had defeated Amīr Dā'ūd outside Āmid, they went and seized Jabal Jūr,[81] Dhu'l-Qarnain[82] and al-Sīwān.[83] These places were taken from Amīr

74. Zangī's attack on Āmid is described in a number of sources: Ibn al-Qalānisī, *Dhail,* 243; Michael the Syrian, *Chronique,* 249-50; Ibn al-Athīr, *al-Kāmil,* XI, 6-7; *idem, Atabegs,* 48. Cf. also M. H. Yinanc, "Diyarbekir", *IA,* 614.

    According to Ibn al-Qalānisī, Dā'ūd met Zangī and Temür-Tash outside Āmid. Dā'ūd was routed, some of his sons were taken prisoner and many of his men killed. The battle took place on the last day of Jumādā II, 528/April 1134. Zangī then laid siege to Āmid but was unsuccessful and withdrew (*Dhail,* 243).

75. Cahen points out that there were two places with very similar names, Ṭanza and Ṭanzī. Ṭanza was situated near Hattākh, to the north of Mayyāfāriqīn, although Cahen is not sure of its exact position ("Diyār Bakr", 224-5). The other, better-known place was in the region of Is'ird (cf. V.F. Minorsky, "Kurds", *EI*[2]).

76. Cf. Ibn al-Athīr, *al-Kāmil,* XI, 6-7; *idem, Atabegs,* 48; al-'Aẓīmī, "Chronique", 409; Ibn al-Qalānisī, *Dhail,* 243.

    For Kafartūthā, cf. Canard, *H'amdanides,* 99; Le Strange, *Lands,* 97.

77. Shams al-Daula Ṭoghan Arslan al-Aḥdab fought as the vassal of İl-Ghāzī. He was the ruler of Arzan and Bitlīs. Ibn al-Qalānisī puts his death in 532/1137-8 (*Dhail,* 267).

78. For a definition of the term *rabaḍ* (plural *arbāḍ),* cf. E. Lévi-Provençal, "rabaḍ", *EI*[1]. Lévi-Provençal defines a *rabaḍ* as the district of a town situated outside the central part, the *madīna.*

79. For a description of this part of Mayyāfāriqīn, which had its own mosque, bazaars and *khāns,* cf. Ibn Shaddād, *Jazīra,* f.71a.

80. Ms.B and Ibn Shaddād state that the work of demolition began on 9 Muḥarram, 530 (19 October 1135). Presumably these two areas of Mayyāfāriqīn were destroyed as a preventive measure since Temür-Tash could not defend it satisfactorily against the depredations of his cousin Dā'ūd.

81. Jabal Jūr was to the north of Mayyāfāriqīn near al-Ṣīwān and Dhu'l-Qarnain.

82. The scribe of Ms.A consistently writes the name of this citadel as *bi'l-Qarnain.* Ibn Shaddād calls it Ḥiṣn Dhi'l-Qarnain (*Jazīra,* f.65b).

    The source of the Tigris lay below a castle called Dhu'l-Qarnain, north of Mayyāfāriqīn (Quatremère, *Mongols,* 362).

    In 516/1122 a copper mine was discovered near the citadel and from that date onwards its resources were exploited (Ibn al-Athīr, *al-Kāmil,*

Arslan[84] b. ʿAbd al-Jabbār b. Artuq and were handed over by Zangī to al-Saʿīd Ḥusām al-Dīn. Amīr Arslan ran away and entered the service of Amīr Dāʾūd.

¶ In (5)28 (1133-4) Amīr Dāʾūd plundered the *rabaḍ* of Ṭanzī, taking its inhabitants captive, plundering their possessions and raping the women more disgracefully than even the Franks would have done. In (5)28 (1133-4), al-Saʿīd Ḥusām al-Dīn took possession of al-Hattākh, as we have already related.[85] He took al-Hattākh[86] from Amīr Shams al-Daula ʿĪsā b. Aḥmad b. Niẓām al-Dīn b. Marwān.[87]

¶ In 531 (1136-7) al-Saʿīd came to Mayyāfāriqīn, accompanied by Ḥabashī b. Ḥabashī,[88] who conducted a financial inspection of the

X, 215). Taylor visited this place in 1862-3 (J. G. Taylor, "Travels in Kurdistan, with Notices of the Sources of the Eastern and Western Tigris, and Ancient Ruins in their Neighbourhood", *The Journal of the Royal Geographical Society* 35 [1865], 21-58.)

83. Jabal Jūr, Dhu'l-Qarnain and al-Sīwān were all three the possessions of Dāʾūd and were handed over to Temür-Tash. No doubt Dāʾūd's hostility in 530/1135-6 may be attributed to this. Ibn al-ʿAdīm lists Zangī's conquests as al-Ṣūr, Bārʿiya, Jabal Jūr and Dhu'l-Qarnain and says that Zangī presented them all to Temür-Tash. He kept only Ṭanzī for himself (*Zubda,* 235).

84. Cf. Appendix B.

85. In an earlier passage, Ibn al-Azraq implies that the capture of al-Hattākh was in 528/1133-4 (ʿAwaḍ, 254). Cf. C. Hillenbrand, "Marwānids", *EI*².

86. According to Michael the Syrian, the fortress of al-Hattākh had not yet been in Turkish hands but had remained in the possession of the Banū Marwān (*Chronique,* 264).

In 355/965-6, al-Hattākh was considered the frontier of Byzantine territory. According to Canard, it was six *farsakhs* north-east of Mayyāfāriqīn (*H'amdanides,* 256). According to Honigmann, it lay some 20 kms to the NW of Mayyāfāriqīn and is probably to be identified with modern Hazro (*op.cit.,* 166). Cf. also Tihrānī, *Kitāb-i Diyārbakriyya* II, 210, 388; Markwart, *Südarmenien,* 249. Taylor visited the ruins of this place in 1862-3 (*op.cit.,* 39).

87. Sibṭ b. al-Jauzī relates that in 531/1136-7 the lord of Mārdīn took the citadel of al-Hattākh, the last remaining possession of the Marwānids in Diyār Bakr (*Mirʾāt,* 161). The date of 531 for Temür-Tash's capture of the citadel is confirmed by Ibn Abī Ṭayyi' in Ibn al-Furāt, *Duwal,* f.93b.

In an earlier passage, Ibn al-Azraq says that many of the members of the Marwānid family stayed in the service of Temür-Tash (ʿAwaḍ, 254).

88. Ḥabashī had entered Temür-Tash's service in 528/1133-4 after being in Ḥamā with Ṣalāḥ al-Dīn Muḥammad al-Yaghī-Sīyanī (Ms.A, f.164b).

ummāl[89] and the *mutaṣarrifūn.*[90] Ḥabashī mulcted the inhabitants of the city, uprooted them (from their homes) and did them great harm. The people met at his hand abuse, injustice and oppression of an indescribable severity and he inflicted extreme tyranny and hardship on them. Ḥabashī seized al-Nāṣiḥ al-Āmidī, who was a *mutawallī* in the *dīwān* of Mayyāfāriqīn, and his son Abū Naṣr. Al-Mu'ayyid b. Mukhtār, who was (also) a *mutawallī,* fled from the hand of Ḥabashī and went to the Jazīra, but the latter arrested his brother Abū Sa'īd. Ḥabashī released the *'amīd*[91] Abū Ṭāhir b. al-Muḥtasib from prison where he had been incarcerated for a while, and he appointed him *muḥtasib*[92] of the people. They encountered from him unspeakable severity and hardship.

In that year I was in the Jazīra where I lived for a while before returning to Mayyāfāriqīn. I passed through Naṣībīn where I saw Atābeg Zangī.

In (5)29 (1134-5) Shihāb al-Dīn Mālik b. Sālim[93] died in Qal'at (Ja'bar) and Atābeg Zangī took al-Raqqa from Amīr Musayyib.[94] He went on to Damascus, besieged it for a while and then entered it.[95] Mālik's son Badrān[96] was in Qal'at (Ja'bar) for a while, remaining

89. The *'ummāl* (sing. *'āmil)* were the tax-collectors from the *dīwān-i istīfā-yi mamālik* of Saljuq Iran. They were responsible to the local *mustaufī* for the collection of taxes in a particular area. According to Lambton, Niẓām al-Mulk recommended that the *'ummāl* should be changed every two or three years to prevent their becoming too powerful locally (*op.cit.,* 254, 258, 260).
90. The *mutaṣarrifūn* were the subordinates of the *'ummāl* (*ibid.,* 258).
91. The *'amīd* was another term for *'āmil* (Klausner, *op.cit.,* 20).
92. The word *muḥtasib* is only a tentative suggestion. The Ms. is damaged here.
93. Ms.A: Najm al-Daula Mālik b. Mālik. This should read Shihāb al-Dīn Mālik b. Sālim.
94. The conquest of al-Raqqa by Zangī has already been mentioned on f.167a.
95. Cf. Ibn al-'Adīm (*Zubda,* 258). Zangī attempted unsuccessfully to take Damascus on this occasion.
96. Badrān b. Mālik was the son of the union between his father and a beautiful Frankish girl who had been taken prisoner on a pilgrimage to Afāmiyya. After her husband's death (in 529), Badrān's mother left Qal'at Ja'bar, went to Sarūj, which was in Frankish hands, and married a shoemaker (Ibn Shaddād, *Jazīra,* f.34a).

until the beginning of (5)30 (October 1135) when his brother Amīr ʻAlī b. Mālik killed him and took over the citadel.[97]

97. According to Ibn Shaddād, ʻAlī b. Mālik killed his brother in 533/1138-9 and then remained in the citadel until Zangī attacked it in Dhu'l-Ḥijja 540/May-June 1146 (*Jazīra,* f.34a).
A tentative genealogy of the late ʻUqailids might be as follows:

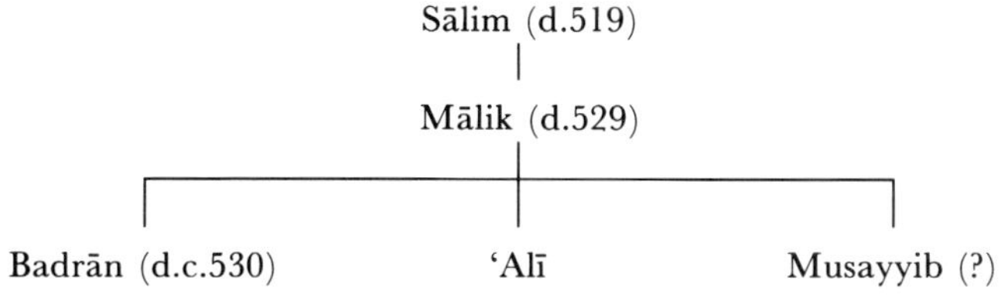

Chapter 5

An excursus into Maghribī history and further developments in the Jazīra

In 528 (1133-4) 'Abd al-Mu'min conquered the Maghrib.[1] I will mention something about him and about the information which has reached me about him. The story goes as follows: Muḥammad b. Tūmart who was from the Maṣmūda (tribe)[2] went to the countries of the east.[3] He was the *shaikh* of 'Abd al-Mu'min b. 'Alī al-Kūmī[4] who

1. This digression into North African history is unusual for Ibn al-Azraq. Normally, he looks no further than Egypt. He displays none of the scruples shown by Ibn al-Qalānisī in his account of the rise of the Almohads. The latter historian is aware of the unreliability of some of his sources but nevertheless devotes much space to Maghribī material (*Dhail,* 291-3).
   It seems probable that to contemporary Muslims the religious significance of these events transcended the remote area in which they occurred and impressed Muslims as far away as Syria and the Jazīra. Ibn al-Athīr devotes a much longer section than Ibn al-Qalānisī to the rise of the Almohads (*al-Kāmil,* X, 400-14).
2. *al-Maṣāmida*. Cf. *EI*[1] s.v. "Maṣmūda". A broken plural *Maṣāmida* is also found. The Maṣmūda were one of the principal Berber ethnic groups. Their home was the High Atlas mountains of Morocco.
3. There is great uncertainty about the chronology of the early events of the life of Ibn Tūmart. He was born between 471/1078-9 and 474/1081-2 (A.H. Miranda, *Historia Politica del Imperio Almohade* [Tetuan, 1956], I, 24). According to al-Marrākushī, he went on his important journey to the east in 501/1107-8 ('Abd al-Wāḥid al-Marrākūshī, *Kitāb al-Mu'jib fī talkhīs akhbār al-Maghrib*, ed. R.P.A. Dozy [Leiden, 1847], 129).

came from the mountains of Sūs in the Maghrib.[5] Muḥammad b. Tūmart al-Idrīsī al-Ḥusainī had gone (f.168b) to the east where he remained for a while before returning to the Maghrib in 519 (1125-6).[6]

While he was staying in Marrākush, a group of *fuqahā'* met him.[7] He engaged in debate with them and there occurred between them things which did not usually happen amongst the Maghribīs and which were outside their way (of thinking). Both parties disowned the other.[8] Then the *fuqahā'* held a meeting with the *amīr al-muslimīn*[9] 'Alī b. Yūsuf b. Tāshufīn[10] at which they said to him, "Send this man away from us. If you don't, he will corrupt and ruin the people." 'Alī therefore ordered him to leave,[11] which he did in 520 (1126-7).[12] 'Alī

4. The full name of 'Abd al-Mu'min was 'Abd al-Mu'min b. 'Alī b. 'Alawī al-Kūmī (al-Marrākushī, *op.cit.*, 141).
For an account of the momentous encounter between Ibn Tūmart and 'Abd al-Mu'min, cf. *ibid.*, 130.
5. Ms.A: *al-Sūs al-Aqṣā bi'l-Maghrib*. This is a reference not to Sūs in Tunisia but to the place of the same name in Morocco.
6. The date of 519/1125-6 given by Ibn al-Azraq is much too late. Miranda puts the return of Ibn Tūmart to the Maghrib in 511/1117-8 (*op.cit.*, I, 38).
7. According to Julien, the majority of chroniclers give 514/1120-1 as the date for the arrival of Ibn Tūmart in Marrākush (C. A. Julien, *History of North Africa*, tr. J. Petrie [London, 1970], 100).
Marrākush was not Ibn Tūmart's first port of call. He had already visited Tripoli, al-Mahdiyya, Tūnis, Būjiyya, Fās and Sāla (Miranda, *op.cit.*, I, 39-46). Whilst at Fās, he had engaged in theological debate and the *fuqahā'* had recommended his expulsion "lest he should corrupt the minds of the populace" (al-Marrākushī, *op.cit.*, 132).
8. According to Miranda, Ibn Tūmart met 'Alī b. Yūsuf b. Tāshufīn in the mosque at Marrākush and told him to correct the wrongs committed in his country. Ibn Tūmart then met the *fuqahā'* of Marrākush. These men were mere casuists, used only to dealing with practical legal matters. They could not maintain a theological discussion with Ibn Tūmart. The exception amongst them was Abū 'Abdallāh Mālik b. Wuhayb (*op.cit.*, 53-4).
9. Yūsuf b. Tāshufīn had assumed the title of *amīr al-muslimīn* after his first major victory against the Castilians in 1086 (J. M. Abun-Nasr, *A History of the Maghrib* [Cambridge, 1971], 98). Cf. also Ibn Khallikān, *Wafayāt*, III, pt.1, 207-9.
10. 'Alī b. Yūsuf b. Tāshufīn ruled the Almoravid empire from 500/1106 - 537/1142 (C. E. Bosworth, *The Islamic Dynasties* [Edinburgh, 1967], 28).
11. Mālik b. Wuḥayb was persuaded by the envious *fuqahā'* to denounce Ibn Tūmart as a dangerous innovator, who would corrupt morals and rebel against the Almoravid empire, thus provoking its ruin. Mālik therefore advised 'Alī to imprison Ibn Tūmart. 'Alī, however, opted for the compromise solution of expulsion (Miranda, *op.cit.*, 54-5). According to al-Marrākushī, Mālik advised 'Alī to kill Ibn Tūmart (*op.cit.*, 133).
12. The year 520/1126-7 is much too late for Ibn Tūmart's expulsion from Marrākush. Miranda gives 514/1120-1 (*op.cit.*, I, 59).

banished him to the mountain area, to the Maṣmūda, a group of Berbers who were his own tribe.[13] He lived amongst them and incited them to abandon their allegiance to the *amīr al-muslimīn.*[14] Thereupon the *amīr al-muslimīn* took the field against him and Ibn Tūmart met him (in battle and) defeated him. The commander of the troops, 'Abdallāh b. Malwīya, was killed. The *amīr al-muslimīn* therefore went out in person and, having assembled his troops, he met Ibn Tūmart on the battlefield and defeated him.[15]

Ibn Tūmart consolidated his position in the mountain area, which is a journey of a month or two.[16] This mountain area is called Daran[17] and is in the province of Marrākush and Sūs. A great many people

13. Ibn Tūmart's tribe was the Hargha (al-Marrākushī, *op.cit.,* 128). The Hargha were one of the Maṣmūda tribes (Abun-Nasr, *op.cit.,* 103).
14. Ms.B adds "they refused to fulfil the obligations imposed on them" (f.118b).

    After leaving Marrākush, Ibn Tūmart went to Aghmat and Tīnmāl. The latter was the heart-land of the Maṣmūda tribes and afforded him an excellent strategic position (Miranda, *op.cit.,* 59-61; Julien, *op.cit.,* 101). In the Atlas mountains, he organised a regular state with revenues drawn from taxation and fanatical troops ready for war (*ibid.,* 103).
15. The meaning of these lines is confused by the ambiguity of the personal pronouns used. There would appear to have been two encounters between the troops of the *amīr al-muslimīn* and the forces of Ibn Tūmart. On the first occasion, it seems that Ibn Tūmart was victorious since the *amīr al-muslimīn* thereafter took the field in person. In this second encounter, it was probably the *amīr al-muslimīn* who won, although it is by no means clear from the Arabic text.

    Information is sparse about the early conflict between the Almohads and the Almoravids. Abun-Nasr says that the struggle between them began in earnest only in the last year of Ibn Tūmart's life (*op.cit.,* 106). Julien mentions one encounter between them, in 516/1122-3 when Ibn Tūmart's forces were victorious (*op.cit.,* 103). Miranda also describes a skirmish in 517/1123-4 between 'Alī's army, under the leadership of Ibrāhīm b. Ta'aiyast, and Ibn Tūmart's forces. In the ensuing battle Ibn Tūmart achieved a great victory (*op.cit.,* 61, 68-9). The name given in Ms.A as 'Abdallāh b. Māwiya is written by Miranda as 'Abd Allāh b. Ya'lā b. Malwīya. This man was certainly not killed in these early fights since he took part in the campaign against Marrākush in 524/1130 (*ibid.,* 84).
16. After the fighting in 517/1123-4, Ibn Tūmart spent the next year organising his affairs. He strengthened the citadel at Tīnmāl. The winter of 523-4/1128-9 was spent in preparation for the attack on Marrākush (*ibid.,* 71-9).
17. Mss. A and B both have the mountain of Aran (*Arn*). Ibn al-Qalānisī correctly writes Daran (*Drn*) (*Dhail,* 292). Mount Daran is in the High Atlas (Abun-Nasr, *op.cit.,* 216).

rallied to him. Muḥammad b. Tūmart remained (there) until his death in 523 (1128-9).[18] His place was taken by ʿAlī al-Wansharishī who equipped troops and later laid siege to Marrākush in 524 (1129-30).[19] After the *amīr al-muslimīn* had defeated him and hounded him from Marrākush, he fled to the mountains and strengthened his position there. The situation between him and the *amīr al-muslimīn* remained more or less unchanged until 528 (1133-4) when ʿAlī al-Wansharishī died.

He was succeeded by ʿAbd al-Mu'min b. ʿAlī al-Kūmī.[20] He was one of the companions, disciples, friends and helpers of Muḥammad b. Tūmart. Having mobilised troops, he met the *amīr al-muslimīn* in battle and defeated him. He took possession of the whole mountain area, seizing another province too before going down into the desert in 530 (1135-6).[21] He conquered most of the lands of the *amīr al-muslimīn* and he possessed the Ṣūfī convents.[22] He conquered most of Ifrīqiyya and

18. Ibn al-Azraq's facts are extremely inaccurate here. Ibn Tūmart died *after* the siege of Marrākush, not before.

According to al-Marrākushī, Ibn Tūmart sent out an army to Marrākush in 524/1129-30, under the leadership of ʿAbd al-Mu'min. In the ensuing battle between the Almoravids and the Almohads which took place at Buḥaira, the Almohads were defeated. That same year, Ibn Tūmart died (*op.cit.*, 138-9).

Julien puts the siege of Marrākush and the ensuing defeat of the Almohads at an earlier date, 522-3/1128 (*op.cit.*, 103). Miranda, however, gives the exact date of the battle as Saturday, 2 Jumādā I, 524 (13 April, 1130). Ibn Tūmart died in Ramaḍān, 524/August, 1130 (Miranda, *op.cit.*, 83-4, 87). Ibn Tūmart's death was apparently concealed for more than two years (Julien, *op.cit.*, 104).

For the life of Ibn Tūmart, cf. also Ibn Khallikān, *Wafayāt,* III, pt.1, 209-21.

19. Ms.A: ʿAlī al-Waranshī. The correct name of this associate of Ibn Tūmart is ʿAbdallāh b. Muḥsin al-Wansharishī (Miranda, *op.cit.*, 46). He joined the service of Ibn Tūmart shortly after ʿAbd al-Mu'min. He would probably have succeeded Ibn Tūmart if he had not been killed at Buḥaira, thus allowing ʿAbd al-Mu'min to step into the limelight (*ibid.*). Al-Wansharishī was commonly known as al-Bashīr.

Ibn al-Azraq is right to say that al-Wansharishī participated in the siege of Marrākush. Indeed, according to Abun-Nasr he led the troops jointly with ʿAbd al-Mu'min (*op.cit.*, 106). But al-Wansharishī did not take over the Almohad leadership after the death of Ibn Tūmart, as Ibn al-Azraq states, since he was himself killed at the battle of Buḥaira.

20. ʿAbd al-Mu'min succeeded Ibn Tūmart but concealed his death until his own authority was stronger (Julien, *op.cit.*, 104).

21. Ms.A has 503.

22. ʿAbd al-Mu'min first stayed in the mountain area, where he was stronger, and gradually conquered southern Morocco (Julien, *op.cit.*, 104; Abun-Nasr, *op.cit.*, 107). He gradually absorbed the lands of the

the lands of Spain,[23] taking most of the lands of the *amīr al-muslimīn* and conquering many places from the Franks. Then in 540 (24 June 1145 - 12 June 1146) he met the *amīr al-muslimīn*, Tāshufīn b. 'Alī Yūsuf, defeated him and killed many people.[24] He imprisoned and killed the *amīr al-muslimīn*.[25] He gained a strong hold of the country; he conquered most of the Maghrib and the people went in terror of him. Whenever he conquered a city he would kill all its inhabitants, and he used to say: "I am the Lord of the Age."[26] In (5)42 (2 June 1147 - 21 May 1148) he took the city of Tūnis[27] which is one of the mightiest cities of the Maghrib.[28] According to the *Kitāb al-Masālik wa'l-Mamālik* the circumference of its walls is 21 *mīls*.[29]

In the year (5)31,[30] on 4 Dhu'l-Qa'da (24 July 1137), the *amīr* Dā'ūd took over control of Ḥānī from the *amīr* Shāhrukh[31] and granted it (back) to him as an *iqṭā'*. Shāhrukh remained in (his) service in the *rabaḍ* of Ḥānī until he died. He was buried in Ḥānī.

Almoravids until only Marrākush remained (al-Marrākushī, *op.cit.*, 145).

It is likely that the term *biqā'* (the plural of *buq'a)* means "Ṣūfī convents" in this context. Cf. *EI²*, *Supplement*, s.v. "buq'a" (C. E. Bosworth); B. O'Kane, "Tāybād, Turbat-i Jām and Timurid vaulting", *Iran* (XVII), 1979, 94-6.

23. The order of events is wrong here. The conquest of Spain and Ifrīqiyya occurred after the death of Tāshufīn b. 'Alī and the conquest of Marrākush.

For the conquest of Ifrīqiyya, cf. al-Marrākushī, *op.cit.*, 162-4. For the conquest of Spain, cf. *ibid.*, 151 and 159.

24. 'Alī b. Yūsuf b. Tāshufīn had died in 537/1142-3 and had been succeeded by his son, Tāshufīn (al-Marrākushī, *op.cit.*, 145). The date given by Ibn al-Azraq for the death of Tāshufīn tallies with that of al-Marrākushī - 540/1145-6 (*ibid.*, 146).
25. Tāshufīn died by accident. Julien says it was as a result of falling off a horse (*op.cit.*, 105). One report said that the Almohads crucified his dead body (al-Marrākushī, *op.cit.*, 146).
26. This is possibly a Ṣūfī term.
27. The year 542/1147-8 is much too early for 'Abd al-Mu'min's conquest of Tūnis. This occurred in 554/1159-60 (al-Marrākushī, *op.cit.*, 163).
28. Al-Marrākushī describes Tūnis as "the capital of Ifrīqiyya after al-Qairawān, and the seat of its government" (*op.cit.*, 162).
29. Cf. Abu'l-Qāsim 'Ubaidallāh b. 'Abdallāh b. Khurdādhbih, *Kitāb al-masālik wa'l-mamālik*, ed. M. J. de Goeje (Leiden, 1889), 87.
30. This sudden return to the history of the Jazīra before the Maghribī episode is finished is typical of Ibn al-Azraq's disordered approach.
31. Ms.A gives this name as *Shārūḥ*. It is probably intended to be Shāhrukh, although Ibn Shaddād calls him *Siyā Rukh*.

This *amīr* had ruled Ḥānī as early as 497/1103-4 and had served Duqaq ('Awaḍ, 268-9). No doubt because of his advanced age, Dā'ūd allowed him to remain in Ḥānī until he died.

¶ In 531 (29 September 1136 - 18 September 1137)[32] 'Abd al-Mu'min seized the territory of the Banū Ḥammād, driving them out of that area.[33] In 532 (1137-8) he conquered and took possession of al-Mahdiyya;[34] there remained no-one who opposed him, was hostile to him or resisted him. He built two great cities, one of which was Brīnī which he called al-Mahdiyya (f.169a) and the other was Brīnī (?).[35]

32. Although the Ms. has the year 541 it is probable that 531 is intended, in view of the subsequent dates in the text.
33. Cf. al-Marrākushī, *op.cit.,* 106.
34. The date of 532/1137-8 is much too early for the capture of al-Mahdiyya. This city was taken some time after the end of 553/1158-9 during the campaign which gave 'Abd al-Mu'min Tūnis and Tripoli too (al-Marrākushī, *op.cit.,* 163-4). Julien gives the exact date of 22 January 1160 for the conquest of al-Mahdiyya but he does not state his source (*op.cit.,* 112).
35. The text is almost certainly corrupt here. It appears to read: *wa-banā madīnatain 'aẓīmatain iḥdāhumā brīnī (?) wa-sammāhā al-Mahdiyya wa'l-ukhrā brīnī (?).* The word *brīnī* is clearly not an adjective since correct grammar would necessitate a feminine ending here. Yet it is not an isolated slip of the pen, since the very same word is repeated in exactly the same form later in the sentence. The word must be a noun or a proper name.

Various possibilities exist, none of which are satisfactory - and some may even appear fanciful :

i) 'Abd al-Mu'min built two cities (i.e. fortified two existing cities). They both bore the same name (*brīnī* (?)), so he named one of them al-Mahdiyya.

This hypothesis is unlikely. This second mention of al-Mahdiyya by Ibn al-Azraq does not refer to the city of that name (mentioned in n. 34), which is on the east coast of Tunisia, between Sousse and Sfax. Instead, it is a reference to the present city of Rabāṭ, which for a short time bore the name al-Mahdiyya when it was a small military station founded by 'Abd al-Mu'min (cf. G. Marçais, "al-Mahdiyya", *EI*¹; E. Lévi-Provençal, "Rabāṭ", *EI*¹). There is no resemblance between the words *brīnī* (?) and *rabāṭ*. Nor was Rabāṭ called anything resembling *brīnī*. Besides, the text mentions "two huge cities".

ii) *brīnī* should be read as *marsan* (port).

This idea, however, necessitates too great a distortion of the letters as they appear in the manuscript.

iii) *brīnī* should be read as Mursiya (Murcia) or al-Mariyya (Almeria), both of which are mentioned by Ibn al-Athīr as having been conquered by 'Abd al-Mu'min (*al-Kāmil,* X, 124 and 127).

This hypothesis is also weak since neither of these cities was known as al-Mahdiyya.

It is difficult to say what the other city mentioned by Ibn al-Azraq might be. 'Abd al-Mu'min founded many towns and restored a great number of others. He also repaired several sea-ports to shelter his fleet (E. Lévi-Provençal, "'Abd al-Mu'min", *EI*²).

iv) *brīnī* should be read as *bīrni* (walled town) (cf. E. W. Bovill, *The golden trade of the Moors* [Oxford, 1970], 225).

His sovereignty became established and he continued conquering the lands of the Franks bit by bit until his death in 540 (1145-6).[36] His sons remained in power after him. It is said that he left some forty male children.[37]

¶ In 532 (1137-8) the Byzantine emperor left Constantinople for Syria.[38] He seized Buzā'ā,[39] taking all its inhabitants away into captivity and plundering the property there. He (then) encamped before Aleppo and laid siege to it.[40] Although Atābeg Zangī joined battle with him, he remained fixed on his goal; but when all the troops of Diyār Bakr and Diyār Rabī'a came and Amīr Dā'ūd sent his son with Turcoman troops,[41] the Byzantine emperor left Aleppo and returned to his own country.[42]

This is an attractive hypothesis but it is not very likely that this West African word was used in the Maghrib.

v) *brīnī* is a corruption of *bīrūnī* and denotes the idea of "suburb".

It has to be admitted that none of these suggestions are satisfactory, that the text is almost certainly corrupt and that the original meaning of this sentence is now lost.

36. 'Abd al-Mu'min died not in 540/1145-6 but on 27 Jumādā II, 558/2 June, 1163 (al-Marrākushī, *op.cit.*, 168).
37. It is interesting to note that Ibn al-Azraq's attitude to Ibn Tūmart and the Almohads remains neutral. He does not indulge in the hostile invective of Ibn al-Qalānisī who dwells more on the religious implications of the movement. Ibn al-Qalānisī is of course closer in time to the events than Ibn al-Azraq and the former deals only with the beginnings of the Almohad state.
38. Ibn al-Azraq's account broadly tallies with other accounts of the Byzantine emperor's campaign into Syria. The Byzantine emperor at that time was John Comnenus. Cf. Ibn al-'Adīm, *Zubda,* 262-8; Sibṭ b. al-Jauzī, *Mir'āt,* 161-3; Ibn al-Qalānisī, *Dhail,* 264-5; al-'Aẓīmī, "Chronique", 414; Ibn al-Athīr, *Atabegs,* 55-6.
39. Buzā'ā was 45 km. north-east of Aleppo. Cf. J. Sourdel-Thomine, "Buzā'ā", *EI*².
40. Sibṭ b. al-Jauzī, who puts the conquest of Buzā'ā in 531/1136-7, mentions under the following year that the people of Aleppo and Buzā'ā were in an uproar in the mosque because of the treatment they had received at the hands of the Byzantines (*Mir'āt,* 163).

    According to Ibn Shaddād, Buzā'ā was attacked by the Byzantines in two successive years, 531/1136-7 and 532/1137-8. On the second occasion the inhabitants surrendered peacefully (Eddé, *Description,* 75-6). The campaign was conducted jointly by John Comnenus and Raymond of Antioch. Buzā'ā was subsequently handed over to Jocelyn of Edessa. Cf. also Ibn al-Athīr, *al-Kāmil,* XI, 56; Ibn al-'Adīm, *Zubda,* II, 265; Ibn al-Qalānisī, *Dhail,* 265.
41. According to Ibn al-'Adīm, Zangī did not ask for help from Dā'ūd. On the contrary, Zangī sent Qara Arslan b. Dā'ūd specific orders to rejoin his father, saying that he did not need him (*Zubda,* 268).
42. For an analysis of this Byzantine campaign, cf. Cahen, *Syrie,* 359-60.

In this year Bahā' al-Dīn Abu'l-Ḥasan b. 'Alī al-Shahrazūrī[43] died in al-Raqqa, where he was buried. News of his death came to the Jazīra while I was staying there. That year I lived there for a while before returning to Mayyāfāriqīn. In (5)32 (1137-8) Zangī made peace terms with the ruler of Damascus whose mother he (then) married.[44] In that year Zangī took Ḥimṣ and killed Qïr-Khān, its ruler.[45] In that year Shihāb al-Dīn, ruler of Damascus,[46] was killed and was succeeded by his son.[47]

¶ In 533 (1138-9) Amīr Dā'ūd looted Arzan, taking all its inhabitants into captivity and plundering their possessions - all of which he made lawful for the soldiers to take.[48] While he was there, atrocities worse than those at Ṭanzī were committed on the population, and the people received indescribable treatment at his hands. When al-Sa'īd Ḥusām al-Dīn arrived in Mayyāfāriqīn, Ḥusām al-Daula Qurtï[49] b. al-Aḥdab, lord of Arzan, joined him.

¶ In Shawwāl (5)33 (1-29 June 1139) Sav-Tegin al-Karjī,[50] lord of

43. Cf. Ibn al-Athīr, *Atabegs,* 57; Ibn al-Qalānisī, *Dhail,* 266; Sibṭ b. al-Jauzī, *Mir'āt,* 65. Ibn Khallikān gives a precise date: Saturday, 6 Ramaḍān, 532 (*Wafayāt,* I, 541).
44. Cf. Ibn al-'Adīm, *Zubda,* 262; Sibṭ b. al-Jauzī, *Mir'āt,* 165; Ibn al-Qalānisī, *Dhail,* 266-7.
45. According to Ibn al-Qalānisī, Zangī took Ḥimṣ in Ramaḍān 533/May 1138 (*Dhail,* 266).
    Qïr-Khan had been Zangī's prisoner for some years.
46. Shihāb al-Dīn Maḥmūd was murdered on 23 Shawwāl,533/23 June, 1139 (Ibn al-Qalānisī, *Dhail,* 268-9; Ibn al-'Adīm, *Zubda,* 272; Sibṭ b. al-Jauzī, *Mir'āt,* 169, 171-2).
47. Shihāb al-Dīn was in fact not succeeded by his son, as Ibn al-Azraq says, but by his brother, Jamāl al-Dīn Muḥammad, whom Mu'in al-Dīn Unur placed in power, having summoned him from Ba'albak (Ibn al-'Adīm, *Zubda,* 272; Ibn al-Qalānisī, *Dhail,* 269).
48. Ms.A: *wa-abāḥa al-jund kullahā.* Ms.B: *wa-abāḥa al-'askar al-nās wa-amwālahum wa-nisā'ahum. abāḥa* "the making of a thing allowable; lawful taking; it bears a meaning similar to spoliation" (Lane, *op.cit.,* I, 273).
49. Ḥusām al-Daula Qurtï had succeeded his father as ruler of Arzan and Bitlīs in 533/1138-9 (or in 528/1133-4, if Ibn al-Azraq's date is to be trusted).
    For further details on this ruler, cf. Minorsky, *Studies,* 85-6. Citing Vardan, Minorsky relates how Qurtï, whose brutality is also described by Ibn al-Qalānisī, placed the skulls of his enemies' heads on the ledges of a minaret (*ibid.,* 86).
50. This name appears in Ms.A as *M.rjī.* Ibn al-'Adīm, on the other hand, has *K.rjī.*
51. The death of Sav-Tegin (?) al-Karjī and Zangī's subsequent acquisition of Ḥarrān are recorded in 533/1138-9 by Ibn al-'Adīm, *Zubda,* 271.
    Ḥarrān was an important town in Diyār Muḍar. It was the centre of the Sabians and was situated four *farsakhs* from Edessa (Canard, *H'amdanides,* 93).

Ḥarrān, died. Atābeg (Zangī) attacked and took possession of the city.[51] In this year Ḥusām al-Dīn defeated the Franks in Shabakhtān and captured the caravan outside Edessa.[52] In that year I was in Āmid. In that year al-Sa'īd Ḥusām al-Dīn and Zangī made peace. Zangī took Dārā and married Ṣafiyya Khātūn, daughter of al-Sa'īd Ḥusām al-Dīn.[53] She was brought to Mosul in 534 (1139-40) while I was there.

I stayed in Mayyāfāriqīn until the end of 5(3)3 (1138-9) before going down to Baghdad, where I met al-Sa'īd Mu'ayyid al-Dīn Abū 'Abdāllah Muḥammad b. al-Anbārī, may God have mercy on him.[54] I arrived in Baghdad (only) in Rabī' I, 534 (26 October - 24 November 1139) because I had spent some time in the Jazīra and Mosul. I lived in Baghdad for six months and I saw the caliph al-Muqtafī when Khwāja 'Izz al-Mulk took the oath of allegiance to him. (It was at that time that) the caliph al-Muqtafī consummated his marriage with the *sulṭān's* sister.[55] While I was in Baghdad, I was at the *Bāb al-Ḥujra*[56]

As is his custom, Ibn Shaddād lists the rulers of Ḥarrān. They are as follows:

497/1103-4	Chökermish
502/1108-9	İl-Ghāzī
516/1122-3	Balak
521/1127-8	Zangī, who granted the town as an *iqṭā'* to Sav-Tegin (the date of his death is not given)
544/1149-50	Quṭb al-Dīn Maudūd
547/1152-3	Zain al-Dīn 'Alī Küçük (*Jazīra,* f.16b).

52. Cf. Michael the Syrian, *Chronique,* 246; Anon. Syr. Chron., 278.
53. Ibn Shaddād relates that in (5)33/1138-9 Zangī and Temür-Tash quarrelled and that Ṣalāḥ al-Dīn travelled from Ḥamā to Mārdīn to make peace between them (*Jazīra,* f.103b).
Later on in his obituary notice about Temür-Tash (Ms.A, f.176b), Ibn al-Azraq explains that the disagreement arose because Zangī was angered by Temür-Tash's refusal to hand over Amīr Abū Bakr, lord of Naṣībīn, who had taken refuge with him.
Presumably the marriage with Temür-Tash's daughter and the acquisition of Dārā formed part of the peace-treaty. Cf. also al-'Aẓīmī, "Chronique", 417; Ibn al-'Adīm, *Zubda,* 271. Ibn al-'Adīm says that Zangī took Rā's 'Ain (*sic*), Jabal Jūr and Dhu'l-Qarnain at the same time (*ibid.*).
54. This man was a valuable informant for Ibn al-Azraq.
55. For the marriage of al-Muqtafī to Fāṭima, the daughter of Sulṭān Muḥammad and sister of Sulṭān Mas'ūd, and for other details about this woman, cf. Ibn al-Athīr, *al-Kāmil,* XI, 31; Sibṭ b. al-Jauzī, *Mir'āt,* 161; Ibn al-Jauzī, *Munṭaẓam,* X, 67, 72; Ibn Khallikān, *Wafayāt* III,

at the time of the engagement[57] of Sulṭān Mas'ūd to the daughter of the caliph al-Muqtafī.[58] The chief *qāḍī* al-Zainabī,[59] may God have mercy on him, preached a sermon. Sharaf al-Dīn 'Alī b. Ṭirād al-Zainabī[60] was vizier and Kamāl al-Dīn was the treasurer.[61]

I visited a group of the famous people of Iraq. I studied the *Farā'id*[62] under Shaikh Abu'l-Muẓaffar b. al-Shahrazūrī al-'Aṭṭār.[63] (f.169b) I studied the *Faṣīḥ*[64] and the *'Umda*[65] with Shaikh Abū Manṣūr al-

pt.1, 239. Sibṭ b. al-Jauzī, Ibn Khallikān and Ibn al-Athīr say the marriage took place in 531/1136-7. Ibn Khallikān says Fāṭima could read and write.

56. The *Bāb al-Ḥujra* was the Privy Chamber Gate. The caliph al-Mustarshid added a great hall to the Tāj Palace in Baghdad and this was called by the name of its gateway. He and succeeding caliphs used to sit there bestowing robes of honour on their favourites or ministers (Le Strange, *Baghdad*, 259-60).

57. *amlāk* "fiançailles" (Dozy, *Supplément*, II, 614).

58. Amongst Sulṭān Mas'ūd's other wives were the daughter of Dubais (Ms.A, f.165b; Sibṭ b. al-Jauzī, *Mir'āt*, 164) and the daughter of his uncle Qavurt Beg (*ibid.)*.

Sibṭ b. al-Jauzī puts the marriage of Sulṭān Mas'ūd to the daughter of al-Muqtafī in 532/1137-8 (*ibid.)*.

Lambton points out that marriage alliances and occasionally appointments to the vizierate (that is, the caliphal vizierate) were a means of controlling the caliph in Saljuq times (*op.cit.*, 212).

59. Cf. n.34 (Chapter 4).

60. Sharaf al-Dīn al-Zainabī had been the person responsible for the appointment of al-Muqtafī, who was his son-in-law. He was therefore rewarded with the post of vizier to the caliph, a function which he had also performed under al-Mustarshid (Chapter 3, n.106).

61. Here Ibn al-Azraq correctly calls this important official Kamāl al-Dīn, rather than Jamāl al-Dīn (Chapter 3, n.107).

62. From the context, Ibn al-Azraq probably studied works on *fiqh*. Two Shāfi'ite works with this title and of the correct historical period are listed by Brockelmann. These are the *Kitāb al-Talkhīs fī 'ilm al-farā'iḍ*, written by Abū Ḥakīm 'Alī b. Ibrāhīm b. 'Alī al-Khabrī (d.476/1083-4) and *Al-Ushnuhīya fi'l-farā'iḍ* by Abu'l-Faḍl 'Abd al-'Azīz b. 'Alī b. 'Abd al-'Aziz al-Ushnuhī, who flourished around 505/1111-2 (C. Brockelmann, *Geschichte der arabischen Literatur* (Leiden, 1943), I, 486 and 489).

63. This is probably a reference to Abū Manṣūr al-Muẓaffar al-Shahrazūrī who is mentioned by Ibn Khallikān. He was born in 457/1064-5 and became *qāḍī* of Sinjār "at a very advanced age" (Ibn Khallikān, *Wafayāt*, II, 498).

64. The *faṣīḥ* refers to the *Kitāb al-Faṣīḥ* of Tha'lab, which was studied at this time in the Niẓāmiyya *madrasa* (Fück, *'Arabīya* [Paris, 1955], 179).

65. The work referred to by Ibn al-Azraq as the *'Umda* is probably the *Kitāb al-'Umda fī furū' al-Shāfi'iyya*, which was composed by Abū Bakr Muḥammad al-Mustaẓhirī (d.507/1113-4) (Brockelmann, *op.cit.*, I, 489 and *Supplement*, I, 674).

Jawālīqī[66] and I studied the *Tanbīh* with Shaikh Abū Ḥasan b. al-Khall.[67] I met Shaikh Abū Manṣūr al-Razzāz[68] and a group of the *fuqahā'*, amongst whom were Shaikh[69] 'Abd al-Qādir b. al-Narāwī[70] and the sons of the chief *qāḍī* al-Dāmghānī[71] and Yūsuf al-Dimishqī[72] and a group of *ḥadīth* scholars, including the *qāḍī* Abū Bakr, who was the *qāḍī* of the *bīmāristān*,[73] Ibn al-Samarqandī,[74] 'Abd al-Wahhāb al-Anmāṭī[75] and many others. I listened to them and I studied the Qur'ān with Shaikh Abū Muḥammad b. Nabt (?) and the *Khifāf* with Shaikh 'Abd al-Wahhāb. I stayed in Baghdad and visited all the *mashhads* there. I went down to al-Madā'in[76] and visited the tomb of

66. Al-Jawālīqī (466/1073-4 - 539/1144-5) wrote a number of works, including a dictionary of foreign words called *al-Mu'arrab*. He also taught at the Niẓāmiyya *madrasa* in Baghdad *(ibid.)*. Cf. also Brockelmann, *op.cit.*, I, 126; Ibn Khallikān, *Wafayāt*, III, 498-502; *EI*², s.v. "al-Djawālīḳī".

67. Abu'l-Ḥasan Muḥammad b. Abi'l-Bakā al-Mubārak b. Muḥammad, also called Ibn al-Khall, was born in 482/1089-90 and died in 552-3/1157-9. He was a doctor of the Shāfi'ites and wrote a work in the form of a commentary on Abū Isḥāq al-Shīrāzī's book, the *Tanbīh*. Ibn al-Khall called his own commentary *Taujīh al-Tanbīh* (Ibn Khallikān, *Wafayāt*, II, 631-3).

According to Ibn al-Furāt, Ibn al-Khall resided in a *madrasa* built by (Kamāl al-Dīn) Ibn Ṭalha (*Duwal*, f.129b).

68. According to de Slane, al-Razzāz was the head of the Shāfi'ites at Baghdad. He was born in 462/1069-70 and died in Dhu'l-Ḥijja 539/May-June 1145 (Ibn Khallikān, III, pt.1, 312, n.2). 'Imād al-Dīn al-Iṣfahānī studied at the Niẓāmiyya under al-Razzāz (*ibid.*, 306).

69. Ms.A: *jamā'a al-fuqahā' min al-shaikh*. The word *min* is misplaced. The text has therefore been amended to read: *jamā'a min al-fuqahā' minhum al-shaikh*. The word *minhum* has been added.

70. 'Abd al-Qādir Gīlānī (d.562-3/1166) was the famous spiritual leader who gave his name to the Qādiriyya branch of *Ṣūfīs* (A. Bausani, "Religion in the Saljuq Period", *CHI*, V, 297).

71. Abu'l-Ḥasan al-Dāmghānī was a chief *qāḍī* and also served as deputy vizier to the caliphs al-Mustaẓhir and al-Mustarshid (Klausner, *op.cit.*, 26, citing Ibn al-Jauzī, *Muntaẓam*, IX, 208). Cf. also Ibn Khallikān, *Wafayāt*, II, 232. His descendants were conspicuous in the office of chief *qāḍī* (Klausner, *op.cit.*, 128). Cf. also Sibṭ b. al-Jauzī, *Mir'āt*, 179.

72. For this *faqīh*, cf. Ibn al-Jauzī, *Muntaẓam*, X, 115-6.

73. According to Sibṭ b. al-Jauzī, a person whom he designated *Qāḍī al-Māristān* died in 535/1140-1 (*Mir'āt*, 178).

74. According to Ibn Khallikān, 'Imād al-Dīn al-Iṣfahānī studied *ḥadīth* with Abu'l-Mukārim al-Mubārak b. 'Alī al-Samarqandī (*Wafayāt*, III, 307).

75. 'Abd al-Wahhāb al-Anmāṭī is also mentioned by Sibṭ b. al-Jauzī (*Mir'āt*, 148-9). His obituary notice is given by Ibn al-Jauzī (*Muntaẓam*, X, 108-9) and repeated by Ibn al-Furāt (Shayyāl, 315). He died in Baghdad on 11 Muḥarram 538 (26 July 1143).

76. For al-Madā'in, the ancient Ctesiphon, cf. Le Strange, *Lands*, 33-5.

Salmān al-Fārisī. I stayed in Baghdad until 5 Muḥarram 535 (21 August 1140).

At the end of 534 (August 1140), Sharaf al-Dīn al-Zainabī, who was vizier, became angry, went off in high dudgeon to the *sulṭān's* palace[77] and took up residence there.[78] The caliph sent the *sulṭān* a slave (whose name was Najāḥ) requesting the *sulṭān's* permission to dismiss the vizier. The chief *qāḍī* al-Zainabī deputised as vizier for a while and was succeeded as deputy by Mu'ayyid al-Dīn Sadīd al-Daula.[79] The order from the *sulṭān* dismissing Sharaf al-Dīn arrived in 535 (17 August 1140 - 5 August 1141).[80] Niẓām al-Dīn Abu'l-Muẓaffar b. al-Za'īm b. Jahīr, who had been *ustādh al-dār*,[81] was appointed vizier and he became established in the post.[82]

¶ In 534 (28 August 1139 - 16 August 1140) Atābeg Zangī took the citadel of Ba'albak.[83] After he had camped before Damascus and besieged it for a while, the people handed over to him the citadel of Buṣrā.[84]

77. In his obituary notice of 'Alī b. Ṭirād al-Zainabī, Ibn al-Jauzī also records this cooling of relations between him and the caliph. Ibn al-Jauzī outlines the career of al-Zainabī, mentioning that he had recommended the appointment of al-Muqtafī who had made him his vizier. Then al-Muqtafī's attitude changed towards him and al-Zainabī sought refuge in the *sulṭān's* palace (*Muntaẓam,* X, 109).

    As subsequent events proved, al-Muqtafī was by no means as malleable and docile as Sulṭān Mas'ūd had hoped (cf. Ms.A, f.165b). No doubt the clash between al-Zainabī and his protégé also arose because al-Muqtafī began to manifest signs of independence.
78. Ms.B adds: "He took up residence in the house of Najm al-Dīn Rashīd al-Jāmdār" (f.117a).
79. This person is Ibn al-Anbārī.
80. For the dismissal of al-Zainabī, cf. al-'Aẓīmī, "Chronique", 418; Ibn al-Furāt, *Duwal,* f.129b.
81. This office existed amongst the 'Abbāsids, Khwarizmshāhs and Mamlūks, as well as the Saljuqs of Rūm. The *ustādh al-dār* looked after the *sulṭān's* valuables (Uzunçarşili, *Osmanli devleti,* 87).
82. For the appointment of Niẓām al-Dīn as vizier, cf. Ibn al-Furāt, *Duwal,* f.129b; al-'Aẓīmī, "Chronique", 418; Ibn al-Qalānisī, *Dhail,* 273. Ibn al-Furāt confirms that he had previously been *ustādh al-dār.*
83. Zangī took Ba'albak in 534/1139 (Ibn al-Qalānisī, *Dhail,* 269; Sibṭ b. al-Jauzī, *Mir'āt,* 172; Ibn al-'Adīm, *Zubda,* 272-3). Ibn al-Athīr gives the date of Dhu'l-Qa'da, 533/June-July, 1139 (*al-Kāmil,* XI, 45).
84. This sequence of events, in which Zangī proceeded from Ba'albak to Damascus, is followed by Ibn al-'Adīm. Zangī was unsuccessful in this attempt on Damascus and after protracted negotiations had to be content with the moral truimph of having his name mentioned in the *khuṭba* and receiving a vague recognition of suzerainty from the new ruler of Damascus, Mujīr al-Dīn Abaq (Ibn al-Qalānisī, *Dhail,* 271-3; Ibn al-Athīr, *Atabegs,* 58-9; *idem, al-Kāmil,* 48-9; Ibn al-'Adīm, *Zubda,* 273-4). For Buṣrā, cf. Markwart, *Südarmenien,* 274.

¶ The treasurer Kamāl al-Dīn resigned from office and went to Mecca. His son, Qawām al-Dīn b. Ṣadaqa, was appointed to succeed him. Sharaf al-Dīn al-Zainabī did not leave his house.[85] Ṣafī al-Dīn b. al-Zuwān al-Hāshimī was the *ṣāḥib al-dīwān*[86] and Niẓām al-Dīn became established as vizier.

Then I returned to Mayyāfāriqīn early in Muḥarram 535 (c.17 - 20 August 1140), passing through Mosul and Ḥiṣn Kaifā, where I happened to meet Amīr Dā'ūd. A quarrel had arisen between him and al-Sa'īd Ḥusām al-Dīn.[87] Having pillaged the district of Mayyāfāriqīn in Muḥarram (5)36 (6 August - 4 September 1141) Dā'ūd camped outside the city gate where he remained for eight days and then withdrew. He had raided the whole district and had gone to Tall Shaikh, taken it, and distributed the town as an *iqṭā'*. Al-Sa'īd Ḥusām al-Dīn had destroyed the citadel of Bushāt.[88] Dā'ūd took it, erected (new) buildings in it[89] and seized all Jabal (Jūr) as an *iqṭā'*. He spent each day raiding from the two places[90] as far as the gate of the city, stealing people's clothes during the day.[91] Ḥabashī was in (charge

85. Sharaf al-Dīn al-Zainabī remained in disgrace until his death at the age of seventy-six on Wednesday 1 Ramaḍān, 538/8 March, 1144 (Ibn al-Jauzī, *Muntaẓam*, X, 109). Cf. also al-'Aẓīmī, "Chronique", 424.
86. This is probably a reference to the head of the finance ministry who under the Saljuqs of Rūm was called *ṣāḥib dīwān istīfā'* (Uzunçarşili, *Osmanli devleti*, 103). However, the precise definition of administrative offices in late Saljuq times is very difficult.
87. Cahen tentatively suggests that this quarrel between the two Artuqid cousins had been caused by Zangī's seizure of Bahmard, which had belonged to Dā'ūd, in the previous year ("Diyār Bakr", 247).
88. Both Mss. write *F.shāṭ;* so too does Cahen *(ibid.)*. This is, however, surely a reference to the citadel of Bushāṭ (cf. Honigmann, *Ostgrenze*, 152-3). Lehmann-Haupt described it as a Kurdish stronghold, standing to the north of Mayyāfāriqīn on the road to Inner Armenia (*op.cit.*, 419). It was visited by Taylor, who described it as "a very ancient strong fort called Boshat" (*op.cit.*, 40).
89. Ms.A: *wa-kāna al-Sa'īd Ḥusām al-Dīn qad kharaba qal'a Bushāṭ wa-akhadhahā wa-banā bihā*. Cahen interprets this sentence to the effect that Temür-Tash had destroyed the citadel, as he could not defend it, but that he restored it ("une forteresse que Timurtāš, ne pouvant la défendre, avait détruite mais qu'il restaura").

    It would make at least equally good sense to insert a concessive notion here: "although he (Temür-Tash) had taken and built in it". It is also possible to assume that Dā'ūd captured and re-built the citadel. This hypothesis makes more sense in the context of a narrative cataloguing the alleged misdeeds of Dā'ūd.
90. I.e. Tall Shaikh and Bushāṭ.
91. Ms.A *al-nahār;* Ms.B *al-nahr*. Either of these words makes some sense here. Ibn al-Azraq harps on the raiding of Dā'ūd since he is always

of) the area with the *ḥājib* Yūsuf İnāl as *wālī*. He governed the people and protected (the town).[92] The situation remained like that until the end of 535 (August 1141). In 536 (6 August 1141 - 26 July 1142) Amīr Dā'ūd and al-Sa'īd Ḥusām al-Dīn made peace and Amīr Dā'ūd came to Mayyāfāriqīn and went in (through the gate of) the citadel. An agreement was then established between them.

¶ Half-way through Jumādā I, 536 (16 December 1141) Amīr (f.170a) Sa'd al-Daula İl-aldï[93] b. Ibrāhīm, lord of Āmid, died whilst Mu'ayyid al-Dīn[94] was (still) *mutawallī* in Āmid. He put İl-aldï's son Shams al-Mulūk Maḥmūd in power and the latter became established in it. His mother was Yumnā Khātūn, daughter of Najm al-Dīn İl-Ghāzī, and Ḥusām al-Dīn was his maternal uncle.[95] I was in Āmid that year with my father, may God have mercy on him.[96]

biased in favour of Temür-Tash. It would be possible to interpret the text as referring to the theft of clothes, either in the day-time or from the river, although Ms.B's reading is more plausible.

92. Ms.A: *wa-ḥafaẓa al-K..... wa (?)*. Ms.B: *fa-dabbara Ḥabashī amr al-'askar wa'l-balad*. The word *balad* seems appropriate, therefore, to the context, although it is not justified by the partially legible word in Ms.A.

93. Ms.A: *bālīldī* (?). In one of the Āmid inscriptions analysed by Van Berchem, the form of this name appears as *aylldī*. Van Berchem reads the name as İl-aldï (*Amida*, 57).
For an account of İl-aldï's death in 536/1141-2, cf. Ibn al-Qalānisī, *Dhail*, 275; al-'Aẓīmī, "Chronique", 420; Ibn al-Furāt, *Duwal*, f.136b.

94. Ms.B adds "Ibn Nīsān" here (f.122a). The most important members of the Nīsānid family were Mu'ayyid al-Dīn Abū 'Alī al-Ḥasan b. Aḥmad, who became *de facto* master of Āmid in 536/1141-2, and Jamāl al-Daula Kamāl al-Dīn Abu'l-Qāsim, who succeeded his father and who died in 551/1156-7 (van Berchem, *Amida*, 55).

95. The history of the family of Ïnal at Āmid is traced by van Berchem (*ibid.*, 54-5) and is also discussed in some detail in Yinanc's article "Diyarbekir" which is based to a great extent on Ibn al-Azraq's text.
The Turcoman chief Ïnal founded his own small dynasty at Āmid around 490/1096-7. Thereafter, his family intermarried with the Artuqids. Van Berchem's genealogical table is reproduced below:

Ïnal | İl-Ghāzī
Fakhr al-Daula Ibrāhīm
Sa'd al-Daula Ïl-aldï married Yumna Khatun | Temür-Tash
Jamāl al-Dīn Shams al-Mulūk Maḥmūd married Ṣafiyya Khatun

(*op.cit.*, 55). Whilst this family lasted in power in Āmid for four generations, until the conquests of Saladin, they became increasingly dominated by their viziers, who came from the Nīsānid family (*ibid.*).

96. A very interesting description of Āmid in 534/1139-40 exists from the

¶ In 536 (1141-2) Shams al-Mulūk was killed in Damascus.[97]

¶ Sharaf al-Dīn al-Ḥabashī and the *'amīd* Abū Ṭāhir b. al-Muḥtasib were (in power)[98] when al-Mu'ayyid Abu'l-Ḥasan b. al-Mukhtār[99] returned to the service of al-Sa'īd Ḥusām al-Dīn. Ḥabashī seized him in (5)34 (1139-40) and he remained under arrest. Ḥabashī killed his brother al-Ra'īs Abū Sa'īd under torture. Ḥabashī remained (in power) until the end of (5)36 (July 1142) when Atābeg Zangī got in touch with Ḥusām al-Dīn saying: "If we send messengers to one another, they do not keep faith with you or me.[100] If you want to come to an agreement, send Ḥabashī to me." So Ḥusām al-Dīn sent Ḥabashī to him, accompanied by the *ḥājib* Nāṣir and others. When they met Zangī, he asked them to stay. After three days he appointed Sharaf al-Dīn Ḥabashī to the *(dīwān) al-istīfā'*[101] and bestowed upon him a satin *jubba,* a garment (studded) with 'Irāqī gold and a horse with a (decorated) saddle.[102] The envoys who had gone with Ḥabashī returned home. Then Ḥabashī assured Atābeg Zangī that he could take the country[103] and Zangī cut him short in that. So Ḥabashī said:

pen of an anonymous writer who visited the city at that time. His account is written in the margin of a manuscript of Ibn Ḥauqal and has been translated by Kramers and Wiet. Although the testimony of this unknown writer is biased in favour of the Artuqids, he emphasises the devastation and the chaotic social conditions prevalent in the city, where "not a sign of life was to be found". Because of this tyranny of the Nīsānids, the *'ulamā'* and other inhabitants had been forced to move elsewhere (J. H. Kramers and G. Wiet, *Configuration de la Terre* [Beirut and Paris, 1964], I, 217).

97. Shams al-Mulūk Ismā'īl b. Tāj al-Mulūk Būrī had been killed in 529/1134-5 (Ibn al-Qalānisī, *Dhail,* 246). He was succeeded by his brother, Shihāb al-Dīn Maḥmūd b. Būrī, who was killed in 533/1139 (cf. Chapter 5, n.47).

    Ibn al-Azraq has confused these two rulers and the order in which they ruled at Damascus.

98. The phrase in Ms.A is incomplete, so *fi'l-wilāya* has been added.
99. He had fled Ḥabashī's tyranny in 531/1136-7 (cf. f.168a).
100. Cahen attributes this demand by Zangī to see Ḥabashī as an indication of the deterioration in relations between Zangī and Temür-Tash, following the *rapprochement* between the latter and his cousin, Dā'ūd ("Diyār Bakr", 247).
101. According to Ibn al-'Adīm, Zangī made Ḥabashī his vizier in 538/1143-4 (*Zubda,* 278).
102. *al-markab.* Under the Mamlūks, a gift from a ruler included a fully caparisoned horse, covered with a *kunbūsh* of gold (C. Huart, "Khil'a", *EI*[1]).
103. Ḥabashī was clearly already won over to Zangī's side. Ms.B makes good sense here: "It was said that Ḥabashī gave the *atābeg* the idea of taking the country".

'I have people who have sworn oaths (of loyalty) to me and when we reach the country I will hand it over to you.'

In this year al-Sa'īd Ḥusām al-Dīn seized the most excellent (al-Ajall) Abu'l-Rijā b. Saraṭān[104] and he was imprisoned for a while. Then he tore out his eyes and threw him from the top of the citadel of Mārdīn into the *maidān.*

¶ In 537 (27 July 1142 - 15 July 1143) Atābeg Zangī went up to Diyār Bakr and entered the territory of Amīr Ya'qūb b. Qïzïl[105] Arslan. He attacked Khīzān,[106] al-Ma'dan,[107] Īrūn[108] and Qaṭalbas[109] and took the whole region.[110] That year I was in Mosul.

In 538 (16 July 1143 - 3 July 1144) Zangī turned towards the country (Diyār Bakr), arrived in the district of Mārdīn and came to

104. Ms.A is very uncertain of this name which is given as *Abu'l-Wafā' b. al-R.ṭān.* The version in Ms.B is partially correct: *Abu'l-Wafā' b. al-S.rṭān.* The real name of this official would appear to be *Abu'l-Rijā' b. al-Saraṭān.* Al-'Aẓīmī says that he was Temür-Tash's vizier and that he was seized in 537/1142-3 ("Chronique", 422). The biography of Sa'd Allāh b. al-Saraṭān is given by Ibn al-'Adīm. He was made vizier to Badr al-Daula Sulaimān, the nephew of Īl-Ghāzī, at Aleppo in 517/1123-4. Ibn al-'Adīm does not know where and when Ibn al-Saraṭān died (*Bughyat,* 197-9).

105. It is not clear from the sources whether Zangī made two campaigns or one to Diyār Bakr and whether he went in 537/1142-3 or 538/1143-4.
Qïzïl Arslan (*al-sab' al-aḥmar*) was a vassal of Īl-Ghāzī and ruled territories south of Lake Van, such as Is'ird, Ṭanzī and Bahmard ('Awaḍ, 269). Dā'ūd of Ḥiṣn Kaifā snatched most of these territories from Qïzïl Arslan's son, Ya'qūb (Cahen, "Diyār Bakr", 248). The remainder were now seized by Zangī: Khīzān, al-Ma'dan, Īrūn and Qaṭalbas.

106. Khīzān was a fortress south of Lake Van, north-east of Is'ird and south-east of Bitlīs (cf. Markwart, *Südarmenien,* 341; Honigmann, *Ostgrenze,* 78-9, n.12; Michael the Syrian, *Chronique,* 321; Le Strange, *Lands,* 114; Tihrānī, *Kitāb-i Diyārbakriyya,* II, 33).

107. Al-Ma'dan is described by Ibn al-Athīr as the place where the copper of Armenia is worked (*Atabegs,* 66).

108. Ibn Shaddād lists the citadel of Īrūn amongst the fortresses of Diyār Bakr (*Jazīra,* f.65b). Minorsky says it was one of the dependencies of Shīrwān, on the right bank of the Bohtān, below Khīzān, north-east of Is'ird ("Kurds", *EI*[1]).

109. For Qaṭalbas, cf. Ibn Shaddād, *Jazīra,* f.65b.

110. These conquests by Zangī in Diyār Bakr are also described by Ibn al-Athīr. As well as listing the places conquered in 538/1143-4, Ibn al-Athīr mentions that in 537/1142-3 Zangī sent threatening messages to the ruler of Āmid, who had said the *khuṭba* in Dā'ūd's name instead of his. As usual with Zangī's threats, they were taken seriously and the ruler of Āmid submitted to Zangī's wishes (*Atabegs,* 64 and 66; *al-Kāmil,* XI, 62). Cf. also Ibn al-Qalānisī, *Dhail,* 277; Ibn al-'Adīm, *Zubda,* 277.

Tall Bashmī[111] with the intention of going into the province of Āmid and Mayyāfāriqīn. He had already taken possession of Ḥānī, Is'ird, Jabal Jūr, Dhu'l-Qarnain and the whole of that region[112] after the conclusion of the peace-treaty (which Temür-Tash had made) with Amīr Dā'ūd.[113] Zangī made camp in the olive grove at Tall Bashmī. One night Mu'ammil al-Shāqiṣī and Muḥammad b. Abi'l-Mukārim al-Muḥalmī[114] went into Ḥabashī's tent and they struck him down with their swords. They took his head and brought it to al-Sa'īd Ḥusām al-Dīn.[115] There was an outcry and the people and the *'askar* were in uproar. Early the following morning Zangī withdrew and returned to Naṣībīn.

¶ On Sunday 19 Muḥarram 539 (22 July 1144) Amīr Dā'ūd died in Ḥānī and was taken to Ḥiṣn Kaifā.[116] His bier went through (Mayyāfāriqīn) on the Monday and was placed in the Muḥaddatha mosque[117] where the citizens and Qur'ān readers went to visit it. Early the following morning (f.170b), Amīr Dā'ūd was taken to Ḥiṣn Kaifā. His son, Amīr Fakhr al-Dīn Qara Arslan, took possession of Ḥiṣn

111. This was the site of a bishopric mentioned in Syriac sources as still in existence in the eleventh century. It is to be identified with the modern village of Tilbisim, 2 kms to the south of Derik and 40 kms to the west of Mārdīn (Ilisch, *Geschichte*, 195; Canard, *H'amdanides*, 99; Honigmann, *Ostgrenze*, 21). Cahen puts it due south of Mārdīn on his map: "Diyār Bakr", 222).
112. Having conquered the citadels south of Lake Van, Zangī turned towards the north-west of Diyār Bakr and conquered Ḥānī, Dhu'l-Qarnain and Jabal Jūr. Is'ird is clearly misplaced here and should have been mentioned by Ibn al-Azraq in the earlier list of Zangī's conquests (Chapter 5, n. 105).
113. This must refer to the peace treaty between Dā'ūd and Temür-Tash.
114. The names of the murderers of Ḥabashī are much more clearly written in Ibn Shaddād's text than in either Ms.A or Ms.B. In Marsh 333, they appear as *Mu'ammil al-Shāqiṣī* and *Muḥammad b. Abi'l-Makārim* (f.104a).
Al-'Aẓīmī also mentions the murder of Ḥabashī. He says that Ḥabashī was killed in his tent by a group of Kurds ("Chronique", 422).
115. This would appear to imply that the assassins had been sent by Temür-Tash, although it is equally likely that once Ḥabashī had outlived his usefulness to Zangī, who had now made important inroads into Diyār Bakr, Zangī disposed of him.
116. Cahen mistakenly reads this date as 29 Muḥarram, 539, citing only Ibn al-Azraq as his source ("Diyār Bakr", 248).
For an analysis of the events which followed Dā'ūd's death, cf. Setton and Baldwin, *op.cit.*, 460-1; Cahen, "Diyār Bakr", 248-9.
117. The Muḥaddatha mosque was built by the Marwānid ruler Nāṣir al-Daula in 423/1031-2 (Ibn Shaddād, *Jazīra*, f.70a).

Kaifā, Khartabirt and Bālū after him. His son Arslan Ṭoghmïsh took the citadel of Mīzgard.[118]

118. Qara Arslan was not Dā'ūd's eldest son. Arslan Ṭoghmïsh, the eldest, had fled to Zangī (Michael the Syrian, *Chronique,* 258). He had rebelled against his father at Khartabirt (*ibid.,* 237).

On his return from Zangī, Arslan Ṭoghmïsh took Ḥānī (*ibid.*, 258). He then seized Tall Arsanias, enslaving fifteen thousand Christian inhabitants who had long resisted him (*ibid.,* 265).

Chapter 6

Events following the death of the Artuqid, Dā'ūd of Ḥiṣn Kaifā

Atābeg Zangī attacked the territory of Amīr Dā'ūd and captured Is'ird, Bahmard, Ṭanzī, Bātāsā and all the province adjoining the province of al-Ma'dan. He (then) crossed to the other province, i.e. Ḥānī, Jabal Jūr, Dhu'l-Qarnain and al-Sīwān.[1] He (then) went down and took Arqanīn,[2] al-Hālār,[3] Tall Khūm,[4] Charmūk[5] and all that

1. It is not clear if this is a new campaign or a repetition of the one described in Chapter 5.
2. This citadel corresponds to modern Ergani, some 60 kms to the NW of Āmid, half-way to Khartabirt, and situated in front of the entrance to the mountains. In addition to possessing strategic importance,since it controlled the pass northwards, it lay near the town of Ma'dan where iron, copper and silver were mined. Cf. Ilisch, *Geschichte,* 194-5; Markwart, *Südarmenien,* 107, 246, 333; Honigmann, *Ostgrenze,* 136, 178, 183, 185; Canard, *H'amdanides,* 78.
3. It has not proved possible to locate al-Hālār.
4. Tall Khūm lay to the west of the road from Āmid to Malaṭya between Āmid and Arqanīn (cf. Canard, *H'amdanides,* 78; Markwart, *Südarmenien,* 246, 257; Honigmann, *Ostgrenze,* 185). Matthew of Edessa, who is cited by Honigmann, says that Tall Khūm was occupied in the eleventh century mostly by Christians (Honigmann, *Ostgrenze,* 139).
5. Charmūk (also known as Çermik and Djermik) lay on a left tributary of the Euphrates (Canard, *H'amdanides,* 81; Markwart, *Südarmenien,* 251, 257, 346).

area[6] except for Khartabirt, Bālū and Mīzgard which remained in the hands of Dā'ūd's sons.[7]

In this year Sulṭān Dā'ūd was killed in the bazaar at Tabrīz.[8] In this year Arslan Ṭoghmish b. Dā'ūd married Hadiyya Khātūn, daughter of al-Sa'īd Ḥusām al-Dīn, and she was taken to Arslan Ṭoghmish in Mīzgard. (Also in this year) Atābeg Zangī and Ḥusām al-Dīn quarrelled.

Atābeg Zangī went and camped before Edessa. Having laid siege to the city for a while, he conquered it by force on 25 Jumādā II 539[9] which was 23 December (1144).[10] Edessa had been taken by the Franks after the death of Tāj al-Daula (Tutush) in the year 492 (1098-9)[11] and they had held it for forty-seven years. After he had put

6. According to Ibn al-Furāt, Zangī took from Dā'ūd Bahmard, Ṭanzī, Khīzān, Arqanīn, Tall Khūm, Charmūk and Ḥānī (*Duwal*, f.129b). Ibn al-Furāt adds that according to Ibn Abī Ṭayyi', Zangī also took from Dā'ūd the citadel of Qaisūn which he handed to Temür-Tash (*ibid.*).
7. For these events, cf. Ibn al-Furāt (quoting Ibn Abī Ṭayyi') (Shayyāl), 289.
8. According to Bundārī, who also puts Sulṭān Dā'ūd's death in 538/1143-4, Zangī sent Ismā'īlīs to kill Dā'ūd because Sulṭān Mas'ūd had decided to send Dā'ūd to Syria - i.e. into Zangī's own area of influence (*Zubdat*, 195).

   Mas'ūd had nominated Dā'ūd as his successor and sent him to rule Arrān and Armenia (Mustaufī, *Guzīda*, 347-8).

   For Dā'ūd's death, cf. also al-'Aẓīmī, "Chronique", 423; Ibn al-Qalānisī, *Dhail*, 277.
9. Ms.B has *fī shahr Allāh al-aṣabb*. According to Lane *al-aṣabb* is apparently a dialectal variant of *al-aṣamm*, an epithet applied to the month of Rajab (Lane, *op.cit.*, I, pt. 4, 1640). For an epigraphic example of the latter usage, cf. S. S. Blair, "The Inscription from the Tomb Tower at Basṭām," in *Art et Société dans le Monde Iranien*, ed. C. Adle (Paris, 1982), 266.
10. Ibn Khallikān gives exactly the same date as Ibn al-Azraq for the capture of Edessa by Zangī (*Wafayāt*, I, 540). So too does Matthew of Edessa, who says he took Edessa on the feast of St. Stephen, Saturday, 23 December (*Chronique*, 326; the usual date of the Feast of St. Stephen is of course 26 December, which incidentally would fit better with the Christian prophecy).

    For other accounts of this event, cf. Ibn al-Qalānisī, *Dhail*, 279; Ibn al-Athīr, *al-Kāmil*, XI, 64-6; *idem*, *Atabegs*, 66-70; Anon. Syr. Chron., 281-6; Ibn Shaddād, *Jazīra*, f.29a; Michael the Syrian, *Chronique*, 260-4.
11. The year 492/1098-9 would appear to be the correct date of the capture of Edessa by the Franks (Matthew of Edessa, *Chronique*, 218-19; Anon. Syr. Chron., 70-1).

    The reference to Tutush's death is, however, misleading. This had occurred not in 492/1098-9 but most probably in 488/1095 (Ibn al-Athīr, *al-Kāmil*, X, 166; Ibn Khallikān, *Wafayāt*, I, 274). Ibn al-the affairs of the city in order, Zangī withdrew from it and went down to al-Bīra which he besieged for a while.[12] The Christians had been saying that Atābeg (Zangī) would be killed on Christmas night and they were expecting that (to happen) but Zangī took the city on Christmas night and he remained safe and the Christians were lying.

¶ He continued besieging al-Bīra for a while.[13] A few days later, the news reached him that Naṣīr al-Dīn Jaqar,[14] governor of Mosul, had been killed by his *ghulāms* on 8 Dhu'l-Qa'da 539 (2 May 1145).[15] Atābeg (Zangī) withdrew from al-Bīra,[16] went to Mosul and put its affairs in order, placing Zain al-Dīn 'Alī Küçük in charge.[17]

In 539 (1144-5) Amīr Kurj Ghāzī, lord of al-Bāri'a, had died in Āmid.[18]

The people of Mosul had suffered at the hand of Naṣīr al-Dīn extreme injustice, tyranny, murder, mulcting and (the imposition of) illegal taxes (*aqsāṭ*). When Zain al-Dīn become governor, he did away with all that and he treated kindly both the citizens and the people of the whole area. The people received every kindness from him until he died in 564[19] (5 October 1168 - 24 September 1169).

Qalānisī gives the date of 487/1094-5 (*Dhail,* 130).

Ms. B erroneously states that the Franks had held Edessa since 442/1050-1 (f.123b).

12. Al-Bīra was a well-known citadel on the eastern bank of the Euphrates, due west of Edessa and Sarūj. Cf. M. Streck, "al-Bīra", *EI*².
13. Ibn al-Athīr says that Zangī was on the point of taking the citadel when the news of Jaqar's murder reached him (*Atabegs,* 70).
14. As Ms.A makes no sense at all here, the version of the text in Ms.B has been used. Ms.A reads: (*sic*) *fa-waṣalahu al-khabar anna Naṣīr al-Dīn Jaqar wa-awṣala ilā al-Mauṣil wa-qutila.*
15. Jaqar was assassinated at the instigation of the Saljuq *malik,* Alp Arslan b. Maḥmūd, in Dhu'l-Qa'da 539/April-May 1145. Zangī still used this prince as a fainéant ruler to disguise his own power and was apparently awaiting the death of Sulṭān Mas'ūd before trying to instal Alp Arslan as *sulṭān.* Death prevented him from doing this (Ibn al-Athīr, *Atabegs,* 71). Ibn al-'Adīm attributes the plot against Jaqar to the other Saljuq *malik* in Zangī's care, Farrukh-Shāh - erroneously called Farkhān-Shāh by Ibn al-'Adīm (*Zubda,* 280-1).
16. Zangī left al-Bīra because he was now afraid for the safety of Mosul (Ibn al-'Adīm, *Zubda,* 280; Michael the Syrian, *Chronique,* 265).
17. Cf. Ibn al-'Adīm, *ibid.,* 281; Ibn al-Athīr, *Atabegs,* 72-3.
18. The citadel of al-Bār'ia is mentioned by Ibn al-'Adīm in the context of Zangī's siege of Āmid. It must have been situated between Mārdīn and Āmid. Zangī conquered al-Bār'ia at the same time as Ṣūr and Jabal Jūr (Ibn al-'Adīm, *Zubda,* 254). It would appear from Usāma's account that he was personally present when Zangī took the citadel of al-Bār'ia (*Memoirs,* 186). For further information on the later Artuqid history of this citadel, cf. Ilisch, *Geschichte,* 188.
19. The benevolence of the régime of Zain al-Dīn 'Alī Küçük is also stressed

In the month of Rajab 538 (9 January - 7 February 1144) Amīr Ḥusām al-Dīn had summoned 'Alam al-Dīn Abu'l-Fatḥ Muḥammad b. 'Alī b. Nubāta to Mārdīn and made him *qāḍī* of Mārdīn, appointing his brother Bahā' al-Dīn as *khaṭīb* in Mayyāfāriqīn. Majd al-Dīn Dā'ūd, son of the *qāḍī* al-Sadīd, who had been *qāḍī* of Mārdīn, was dismissed in that year and 'Alam al-Dīn was appointed. Al-Mu'ayyid Abu'l-Ḥasan b. Mukhtār al-Mustaufī was responsible for this. Two days later he was appointed *khaṭīb* in Mārdīn, a job he had already held in Mayyāfāriqīn. After 'Alam al-Dīn had been appointed *qāḍī* of Mārdīn, he established his position and took up residence in Mārdīn. He moved his family and children to Mārdīn and there he remains to this day.

¶ Makīn al-Daula (f.171a) Ibrāhīm b. Munqidh had come to Mārdīn from the people of Egypt. He stayed for a while as the guest of al-Sa'īd Ḥusām al-Dīn. Then, two days after the appointment of 'Alam al-Dīn as *qāḍī* of Mārdīn, Ḥusām al-Dīn made him vizier, appointing as his deputy al-Muhadhdhab al-Baghdādī, who was a scribe in the *mashhad* of Mārdīn. His full name was Abū 'Abdallāh Muḥammad b. Muḥammad al-'Irāqī. He used to say: "I am from the Mu'wajj[20] family from the people of Baghdad." That year I was in Mārdīn.

At the beginning of his rule in Mayyāfāriqīn, al-Sa'īd Ḥusām al-Dīn had moved[21] Najm al-Dīn İl-Ghāzī and Shams al-Daula his brother[22] from the Masjid al-Amīr to Mārdīn. Then he buried them in the citadel of Mārdīn in the Khiḍr mosque in the citadel. In that place there was a *turba* in which a group of people[23] who had died at the time of İl-Ghāzī were (buried). İl-Ghāzī and Shams al-Daula were buried there for a while. Then al-Sa'īd Ḥusām al-Dīn erected a beautiful *mashhad* below the *rabaḍ* of Mārdīn at 'Ain Bāqrī in which he built a *turba*. He spent a lot of money on it, established a *waqf* on it and put the tombs there. There were buried all those people who had previously or subsequently been in the citadel.[24] Ḥusām al-Dīn

by Ibn al-Athīr, *Atabegs*, 73. According to Ibn Khallikān, he died in 563/1169 (*Wafayāt,* II, 535).

20. Ibn al-Jauzī gives an obituary of a member of the Mu'wajj family, which must have been prominent in Baghdad (*Muntaẓam,* IX, 51).
21. Ms.A erroneously writes Shams al-Dīn İl-Ghāzī.
22. Shams al-Daula Sulaimān was the brother of Temür-Tash.
23. Ms.A: *jamā'a man māta.* This makes better sense with an extra *min* added.
24. The bodies of İl-Ghāzī and his son, Sulaimān, must have been taken from the *masjid al-amīr* in Mayyāfāriqīn to Mārdīn some time between 518/1124 and 529/1135, since in Ibn al-Azraq's account of the death of

furnished it with rugs, screens and ornaments. He put in it a library supplied with many books which are still there today.

¶ In 539 (1144-5) the structure of the Qarāmān bridge collapsed.[25] It dated from the year 48 (20 February 668 - 8 February 669). In this year the curtain wall[26] inside Mayyāfāriqīn fell down and was rebuilt.

¶ In (5)40 (1145-6) the Egyptian vizier (Ibrāhīm b. Munqidh) was arrested and imprisoned in the citadel of Mārdīn. While in gaol he got hold of pieces of material and escaped from the prison[27] by tying them round his waist, lowering himself from the citadel of Mārdīn and running away. In the morning the people looked for him but could not find him. (When) they saw the material tied (in place), they looked for him and found him on the hill-side. They brought him to al-Sa'īd Ḥusām al-Dīn who let him go and sent him away without harming him.

¶ In 540 (1145-6) al-Sa'īd Ḥusām al-Dīn defeated Fakhr al-Dīn Qara Arslan at Bāghīn.[28] It was a great and memorable day. The victory and conquest belong to Shihāb al-Dīn Muḥammad b. Ayāz b. İl-Ghāzī since he was at the head of the troops with his uncle, Ḥusām al-Dīn. In (5)40 (1145-6) Atābeg Zangī came to Mayyāfāriqīn, took Tall Shaikh and harassed Mayyāfāriqīn for a while before withdrawing.

Dubais in 529/1134-5 he relates that Dubais' body was taken to Mārdīn and buried beside İl-Ghāzī (Ms.A, f.165b).

Ibn al-'Adīm states in his biography of Dubais: "I saw the *mashhad* in which Dubais is buried. It is to the west of the city of Mārdīn.... The daughter of İl-Ghāzī b. Artuq, the wife of Dubais, built it" (*Bughyat,* 250).

It seems probable that İl-Ghāzī was finally buried in Mārdīn. According to Ibrāhīm Artuk, 'Abd al-Salam, the former *müfti* of Mārdīn, writes that İl-Ghāzī is buried in a *hücre* in the Aṣfar mosque opposite the hospital in Mārdīn (*op.cit.,* 61). Gabriel also mentions the *Jāmi' al-Aṣfar* which, he says, according to some traditions housed the tomb of İl-Ghāzī (A. Gabriel, *Voyages archéologiques dans la Turquie orientale* [Paris, 1940] I, 11).

25. The whole question of the Qaramān bridge is discussed in greater detail by Ibn al-Azraq on f.171b. Cf. n. 41 below.

26. Ms.A: *inhadamat al-badana.* Presumably the wall of the citadel is meant here.

27. The Egyptian vizier was not the first prisoner to escape with make-shift ropes from the lofty citadel of Mārdīn. Sulṭān-Shāh b. Riḍwān escaped with ropes from a window of the citadel in 518/1124-5 (*Zubda,* 220).

28. Bāghīn was a citadel north-west of Mayyāfāriqīn. It is listed by Ibn Shaddād amongst the citadels of Diyār Bakr. He calls it Qal'at Bāghīn al-Suflā (*Jazīra,* f.65b). Cf. also Honigmann, *Ostgrenze,* 178, 185; Cahen, "Diyār Bakr", 226.

¶ In 540 (1145-6) Shaikh Nūr al-Hudā Sulaimān b. 'Umar the 'Alid came from Is'ird to Mayyāfāriqīn[29] while Ḥusām al-Dīn was staying in the town.[30] The inhabitants of Mayyāfāriqīn all went out to meet him about a *farsakh* (outside the town), and then the *amīr* went and met him at the Qubbat al-Sulṭān, for Sulaimān was distinguished and learned. He stayed with Tāj al-Dīn, may God have mercy on him, in the house of 'Alam al-Dīn. After one day the *amīr* went in to see him and Sulaimān did not stand up for him. He sat in the mosque and preached and spoke. The people were captivated by him, he attained a considerable degree (of influence)[31] and he acquired the highest possible[32] position. His status became such that if the *amīr* was in Mayyāfāriqīn, Sulaimān was with him. If the *amīr* went to Mārdīn, he would go with him; (indeed) he lived wherever (f.171b) the *amīr* lived. He was so much in his confidence that during the whole time he stayed with the *amīr* he never stood up for him.[33]

He began to act in a way which was inappropriate for the likes of him. He lost favour with the people and went off to Syria, where he remained a while and took the citadel of Abū Qubais.[34] He then had a disagreement with the Ismā'īlīs and returned to al-Sa'īd Ḥusām al-Dīn with whom he remained for a time. He had encouraged al-Sa'īd Ḥusām al-Dīn to become interested in alchemy, but he achieved no results.[35] He went to Is'ird where he remained for a while until the month of Rabī' I 546 (18 June 1151 - 17 July 1151). As he was going into the mosque one Friday, two Ismā'īlīs attacked him. One of them struck him with a dagger; the *shaikh* hit back at him with a sword which he had in his hand, (but) the other man[36] leapt on him striking him with a knife and he fell down. The people were in uproar and his

29. This anecdote is an interesting reminder of continuing Ismā'īlī activity in Diyār Bakr.
30. Temür-Tash obviously paid regular visits to Mayyāfāriqīn from his base at Mārdīn.
31. Ms.A: *wa-balagha al-amīr mablaghan 'aẓīman.* A more normal construction here would be the use of *'inda* with *al-amīr*.
32. Literally: "the most perfect" (*aufā).*
33. I.e. in the *amīr's* presence.
34. This is one of the castles of the Ismā'īlīs listed by Dimishqī (G. Le Strange, *Palestine under the Moslems* [London, 1890], 352, quoting Dimishqī; Gaudefroy-Demombynes, *La Syrie à l'époque des Mamelouks* [Paris, 1923], 114).

    The citadel of Abū Qubais is not mentioned by al-Qalqashandī when he enumerates Ismā'īlī citadels (*Ṣubḥ al-a'shā fī ṣinā'at al-inshā* [Cairo, 1914-28], XIII, 245).
35. Literally: "nothing was substantiated from it".
36. Ms.A: "a man". Ms.B: "another".

assailant and his companion were arrested. He lived until his appointed day and then he died, may God have mercy on him. He was buried in the mosque of Khiḍr (peace be upon him) in Is'ird and his two murderers were killed.

¶ In 540 (1145-6) al-Maulā Najm al-Dīn al-Mālik[37] (Alpï) became joined in marriage to the *khātūn,* daughter of Amīr Aḥmad b. Sukmān, lord of Akhlāṭ. She was the uterine sister of the Shāh-i Arman and the daughter of his paternal uncle.[38] Ṣafī al-Dīn b. Rashīq, Athīr al-Dīn 'Abbād b. Abi'l-Futūḥ, Sirāj al-Dīn b. al-Kāmil Ghāzī and a group of Sukmān's state officials came and stayed a few days in Mayyāfāriqīn, before going on to Mārdīn and then returning home. In 541 (13 June 1146 - 1 June 1147) Qāḍī 'Alam al-Dīn Abu'l-Fatḥ Muḥammad b. Nubāta went to Akhlāṭ with dignitaries of state and fetched the *khātūn.* The wedding took place in Mārdīn and was attended by the state dignitaries from Akhlāṭ.

¶ In 541 (1146-7) al-Sa'īd[39] Ḥusām al-Dīn, may God have mercy on him, began the building of the Qaramān[40] bridge (*jisr*) on the

37. This is a reference to Temür-Tash's son, Najm al-Dīn Alpï.
38. These genealogical facts tally with Turan's family tree of the rulers of Akhlāṭ, which he gives at the back of his history of Eastern Anatolia.

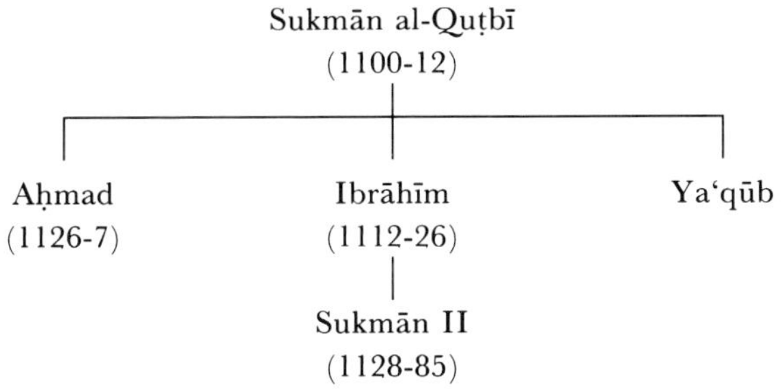

Najm al-Dīn Alpï married the daughter of Aḥmad. Her mother must also have been married to Ibrāhīm, and bore him Sukmān II. On Sukmān al-Quṭbī, who governed Armenia, Akhlāṭ and for a short time Mayyāfāriqīn, cf. 'Awaḍ, 249-50.
39. On almost all the occasions when Ibn al-Azraq mentions Temür-Tash he prefaces the name by the title al-Sa'īd. This is not a common title. Here, however, Ms.A has *'amīd* for *sa'īd.* This is the only time this occurs.
40. The mss. have the forms Aqramān and Qaramān. Sibṭ b. al-Jauzī calls it the Qaramān bridge (*op.cit.,* 188). Quatremère says there is a mention in the history by Rashīd al-Dīn of Āb Qūmān which flowed between Mayyāfāriqīn and Arzan (*op.cit.,* 363). The form Qaramān has therefore been selected.

(earlier) bridge (*qantara*)[41] under the supervision of al-Zāhid b. al-Ṭawīl. After its piles had been firmly fixed on the eastern side, floods

41. i) Ms.A: *jisr Aqrāmān 'alā al-qanṭara*
ii) Ms.B: *jisr Aqrāmān bi'l-Qaisūm*
These two divergent readings raise the question of the identity of the bridge. The reading in Ms.A has been chosen.
Cahen, who reads further into Ms.A into the reign of Najm al-Dīn Alpï, states that the work on the bridge was interrupted twice by floods; once on the occasion analysed in this account and once later, when the bridge was damaged and rebuilt under Alpï.
The stone arch, of more than sixty spans, was one of the wonders of the age (Cahen, "Diyār Bakr", 272, citing Ms.A, f.179b). This later description of Ibn al-Azraq, where the arched bridge is admired, tallies with i). Cahen, on his map of Diyār Bakr, places the Qaramān bridge due east of Mayyāfāriqīn on the Satidāmā (*ibid.*, 222). The Satidāmā (also called the Nymphaeus) is the Batman Su and flows five miles east of Mayyāfāriqīn (Taylor, *op.cit.*, 49).
Further confirmation that the bridge in question was on the Satidāmā/Batman Su is given by Gabriel, who mentions a monumental bridge going back to medieval times which crosses the Batman Su, a tributary of the Tigris, to the east of Mayyāfāriqīn (A. Gabriel, *Voyages archéologiques dans la Turquie Orientale* [Paris, 1940], 231).
Gabriel gives a detailed analysis of the bridge, which he also sketches, and says that Sauvaget, who read the inscriptions, established with certainty the name Temür-Tash and the year 542 on the bridge (*ibid.*, 236). Gabriel believes that the bridge which remains corresponds to the initial building project begun in 541/1146-7 (*ibid.*).
In a later description of the bridge, Ibn al-Azraq writes: "Al-Sa'īd Ḥusām al-Dīn had begun the building of the Qaramān bridge on the Satidāmā river. He built most of it, leaving unfinished some of the work for the completion of the arch. After his death, al-Mālik Najm al-Dīn set about completing it. He built and repaired it and completed the joining of the arch" (Ms.A., f.179b). Ibn al-Azraq then describes how this bridge became the model for other bridges in the area, especially the one built by Fakhr al-Dīn Qara Arslan on the Tigris at Ḥiṣn Kaifā (*ibid.*).
ii) The version of Ms.B remains a problem: "the Qaramān bridge on the Qaisūm" (*sic*).
It is difficult to assess why Ibn al-Azraq, as a native of Mayyāfāriqīn and its chronicler, would write this, since he must have been extremely familiar with the topography of the area. This variant reading must be due to scribal tampering. One possible interpretation of the reading in Ms.B is that the area Qaiṣūm is meant. Qaiṣūm lay to the west of the Euphrates, in the area of Ḥiṣn Manṣūr, due west of Āmid. In this area was an older, even more famous bridge which according to Ibn Ḥauqal was one of the wonders of the world (Le Strange, *Lands*, 123).
For an analysis of early bridges in this area, cf. also F. İlter, "Eine Gruppe der frühtürkischen Brücken in Südostanatolien", *IVème Congrès International d'Art Turc* (Aix and Paris, 1976), 99. İlter calls the Qaramān bridge the "Malabadi" bridge, dates it between 1145-54 (540-9) and publishes a photograph of it.

uprooted and destroyed it because of its defective craftsmanship.[42] Al-Zāhid demanded that he (Temür-Tash) should pay for the flood (damage), so a toll was made payable on it (the bridge).[43] Then he (Temür-Tash) put Amīr Saif al-Dīn Shīrbārīk Maudūd b. 'Alī (b. Alp-Yaruq) b. Artuq in charge of it.[44] He began building it under the supervision of Abu'l-Khair al-Fāsūl, who brought unusually large pieces of wood and began work constructing it.[45] It is one of the marvels built in this age and work continued on it.

In 541 (1146-7) Atābeg Zangī attacked Qal'at Ja'bar where Saif al-Daula Abu'l-Ḥasan 'Alī b. Mālik was.[46] He prosecuted the siege vigorously and it was on the verge of being taken. Jamāl al-Dīn Qurtï(?),[47] the son of al-Sa'īd Ḥusām al-Dīn, was in his service with an *'askar* but he had seized Jamāl al-Dīn and imprisoned him in the church (*bī'a*) in the *rabaḍ* of the citadel.

(When I was) in Mosul in 544 (11 May 1149 - 29 April 1150) I asked the *wālī* al-Maṣdar al-Kāmil Qāḍi'l-Quḍāt, Kamāl al-Dīn Abu'l-Faḍl Muḥammad b. 'Abdallāh al-Shahrazūrī,[48] may God perpetuate his shadow, about the killing of the *atābeg* (f.172a) (Zangī) and what happened. He said: "After we had been besieging the citadel for a while, Amīr Ḥassān al-Manbijī[49] went out one day and

42. Ms.A: *wa-akhrabahu wa-ḍa'ufa 'amaluhu wa-akhrabahu*
Ms.B: *wa-akhrabahu li-ḍa'fi 'amalihi*
The version of Ms.B has been used since it makes better sense.
43. i) Ms.A: *wa-alzamahu al-Zāhid bi-'imāratihi fa-akhraja (*or *ukhrija) 'alaihi*
ii) Ms.B: *wa-alzama al-Zāhid al-gharāma* (f.126a). There is a problem of the translation of *akhraja* (or *ukhrija) 'alaihi.* In view of the context, it would be attractive to render this by "he was removed *(ukhrija)* from it (the job)". However, such a meaning would normally necessitate *minhu* rather than *'alaihi.* Accordingly, the phrase has been translated as "tax (i.e. a toll) was raised on it" (*ukhrija 'alaihi*). In point of fact, tolls on bridges were common at this time.
44. Ms.A: *Saif al-Dīn Shīrbārīk Mamdūd b. 'Alī b. Artuq.* The correct form of this name is Saif al-Dīn Shīrbārīk *Maḥmūd* b. 'Alī *b. Alp Yaruq* (cf. the genealogical table of the Artuqids).
45. "And he worked on it until 548"/1153-4 (Ms.B, f.126b).
46. The 'Uqailid ruler of the citadel, cf. Chapter 4, n.97.
47. This name presents some difficulties. Cahen calls this son of Temür-Tash Jamāl al-Dīn Tafratī ("Diyār Bakr", 251) but he is tentative about his reading. Artuk reads "Tughrati" (I. Artuk, *op.cit.*, unnumbered last page). The disposition of the letters would also permit the reading Qurtï. This is a well-known name amongst the Turcomans and Kurds.
48. Cf. n. 96.
49. Ibn al-Athīr relates that Ḥassān was sent to try to persuade 'Alī b. Mālik to surrender the citadel. He was chosen because of his friendship with 'Alī. He was told by Zangī to offer 'Alī inducements and gifts (*Atabegs,* 74).

shouted: 'I want to speak to Amīr 'Alī.' When 'Alī appeared in front of him on the walls, he said to him: 'You know what (friendship) exists between us and you know what sort of man Zangī is. You have no-one with whom to take refuge and no-one to defend you against Zangī. The best thing to do is to surrender; if not, he will take the citadel by the sword in a way which you will be powerless to resist. After such an eventuality what fate can you expect?" 'Alī replied: 'Amīr Ḥassān! I am expecting relief from God most high and what you were expecting at Manbij when Amīr Balak was besieging it - and God took care of him for you.'"[50]

Kamāl al-Dīn said: "By God, hardly had half of that night passed (it was Wednesday, 5 Rabī' II (14 September 1146) or, according to another report, the 9th (of that month), 541 (18 September 1146)[51] when the town-crier shouted from the citadel: 'Atābeg (Zangī) has been killed.[52] What good news for you, Ibn Ḥusām al-Dīn!' People

50. Ibn al-Athīr's account is broadly similar to that of Ibn al-Azraq. Ibn al-Athīr also explains the point of 'Alī's pithy comment about Balak and the latter's fortuitous death at Manbij, where Ḥassān was governor (*Atabegs*, 64).

Ibn Shaddād's account is slightly different: "'Alī said: 'Give me until tomorrow.' So Ḥassān said to him: 'What can happen to you tomorrow?' 'Alī replied: 'What happened to Balak...while he was besieging you at Manbij'" (*Jazīra*, ff.34a-b).

Ibn al-'Adīm suggests that Zangī's offer of money to 'Alī had been accepted but that Zangī subsequently broke faith with him (*Zubda*, 282). Ibn al-'Adīm also relates the anecdote about Balak (*ibid.*, 283).

51. The dates given in the sources for Zangī's death may be tabulated as follows:

Ibn al-Azraq:	5 or 9 Rabī' II, 541 (14 or 18 September 1146)
Ibn Shaddād:	Monday, 6 Rabī' II, 541 (15 September 1146) (*Jazīra*, f.34b)
Michael the Syrian:	Sunday, 15 September, 1146 (Rabī' II, A.H. 541) (*Chronique*, 268)
Ibn Khallikān:	Wednesday, 15 Rabī' II, 541 (24 September 1146) (*Wafayāt*, I, 541)
Ibn al-Qalānisī:	Sunday, 6 Rabī' II, 541 (15 September 1146) (*Dhail*, 285)
Ibn al-Athīr:	5 Rabī' II, 541 (14 September 1146) (*al-Kāmil*, XI, 72 *Atabegs*, 74)
Anon. Syr. Chron.:	The night before Sunday, 14 September, 1146 (291).

52. The death of such an important figure as Zangī is overlaid in the sources with a wealth of details and apocryphal anecdotes. In one such

shouted and were in an uproar. It had come about because while Atābeg (Zangī) had been spending the night in his tent, a slave was with him but no-one else. When he was asleep that night in his tent, the slave killed him. Taking the knife covered in blood he left, went up to the *rabaḍ* below the citadel and shouted to the people, 'I have killed Atābeg (Zangī).'[53] When they did not believe him, he showed them the knife and another token which he had taken from Zangī's possessions. So they let him come up to them, verified his story and called out (the news). The people were in great confusion and at odds with each other.[54] They went to the camp of Jamāl al-Dīn the vizier.[55] It was pillaged and he ran away and came to me. The *amīrs* and prominent people sought me out. When I rode up, they asked: 'What does the *malik* think?' We made our way to the tent of Malik Alp Arslan b. Maḥmūd and there I spoke as follows: 'The people, the Atābeg and I are the servants of the *malik* (i.e. you) and the country belongs to him. We are all his servants and the slaves of the *sulṭān*.'[56]

anecdote, Ibn Khallikān relates that the poet Ibn Munīr al-Tarabalūsī always brought misfortune to those who were with him. Zangī liked his verses when they were read out to him during the siege of Qal'at Ja'bar and he summoned the poet to him. The night Ibn Munīr arrived, Zangī was murdered (*Wafayāt,* I, 138-43).

53. Ibn al-Qalānisī says that Zangī was murdered by a slave of Frankish origin. He waited until Zangī was drunk and then killed him in his sleep. He fled to 'Alī in the citadel, who did not believe that he had murdered Zangī but welcomed him (*Dhail,* 285).

Certainly the most likely person to have murdered Zangī would appear to have been 'Alī, especially since Zangī had apparently not kept faith with him. On the other hand, he could have been killed by partisans of Alp Arslan b. Maḥmūd. It is equally possible that the murderer had some private score to settle with him; Zangī's ferocity was a legend in his own time and he must have been more vulnerable than most contemporary rulers to such personal grudges.

54. The confusion and chaos after Zangī's death is described most graphically by the anonymous Syriac Chronicle: "Fear and confusion fell on the camp; they plundered one another, and each who had a grudge against his neighbour and had the power took vengeance on him.... The guards sacked the tent and camp of Zangī..... All went their own ways" (*op.cit.,* 291).

55. Jamāl al-Dīn al-Jawād al-Iṣfahānī was one of the most important officials employed in high positions by Zangī and by his sons, Saif al-Dīn Ghāzī and Quṭb al-Dīn Maudūd (cf. Sibṭ b. al-Jauzī, *Mir'at,* 248-50; Bundārī, *Zubdat,* 211-3).

56. These details are borrowed almost *verbatim* by Ibn Khallikān from Ibn al-Azraq. Ibn al-Azraq does not see any need to explain that the real intention of Jamāl al-Dīn and Kamāl al-Dīn was to conciliate Alp Arslan until Saif al-Dīn Ghāzī could reach Mosul and assume power.

The people agreed on the *malik*[57] and Jamāl al-Dīn Qurtï(?) was released from the church and taken to Mārdīn.

The people divided into two factions. Salāḥ al-Dīn[58] Muḥammad al-Yaghï-Sïyanī took Nūr al-Dīn Maḥmūd b. Atābeg (Zangī) and the Syrian *'askar,* went to Syria and seized Aleppo, Ḥamā, Manbij, Ḥarrān, Ḥimṣ and all Zangī's possessions in Syria. Thus Nūr al-Dīn became established there.[59] As for us, we took the *malik* and the *'askars* of Diyār Rabī'a and made our way to Mosul.[60]

When we arrived in Sinjār,[61] the *malik* ran away, making for the Jazīra. My brother Tāj al-Dīn Abū Ṭāhir Yaḥyā,[62] may God have mercy on him, and 'Izz al-Dīn Abū Bakr al-Dubaisī caught up with him, made promises to him and brought him back to the camp, and we then continued down to Mosul. Saif al-Dīn Ghāzī b. Atābeg (Zangī) came from the town of Shahrazūr[63] which had been given to him as an *iqṭā'* by the *sulṭān* and he took possession of the whole of Diyār Rabī'a. The *malik* was taken to the citadel of al-Thalū at Sinjār.[64] Saif al-Dīn Ghāzī took Mosul and the whole country. He appointed as vizier Jamāl al-Dīn Muḥammad b. al-Iṣfahānī who had been *mustaufī*[65] of the *dīwān* in his father's time and (f.172b) he granted the Jazīra as an *iqṭā'* to 'Izz al-Dīn Abū Bakr al-Dubaisī.[66] He became established in the land."[67]

57. The term *malik* has not been translated here and on the other occasions where it appears in Ibn al-Azraq's text. Saljuq princes were known as *maliks* in contradistinction to the chief ruler, the *sulṭān* (cf. Lambton, *op.cit.,* 218).
58. Ṣalāḥ al-Dīn Muḥammad al-Yaghï-Sïyanī was certainly not the same person as Ṣalāḥ al-Dīn b. Ayyūb, as Ms.A mistakenly suggests.
59. The division of Zangī's forces into two factions is confirmed by other sources (Ibn al-'Adīm, *Zubda,* 285; Michael the Syrian, *Chronique,* 268). For the establishment of Nūr al-Dīn at Aleppo, cf. Ibn al-'Adīm, *Zubda,* 289-90; Anon. Syr. Chron., 292.
60. Cf. Ibn al-'Adīm, *Zubda,* 289-90; Anon. Syr. Chron., 292; Ibn al-Qalānisī, *Dhail,* 285-6; Ibn al-Athīr, *al-Kāmil,* 74.
61. For Sinjār, a city in the Jazīra, cf. Le Strange, *Lands,* 98-9, 124; Ilisch, *Geschichte,* 206.
62. Cf. nn. 96 and 97.
63. For references to Shahrazūr in the medieval geographers, cf. Le Strange, *Lands,* 190-1.
64. Ms.B adds: "It is said that he killed the *malik*".
65. The *mustaufī* was the head of the *dīwān al-istīfā'* (Uzunçarşïlï, *Osmanlï devleti,* 45 and 103).
66. Cf. Ibn Shaddād (*Jazīra,* f.59a).
67. The immediate descendants of Zangī who now enter Ibn al-Azraq's history are as follows:

Zangī

Saif al-Dīn Ghāzī | Nūr al-Dīn Maḥmūd | Nuṣrat al-Dīn Amīr Amīrān | Quṭb al-Dīn Maudūd | daughter

Salāḥ al-Dīn (Muḥammad al-Yaghï-Sïyanī) and Asad al-Dīn Shīrkūh[68] assumed responsibility for Amīr Nūr al-Dīn, whilst he appointed Majd al-Dīn Abū Bakr b. al-Dāya as *ḥājib*. The latter's mother had been the wet-nurse (*dāya*) of Nūr al-Dīn, which was a post of some standing, and Majd al-Dīn had served him from his youth onwards. When the *amīr* (Nūr al-Dīn) took power, he handed command back to him and made him governor of Aleppo.[69] He then established his position in Syria.

A few days after the murder of Zangī, the Armenian population of Edessa attacked the Muslim inhabitants of the city, killing a number of them. 'Izz al-Dīn Dubaisī and Ḥassān, lord of Manbij, arrived with a group of Turcomans. They joined forces against the city, plundered and conquered it. A great number of people were killed and a group (of the conquerors) remained in the city.[70]

At the time of the murder of Atābeg (Zangī), al-Sa'īd Ḥusām al-Dīn was in Mayyāfāriqīn. The news reached him one afternoon when he was in the citadel garden, whereupon he left immediately. Before that day, he had received the news that his son Jamāl al-Dīn had been arrested and this had distressed him greatly. When he heard the news that Zangī had been murdered, he went to Ḥānī and laid siege to the town for a time and then took possession of it. Its ruler was Amīr Ghāzī b. al-Mihrī. Ḥusām al-Dīn took Ḥānī on 23 Rabī' II, 541 (2 October 1146). Thereafter he went and seized al-Sīwān, Jabal Jūr and

68. For this well-known figure of Crusader history, cf. *EI*[1] "Shīrkūh".

69. It was to Majd al-Dīn Ibn al-Dāya that Joscelin II was handed over after his capture in a Turcoman ambush in 545/1150 (cf. N. Elisséeff, *Nūr al-Dīn, un grand prince musulman de Syrie aux temps des Croisades* [Damascus, 1967] II, 389).

70. For Edessan affairs at the beginning of the sixth/twelfth century, cf. C. J. F. Dowsett, "A twelfth-century Armenian inscription at Edessa", *Iran and Islam. In memory of the late Vladimir Minorsky*, ed. C. E. Bosworth (Edinburgh, 1971), 197-227.

For other accounts of the Armenian revolt at Edessa, cf. Michael the Syrian, *Chronique,* 270; Matthew of Edessa, *Chronique,* 328-9; Bar Hebraeus, *Chronography,* 272; Ibn al-'Adīm, *Zubda,* 290; Ibn al-Qalānisī, *Dhail,* 288; Ibn al-Athīr, *al-Kāmil,* XI, 75.

What Ibn al-Azraq fails to mention in his account is the complicity of Joscelin, who saw the period immediately following the death of Zangī as a propitious moment for the capture of Edessa. An even more important omission by Ibn al-Azraq is the fact that it was Nūr al-Dīn who took Edessa, whilst 'Izz al-Dīn al-Dubaisī arrived before the city too late. Thus it was Nūr al-Dīn, not his brother Saif al-Dīn Ghāzī from Mosul, whose associate 'Izz al-Dīn al-Dubaisī was, who had acquired the important possession of Edessa (Ibn al-'Adīm, *Zubda,* 290; Ibn Shaddād, *Jazīra,* f.29b).

Dhu'l-Qarnain before going down to take Shabakhtān, al-Muwazzar,[71] Tall Mauzan,[72] Jamalīn[73] and Ra's 'Ain al-Khābūr.[74] He then returned home. That year I was in Mārdīn.

Fakhr al-Dīn Qara Arslan went and took Arqanīn, Charmūk, Tall Khūm, al-Hālār and all the fortresses which Atābeg (Zangī) had taken from his father, Amīr Dā'ūd. He took the eastern side of Is'ird as well as Bahmard, Bātāsā, Ṭanzī, al-Rūq, Qaṭalbas, the town of Ṣāf and the citadel of al-Haithum[75] which is in the mountainous area of the Ṭūr 'Abdīn.

The lord of Akhlāṭ, the Shāh-i Arman,[76] went down and took Khīzān, al-Ma'dan, Īrūn and the whole area which Zangī had taken from Amīr Ya'qūb.[77]

In this year, which was 542 (1147-8), al-Sa'īd Ḥusām al-Dīn struck copper coins, after I had gone to al-Ma'dan and bought copper for the coins.[78]

71. Ibn Shaddād mentions the two citadels of al-Muwazzar and Jamalīn (or Jumulīn) together. He states that they were situated between Diyār Muḍar and Diyār Bakr, at a distance of one day's journey from Ḥarrān. They were held by the Franks after their capture of Edessa and later by the Artuqids. Zangī fortified al-Muwazzar in 535/1140-1 and Jamalīn in 538/1143-4. After Zangī's death, they were re-captured by the Artuqids (f.21b). Ilisch gives more precise information on Jamalīn (Cimlin Kalesi), stating that it lies 57 kms to the east of Edessa and that it was built to defend the eastern frontier of the Crusader principality (*op.cit.,* 188).

    For Zangī's capture of al-Muwazzar, cf. also Ibn al-Furāt, *Duwal,* f.129b. Ilisch spells the name of the citadel as al-Muwazar (*Geschichte,* 211).
72. Tall Mauzan was situated on the road from Edessa to Mārdīn. It was a town built of black stones (Canard, *H'amdanides,* 93; Markwart, *Südarmenien,* 257; Honigmann, *Ostgrenze,* 22).
73. Cf. n.71 above.
74. The death of Zangī allowed the minor rulers of Diyār Bakr a new lease of life. Temür-Tash profited at once from this power vacuum to seize these citadels. Ra's al-'Ain (modern Resülayn) lies some 80 kms SW of Mārdīn at the source of the Khābūr on the Turkish-Syrian border (Le Strange, *Lands,* 95; Ilisch, *Geschichte,* 203).
75. The citadel of al-Haithum is mentioned by Ibn Shaddād (*Jazīra,* f.65b).

    Michael the Syrian says that Qara Arslan invaded the Ṭūr 'Abdīn, which had previously belonged to his father and which Zangī had seized. After numerous massacres he established his power over the area (*op.cit.,* 268).
76. The Shāh-i Arman at this time was Sukmān II.
77. Cf. Chapter 5, n.105.
78. It would appear that Temür-Tash minted only one issue of coins, which were copper. The few examples that have been found were discussed by Lane-Poole. He mentions four such coins, none of which have a date or

In (5)43 (22 May 1148 - 10 May 1149) Arslan Ṭoghmïsh b. Amīr Dā'ūd died.[79] Al-Sa'īd Ḥusām al-Dīn laid siege to Is'ird for several days and took possession of it. Jamāl al-Dīn Maḥmūd, lord of Āmid, and Jamāl al-Dīn Abu'l-Qāsim b. Nīsān, who was with him at Is'ird, joined his service.[80] After Ḥusām al-Dīn had taken Is'ird, he returned to Mayyāfāriqīn. After a while he handed Is'ird back to Fakhr al-Dīn Qara Arslan, who during this period had taken Mīzgard. Hadiyya Khātūn returned to Mayyāfāriqīn.[81] In this year al-Sa'īd Ḥusām al-Dīn and Zangī's son, Saif al-Dīn Ghāzī, quarrelled and Saif al-Dīn plundered the district of Mārdīn[82] and (took away) a number of the *mamlūks*[83] (of Ḥusām al-Dīn).

In this year the *khātūn,* daughter of 'Izz al-Dīn Saltuq,[84] lady of Akhlāṭ, came to Ḥiṣn Kaifā on her way to the Ḥijāz.[85] Fakhr al-Dīn Qara Arslan gave her hospitality (f.173a) and spared no effort in his kind treatment of her. (Then) the vizier Bahā' al-Dīn and Athīr al-Dīn 'Abbād and 'Alam al-Dīn b. Ṭabar, the *qāḍī* of Arjīsh, arrived

the place where they were minted (S. Lane-Poole, *The Coins of the Turkman Houses of Seljook, Urtuk, Zengee, etc. in the British Museum* [London, 1877], 139-40).

79. Arslan Ṭoghmïsh was the ruler of Mīzgard.
80. The declaration of suzerainty to Temür-Tash by the lord of Āmid and his vizier and their participation in the attack on Is'ird had probably been prompted by fear of Qara Arslan who had attacked Āmid around this time (Michael the Syrian, *Chronique,* 288).
81. Hadiyya Khātūn, Temür-Tash's daughter, returned to Mayyāfāriqīn after the death of her husband, Arslan Ṭoghmïsh b. Dā'ūd. She had married him in 539/1144-5.
82. A quarrel between Temür-Tash and Saif al-Dīn Ghāzī was inevitable as soon as the latter had established himself firmly at Mosul. Temür-Tash had, after all, taken back Zangī's possessions after Zangī's death in 541/1146.

    Temür-Tash had re-annexed Dārā but in 544/1149-50 Saif al-Dīn Ghāzī re-conquered it. He extended his authority over a large section of the territory around Mārdīn. He then besieged Mārdīn itself and pillaged the countryside. Temür-Tash was obliged to sue for peace and handed over his daughter Zumurrud Khātūn in marriage to Saif al-Dīn Ghāzī (Ibn al-Athīr, *Atabegs,* 91; Ibn al-Furāt [Shayyāl], 352).

    Significantly, Ibn al-Azraq maintains a discreet silence over a defeat incurred by Temür-Tash, his former master.
83. Ms.A: *wa-n.h.ba mamālīkan (sic) jamā'a.*

    Since the plural given here is the plural of *mamlūk,* it has been translated accordingly as "slaves". The proximity of the word *jamā'a* "group" (of people) strengthens this hypothesis.
84. 'Izz al-Dīn Saltuq was the ruler of Erzerum from 1132-68. He married his daughter to the ruler of Akhlāṭ, Sukmān II (O. Turan, *Doğu Anadolu Türk Devletleri Tarihi* [Istanbul, 1973], 9-10).
85. Ms.B adds that she wanted to perform the pilgrimage.

and stayed in the house of al-Mu'ayyid b. Mukhtār in Mayyāfāriqīn, remaining several days.[86] Al-Sa'īd Ḥusām al-Dīn got in touch with Fakhr al-Dīn and they stopped the *khātūn* from going to the Ḥijāz,[87] which was what the Shāh-i Arman had asked them to do, and they questioned the *khātūn,* as a result of which they all went back to Akhlāṭ.

In this year al-Mu'ayyid al-Mustaufī Abu'l-Ḥasan al-Mubārak b. Mukhtār died.[88] He was the *mutawallī* of the *dīwān,* with al-Muhadhdhab al-'Irāqī as *mushrif*[89] for him. Ibn Mukhtār was buried in Mārdīn in the mausoleum which he had built[90] and he was succeeded by his son, al-Ajall Karīm al-Daula Abū Manṣūr Khālid,

86. The text does not use the dual verb form here. Presumably these two dignitaries arrived with a retinue.
87. The *Khātūn* was probably prevented from performing the pilgrimage because of the existence of *ḥadīths* which forbid a woman to travel alone. She should be accompanied by male relatives. The *Khātūn* of Akhlāṭ was obviously a woman of independent spirit. As Spuler points out, although women had enjoyed a notable lack of restriction in early Islamic times, they had lost this to a great extent thereafter. He goes on to say that much of the later impetus towards greater freedom for women can be attributed to the irruption of the nomadic Turks into the Near East (B. Spuler, *Iran in früh-islamischer Zeit* [Wiesbaden, 1952], 380-3).
88. The proper title of this man was al-Mustaufī Mu'ayyid al-Daula Abu'l-Ḥasan b. al-Mukhtār. He had first come to Mayyāfāriqīn to take over the *dīwān al-istīfā'* in 510/1116-7 ('Awaḍ, 283).
89. In the province, the *mushrif* was the head of the *dīwān al-ishrāf* which was the accounting department. The *mushrif* worked closely with the *dīwān al-istīfā'* (Horst, *Staatsverwaltung,* 51-2).
90. *fi'l-bī'a allatī banāhā.*
    Several possibilities may be adduced here:
    i) The word *bī'a* may have a more general meaning than "church".
    ii) The word may be read as *buq'a* (mausoleum, Ṣūfī convent).
    iii) Ibn Mukhtār was a Christian and remained one, although he adopted Muslim names.
    iv) Ibn Mukhtār was a Muslim but was buried in a Christian building.
    Of these possibilities, the third is certainly plausible. Mārdīn was a very important centre of Christianity and Christians would certainly have outnumbered Muslims at this time. High administrative posts were often held by Christians. Even at the time when Niebuhr visited Mārdīn, he found that one-third of the population of the city was still Christian (V.F. Minorsky, "Mārdīn", *EI*[1], 276). The most attractive reading, however, must be *buq'a,* a term which connotes a mausoleum and a communal institution for Ṣūfī life. The word gained acceptance in Anatolia, as well as Iran, and is found in inscriptions of the 7th and 8th centuries A.H. at Akhlāṭ and Erzerum, i.e. the very area under discussion (O'Kane, *op.cit.,* 84-5).

who adopted as a *laqab* the *laqab* of his father, Mu'ayyid al-Daula[91] Karīm al-Mulk. He remained within his conditions of service and followed what was incumbent upon him to do. (Then) he took sole command and went beyond what people expected of him, with all administrative matters coming under his control.

¶ In 542 (1147-8) the caliph al-Ḥāfiẓ[92] died in Egypt and was succeeded by his son al-Manṣūr Ismā'īl, whose *laqab* was al-Ẓāfir,[93] but the real ruler was the *amīr al-juyūsh* al-'Ādil (b.) al-Sallār[94] from the Zarzārī (tribe)[95] who established the state and put the army in order. Al-Ẓāfir became established as caliph.

¶ In 542 (1147-8) Atābeg Ghāzī seized the *qāḍī* Kamāl al-Dīn[96] and Tāj al-Dīn, the sons of 'Abdallāh al-Shahrazūrī. He (Kamāl al-Dīn)[97]

91. Ms.A has al-Mu'ayyid al-Daula. The *al-* has been deleted.
92. Al-Ḥāfiẓ died on 5 Jumādā II, 544/10 October, 1149 (Wüstenfeld, *Faṭimiden-Chalifen,* 310).
93. Abu'l-Manṣūr Ismā'īl was the youngest son of al-Ḥāfiẓ. He was born in 527/1132-3 so he succeeded to the throne when he was only seventeen (*ibid.,* 312; Ibn Khallikān, *Wafayāt,* I, 222).
94. According to Usāma, this man's full name was Saif al-Dīn b. al-Sallār. After al-Ẓāfir had been forced to appoint him as vizier, Ibn al-Sallār assumed the title al-Malik al-'Ādil. In Ramaḍān 544/2-31 January 1150, al-Ẓāfir had Ibn al-Sallār put to death (*Memoirs,* 31-3). Cf. also Ibn Khallikān, *Wafayāt,* II, 550.
   Wüstenfeld corrects this last date to 6 Muḥarram, 548 (*Faṭimiden-Chalifen,* 317).
   Sallār, the father of the vizier of al-Ẓāfir, was a Kurd. He had served in the *'askar* of Sukmān b. Artuq. When al-Afḍal took Jerusalem, he joined the Egyptian army (*ibid.,* 312).
95. Ms.A: *wa-kāna al-sulṭān amīr al-juyūsh al-'Adīl al-Sallār min al-mukhtafī* (?).
   The difficulty is the reading *al-mukhtafī* which is not very satisfactory. The word might be *al-mukhtabī* or *al-mukhtanī.* None of these readings yield much sense. A bold emendation to *Ẓarzārī* has been made here since the details supplied by Ibn Khallikān are unambiguous: "He was of Kurdish origin and belonged to the tribe of Zarzārī" (*Wafayāt,* II, 350).
96. Kamāl al-Dīn al-Shahrazūrī was one of the most famous officials of the age. He exercised great power, first at Mosul and then at Damascus. He and his brother, Tāj al-Dīn Abū Ṭāhir Yaḥyā, had been with Zangī at Qal'at Ja'bar and after the latter's assassination they had been instrumental in putting Zangī's son, Saif al-Dīn Ghāzī, in power. Saif al-Dīn had handed over the running of affairs in Mosul to these two brothers. Kamāl al-Dīn al-Shahrazūrī later served the Ayyūbids in Syria and founded *madrasas* in Mosul and Naṣībīn (Ibn Khallikān, *Wafayāt,* II, 646-9; Ibn al-Jauzī, *Muntaẓam,* X, 268; al-Subkī, *Ṭabaqāt,* VI, 117-21).
97. Kamāl al-Dīn al-Shahrazūrī seems to have been the more powerful of the two brothers.

had kept control of the state since the murder of Atābeg Zangī. The vizier, Jamāl al-Dīn and Zain al-Dīn (all)[98] had a hand in their arrest. After Saif al-Dīn Ghāzī had seized them, they were taken up to the citadel of Mosul. He summoned from al-Raḥba[99] the *qāḍī* Najm al-Dīn Abū 'Alī b. Bahā' al-Dīn b. al-Ḥasan b. 'Alī b. al-Qāsim al-Shahrazūrī,[100] who administered the law there. When Bahā' al-Dīn al-Shahrazūrī had died in 532 (1137-8) in al-Raqqa as we have already mentioned,[101] his son the *qāḍī* Najm al-Dīn Abu'l-Ḥasan b. 'Alī took over as *qāḍī* of the whole of Atābeg (Zangī's) territories. The nephew of Bahā' al-Dīn, Shams al-Dīn Abū Aḥmad, succeeded at Mosul. Kamāl al-Dīn became *qāḍī* of Naṣībīn and *qāḍī al-'askar.* Tāj al-Dīn Abū Ṭāhir took over as *qāḍī* of the Jazīra and Sharaf al-Dīn, the brother of Bahā' al-Dīn, became *qāḍī* of Sinjār. All these people exercised independent control, without deputies. (This came about) because they had all been in these posts as deputies for Bahā' al-Dīn, and when Bahā' al-Dīn died, these men took over these districts (in their own right).[102]

Najm al-Dīn, the son of Bahā' al-Dīn, ruled all the remaining territories with the *qāḍīs* as his deputies. He remained (in power) until 533 (1138-9), when Shams al-Dīn Abū Aḥmad took over in Mosul as chief *qāḍī.* Having paid money[103] to Najm al-Dīn he took the post of *qāḍī* of Mosul in addition to what he already had. The situation remained like that until 535 (1140-1) when Najm al-Dīn, (who was now) *mutawallī* of Naṣībīn, was seized. He was mulcted, imprisoned and severely tortured. (f.173b) About 130,000 Amīrī[104] *dīnārs* were extorted from him. Kamāl al-Dīn Abu'l-Faḍl Muḥammad b.

98. Jamāl al-Dīn al-Iṣfahānī and Zain al-Dīn 'Alī Küçük had been the faithful associates of Zangī. When Saif al-Dīn Ghāzī came to power in Mosul, Jamāl al-Dīn stayed as vizier and Zain al-Dīn was governor and commander of the *'askar* (Elisséeff, *op.cit.,* II, 437). Relations between these two men and Kamāl al-Dīn al-Shahrazūrī appear to have become strained and the latter was imprisoned by Saif al-Dīn.
99. For al-Raḥba, cf. E. Honigmann, "Raḥba", *EI*[1]; Le Strange, *Lands,* 105, 124.
100. Cf. Chapter 3, n.14 and n.15.
101. Cf. f.169a.
102. This rather complicated description of the administrative posts held by the Shahrazūrī family has been rendered more comprehensible by the occasional addition of nouns instead of ambiguous pronouns.
103. For this use of the verb *khadama,* cf. Dozy, *Supplément,* I, 354.
104. At the time of the Crusades, there were several kinds of *dīnār* (gold coins): *Imāmī dīnārs* struck at Baghdad by the caliph; *Amīrī dīnārs* struck by the *amīrs; Ṣūrī dīnārs* struck by the Faṭimids and red *dīnārs* possibly struck by the Saljuqs (*Recueil des Historiens des Croisades, Historiens Orientaux* [Paris, 1887], II, 115, n.1).

'Abdallāh al-Shahrazūrī took control of the whole area, seizing power independently. The administration of the law, the lands, the troops and of all (other) affairs was handed back to Kamāl al-Dīn until the death of Zangī, as we have already mentioned.

Najm al-Dīn remained in prison for four years until the *qāḍī* Kamāl al-Dīn obtained his release and appointed him *qāḍī* of al-Raḥba, (an office which he had held) in the days of his father Bahā' al-Dīn.[105] He remained in the post until Kamāl al-Dīn was arrested, as we have already mentioned. (Then) Najm al-Dīn came and took over Mosul, appointing his eldest son Bahā' al-Dīn in al-Raḥba, as we have already said.[106] Najm al-Dīn established himself in Mosul and Kamāl al-Dīn and Tāj al-Dīn stayed imprisoned for a time in the citadel at Mosul.

The *imām,* the caliph al-Muqtafī, may God's mercy be upon him, sent a group of messengers to Mosul and they obtained permission for the two of them to be sent back to their homes. Najm al-Dīn put two Khurāsānīs at each of the two men's doors so that no-one could go in or out, and the son of Kamāl al-Dīn Abū Aḥmad al-Jalāl[107] and (the son of) Tāj al-Dīn, Abu'l-Faḍā'il al-Ḍiyā',[108] were taken and imprisoned in the citadel at Mosul. Najm al-Dīn acquired sole power as *qāḍī* of Mosul.[109] He gave 'Izz al-Dīn Abū Bakr al-Dubaisī the Jazīra as an *iqṭā'* and appointed a *qāḍī* there for a while. His name was Ibn Ḥamza and he came from Daqūqā.[110]

¶ In 536 (1141-2) the vizier Niẓām al-Dīn Abū Ja'far, whom another report calls al-Muẓaffar Muḥammad b. al-Za'īm b. Jahīr, was appointed as vizier to the caliph, after Sulṭān Mas'ūd's permission to dismiss Sharaf al-Dīn al-Zainabī had been obtained. Qawām al-Dīn b. Ṣadaqa was made treasurer as we have already mentioned.[111] The vizier remained in office until 541 (1146-7), when he went to Mecca, performed the pilgrimage and then returned to Baghdad.

In this year Bahā' al-Dīn Abū Ṭāhir b. 'Aqīl b. Nubāta set out on the pilgrimage from Mayyāfāriqīn. When he arrived in Baghdad, he

105. *fīhi* has been added here to make any sense of the text.
106. The fact that Najm al-Dīn appointed his son, Bahā' al-Dīn, as *qāḍī* of al-Raḥba has not been mentioned before.
107. Ibn Khallikān, who borrows this incident from Ibn al-Azraq, corrects the name of Kamāl al-Dīn's son to Jalāl al-Dīn Abū Aḥmad b. Kamāl al-Dīn (cf. Hillenbrand, "Approaches", 210, n.50).
108. Ibn Khallikān also corrects the name of the son of Tāj al-Dīn to read Ḍiyā' al-Dīn Abu'l-Faḍā'il al-Qāsim b. Tāj al-Dīn *(ibid.)*.
109. This anecdote is written as a continuous narrative by Ibn Khallikān. Ibn al-Azraq resumes the story on f.174b.
110. For Daqūqā, cf. Yāqūt, *Reisen,* 440; S.H. Longrigg, "Daḳūḳā", *EI*².
111. This is a repetition of events already described on f.169b.

visited the caliph's palace and pronounced a judicial decision[112] in the presence of the vizier Niẓām al-Dīn and Sadīd[113] al-Daula b. al-Anbārī, may God have mercy on them both. He made another visit after the state officials of the caliph had assembled, and the caliph put a robe of honour on him. He was attended by the *qāḍīs* and Abu'l-Fatḥ b. al-'Umrānī. After the vizier[114] had returned to Baghdad, he remained (in power) for a while before being dismissed from the vizierate.[115] Qawām al-Dīn b. Ṣadaqa succeeded him as vizier[116] and Za'īm al-Dīn b. Ja'far took over as treasurer, whilst al-Ajall Jamāl al-Dīn Abu'l-Muẓaffar b. Hiba inherited the *dīwān*.

112. Ms.A: *wa-awrada faṣlan*.
The normal usage would be *ḥakama faṣlan*. The phrase might also mean "delivered a section (of the Qur'ān)."
113. Ms.A: Rashīd al-Daula b. al-Anbārī. This should read Sadīd al-Daula (cf. Chapter 3, n.103.)
114. The vizier in question is still Niẓām al-Dīn, after his completion of the pilgrimage.
115. For the vizierate of Niẓām al-Dīn Abū Naṣr Muẓaffar b. 'Alī b. Muḥammad b. Jahīr, cf. Ibn al-Ṭiqṭaqā, *al-Fakhrī*, 533-4; Sibṭ b. al-Jauzī, *Mir'āt*, 195).
116. Ibn al-Ṭiqṭaqā writes that the vizier Niẓām al-Dīn was succeeded by *Mu'taman al-Daula* Abu'l-Qāsim 'Alī b. Ṣadaqa (*al-Fakhrī*, 534).

Chapter 7

The latter part of the reign of Temür-Tash

¶ In 543 (1148-9) the *khātūn,* Fāṭima, wife of the caliph al-Muqtafī, died in Baghdad.[1] In 543 (1148-9) Shaikh Sharaf al-Dīn b. Sa'd b. 'Aṣrūn[2] came from Mosul and concluded the marriage between Zumurrud Khātūn, daughter of al-Sa'īd Ḥusām al-Dīn, (f.174a) and Atābeg Ghāzī.[3] The engagement ceremony had been in the citadel of Mayyāfāriqīn for (a dowry of) 20,000 *dīnārs,*[4] with Shaikh 'Izz al-Shuyūkh Abu'l-Qāsim b. Ḥabashī as *wālī.*[5]

In Sha'bān 543 (15 December 1148 - 12 January 1149) 'Izz al-Daula Abū Naṣr b. Nīsān came to Mayyāfāriqīn and concluded the

1. Ibn al-Jauzī says that Fāṭima Khātūn bint Sulṭān Muḥammad died in Baghdad in Rabī' I, 542/31 July - 29 August 1147 (*Muntaẓam,* X, 128).
   Ibn Khallikān gives the exact date of her death as 22 Rabī' II, 542/20 September 1147 (*Wafayāt,* III, pt. 1, 239). For details of her marriage to the caliph al-Muqtafī, cf. Ibn al-Athīr, *al-Kāmil,* X, 31; Ibn al-Jauzī, *Muntaẓam,* X, 67.
2. Sharaf al-Dīn b. Abī 'Asrūn was a Shāfi'ite doctor. He was born in 492/1099 and died in 585/1182 (Ibn Khallikān, *Wafayāt,* II, 32-6). Cf. also Ibn al-'Adīm, *Ẓubda,* 294.
3. The name Atābeg Ghāzī refers to Saif al-Dīn Ghāzī b. Zangī.
4. This marriage had been arranged after Saif al-Dīn Ghāzī had attacked Mārdīn (cf. Chapter 6, n.82).
5. Ms.A: *wa-kāna al-wālī al-shaikh 'Izz al-Shuyūkh.*
   The use of the word *wālī* presents problems here.
   A bride is accompanied by a close male relative (*walī).* In certain *madhhabs,* the governor (*wālī)* would deputise at a marriage, if the bride had no close male relative (*walī).* Cf. R. Levy, *The social structure of Islam*(Cambridge, 1971), 1971, 109-112. Probably the concept *walī* is intended here and the word *wālī* is a scribal error.

marriage between Ṣafiyya Khātūn, daughter of al-Sa'īd Ḥusām al-Dīn, and Jamāl al-Dīn Shams al-Mulūk Maḥmūd b. İl-aldï, lord of Āmid, for (a dowry of) 5,000 *dīnārs* with the *khaṭīb* Tāj al-'Ulamā' al-Khaṣlaqī (?)[6] as the *wālī*.[7] He took her to Āmid in the last few days of Sha'bān.

In 543 (1148-9) Amīr Bahā' al-Dīn Sevinch b. Kuhmïsh (?) and the vizier Ḍiyā' al-Dīn came on behalf of Amīr Fakhr al-Dīn Daulat-Shāh b. Ṭoghan Arslan, lord of Arzan and Bitlīs, and drew up a marriage contract between (him and) Nūra Khātūn, daughter of al-Sa'īd Ḥusām al-Dīn, for 50,000 *dīnārs* and the *wālī* was present and the marriage (contract was drawn up) in Mayyāfāriqīn. In 538 (1143-4) Ḥusām al-Daula Qurtï had died in Arzan and was succeeded by his brother Shams al-Dīn Yāqūt Arslan who held power until 540 (1145-6).[8] He sent his brother Daulat-Shāh to work for Atābeg Zangī when he crossed over and took the territory of Amīr Dā'ūd after Dā'ūd died. Then Yāqūt Arslan died on a Saturday at the beginning of Ramaḍān 540 (15 February - 16 March 1146). Ḍiyā' al-Dīn Ayyūb went to Zangī's camp, fetched[9] Amīr Daulat-Shāh, whose *laqab* was Fakhr al-Dīn, and brought him to Mayyāfāriqīn. He (then) went to Arzan and took possession of the area. He assumed sole command and conquered all the territory of his father and his brothers. Ḍiyā' al-Dīn Ayyūb had married Daulat-Shāh's mother. Daulat-Shāh joined up with[10] al-Sa'īd

6. Ms.A: *al-Ḥ.ṣlqī*. Perhaps it would not be too fanciful to read this as *al-Ḥ.ṣnk.fī* (the *nisba* of the nearby town of Ḥiṣn Kaifā).
7. Again the word used is *wālī*.
8. Ḥusām al-Daula Qurtï and his family are discussed by Minorsky (*Studies in Caucasian History*, 85-6). These *amīrs* ruled Arzan and Bitlīs. Their genealogy is as follows:

Ṭoghan Arslan al-Aḥdab
- Ḥusām al-Daula Qurtï
- Yāqūt Arslan
- Fakhr al-Dīn
  - Arslan Ṭoghmïsh
- Daulat- Shāh

Minorsky misreads Ibn al-Azraq's text here (he follows the transcription of part of the text by Amedroz). Minorsky says that Daulat-Shāh died in 539/1144 (*ibid.*, 90, n.1). In fact, Ibn al-Azraq relates that Dā'ūd of Ḥiṣn Kaifā died in 539/1144.
9. Ms.A: *fa-jābū al-amīr*. Ms.B makes better sense and retains a singular verb: *wa-'āda bi-hi ilā Arzan*.
10. Ms.A: *ittiṣala ilā*. Ms.B: *intaqala ilā*. The version of Ms.B has been preferred here, since *intaqala* is usually followed by *ilā*, whereas *ittiṣala* takes *bi*.

Ḥusām al-Dīn and in Dhu'l-Ḥijja (15 May - 12 June 1146) they (Daulat-Shāh's officials) came to Mayyāfāriqīn and fetched (Nūra) Khātūn and took her to Arzan, the wedding having taken place in Mayyāfāriqīn.

In 543 (1148-9) Tāj al-Dīn Abū Sālim Ṭāhir b. Nubāta went to the Ḥijāz. When he arrived in Baghdad he went to the *dīwān* of the caliph.[11] In 543 (1148-9) the vizier Makīn al-Dīn al-Miṣrī returned to Mayyāfāriqīn where al-Sa'īd Ḥusām al-Dīn appointed him vizier.[12] That year I was *mutawallī ishrāf*[13] outside the town of Mayyāfāriqīn. After a while Makīn al-Dīn seized al-Mu'ayyid and al-Muhadhdhab and tortured them in the citadel for a few days. Then he appointed al-'Amīd b. Abī Ṭāhir b. al-Muḥtasib to audit the *dīwān*. He held office for only two days before al-Sa'īd Ḥusām al-Dīn gave orders that he should be dismissed, slapping him, shaving off his beard, putting him on a donkey and having him led round the town. He was (then) banished and driven from the town. After a few days, the vizier left one afternoon with his *ghulām* in attendance. He was taken round the town and then made for the Ḥiṣn Kaifā road and departed. When al-Sa'īd Ḥusām al-Dīn was told that the vizier had fled, he said 'He has taken nothing from us, so do not go out looking for him'. So he got away and the following morning al-Mu'ayyid and al-Muhadhdhab were reinstated in the *dīwān*, their position became established and they regained the highest office.

¶ In 544 (1149-50) Zangī's son Ghāzī went (f.174b) as far as Naṣībīn[14] and sent Amīr Julduk (?) al-Khalīfatī to Mārdīn, whence he brought Zumurrud Khātūn as far as Naṣībīn, accompanied by Ṣamṣām al-Dīn.[15] (Then) Zangī's son Saif al-Dīn Ghāzī fell ill[16] and

11. This may be the same person whose pilgrimage is recorded on f.173b.
12. The text is repetitive here: *baqiyā ayyāman...baqiyā muddatan*. The first of these has therefore been omitted.
13. The *dīwān al-ishrāf*, as well as holding responsibility for the collection of taxes, also administered *waqfs* (Lambton, *op.cit.*, 259).

    Ibn al-Azraq's post was probably that of supervising *waqfs*. Yet again, however, problems are caused by the use of imprecise administrative terminology in this period.

    Amedroz erroneously refers to Ibn al-Azraq's post as the *mutawallī ashrāf* (H. F. Amedroz, "Three Arabic MSS. on the History of the City of Mayyāfāriqīn", *JRAS* [1902], 787). *Ashrāf* is the plural of *sharīf*.
14. Saif al-Dīn Ghāzī was probably at Naṣībīn during his campaign into Diyār Bakr in 544/1149-50 (Ibn al-Athīr, *Atabegs*, 90-1).
15. Ṣamṣām al-Dīn Bahrām was the brother of Zumurrud Khātūn and the son of Temür-Tash.
16. When Zumurrud Khātūn arrived in Mosul, her husband was already seriously ill, suffering from colic (Ibn al-Athīr, *Atabegs*, 92; Ibn al-

she was taken to Mosul where she stayed in Darb Durrāj and in the house of the *khātūn*, the daughter of Sukmān[17] and wife of Atābeg Zangī. Saif al-Dīn Ghāzī, who was seriously ill, came back and stayed in Mosul. He had sent people to Baghdad who brought back the doctor Abu'l-Barakāt. Although this man arrived and treated him for several days, he died in Ṣafar 544 (10 June - 8 July 1149).[18] His brother, Quṭb al-Dīn Maudūd[19] b. Zangī, took command and stabilised his position. The state was administered by the vizier Jamāl al-Dīn, Zain al-Dīn and 'Izz al-Dīn.[20] Saif al-Dīn Ghāzī was buried in the 'Imādiyya *madrasa*.[21]

After the death of Saif al-Dīn, the *qāḍī* Kamāl al-Dīn and his brother were released from their homes and summoned to the *maidān*.[22] That year I was in Mosul working for al-Sa'īd Ḥusām al-Dīn by selling iron, and I was in the *maidān* (that day). The vizier Jamāl al-Dīn had sent them two she-mules, so they came riding into the *maidān* inside Mosul. When they came through the gate of the *maidān* - having changed their clothes and riding without *ṭarḥas*[23] - they dismounted. When Atābeg Quṭb al-Dīn saw them, he went towards them and dismounted to (speak to) them. They went up to meet him, complained to him about his brother and congratulated him on his assumption of power. Then they remounted and stopped beside him, remaining (there) an hour, before returning home. The soldiers were (then) removed from their doors.[24] The two brothers began riding out

Qalānisī, *Dhail*, 306). Their marriage was not consummated (Ibn al-Athīr, *Atabegs*, 91).

17. Zumurrud Khātūn stayed in the house of the daughter of Sukmān al-Quṭbī of Akhlāṭ. She had married Zangī after both he and Ḥusām al-Daula Qurtī from Arzan had asked for her hand (Usāma, *Memoirs*, 118-9; Ibn al-'Adīm, *Zubda*, 254).
18. Saif al-Dīn Ghāzī died at the end of Jumādā II, 544/ November 1149 (Ibn al-Athīr, *Atabegs*, 92). According to Ibn al-Athīr, the best doctor of the time was summoned but to no avail (*ibid.*).
19. Ms.A: Mamdūd. This has been corrected to Maudūd.
20. Quṭb al-Dīn Maudūd, another of Zangī's sons, was put in power at Mosul by Jamāl al-Dīn al-Iṣfahānī, the vizier, and by Zain al-Dīn 'Alī, the commander of the *'askar*. They saw that his malleability would be in their own interests (Ibn al-Athīr, *Atabegs*, 94; *al-Kāmil*, XI, 91-2).
21. According to Ibn al-Athīr, Saif al-Dīn Ghāzī was buried in a *madrasa* which he himself had founded at Mosul (*Atabegs*, 92).
22. This is the resumption of the story begun on f.173b.
23. The *ṭarḥa* was a kind of hood worn by the chief *qāḍīs* of the Shāfi'ite sect (Ibn Khallikān, *Wafayāt*, II, 649 - n.1 by de Slane quoting M. de Sacy in his *Chrestomathie*, II, 269).
24. I.e. from the doors of the two brothers. The active verb *azālū* has been rendered here as a passive.

every week in the service of Quṭb al-Dīn, Zain al-Dīn and Jamāl al-Dīn. After a while they approached al-Sa'īd Ḥusām al-Dīn and arranged matters and the marriage contract was drawn up for Atābeg Quṭb al-Dīn to Zumurrud Khātūn after the completion of her period of widowhood.[25] Quṭb al-Dīn consummated the marriage with her in Mosul.

At the end of (5)44 (April 1150) al-Sa'īd Ḥusām al-Dīn attacked the city of Dārā but the *wālī* refused to surrender it. After he had laid siege to it for a while, the *wālī* surrendered it to him on Wednesday, 12 Dhu'l-Ḥijja (12 April 1150). After he had taken possession of the city he appointed the *ḥājib* Ibn Baqsh (?) al-Dunaisirī as governor there. I was in the camp, working for al-Sa'īd Ḥusām al-Dīn, until he conquered the city.[26]

In this year, that is (5)44 (1149-50), the domed bazaar in Mayyāfāriqīn was burned. (Also) in this year, in Dhu'l-Ḥijja (1-29 April 1150) there was disagreement between the sons of the *'amīd* Tāj al-Dīn Abū Sālim b. Nubāta. Ḍiyā'al-Dīn went to Dārā, met al-Sa'īd Ḥusām al-Dīn, paid his respects and took the post of *qāḍī* before returning to Mayyāfāriqīn. On 12 Muḥarram, 544 (22 May 1149) Quṭb al-Dīn Īl-Ghāzī, son of al-Mālik Najm al-Dīn, was born. May both their shadows be preserved.

In 544 (1149-50) the Christians *(al-Afranj)* took Almeria (f.175a) from the Muslims.[27] The city was plundered and loot from it was taken and sold in the lands of Egypt, the Sāḥil and Syria.

In 545 (30 April 1150 - 19 April 1151) Ṣamṣām al-Dīn Bahrām b. al-Sa'īd Ḥusām al-Dīn became engaged to Zangī's daughter, the sister of Quṭb al-Dīn, and I was in Mosul at the time of the engagement ceremony.

In 545 (1150-1) the Bedouin, the Banū Za'b and others, as well as scum and dissolutes (?), plundered the last (caravan) of the

25. Ms.A: *ba'da inqiḍā' mudda al-wafā'*. This period is normally called the *'idda*. It is a prescribed period of four months, ten days in which widows cannot contract a new marriage (cf. T.W. Juynboll, "'idda", *EI*[1]).

26. Dārā was constantly changing hands. Zangī had taken it; and, when he died, Temür-Tash took it back. Thereafter Saif al-Dīn Ghāzī captured it in 544/1149-50 (Ibn al-Athīr, *Atabegs,* 90; Michael the Syrian, *Chronique,* 275). No doubt the capture of Dārā by Temür-Tash recorded here was the immediate result of the news of Saif al-Dīn Ghāzī's death.

27. From around 539-42/1144-7, King Alfonso VII of Castile made raids into Andalusia, pillaging the country as far as Almeria (Julien, *op.cit.,* 91).

pilgrimage,[28] taking all their possessions between Mecca and Medina at a place called Sadd, and a great number of people perished. This is an occurrence which is unheard of except in the distant past. Only a very small number of people escaped alive. That year I was living in Mosul.

Ḥusām al-Dīn with his sons conquered all the *amīrs* of Diyār Bakr, Diyār Rabī'a and Armenia and attached them to himself.[29] After Atābeg Zangī (had been killed) no *amīr* other than Ḥusām al-Dīn remained[30] independent, unopposed, unchallenged and governing alone.

In 545 (1150-1) Mu'īn al-Dīn Unur died in Damascus.[31] Also in that year Nūr al-Dīn Maḥmūd b. Zangī, ruler of Syria, met the Franks and defeated them roundly. Joscelin's son, the lord of Edessa and its surrounding area, was taken prisoner and all his lands were seized. (Then) Nūr al-Dīn took Tall Bāshir and its environs and Tall

28. Ms.A: *nahaba al-'Arab Banū Ẓa'b wa-ghairuhum wa-dh.bāb wa-baṭrān ākhir al-ḥājj*. Ms.B: *nahaba al-'Arab al-ḥājj*

The meaning of *dh.bāb wa-baṭrān* presents problems. These words may be tribal names. More plausibly, they may be terms of abuse. Lane gives examples of the use of *dhubāb* (fly), such as Abu'l-Dhubāb with an obvious pejorative meaning, *Lexicon,* I, 952). *Baṭrān* may come from *baṭara* (to behave insolently).

The hypothesis that these are terms of abuse is supported by Ibn al-Qalānisī who also records this incident under the year 545 and mentions that the pilgrims were seized by a group of Bedouin infidels, riff-raff *(zuṭṭ)* and dregs *(aubāsh)* (*op.cit.*, 310).

29. Ms.A: *malaka Ḥusām al-Dīn bi-awlādihi jamī' umarā' Diyār Bakr wa-Diyār Rabī'a wa-Arminiyya wa-ittiṣālahu bi-him.*

The last phrase is rather strange. Perhaps it should read *ittaṣala bi-him.*

30. This is a fine piece of pro-Artuqid propaganda. Temür-Tash had in fact already proved powerless to resist the onslaught of Saif al-Dīn Ghāzī in 544/1149-50. No doubt Ibn al-Azraq deliberately suppressed the circumstances of this affray. There was a certain falling off of interest on the part of both Nūr al-Dīn and Quṭb al-Dīn, his brother, in Diyār Bakr. Thus it would be true to say that of the petty rulers of that area, Temür-Tash was the master for a brief time - some three years - until his death in 547/1152-3. Qara Arslan of Ḥiṣn Kaifā was the faithful ally of Nūr al-Dīn and answered his appeals for help (*Atabegs*, 96).

31. This event is mentioned without comment by Ibn al-Azraq on two occasions. Mu'īn al-Dīn Unur was the *de facto* ruler of Damascus, rather than the Būrid family behind whom he wielded his power. He died on 23 Rabī' II, 544/29 August, 1149 (Ibn al-Qalānisī, *Dhail,* 306).

Khālid and its neighbourhood.[32] Ḥusām al-Dīn seized Sumaisāṭ[33] and on 6 Rabīʿ I (3 July 1150) took al-Bīra.[34]

In the defeat in (5)46 (20 April 1151 - 7 April 1152) the *ḥājib* ʿUmar al-Khāṣṣ,[35] who was in the employ of Nūr al-Dīn, was killed. Fakhr al-Dīn Qara Arslan[36] took Ḥiṣn Manṣūr[37] and Bābalū,[38] both in the territory of Joscelin's son, and seized the citadel of Gargar[39] from

32. As usual with Ibn al-Azraq's narrative, this is a blend of inaccuracies and sound information. "Joscelin's son" is Joscelin II, the son of Joscelin of Courtenay. Joscelin II ruled the county of Edessa from 525/1131 to 545/1150. Ibn Shaddād refers to him as the "King of the Armenians", no doubt because of the large Armenian population in his territory (cf. Eddé, *Description,* 68). It would appear probable that Joscelin's capture took place during the first days of Muḥarram 545 (early May 1150). Cf. Ibn al-ʿAdīm, *Zubda,* 301-2.

It is difficult to identify the victory of Nūr al-Dīn over the Franks mentioned here by Ibn al-Azraq as preceding the capture of Joscelin. Joscelin was seized in an ambush laid by Turcoman troops; at the time Nūr al-Dīn, however, was moving north from Damascus and was not involved in the incident. After Joscelin's capture, Tall Bāshir and other Edessan fortresses were sold to Manuel Comnenus in the summer of 545/1150. It was only in the following year that Nūr al-Dīn seized Tall Bāshir, the last remnant of the county of Edessa, on 25 Rabīʿ I,546/12 July, 1151. Cf. the discussion in Baldwin, I, 624; Elisséeff, 453-4; Stevenson, 167.

Ibn al-Athīr puts the capture of Joscelin in 546/1151 and speaks of a defeat inflicted on Nūr al-Dīn by Joscelin a year earlier. This chronology differs from that of the other sources (*Atabegs,* 101-2).

For Tall Bāshir cf. Eddé, *Description,* 61-7; for Tall Khālid, cf. *ibid.,* 63.

33. For this important town on the left bank of the upper Euphrates, cf. the detailed description given by Ibn Shaddād (Eddé, *Description,* 114-8).

34. According to Ibn Shaddād, Temür-Tash kept al-Bīra until Nūr al-Dīn took it from him and gave it as an *iqṭāʿ* to Shihāb al-Dīn Muḥammad b. Ayāz b. İl-Ghāzī, who held it until he died in 577/1181-2 (*Jazīra,* f.36b).

35. Cf. f.178a.

36. Qara Arslan had begun the attacks on Joscelin's territory. He took Bābālu and invaded the area around Gargar as early as 543/1148-9 (Michael the Syrian, *Chronique,* 290).

37. For Ḥiṣn Manṣūr (present-day Adiyaman), cf. Eddé, *Description,* 109-110; F. Taescher, "Adiyaman", *EI*². It is situated to the NW of the Nahr al-Azraq (Gök Su), a tributary of the Euphrates.

38. Bābālu is listed by Ibn Shaddād (*Jazīra,* f.65b). Michael the Syrian says the fortress was on the bank of the Euphrates (*Chronique,* 290). Cahen places it opposite Charmūk, between Gargar and Khanzīt ("Diyār Bakr", 226).

39. Gargar was called Karkaron by the Byzantines. It was situated on the Euphrates (cf. Honigmann, *Ostgrenze,* 116, 133; Markwart, *Südarmenien,* 255; Canard, *H'amdanides,* 264; Gaudefroy-Demombynes, *op.cit.,* 87).

the Armenians. Sulṭān Qïlïch Arslan[40] took Maʿrash[41] and Kaisūn[42] and its neighbourhood. Joscelin's son had no territory left except Qal'at al-Rūm which Ḥusām al-Dīn would have taken if he had lived.[43]

In 545 (1150-1) Mu'īn al-Dīn Unur died in Damascus.[44]

In 546 (1151-2) I travelled to Akhlāṭ and went down to Baghdad again, where I arrived on 27 Ramaḍān (6 January 1152), and I stayed there (for a while). In 546 al-Sa'īd Ḥusām al-Dīn circumcised[45] the sons of Amīr Jamāl al-Dīn Qurtï (?) in Mayyāfāriqīn.

In (5)47 (8 April 1152 - 28 March 1153) an edict came to al-Sa'īd Ḥusām al-Dīn from the *sulṭān* and the caliph, which was read from the *minbar* throughout the land. Robes of honour arrived (too).[46] Two nights later, that is to say, the night of Monday, 22 Rabī' I 547 (27

40. According to Ibn Shaddād, it was Mas'ūd b. Qïlïch Arslan who took these places in 544/1149-50. They remained in the possession of his son Qïlïch Arslan until Nūr al-Dīn seized them in 550/1155 (Eddé, *Description,* 104). According to Michael the Syrian, Mas'ūd sent his son Qïlïch Arslan to attack Mar'ash (*Chronique,* 290). There is no mention, however, of Kaisūn. Ibn al-Athīr says that it was Nūr al-Dīn who took Mar'ash (*Atābegs,* 103).
41. On this frontier post in the Jazīra, cf. Eddé, *Description,* 101-5; E. Honigmann, "Maʿrash", *EI*¹.
42. Ms.A: Kaisūm. This must be a mistaken reference to Kaisūn, which Cahen describes as a prosperous little town between Qal'at al-Rūm and the Aq-Su. The citadel of Kaisūn, which was originally of mud brick, was partially re-built of stone by Baldwin of Mar'ash (Cahen, *Syrie,* 120).
43. Cahen implies that Ibn al-Azraq says that Temür-Tash actually occupied Qal'at al-Rūm ("Diyār Bakr", 254, n.1). He must have misread the text. On the position of Qal'at al-Rūm at the convergence of the Merzmen Su and the Euphrates, cf. Cahen, *Syrie,* 122; Elisséeff, *Nūr al-Dīn,* 165; E. Honigmann, "Rūm Ḳal'a", *EI*¹.
44. This is a repetition of f.175a.
45. Ms.A: *ṭahhara al-Sa'īd Ḥusām al-Dīn al-amīr Jamāl al-Dīn aulād.*
    The sons of Jamāl al-Dīn were the grandsons of Temür-Tash. For circumcision, cf. A.J. Wensinck, "khitān", *EI*². For *ṭahhara* cf. Lane, *Lexicon,* I, 187.
46. The *manshūr* was the patent of appointment, sent by the caliph, which assigned to a new *amīr* all the territories which his father had held or which he himself might have acquired. The *manshūr* was read out before a large gathering and the ceremony ended with the donning by the *amīr* of a *khil'a* (a robe of honour) sent by the caliph (R. Levy, *The Social Structure of Islam* [Cambridge, 1971], 372).
    Since Temür-Tash had ruled Mārdīn for thirty years by this date, it is probable that the arrival of this edict from Baghdad finally recognising his authority in Diyār Bakr represented the apogee of his power, the brief moment when, unfettered by submission to the Zangids of Mosul, he enjoyed a small degree of independence.

June 1152), the *minbar* area and the arcades[47] of the mosque in Mayyāfāriqīn collapsed.[48]

(In this year) I was in Baghdad where I met Quṭb al-Dīn al-'Abbādī the preacher. I was in his company for a time and I wrote down a lot of discourses from him.[49]

At the end of (5)44 (1149-50) 'Aun al-Dīn al-Muẓaffar Muḥammad b. Yaḥyā b. Hubaira became the (caliph's) vizier after the dismissal of Qawām al-Dīn b. Ṣadaqa.[50] 'Aun al-Dīn became established in the post. He had (previously) been in charge of the *dīwān al-zimām wa'l-istīfā'*.[51] Jalāl al-Dīn (f.175b) b. Ja'far, the brother of the treasurer, took over the *dīwān al-zimām*. Their father (Ja'far) had come from the small village of Ba'qūbā and had served as vizier to Mujāhid al-Dīn[52] Bihrūz until he died. The caliph remained in control of affairs.

In (5)46 (1151-2) Sulṭān Mas'ūd arrived in Baghdad, where he stayed all winter.[53] I saw him that year in Baghdad when I (also) saw

47. The space between two rows of pillars in a mosque was called *riwāq* (plural *arwiqa* or *riwāqāt)* (cf. J. Pedersen, "Masdjid", *EI*[1]). The term also means "arcade".
48. Ibn Shaddād adds here: "The rest of it (the mosque) was pulled down, Then he (Temür-Tash) ordered that it should be re-built" (*Jazīra*, f.104b).
49. Quṭb al-Dīn al-'Abbādī had come to Baghdad in 541/1146-7 on a mission from Sulṭān Sanjar to the caliph, and people flocked to hear his sermons. He died in 546/1151-2 whilst in Khūzistān as an envoy from the caliph to Muḥammad b. Maḥmūd (Amedroz, "Three Arabic MSS.", 790, n.1, citing Ibn al-Athīr, *al-Kāmil,* XI, 78 and 103).
50. The appointment of Ibn Hubaira to the caliphal vizierate after Ibn Ṣadaqa is confirmed by Ibn Ṭiqṭaqā (*al-Fakhrī,* 534-5). Ibn al-Athīr also gives the date as 544/1149-50 (*al-Kāmil,* XI, 96). Ibn Hubaira was one of the principal architects of the reassertion of caliphal authority after the death of Sulṭān Mas'ūd. In 549/1154-5 al-Muqtafī, in recognition of his vizier's services, accorded him the titles *Sulṭān al-'Irāq* and *malik al-juyūsh* (Ibn al-Jauzī, *Muntaẓam,* X, 157). Cf. also Bundārī, *Zubdat,* 234-5; Ibn Khallikān, *Wafayāt,* IV, 114.
51. The *dīwān al-zimām wa'l-istīfā'* was the Treasury department (Uzunçarşili, *Osmanli devleti,* 45). In Saljuq Iran it was also called the *dīwān-i istīfā'-yi mamālik* (Lambton, *op.cit.,* 257). For an analysis of the functions of this department under the Great Saljuqs, cf. Horst, *Staatsverwaltung,* 36-8.

    Ibn Hubaira had been given charge of the *dīwān al-zimām* in 542/1147-8 (Ibn al-Athīr, *al-Kāmil,* XI, 81).
52. Under the biography of Saladin given by Ibn Khallikān there are many details about Mujāhid al-Dīn Bihrūz who was *shiḥna* of Iraq for Mas'ūd (*Wafayāt,* IV, 481-3).
53. According to Bundārī, Mas'ūd spent the winter of 545/1150-1 in Baghdad. Thereafter he never returned there again (*Zubdat,* 226).

the elephant, the parrot and the monkey.[54] The *sulṭān* moved on to Hamadhān, where he fell ill in Jumādā I (5)47 (4 August - 2 September 1152). He hung on until 11 Jumādā II (13 September 1152) when he died outside Hamadhān. He was (then) taken to Iṣfahān.[55] I remained in Baghdad until 1 Rajab (2 October 1152) that year before I went to Mayyāfāriqīn. When we reached Takrīt the news broke that the *sulṭān* had died. The people were in turmoil.[56] We moved on to Mosul.

The caliph rose up in rebellion, occupied the *sulṭān's* palace and seized control of Baghdad.[57] Mas'ūd Bilāl, who was *shiḥna* in Baghdad,

54. This reference to the animals in Mas'ūd's retinue may have been mentioned by Ibn al-Azraq because of its curiosity value. Perhaps Mas'ūd paraded such animals to excite awe and admiration amongst the populace. Certainly, even as late as Timur's time, the presence of elephants in his attack on Aleppo provoked panic amongst the inhabitants of that city. Monkeys could be used to detect poison in food and drink, as well as in menageries and public ceremonies. Cf. F. Viré, "ḳird", *EI*²; G.M. Meredith-Owens, "fīl", *EI*².

The possession of elephants was a jealously guarded royal prerogative (C.E. Bosworth, *The Ghaznavids, their empire in Afghanistan and Eastern Iran. 994:1040* [Edinburgh, 1963], 115-7).

55. Ibn Khallikān has exactly the same date as Ibn al-Azraq for the death of Mas'ūd (*Wafayāt,* III, pt. 1, 363).

For other accounts of Mas'ūd's death, cf. Ibn al-Athīr, *Atabegs,* 105; *idem, al-Kāmil,* XI, 105; Rāwandī, *Rāḥat,* 205; Bundārī, *Zubdat,* 226-7; Ibn al-Jauzī, *Muntaẓam,* X, 151; Mustaufī, *Guzīda,* 357.

The *Tārīkh-i Guzīda* states that Mas'ūd was buried in a *madrasa* in Hamadhān, having died on 1 Rajab (*ibid.*). Ibn Khallikān says he was buried in a *madrasa* built by Jamāl al-Dīn Iqbāl al-Khādim (*Wafayāt,* III, pt. 1, 364).

56. Ibn al-Azraq is unusually precise about his dates here. If they are correct, the implication is that the news of Sulṭān Mas'ūd's death took three weeks to reach Baghdad. Perhaps the event had been deliberately kept hidden, as was often the case.

57. Al-Muqtafī chose Mas'ūd's death as the most appropriate moment to manifest firm signs of his desire for independence, although there had been inklings right from the outset of his caliphate that he did not fit Sulṭān Mas'ūd's blueprint for a puppet caliph (cf. f.165b).

Ibn al-Athīr relates a significant anecdote about al-Muqtafī immediately after his accession. The new caliph gave a particularly clever and subtle reply to a question asked him by the sulṭān's vizier who wanted to know what his household requirements would be. The vizier returned to the sulṭān and said: "It would have been prudent to steer clear of this man... I have seen in him indications of great intellect, an ability to achieve his aims and a high degree of knowledge" (*Atabegs,* 54).

fled to Takrīt.[58] He had organised the *ḥajj* for some years and had treated the people with great kindness and leniency.[59] The caliph mobilised the *junūd* and the *'askars*[60] and he removed the *mu'an*[61] and the *a'shār* which the *sulṭān's* officials had taken. He was kind to the people and treated his subjects justly. He acquired Iraq and appropriated all its revenues.[62] The *sulṭān,* the royal ladies and the *sulṭān's* officials in Iraq had possessed an income (sufficient to support) 20,000 horsemen. So all that reverted to the caliph.

When Sulṭān Mas'ūd died outside Hamadhān, Sulṭān Muḥammad-Shāh b. Maḥmūd, who was his son-in-law - being married to his daughter - was in Khūzistān. The brother of Muḥammad-Shāh, Malik-Shāh b. Maḥmūd, was with him (Mas'ūd) in the camp,[63] so Khāṣṣ Beg b. Palang-Eri[64] made him *sulṭān* for a

58. This man is normally called Mas'ūd al-Bilālī. After his departure from Baghdad to Takrīt, the caliph set about ransacking the houses of Saljuq officials in the city (Ibn al-Athīr, *al-Kāmil,* XI, 106).
59. Sibṭ b. al-Jauzī stresses the tyranny of Mas'ūd al-Bilālī during his period as *shiḥna* of Baghdad. He had been appointed in 541/1146-7 and thereafter the populace suffered (*Mir'at,* 186).
60. The *'askar* were the standing army of the ruler. The *jund* came from a second line of troops who were called up to fight on more important occasions (Gibb, *Damascus Chronicle,* 34-6).
61. Ms.B adds *mukūs* to this list (f.117b). For a definition of this term, cf. R. Le Tourneau, *Damas de 1075 à 1154* (Damascus, 1952), 14, n.1.
62. *ishtaghala irtifā' al-'Irāq jamī'ihi* (*sic*).
Ms.B: *wa-ishtaghala bi-irtifā' al-'Irāq jamī'ihi.* Ms.B makes much better sense and has been used in the translation given here.
Horst defines *irtifā'āt* as directly-raised taxes (*Staatsverwaltung,* 187).
This may well be a reference to Ibn Hubaira's fiscal policy of making lands once again directly taxable (Bosworth, "Iranian World", 168).
Ms.B specifically states that al-Muqtafī took al-Ḥilla and Wāṣit (f.118a).
63. Bundārī confirms that Malik-Shāh was with his uncle at the time of the latter's death but it is not clear if Mas'ūd had actually appointed Malik-Shāh his heir (*Zubdat,* 227).
64. Ms.A: *Khāṣṣbak b. al-Blnkrī.* This name is given in the *Cambridge History of Iran, Volume 5* as Khāṣṣ Beg Arslan b. Palang-Eri. Since Boyle's system has been the one generally adopted for the transliteration of the Turkish names in this thesis, for the sake of consistency the name above has also been adopted. The transliteration Palang-Eri does, however, seem unsatisfactory.
Khāṣṣ Beg had emerged as an increasingly powerful figure in the last few years of Mas'ūd's reign (Bundārī, *Zubdat,* 198). Khāṣṣ Beg's growing influence prompted Sanjar to go to Rayy in Sha'bān 544/December 1149-January 1150 to try to check the situation (*ibid.,* 224).

while.[65] When Muḥammad-Shāh heard (about that) he left Khūzistān, set out for Hamadhān and seized the sultanate, whereupon his brother Malik-Shāh went and took Khūzistān, Ahwāz and part of Baṣra.[66] After a while Muḥammad-Shāh killed Khāṣṣ Beg b. Palang-Eri and ruled independently as *sulṭān.*[67]

Sulṭān Mas'ūd, may God have mercy on him, was a just *sulṭān,*[68] of mild disposition and so generous that he divided out all his territory amongst his associates, leaving for himself only the name of *sulṭān.* In spite of his mildness, he never fought anyone without defeating them.[69] Amongst the great *amīrs* he killed those whom no-one else could have slain: Mengü-Bars,[70] Qaracha al-Sāqī,[71] lord of Fārs and Shīrāz, and 'Abbās, lord of Rayy.[72] He (also) killed al-Rāshid, al-Mustarshid,[73]

65. Cf. Mustaufī, *Guzīda,* 357; Ibn al-Athīr, *Atabegs,* 105.
After a very short time, Khāṣṣ Beg deposed Malik-Shāh and imprisoned him. Ibn al-Athīr then writes that Khāṣṣ Beg wrote to Muḥammad-Shāh, who was then in Khūzistān, inviting him to come and take over the sultanate. His aim was to arrest him too and thus rid himself of Saljuq contenders who stood in his way (*Atabegs,* 105).
66. Malik-Shāh escaped from prison and withdrew to Khūzistān (Mustaufī, *Guzīda,* 357).
67. Muḥammad accepted Khāṣṣ Beg's invitation to come to Hamadhān but he soon killed Khāṣṣ Beg and took complete control himself. This occurred in 548/1153-4 (Ibn al-Athīr, *Atabegs,* 105).
68. Ibn al-Azraq's obituary notice of Sulṭān Mas'ūd is borrowed almost *verbatim* by Ibn Khallikān (cf. Hillenbrand, "Approaches", 208-9).
69. This description of Mas'ūd's "generosity" to his associates is hollow panegyric, especially in view of the details which follow. Ibn al-Athīr is only too well aware of the strength of Mas'ūd and stresses that with his death, the power of the Saljuq family was irrevocably damaged (*al-Kāmil,* XI, 105).
Whilst *amīrs* such as those listed below managed to acquire autonomy in the outlying provinces of Mas'ūd's empire, Mas'ūd did make positive attempts to bring them to heel.
70. Ms.A: *Mnkwrws.* This must be a reference to Mengü-Bars (cf. Chapter 4, n.22). He was made governor of Fārs in 526/1131-2 by the Saljuq *sulṭān,* who made him *atābeg* to his son (al-Ḥusainī, *Akhbār,* 101). He rebelled and was eventually imprisoned and put to death by Mas'ūd in 532/1137-8 (Ibn al-Athīr, *al-Kāmil,* XI, 39).
71. Qaracha al-Ṣāqī is wrongly placed in this list. He commanded the right wing of the army of Mas'ūd and Saljuq-Shāh in the battle which these two princes lost against their uncle Sanjar on 8 Rajab 526/25 May 1132. Qaracha al-Sāqī was imprisoned and killed by Sanjar (al-Ḥusainī, *Akhbār,* 101).
72. 'Abbās had conspired with Boz-Aba and others against Sulṭān Mas'ūd. For his activities, cf. Bundārī, *Zubdat,* 168, 214-7, Ibn al-Furāt (Shayyāl), 298, 327, 342, 353-4, 357-9; Ibn al-Athīr, *al-Kāmil,* XI, 68-9; Ibn al-Jauzī, *Muntaẓam,* 116, 119.
73. Here Ibn al-Azraq states explicitly that Mas'ūd killed the two caliphs,

Dubais, Boz-Aba,[74] 'Abd al-Raḥmān b. Ṭoghan-Yürek[75] and a group of great *amīrs* and generals. Mas'ūd was blessed with great good fortune. When he died, he left three young sons; Muḥammad-Shāh became established as *sulṭān* and took Hamadhān and Iṣfahān and its environs without being mentioned in the *khuṭba* in Iraq.

¶ In (5)47 (1152-3) Fakhr al-Dīn Qara Arslan took the fortress of Gargar from the Armenians.[76] In 547 Jalāl al-Mulūk Köpek b. Sulaimān b. 'Abd al-Jabbār (f.176a) b. Artuq married Hadiyya Khātūn, daughter of al-Sa'īd Ḥusām al-Dīn, through the good offices of his mother the princess, daughter of Riḍwān and wife of Ḥusām al-Dīn.

In (5)45 (1150-1) the vizier Zain al-Dīn As'ad b. 'Abd al-Khāliq, the brother of al-Mu'ayyid Zain al-Dīn, the *sulṭān's* vizier, had come to Mārdīn and stayed with Ḥusām al-Dīn, who appointed him vizier. He remained in the *dīwān*, assisted by al-Mu'ayyid the *mustaufī* and al-Muhadhdhab, and appointing as his deputy a scribe whose *laqab* was al-Shihāb.[77] Zain al-Dīn became established as vizier until 546.

In the year 544 (1149-50), Ṣafiyya Khātūn had died in Āmid. At the beginning of (5)46 (1151-2) al-Sa'īd Ḥusām al-Dīn set out and encamped before Āmid and demanded from the inhabitants the dowry (*ṣadāq*) of Ṣafiyya Khātūn.[78] He remained (there)[79] for a while

regardless of his earlier narrative where he presented a number of reports about their death (cf. ff.164b, 165a and 167b).

74. Ms.A: *Bwzbāh.* This name is usually rendered as Boz-Aba. Boz-Aba was the lieutenant of Mengü-Bars in Khūzistān and took Fārs and Khūzistān after the latter's death. He plotted against Sulṭān Mas'ūd with the Saljuq princes Muḥammad, Malik-Shāh and Sulaimān-Shāh, and with 'Abbās, the *wālī* of Rayy. Boz-Aba was executed by Mas'ūd in 542/1147-8 (Bosworth, "Iranian World", 126).

75. Ms.A: *'Abd al-Raḥmān b. Ṭ.ghrbīk.* 'Abd al-Raḥmān Ṭoghan-Yürek was killed by Mas'ūd in 541/1146-7. He was *amīr ḥājib* to Mas'ūd (Ibn al-Athīr, *al-Kāmil,* XI, 76).

76. On f.175a Ibn al-Azraq records that Qara Arslan took Gargar in 546/1151-2.

77. Ms.B adds: "He is now in the *dīwān* of the lord of Arzan."

78. Ṣafiyya Khātūn had married Jamāl al-Dīn Maḥmūd b. İl-aldï, lord of Āmid, in 543/1148-9. The dowry (*ṣadāq*) was 5,000 *dīnārs* and the contract had been drawn up by Ibn Nīsān who came from Āmid to Mayyāfāriqīn.

The *ṣadāq* is a gift made by the bridegroom to the bride when the marriage contract is drawn up and it becomes her property. It also remains hers if the marriage is annulled. (Cf. O. Spies, "mahr", *EI*[1]).

79. Ms.B adds: "He remained on the Hau *(sic)* bridge for a while before going to Tall al-'Alawiyya. Messages went backwards and forwards between them and he (Temür-Tash) took the harvest that year" (f.134a).

and then left Āmid and went back to Mārdīn. After a few days Ibn Nīsān[80] sent two men who stayed in the citadel at Mārdīn for a few days working as labourers (?).[81] Then the vizier Zain al-Dīn went riding one day and on his way up to the citadel, he passed through a narrow place where he was attacked by these two men, one of whom hit him on the head with an axe so that he fell (to the ground). A group of people who were with the vizier went looking for the two men, who said to them: "What do you want? We will go up with you to the *amīr.*" So they went up with the group to the gate of the citadel, with the citizens behind him. When they had gone into the citadel to see the *amīr,* they said: "We have killed the vizier." He said: "Why?" to which they replied "We were ordered to do so." The majority of people said that Ibn Nīsān had plotted against them and killed him. Amīr Ḥusām al-Dīn ordered that the two men should be executed on the vizier's grave. He was buried in Mārdīn. The two men were Ismā'īlīs (*mulāḥida*).

Ḥusām al-Dīn attacked Āmid again and harassed it severely. Bahā' al-Dīn Aus, the vizier of Akhlāṭ, came and met al-Sa'īd Ḥusām al-Dīn outside Āmid, talked to him and interceded on behalf of the people of Āmid. Then Bahā' al-Dīn went into Āmid, met Mu'ayyid al-Dīn b. Nīsān and arranged the matter with him, (whereupon) Mu'ayyid al-Dīn went out to the *amīr* and they made peace. The garrison of Āmid went out to al-Sa'īd Ḥusām al-Dīn and they joined his service and (came) under his command. (Then) he left them.

80. The name of Ibn Nīsān, the vizier of Āmid, as well as that of his "master", Maḥmūd b. Īl-aldï, is mentioned in the inscriptions of 550/1155-6 in the Great Mosque at Āmid (van Berchem and Strzygowski, *Amida,* 61). Van Berchem points out that the protocol of one of these inscriptions is an indication of the true political situation at Āmid at this time. The name of the vizier is mentioned first. Although he has no title, he takes precedence in the inscription over his nominal master, for all the latter's titles (*ibid.,* 62).

81. Ms.A: *fa-aqāmā bi'l-qal'at Mārdīn ya'malāni bi'l-fā'il.*

The precise meaning of this sentence and indeed of this whole anecdote is difficult to grasp. The translation given here represents one possibility, but other solutions could be proposed.

Presumably, the money which Temür-Tash was re-claiming was not to be found; either an unknown party, such as the vizier Zain al-Dīn, had appropriated it and hidden it away somewhere, or Ibn Nīsān, the vizier of Āmid, was unwilling to hand it back and sent assassins to kill the vizier who had possibly prompted Temür-Tash to ask for it in the first place.

Alternatively, it could be argued that *fā'il* means "criminal, guilty party" (cf. Dozy, *Supplément,* II, 271) and that *'amila bi* contains the nuance of "to work secretly or under cover" (Dozy, *Supplément,* II, 173). The sentence would then be translated as: "They stayed in the citadel for a few days (secretly) working for the guilty party."

In the last ten days of Rajab 546 (3-12 November 1151), Nūra Khātūn, daughter of Ḥusām al-Dīn, died at the house of the lord of Arzan, leaving a son who outlived her by a few days before he (too) died. She was buried in Arzan. Al-Sa'īd Ḥusām al-Dīn grieved at her death.[82]

After the murder of the vizier Zain al-Dīn, Ḥusām al-Dīn remained without a vizier. He was content with (the services of) al-Ajall Mu'ayyid al-Daula Abū Manṣūr Khālid b. al-Mubārak b. Mukhtār until he (Ḥusām al-Dīn) died. Mu'ayyid al-Daula performed his task most admirably. Al-Sa'īd Ḥusām al-Dīn remained in power until Thursday 2 Dhu'l-Qa'da 548 (19 January 1154) when he died in Mārdīn.[83] His illness lasted from Saturday until Thursday 2 Dhu'l-Qa'da. He was buried in the *mashhad* below Mārdīn. He ruled Mayyāfāriqīn for 30 years and Mārdīn for 32 years. (f.176b) May God be pleased with him. Ḥusām al-Dīn was a knowledgeable *amīr*, well versed in all the branches of religious knowledge. He liked the *'ulamā'*, maintaining close contact with them, and he honoured skilled craftsmen in every trade. He was generous, munificent and bountiful. He only contemplated killing when it was a necessity and he provided security and protection to an extent which was unknown (even) amongst the pure-blooded Arabs. Amīr Abū Bakr, lord of Naṣībīn, had come to him when he fled from Atābeg Zangī. Ḥusām al-Dīn gave him refuge and when Zangī asked him to hand him over, he would not do so. A serious disagreement between them ensued and Zangī took Dārā and plundered the country. Although al-Sa'īd Ḥusām al-Dīn lost a lot of money, he still would not hand Abū Bakr over, and that man was the reason for the estrangement between al-Sa'īd and Zangī. When Abū Bakr left Ḥusām al-Dīn, he went to

82. Two daughters had now pre-deceased Temür-Tash.
83. For some reason Cahen does not accept this date. He writes that Temür-Tash died at the end of 547/1152 or perhaps in 548/1153 ("Diyār Bakr", 254).
The dates given by other sources for the death of Temür-Tash are as follows:

Ibn al-Qalānisī:	1 Muḥarram, 549/18 March 1154 (*Dhail,* 329)
Bundārī:	1 Muḥarram, 549/18 March 1154 (*Zubdat,* 244)
Sibṭ b. al-Jauzī:	2 Dhu'l-Qa'da 548/19 January 1154 (*Mir'āt,* 218-9)
Ibn al-Athīr:	548/1153-4 (*Atabegs,* 106).

Sulṭān Mas'ūd who seized him and sent him to Zangī. Zangī (then) killed him.[84]

Al-Sa'īd Ḥusām al-Dīn, may God have mercy on him, used to show deference to the members of (important) families and to look after their affairs. He did not contemplate the uprooting of the ancient families. If a member of the turbaned class and the *'ulamā'* came to him, he would give him hospitality, honour him, treat him kindly and minister to all his needs. If he detected a knowledge of any of the religious sciences in a man he would bid him approach, present gifts to him and ask him about what he knew of his science or craft.

When Ḥusām al-Dīn died, I was in the province of the Gurj in the service of the king of the Abkhāz, Dīmīṭrī b. Dā'ūd, the king of the whole area, for I had come to Tiflīs in (5)48 (1153-4) and entered his employ. I accompanied him to the province of al-Lān and of the Abkhāz and to Darband. One day we were near the town of Darband - it was 4 Muḥarram 549 (21 March 1154) - when the king summoned me and said: "Your master Ḥusām al-Dīn has died. I received the news today."

A number of people held the office of governor of Mayyāfāriqīn during the lifetime of Ḥusām al-Dīn. Amongst them were al-Ḥājib Abū Bakr, Bairam and 'Uthmān b. Khumar-Tash al-Ḥājj, each of whom was governor once, except for al-Ḥājib Bairam who held office twice. Thereafter al-Ḥājib 'Abd al-Karīm became governor, and was then dismissed. (He was succeeded by) al-Ḥājib Yūsuf İnal, who was subsequently dismissed and given an *iqṭā'* below Dārā which[85] Atābeg Zangī took from him. Then a *mamlūk* belonging to Ḥusām al-Dīn whose name was Oghuzoghlu became governor of Mayyāfāriqīn for a while and he died (in office). Then Amīr Qaimāz, the eunuch, occupied the citadel with al-Ḥājib (Bairam) for a while. Thereafter, al-Ḥājib Yurunqush was made governor for a while and was succeeded by al-Ḥājib Yūsuf İnal who held office a second time and remained in the governorship until 3 Rajab (5)39 (30 December 1144) when he died and was buried in Mayyāfāriqīn. Then Nāṣir al-Daula Ṣandal became governor in Dhu'l-Qada (5)39 (25 April - 24 May 1145) and he remained (in office) until Rabī' I (5)43 (20 July - 18 August 1148) when he died. (Then) his son Ghars al-Daula İnal remained in the *burj al-mulk* and al-Ḥājib Bairam held the citadel for a while. (Then) İnal assumed sole control as governor and he remained

84. This incident is also related by Ibn al-Athīr when he gives his obituary of Zangī. Zangī laid siege to Mārdīn because Temür-Tash refused to hand over Abū Bakr (*Atabegs*, 79-80).
85. Ibn Shaddād says this *iqṭā'* was Sarja (*Jazīra*, f.104b).

in office until al-Sa'īd Ḥusām al-Dīn died, as we have related, God willing (!) (*sic*).

I will relate the genealogy of the Artuqids and what information has come to me about them and what descendants remain of (f.177a) Amīr Artuq, may God have mercy on him.[86]

¶ When Amīr Artuq died he left a number of children; amongst them were Amīr Sukmān, Najm al-Dīn İl-Ghāzī, Bahrām, 'Abd al-Jabbār, Siyāwush, Alp-Yaruq, another son called Bektash and another whose name was Alp-Tash. These sons are the ones who had children whose descendants have remained until now in Diyār Bakr. Artuq left other children besides these, but as I have not heard that they have descendants alive I have omitted to mention them.

As for Sukmān, he took Ḥiṣn Kaifā (and he) remained (there) for a while; then he died in 506 (1112-3). He left Amīr Rukn al-Daula Dā'ūd, and Amīr Ibrāhīm, who ruled Ḥiṣn Kaifā after his father for a while and (then) died. Rukn al-Daula Dā'ūd took the city after Ibrāhīm. Sukmān (also left) Azar Khātūn. Rukn al-Daula ruled Ḥiṣn Kaifā, subsequently conquering other places too. Dā'ūd left four sons: Arslan Ṭoghmïsh, Qara Arslan, Sulaimān and Maḥmūd. As for Arslan Ṭoghmïsh, he died, having taken possession of Mīzgard after his father. Arslan Ṭoghmïsh left a son by the daughter of al-Sa'īd Ḥusām al-Dīn but the son died shortly after his father. As for Sulaimān, he died leaving a son called Ya'qūb, who is now in the service of al-Mālik Najm al-Dīn, and another who is in the service of Jamāl al-Dīn in Ḥānī. As for Maḥmūd, he took Ṭanzī and al-Qarshiyya.[87] When he died, he left a son called Dā'ūd who is now in the service of the sons of his uncle Fakhr al-Dīn in Ḥiṣn Kaifā. As for Fakhr al-Dīn Qara Arslan, he took over the whole of his father's territory after the latter had died, as we have already mentioned.

When he died, he left two sons: Nūr al-Dīn Muḥammad and 'Imād al-Dīn Abū Bakr. It was Nūr al-Dīn who succeeded him and who is now in power. Fakhr al-Dīn (also) left a number of daughters.

As for Bahrām b. Artuq, he left Amīr Nūr al-Daula Balak who held Khartabirt, Bālū and its surrounding area until Shams al-Daula Sulaimān b. İl-Ghāzī seized these possessions from him. When

86. The information provided in the rest of the translation of Ms.A about the genealogy of the Artuqids has been included in Appendix B, where there is a genealogical table. Any other minor comments on the rest of the text or translation are included below.

87. Ms.A: *al-Q.rīsha*. This should be al-Qarshiyya, which is listed by Ibn Shaddād as a fortress in Diyār Bakr (*Jazīra*, f.65b). Cahen does not know precisely where it was situated. He thinks it was near Ṭanzī ("Diyār Bakr", 223).

Sulaimān died, Amīr Dā'ūd took them. Balak had married Princess Farkhundā Khātūn, daughter of Malik Riḍwān, after Najm al-Dīn İl-Ghāzī, and it was Balak who (actually) consummated his marriage with her. He seized territory near the Euphrates and waged war against the Franks until he was killed below Manbij as we have already mentioned. He left a daughter whom Fakhr al-Dīn Qara Arslan married and he died before her.

As for Siyāwush b. Artuq, he left Amīr Yūnus al-Ḥarāmī whom I saw in the service of al-Sa'īd Ḥusām al-Dīn (may God have mercy on him). Yūnus al-Ḥarāmī left sons, some of whom are in the service of Fakhr al-Dīn in Ḥiṣn Kaifā. (Siyāwush also left) Sevinch who is in Ḥānī in the service of Jamāl al-Dīn, the brother of al-Mālik Najm al-Dīn. Sevinch married the daughter of Amīr Shīrbārīk by whom he had a son whose name was Shāh Malik. After she died he married one of her sisters.

As for Alp-Yaruq b. Artuq, he left sons, amongst whom was Amīr 'Alī, the *malik* of Jabal Jūr, who begat Amīr Maudūd - who was (also) called Shīrbārīk - and another son who died, whose name was Maḥmūd. 'Alī also had a son whose name was (Ms. lacuna) who is in Khartabirt. Shāh Malik married the daughter of Shīrbārīk in 507 (*sic)* (1113-4). Shīrbārīk sired Sevinch and Ismā'īl and Ṭoghrïl Beg and a number of daughters. He (also) had a son, whose name was Zangī, from a slave girl. (f.177b) Zangī remained in the service of his father for a while, and (then) went to Egypt where he died in the reign of Shāwar.[88] As for Ṭoghrïl Beg, he died in Ḥiṣn Kaifā and was brought to Mayyāfāriqīn. As for Sevinch, who was the eldest of them, he married Ṣafiyya Khātūn, daughter of Malik Riḍwān, and he died leaving no issue. As for Ismā'īl, he had two sons and he is in the service of al-Mālik Najm al-Dīn. Shīrbārīk remained in the service of Malik Ḥusām al-Dīn until the latter died. (Then) he transferred to the service of Fakhr al-Dīn Qara Arslan and remained with him for a time. (Thereafter) he returned to the service of al-Mālik Najm al-Dīn and he died in Rajab of the year 566 (10 March - 11 April 1170). He was buried in a village belonging to them in the lowest of graves.

As for 'Abd al-Jabbār b. Artuq, he left three sons: Yaghï-Sïyan, Arslan and Sulaimān. As for Yaghï-Sïyan, he moved on and served in the province of Akhlāṭ with the daughter of Sukmān. Whilst he was there, he had two sons, Amīr Aḥmad and another who had the *laqab* 'Izz al-Dīn. He moved to the service of Fakhr al-Dīn Qara Arslan in Ḥiṣn Kaifā with whom he attained a most powerful position. Fakhr

88. Shawār was the famous Egyptian vizier who negotiated with Nūr al-Dīn over the conquest of Egypt (cf. Runciman, *op.cit.*, II, 367-9).

al-Dīn married him to the daughter of his brother Arslan Ṭoghmïsh. Yaghï-Sïyan died of epilepsy, leaving a son who is now in the service of the sons of Fakhr al-Dīn.

As for Alp-Tash, he left Amīr 'Alī al-Ḥarāmī who died in the service of Ḥusām al-Dīn. He left two sons, one of whom was Abū Bakr who became a *Ṣūfī* and was a *faqīr*. He had a long life and he is in the service of the descendants of Fakhr al-Dīn in Ḥiṣn Kaifā.

As for Amīr Arslan b. 'Abd al-Jabbār, he took Jabal Jūr, Dhu'l-Qarnain and al-Sīwān. After a while al-Sa'īd Ḥusām al-Dīn took them from him. He moved to the service of Rukn al-Daula Dā'ūd in Ḥiṣn Kaifā where he died. He left sons, amongst whom were Bulāq and Maḥmūd, and daughters. He gave one daughter in marriage in his life-time to Za'īm al-Daula Musayyib b. Mālik, lord of al-Raqqa, and their descendants remained in the service of Fakhr al-Dīn. Amīr Bulāq moved to the service of al-Mālik Najm al-Dīn where he died.

As for Sulaimān, whose *laqab* was Badr al-Daula, he conquered Aleppo and married the *khātūn*, the princess, the daughter of Riḍwān, who was (also) the wife of Amīr Balak. He had a son by her whose name was Köpek and whose *laqab* was Jalāl al-Mulūk. When Aleppo was taken from him, he went into the service of al-Sa'īd Ḥusām al-Dīn who gave him the town of Qalb as an *iqṭā'*.[89] He fortified the town and he remained in his service until he died. The princess came to Mārdīn after Sulaimān's death accompanied by his son. She settled in Mārdīn and al-Sa'īd Ḥusām al-Dīn married her as we have related. He gave her son Jalāl al-Mulūk in marriage to his daughter, Hadiyya Khātūn, in (5)47 (1152-3). Jalāl al-Mulūk lived until 554 (1159) when he died outside Naṣībīn as we shall relate, if God wills.

As for the other son called Bektash, he sired Arslan Ṭoghmïsh who moved to the service of Atābeg Ṭogh-Tegin, lord of Damascus, for he had a most powerful position with him. He married 'Ā'isha Khātūn, daughter of the brother of the vizier (f.178a) Muḥammad al-Dvīnī, and lived in Damascus until 543 (1148-9) in the service of the descendants of Ṭogh-Tegin. He went to Mosul and lived in the service of its lord for a short time; then he moved to the service of al-Sa'īd Ḥusām al-Dīn who honoured him and gave him many *iqṭā's* at the end of (5)44 (1149-50) when he took Dārā. He remained for a short time and then died, leaving three sons. One of them, who had the *laqab* Shams al-Daula, remained for a period of two years in the service of al-Sa'īd (Ḥusām al-Dīn) after (the death of) his father and then died.

89. Qalb was a fortress in Diyār Bakr (Ibn Shaddād, *Jazīra*, f.65b).

The other two sons, Mas'ūd and Balak, remained. Mas'ūd remained in the service of al-Mālik Najm al-Dīn for a while before transferring to the service of Fakhr al-Dīn Qara Arslan. As for Balak, he remained in the service of al-Mālik Najm al-Dīn until (5)67 (1171-2). (Then) he became an ascetic, breaking away (from worldly things), and he placed himself in the Masjid Yāqūt near the Huwa gate at the top of the *rabaḍ* where he is living to this day.

As for Najm al-Dīn İl-Ghāzī, he had a number of children, including Ayāz and al-Bazm, both killed in his life-time, and Guhar Khātūn. As for Ayāz, he sired Amīr Shihāb al-Dīn Muḥammad b. Ayāz and a daughter from the *khātūn* whom Sa'd al-Daula İl-aldï, lord of Āmid, married. İl-aldï has a son from her in Āmid. As for Shihāb al-Dīn Muḥammad, he grew up in the service of his uncle al-Sa'īd Ḥusām al-Dīn who gave him Tall Bashmī as an *iqṭā'*. He was honoured by Ḥusām al-Dīn until the latter died. He remained a while after his death and then went to Syria, to the service of Nūr al-Dīn. Nūr al-Dīn gave him many *iqṭā's* and he has remained in his service until now. Shihāb al-Dīn has three sons who are now in the service of Nūr al-Dīn.

Najm al-Dīn had a son from a concubine. His name was 'Umar. He married her to Amīr the general (ms. lacuna). His son ('Umar) died leaving no issue. Najm al-Dīn had a son whose name was Naṣr from a slave-girl whom he married to the *ḥājib* 'Umar al-Khāṣṣ. He died and left no issue.

Najm al-Dīn married Guhar Khātūn to Saif al-Daula Dubais. She had by him Amīr 'Izz al-Dīn Muḥammad who remained with her in Mārdīn until Dubais was killed. (Thereafter) he went to al-Ḥilla where he ruled with his brothers. After a while he returned to the service of al-Mālik Najm al-Dīn. He went to and fro several times and died after his mother. She had died in the year 559(1163-4) and she was buried in Mārdīn. 'Izz al-Dīn left a son who is now in the service of Shihāb al-Dīn Muḥammad b. Ayāz.

Najm al-Dīn had a daughter whom he called 'Aina Khātūn and whom Amīr İl-aldï, lord of Āmid, married. He had by her Jamāl al-Dīn Shams al-Mulūk who is now lord of Āmid. When 'Aina Khātūn died, he married the sister of Shihāb al-Dīn as we have related. Najm al-Dīn had a daughter whose name was Safra Khātūn whom Ḥusām al-Dīn Qurtï b. Ṭoghan Arslan, lord of Arzan and Bitlīs, married. She died, leaving a son whose name is Yaghï-Basan (f.178b); he is now in the service of Fakhr al-Dīn Daulat-Shāh, his uncle. Najm al-Dīn (also) sired Shams al-Daula Sulaimān, who ruled Mayyāfāriqīn after his father until he (Sulaimān) died. He left a son called Maḥmūd whom I saw in Mārdīn. He was in a very bad way and I don't know what became of him.

Najm al-Dīn (also) had al-Sa'īd Ḥusām al-Dīn who was the pride of the house and the head of the family. He took possession of Mārdīn, as we have related, after his father and he took Mayyāfāriqīn after his brother. He remained (there) until he died, leaving children: al-Mālik Najm al-Dīn Alpï who ruled after his father; Jamāl al-Dīn Qurtï (?) to whom his brother gave Ḥānī, al-Sīwān and Ḥiṣn Qalb; Ṣamṣām al-Dīn Bahrām, lord of Dārā;[90] Hadiyya Khātūn who is with her brother Jamāl al-Dīn in Ḥānī; Zumurrud Khātūn in Mosul - (whose husband) Quṭb al-Dīn Maudūd b. Zangī died with her, leaving four children by her, including Malik al-Mulūk Saif Ghāzī b. Maudūd, whom we will mention later, God willing - Ṣafiyya Khātūn, wife of the lord of Āmid, and Nūra Khātūn, wife of the lord of Arzan, who died in his life-time, as we have already related. May God have mercy on him and be pleased with him. This is what has reached me of the genealogy of those Artuqids that have remained. God knows best what is true.

90. The territory of Temür-Tash was divided out as follows: Najm al-Dīn Alpï ruled at Mārdīn, Jamāl al-Dīn at Ḥānī and Ṣamṣām al-Dīn at Dārā (Michael the Syrian, *Chronique,* 311).

ذكر ولاية[1] نجم الدين الغازى[2] وملكه في[3] ميفرقين

قيل لما فتح ابن جهير ديار بكر كان الامير ارتق معه فلما استقر ولم يبق له موضع انفصل عنه ومضى لما جاء ملكشاه الى الشام وملك بيت المقدس وما حوله واقام بالساحل ومات هناك وملك بيت المقدس بعده ولداه[4] الامير سكمان والامير نجم الدين الغازى مدة

وسار نجم الدين الغازى الى السلطان محمد وبقى فى خدمته واقطعه حلوان مدة ثم اعطاه شحنكية[5] العراق فاقام ببغداد وملك الافرنج الساحل وبيت المقدس فوصل الامير سكمان الى هذه البلاد وملك حصن كيفا وكان ملك الامير الياقوتي ماردين فوصل نجم الدين الغازى الى هذه البلاد ومات الياقوتي[6] وكان فيها من قبل الياقوتي فدخل تحت طاعة سكمان من حصن كيفا وبقي بها وملكها قيل في سنة ثمان وتسعين واربعمائة مات الامير سكمان وبقي فيها الى ان مات[7] الامير سكمان

وملك بعده ولده الامير ابراهيم بن سكمان فنفذ الى شمس بماردين[8] واخذ ابنا له رهينة وبقي عنده بحصن كيفا مدة ثم بلغه انه اساء[9] الى[10] ولده وحبسه فلما وصل نجم الدين الغازى سلمها اليه

وبقي الامير ابراهيم مدة ثم مات بحصن كيفا وولي موضعه اخوه

[1] Ms. B ذكر ابتداء ولاية
[2] Ms. B uses the form ايل غازى throughout.
[3] Ms. في is written above the line.
[4] Ms. ولده
[5] Ms. سنجر; Ms. B شحنكية
[6] Ms. الباقون
[7] Ms. مات is illegible.
[8] Ms. in the margin بماردين صح
[9] Ms. اسا
[10] Ms. الى is written above the line.

الامير داود بعد اخيه سكمان[11] وبقي مدة وكان الامير شمس وماردين بيده لم يسلمها الى احد وحضر نجم الدين وسلمها اليه في سنة سبع وخمسمائة حصلت للغازى واولاده من ذلك اليوم الى الان

واما الامير شمس فاولد الامير سنقر[12] واولد سنقر يوسف واولد يوسف رسول وقيل ملك ماردين في سنة سبع او[13] ثمان وخمسمائة على ان بقي بها الى سنة اثنتي عشرة وخمسمائة

ثم نفذ الى[14] السلطان يقول له ان ميافارقين خربت واضمحلت وهي بلد لا يرى مثله فنفذ السلطان الى الدزبك[15] رسولا يأمره ان يسلم ميفرقين الى نجم الدين الغازى فحضر وسلمها اليه فدخل اليها في رابع عشر جمادى الاخرة سنة اثنتي عشرة وخمسمائة وملكها وخرج الدزبك ونزل على[16] الروابي واقام ثلثة ايام فلما كان في اليوم الرابع وصله رسول مجد من السلطان يقول له لا تسلم فوجد الامر قد فات واستقر نجم الدين بميفرقين واظهر العدل والاحسان[17] الى الناس وازال عنهم الاثقال والاقساط والانزال[18] من دورها وكان الناس من النزل في دورهم في شدة شديدة

وكان اكثرها خرابا[19] لاختلاف الدول وتغير الاصحاب كل قليل ومن يملكهم يحيف عليهم ويظلمهم ويصادرهم لعلمه انه لا يقيم ولا يدوم ملكه ومن حيث ملك نجم الدين الغازى استقر وطابت قلوبهم واستقر الناس في دورهم

[11] Ms. *sic*.

[12] Ms. يو سنقر

[13] Ms. و

[14] الى added.

[15] This name is very uncertain. Ms. f. 161a, l. 4: الرزبك. Ms. f. 161a, l. 5: الرزبك Marsh 333, f. 101b: زنكي 'Awaḍ, *op. cit.*, 283: الرزبيكي.

[16] Ms. الى on the line, على above it.

[17] Ms. العدل والانصاف والاحسان

[18] Marsh 333 النِزال (f. 102a).

[19] Ms. خراب

وحصلت الاجناد التي ما لهم دور[20] ينزلون بها ويضربون لهم في خرابات المدينة خركاهات[21] لان اكثر المدينة كانت خرابا وكانت الطرقات مخيفة من الحرامية وقطاع الطريق بحيث انه كان لا تقدر القافلة تمضي الى آمد الا ومعها الشحنة والخيل وكذلك الى ارزن وحصن كيفا وحاني وماردين محتاجون من يخفرهم في المسافة القريبة لخراب البلاد والضياع فمن حيث ملك نجم الدين امنت الطرقات والبلاد وانهزمت الحرامية وانعمرت الضياع وبدأت[22] ميفرقين في العمارة وساس الناس احسن سياسة

وبقي الى سنة ست عشرة[23] وخمسمائة وملك حلب ولقي الافرنج وكسرهم كسرة عظيمة[24] وغنم اموالهم واسر منهم خلقا عظيما وهي كسرة البلاط واما حلب فانه اخذها من سلطان شاه بن الملك رضوان وكان اخذها من الامير ابن ملك[25]

قيل وفي سنة ثلث عشرة[26] وخمسمائة احترق جامع آمد

وفي سنة اربع عشرة[27] وخمسمائة ملك نجم الدين نصيبين وسار اليه القاضي علم الدين بن[28] نباتة وجملة من اهل ميفرقين فلقوه بها وهنأوه[29] بفتحها وخلع عليهم واحسن اليهم وعادوا[30] الى ميفرقين

قيل وفي سنة خمس عشرة[31] وخمسمائة نفذ[32] اهل تفليس الى نجم

[20] Marsh 333 مساكن (f. 102a).
[21] Ms. خركاوات; Ms. B خركاهات; Marsh 333 (f. 102a) خركاهات.
[22] Ms. بدت
[23] Ms. ستة عشرة but Ms. B ثلث عشرة
[24] Ms. كسرة is written above the line.
[25] Ms. *sic*.
[26] Ms. ثلث عشر
[27] Ms. اربعة عشر
[28] Ms. B علم الدين ابو الحسن بن
[29] Ms. هنوه
[30] Marsh 333 اجازهم (f. 102a).
[31] Ms. خمسة عشر
[32] Ms. نفذوا

الدين الغازى يستدعونه ليسلموا اليه تفليس وكان لها بيد اهلها مقدار[33] اربعين سنة وكان ملاكها قوما[34] من اهلها يسمون[35] بني جعفر من مقدار[36] مأتي سنة ثم انقرض كبارهم واضمحلوا فعاد امرها (*f. 161b*) الى اهلها[37] وكان كل شهر يلي امرهم واحد منهم[38] وبقوا كذلك مدة اربعين سنة

وكان الملك داود[39] ملك الابخاز والكرج قد ضايقها مضايقة شديدة واضمحلت وكان قد نفذوا الى السلطان طغربك بن السلطان محمد وكان ملك خنزى وآران فنفذ لهم شحنة وزادت[40] مضايقة ملك الكرج لهم وبقوا على هذا مدة فاتفقوا ان يحملوا[41] له في كل سنة عشرة آلاف[42] دينار ويكون عندهم شحنة معه عشرة[43] فوارس[44] فبقوا على ذلك مدة فنفذوا الى نجم الدين الغازى يستدعونه فسار ومعه عساكر عظيمة ومعه دبيس بن صدقة[45] ملك العرب وكان صهر نجم الدين على ابنته كهار خاتون وكان قد وصل اليه في تلك السنة فسار بالعساكر ونفذ الى شمس الدولة طغان آرسلان صاحب ارزن وبدليس وكان له مدينة دوين وامره ان يدخل من شرقي تفليس وسار واخذ معه القاضي علم الدين بن نباتة ومعه ولده القاضي عَلَم الدين ابو الفتح

33 Ms. مقدر
34 Ms. قوم
35 Ms. بنو
36 Ms. مقدر
37 Ms. الى اهلها is repeated.
38 Ms. منهم صح is written above امرهم
39 Ms. B داوود
40 Ms. فنفذ لهم شحنة ذات مضايقة In the right margin is زادت. Amedroz omits ذات too (*op. cit.*, 205). Ms. B ما زالت
41 Ms. يحملون
42 Ms. الف
43 Ms. عشر
44 Ms. B adds لا غير
45 Ms. B المزيدى

الكبير هو الان قاضي ماردين والوزير ابي[46] تمام بن عبدون وسار معه فوصلوا الى ارزن الروم وتخلف القاضي والوزير بارزن الروم

ودخل بالعساكر من ولاية الغرس وطريق ترياليث واتفقوا ان تجتمع العساكر اجمع على باب تفليس وتجهز السلطان طغر[47]بك من ناحية جنزى وسار طغان آرسلان الاحدب من دوين ووصل نجم الدين الى ان بقي بينه وبين تفليس الجبل مقدار[48] نصف يوم وخرج الملك داود ومعه ولده ديميطرى من جانب الغرب في عساكر عظيمة وكان يحدر عليهم من الجبل وهم في لحفه ولم تكن[49] وصلت عساكر السلطان طغربك ولا شمس الدولة الاحدب بمن معه وتقاتلوا قتالا عظيما وكسر نجم الدين وقتل منه خلقا كثيرا وغنم الكفار منهم غنيمة عظيمة وخرج نجم الدين ودبيس[50] في نفر يسير بحيث ان بقي عندهم من الاسرى الى زماننا

القد رأيت موضع الوقعة حين دخلت الى تفليس في سنة ثمان واربعين وخمسمائة فاقمت بها ثم وصلت الى خدمة ملك الابخاز وبقيت عنده وخرجت معه وسرت في ولايته معه مقدار[51] نيف وسبعين يوما واجتاز الى الان[52] وطرف الدربند والى ولاية الابخاز[53] ولقد وصلنا بعض الايام في ولاية الابخاز الى مرج[54] واسع تحت جبل في قلعة شامخة فنزل الملك[55] هناك وقال لي ملك الابخاز يا فلان ان في هذه

[46] Ms. ابو
[47] Ms. *sic.*; Ms. B طغرل
[48] Ms. مقدر
[49] Ms. يكن
[50] Ms. ودبيس صح is written in the margin.
[51] Ms. مقدر
[52] Ms. *sic.*
[53] Ms. الابخاز لقد وصلنا; Ms. B ولقد وصلنا
[54] Ms. برج or مرج
[55] The phrase نزل الملك is barely legible. Ms. B فنزل الملك

القلعة رجلا اسيرا مستغربا[56] من نوبة الغازى فاصعد اليه[57] من الغد وابصره واسأله[58] من اين هو فعولت على ذلك وقلت اطلبه من الملك ليطلقه فبت تلك الليلة فلما كان من وقت السحر ضرب بوق الرحيل[59] لانه وصل اليه الخبر ان بعض ولايته[60] قد تشوشت (*f. 162a*) عليه فحين وصله الخبر رحل ورحل الناس ولم يقدر الله[61] الاجتماع بذلك الرجل

وقيل في سنة خمس عشرة[62] وخمسمائة مات والاول اصح[63] الملك رضوان بحلب ولما كسر نجم الدين وعاد بمن بقي معه[64] رحل ملك الابخاز بالغنائم والاسرى ونزل على تفليس وحاصرها مدة ثم هدم سورها من قبل الغرب ودخلها سيفا واحرقها ونهبها بعد ثلثة ايام امن اهلها وطيب قلوبهم ووعدهم بالجميل

واسقط عنهم تلك السنة الاثقال والمؤن والاقساط والخراج وشرط للمسلمين كلما ارادوه من الشرط الذى هو الان باق بها انه لا يعبر الى جانب المسلمين والمدينة الخنزير[65] ولا يذبح بها ولا في سوقها وضرب لهم الدراهم[66] وعليها اسم السلطان والخليفة في الوجه الواحد وفي الوجه[67] اسم الله واسم النبي عليه السلام واسمه على جانب الدرهم ونادى في البلد انه من آذى[68] مسلما فقد اهدر دمه وشرط لهم الاذان

56 Ms. رجل اسير مستعرب Ms. B مستعرب
57 Ms. فاصعد اليه is repeated.
58 Ms. اسله
59 Ms. B adds من وقته
60 Ms. B بعض الولايات
61 This word is not clear in Ms. A. Ms. B has الله. Amedroz reads على (*op. cit.*, 206).
62 Ms. خمسة عشر
63 Cf. p. 41, n. 81.
64 Ms. B has في عشرين فارسا after عاد
65 Ms. has a lacuna here. Ms. B الخنزير
66 Ms. الدارهم
67 Ms. *sic*.

والصلاة والقراءة ظاهرا وان يخطب يوم الجمعة ويصلى ويدعى[69] للخليفة والسلطان ولا يدعى لغيرهما[70] على المنبر وشرط ان حمام اسماعيل بتفليس لا يدخله[71] كرجي ولا ارمني ولا يهودى ووظف[72] خدمة الكرجي في السنة خمسة دنانير[73] وخدمة اليهودى اربعة دنانير[74] وخدمة المسلم ثلثة[75] دنانير[76] واحسن الى المسلمين غاية الاحسان وجعل لاهل العلم والدين والصوفية اكرم[77] المنازل وما ليس لهم عند المسلمين

ولقد رايت هذه الشروط كلها[78] لما دخلت الى تفليس في سنة ثمان واربعين وخمسمائة ولقد رايت ملك الابخاز ديميطرى الذى كنت في خدمته وقد قدم[79] الى تفليس واقام بها اياما ونزل ذات يوم جمعة الى[80] الجامع وجلس على دكة مقابل الخطيب فوقف موضعه حتى خطب الخطيب . . .[81] سمع الخطبة جميعها ثم خرج واطلق برسم الجامع مأتي دينار احمر[82] وكنت ارى العلماء والوعاظ والاشراف الذين يقصدونه[83] والصوفية والذين يصلون اليه فيكرمهم ويعطيهم ويحترمهم

68 Ms. اذا

69 Ms. يدعا

70 Ms. والسلطان ولا يدعى لغيرهما صح is written in the left margin.

71 Ms. يدخلها

72 Ms. وضف

73 Ms. دنانيرًا

74 Ms. دنانيرًا

75 Ms. ثلث

76 Ms. دنانيرًا

77 Ms. اكرام

78 Ms. ولقد رأيت هذه الشروط جميعا باقية للمسلمين كلها

79 Ms. is damaged here. Ms. B has وقد قدم. Amedroz has نزل الى (*op. cit.*, 206).

80 The Ms. is damaged here. Ms. B has الى

81 The Ms. is damaged here. Amedroz has وكل الناس يسمع الخطبة (*op. cit.*, 206). The subject matter in Ms. B is ordered differently here but mentions that the people prayed. A possible reading here might therefore be صلى الناس

82 Ms. احمرًا

83 The Ms. is illegible here. Ms. B الذين يقصدونه

ويعتمد معهم ما ليس بمثله[84] ولقد كنت ارى لاحترامه للمسلمين ما لو انهم ببغداد ما احترموا تلك الحرمة

قيل وفي سنة ست عشرة وخمسمائة تزلزلت مدينة جنزى وهي كنجة وانخسف طرف منها وانهدم سورها وسار الملك داود باصحابه وخيله ورجاله[85] وقصدها ونهب اموالهم وما كان فيها وقتل منهم خلقا عظيما وسبى[86] منهم خلقا عظيما لا يحصى بحيث دخلت الاسارى الى تفليس على العجل من كثرتهم (*f. 162b*) سيقوا المسلمون[87] مثل قطعات الاغنام اسارى ودخل بهم الى تفليس فاشترى اهل تفليس اكثرهم واطلقوهم وقال لي جماعة من اهل تفليس اننا ما افتقرنا الا من تلك السنة

قيل وفي سنة خمس عشرة[88] وخمسمائة قتل مودود[89] بجامع دمشق ودفن بالبرج

قيل وفي سنة خمس عشرة[90] وخمسمائة عاد نجم الدين الى ماردين[91] واقام بها الى[92] سنة ست عشرة[93] وخمسمائة وخرج الى اوسل[94] الهينة من بلد ميفرقين واقام هناك ومعه زوجته الخاتون بنت تغرتكين[95] صاحب دمشق فمرض وتوفي يوم الخميس سابع عشرين رمضان فحمل ليلا وركب ولده الامير شمس الدولة سليمن والخاتون ووصلوا ميفرقين ليلا ووصلوا الى باب الهوة واجلسوا الامير على فرسه

[84] Ms. مثله
[85] Ms. رجله
[86] Ms. سبا
[87] Ms. المسلمين
[88] Ms. خمسة عشر
[89] Ms. ممدود
[90] Ms. خمسة عشر
[91] Ms. B ميردين
[92] الى is supplied from Ms. B
[93] Ms. ست; Ms. B ست عشرة
[94] The name occurs twice in Ms. B اوسل (f. 104b), اوشل (f. 105a). Marsh 333 اوشل (f. 102b).
[95] Ms. *sic.*; Ms. B طغتكين

ومن ورائه رجل يمسكه وتقدموا وصاحوا فنزل الوالي وكان اسمه كزغلي[96] فدخل شيخ ممن صحب الامير نجم الدين من اول زمانه وكلم· شمس الدولة والخاتون ففتح الباب فقالوا ان الامير مريض فلما حصلوا في ارض القصر صاحوا وضجوا[97] وقالوا مات الامير في هذه الساعة

واصبح الناس وصعد اهل البلد ومن كان بها من الجند الى القصر وغسل الامير وصلي عليه ودفن بالسدلي مدة ثم اخرج ودفن في مسجد الامير شرقي قبة السلطان فدفن هناك

وكان نجم الدين الغازى قد تزوج بفرخندا خاتون بنت الملك رضوان لما ملك حلب وعقد عليها ولم يدخل بها ولا رآها ومات ولم يرها[98] تزوجها بعده الامير بلك بن[99] بهرام بن[100] ارتق

قيل واستقر شمس الدولة سليمن بميفرقين واستوزر عبد الملك بن[101] ثابت ورد الامور اليه واخذ خربرت من الامير بلك وبقيت معه الى ان مات واخذها الامير داود واخذ بلد حزة من الامير داود واخذ الضياع التي[102] اخذها حسام الدولة[103] صاحب ارزن من بلد ميفرقين

وفي سنة سبع عشرة[104] قتل الافضل امير الجيوش بمصر قتلته الباطنية

وترك والي ميفرقين في برج الملك مملوكه ختلج شاه ونفذ خطب سيدة خاتون بنت السلطان قليج آرسلان بن سليمن بن قطلمش ومضى

[96] Ms. *sic*.; Ms. B *sic*.
[97] Ms. B adds وحط الامير after ضجوا
[98] Ms. لم يراها
[99] Ms. ابن
[100] Ms. ابن
[101] Ms. ابن
[102] Ms. الذى
[103] Ms. الدين
[104] Ms. سبعة عشر

القاضي تاج الدين ابو سالم بن نباتة احضرها اليه من ملطية ودخل بها وكان مقامه بميفرقين

وكان لما مات نجم الدين ان السعيد حسام الدين تمرداش[105] ولده[106] بماردين فملك ماردين واستبد بها وكان معه الصاحب الحاجب شمس الحجاب محمد اكديش وكان زوجه نجم الدين الغازى بام السعيد حسام الدين

قيل وفي سادس عشرين ربيع الاخر مات القاضي علم الدين ابو الحسن علي بن[107] يحيى بن[108] نباتة بميفرقين وولي القاضي ولده تاج الدين القضاء وهو ابو سالم رحمه الله وخلع عليه شمس الدولة واكرمه وولاه موضع ابيه واستقر في القضاء وكان ولد لشمس الدولة ابنا اسمه محمود ولقد رأيته بماردين وهو (*f. 163a*) في اسوأ حال من سو طريقته[109] وقبح سيرته في حق نفسه وخروجه عن طاعة اهل بيته[110] ورذالة نفسه وما اعلم ما كان منه وكان شمس الدولة اميرا عادلا حسن السيرة[111] مقداما شجاعا وعاش الى الخميس في سادس[112] شهر رمضان وكان وقت[113] العصر فمات سنة ثمان عشرة وخمسمائة ودفن عند ابيه في مسجد الامير واستبد الوالي ختلشاه بميفرقين وحصلت له وتحت حكمه

105 Ms. *sic*.
106 Ms. وولده
107 Ms. ابن
108 Ms. ابن
109 Ms. A في اسو حال من سو طرقتيه; Ms. B سو حال من سو طريقته (f. 106b).
110 Ms. B adds وقلة همته after بينه
111 Ms. السرية
112 Ms. سادس عادس (?).
113 Ms. واقت

ذكر ولاية حسام الدين

قيل لما مات شمس الدولة استبد ختلشاه بميفرقين والوزير عبد الملك فوصل حسام الدين وحضر بباب المدينة ونزل في خيم ظاهر البلد وراسل[1] ختلشاه وكان الامير داود بن سكمان صاحب حصن كيفا هم بالخروج فسبق السعيد حسام الدين وراسل ختلشاه وحلف له على الذى اراد وحلف ان لا يغير على اهل البلد شيأ وان يستوزر عبد الملك فحلف على ما اقترحوا ودخل البلد في شوال سنة ثمان عشرة[2] وخمسمائة واستوزر عبد الملك واستقر حاله وحصل له جميع ما كان لابيه نجم الدين واحسن الى الناس واحبوه واستبد بالملك

وتزوج بزوجة اخيه الامير اياس بن نجم الدين وكان له منها الامير شهاب الدين محمد بن اياس[3] واولد منها بنتا هي صفية خاتون وهي اول اولاده وبقي مدة وتزوج بالخاتون بنت الامير غازى من ارزن الروم ووصلت الى ميفرقين[4] واولد منها الصاحب نجم الدين آلبي في سنة عشرين وخمسمائة ثم اولد الامير جمال الدين سربي في سنة احدى وعشرين وخمسمائة وملك حسام الدين البلاد ثم اولد هدية[5] خاتون ثم اولد الامير صمصام الدين بهرام في سنة . . .[6] وخمسمائة

وملك حسام الدين حلب وبقيت معه مدة ثم انه عاوض بها . . .[7] او سلم حلب وخرجت عن يده

[1] The Ms. has an initial ا deleted and a second ا placed between the ر and the س

[2] Ms. ثمان عشر

[3] Ms. الياس

[4] Ms. B adds ودخل بها after this name.

[5] Ms. B هده

[6] Ms. has a lacuna.

[7] Ms. is illegible here.

قيل وخرج السلطان محمود الى العراق واراد الدخول فمنعه الخليفة المسترشد وجرى بينهما قتال كثير[8] وكسر المسترشد ونهب ما كان معه ودخل العراق بغير اذنه وبقي مدة واصطلحا جيدا

قيل وفي سنة تسع عشرة[9] او في اول سنة عشرين وخمسمائة[10] قتل البرسقي بجامع الموصل قتلته[11] الباطنية وولي ولده مسعود البلاد من ديار ربيعة وغيرها واجتمع بهاء الدين القاضي الشهرزورى ونصير الدين جقر وصلاح الدين محمد اليغسياني[12] وحصلوا خزانة وخدمة ونزلوا الى بغداد ليخدموا[13] السلطان محمود ويقروا[14] الامير مسعود ولد البرسقي في البلاد لما وصلوا ارتأوا[15] وقالوا ان هذا صبي ولا يقوم (*f. 163b*) بالملك[16] وربما لا يدبر البلاد ويكون الخيف علينا فاقتضى رأيهم انهم اجتمعوا بقسيم الدولة زنكي بن آق سنقر وكان شحنة بغداد في تلك السنة وقرروا معه ما ارادوا من مصالحهم واستحلفوه ان يكون لبهاء الدين قضاء الموصل وجميع البلاد وما فيها من القضاء والامور الدينية له فحلف ان تكون الحجبة وامارة العسكر لصلاح الدين وان تكون ولاية الموصل وجميع البلاد الى نصير الدين ويولى فيها من يراه فحلف لهم على ذلك وتقرر الامر اليهم بينهم ثم انهم خدموا السلطان واصحابه والخليفة واصحابه بالمال الذى وصل معهم وطلبوا[17] زنكي فسلم اليه السلطان ابنيه آلب رسلان[18] والخفاجي وحصل اتابكهما ووقع[19] له

[8] Ms. كثيرًا
[9] Ms. تسعة عشر
[10] Ms. B has في سنة احدى وعشرين وخمسمائة after قيل
[11] Ms. قتله
[12] Ms. B الاغسياني
[13] Ms. ليخدم
[14] Ms. ويقر
[15] Ms. ارتوا
[16] Ms. B adds ولا حمل after بالملك
[17] Ms. B has وطلبوا بعض اولاده وان يكون زنكي اتابك
[18] Ms. *sic.*; Ms. B الب ارسلان
[19] The Ms. is very damaged here. Ms. B has ووقع لهما بالبلاد

بالبلاد وسار الى الموصل وملك الموصل والبلاد اول[20] سنة اثنتين وعشرين وخمسمائة

قيل وفي سنة اثنتين وعشرين وخمسمائة قتل نور الدولة وملك على منبج بالشام وكان محاصرا لها فجاءه سهم فذبحه وملك بلاده خربرت وبالو[21] وميزكرد وما حولها الامير داود وكان الامير بلك قد اخذ هذه الولاية من اولاد[22] جبق ومات ولم يعقب غير بنت تزوجها فخر الدين قرا رسلان[23] بن داود

قيل وفي سنة ثلث وعشرين وخمسمائة مات آتابك طغتكين بدمشق وولي ولده تاج الملوك بورى دمشق وما حولها

قيل وفي يوم[24] خامس شوال سنة اربع[25] وعشرين وخمسمائة مات السلطان محمود صاحب اصفهان وفيها قتل الوزير المزدغاني[26] وبهرام[27] الباطنية اجمع بدمشق ودفن بها وولي السلطان اخوه طغربك[28] السلطنة مدة سنتين ثم مات في اوائل سبع وعشرين وخمسمائة وولي اخوه السلطان مسعود السلطنة

قيل وكان خلف السلطان[29] اولادا جماعة منهم السلطان محمود ولي الامر وحده طغربك[30] وسلطان سليمن شاه ومسعود وسلجوك[31] شاه وبهرام شاه قيل واخذ وخلف السلطان محمود السلطان داود وكان اكبر اولاده وملك اذربيجان وقتل في تبريز في سنة تسع وثلثين وخمسمائة

[20] Ms. B اوائل
[21] Ms. كالوّا
[22] In the Ms. there is no sign of او and the د is written above the لا
[23] Ms. *sic*. ز Ms. B *sic*.
[24] Ms. سنة
[25] Ms. اربعة
[26] Ms. *sic*. Usually known as المزدقاني
[27] Ms. و has been added.
[28] Ms. *sic*.
[29] Ms; i.e. Muḥammad.
[30] Ms. *sic*.
[31] Ms. *sic*.

قتلته[32] الباطنية في وسط السوق ودفن بتبريز وخلف محمد شاه وملك السلطنة بعد عمه مسعود وتزوج ابنته وخلف ملك شاه وكان في حياة[33] عمه مسعود معه في العسكر وملك خوزستان وخلف آلب آرسلان والخفاجي مع آتابك زنكي بالموصل وقتلا بالموصل وخلف بنتا من بنت السلطان سنجر كوهار ملك[34] وعاشت الى ما يقارب سنة سبع وخمسين وخمسمائة

واما سليمن شاه فمات ولم يعقب واما صلجوق[35] فله ابن هو الان بالموصل كان عند مسعود بلال بقلعة تكريت فلما اخذت نقلوه الى الموصل وهو الان بها وله اولاد واما السلطان طغربك[36] فانه خلف آرسلان شاه امه زوجة الامير الدكز وهو (*f. 164a*) الان السلطان من اصفهان وهمذان واذربيجان واران الى مدينة جنزى وشمككوا[37]

وفي سنة اربع وعشرين وخمسمائة كسر حسام الدين وداود على سرجة تحت دارا كسرهما[38] آتبك زنكي

قيل وفي سنة اربع وعشرين وخمسمائة ماتت سعيدة[39] خاتون بنت القليج آرسلان بميفرقين ودفنت في القبة عند ابيها وكانت امها زوجة الامير ركن الدولة داود[40] وبعد ايام حضر اخوها السلطان طغربك[41] من حصن كيفا وكان صحر ركن الدولة داود على ابنته الى ميفرقين واقام بالقبة واخذ دخلها جميعه[42]

32 Ms. قتله
33 Ms. حيوه
34 Ms. *sic*.
35 Ms. *sic*.
36 Ms. *sic*.
37 Ms. *sic*. Possibly شكمور
38 Ms. كسرهم
39 Ms. *sic*. Ms. B الملكة سيدة خاتون
40 Ms. B has وكان الامير داوود تزوج بعائشة خاتون امها after عند ابيها
41 Ms. *sic*. Ms. B الملك طغرل
42 Ms. B has وتسلم ما خلفته instead of اخذ دخلها جميعه

وفي سنة خمس وعشرين وخمسمائة مات الآمر باحكام الله خليفة مصر ولم يخلف ولدا وخلف امرأة حاملا

قيل وفي هذه السنة نفذ السلطان سنجر الى زنكي امره باطلاق دبيس فاطلقه فقصد[43] السلطان مسعود وفي سنة ست [وعشرين][44] وخمسمائة غرقت مراكب الاخلاطية بالبحر بالقسطنطينية . . .[45] فيها جماعة من الاخلاطية وفيها مات نور الدولة صاحب فنك وولي ولده الامير ابو نصر وفيها تسلم الامير داود قلعه قطلبس وباتاسا

قيل واختلف اهل مصر وماجوا وقالوا هذا[46] البيت لا يموت الامام منهم الا وقد خلف ولدا ذكرا منصوصا عليه بالامامة وهذا لم يخلف ولدا ولا نص الا حملا وكان قبل موته نص على الحمل فقالوا يجوز النص على الحمل ويمكن ان يكون ذكرا فبقوا ينتظرون الحمل الى ان وضع فوضعت بنتا فاختلف[47] الناس وماجوا واخرجوا رجلا من القصر من اولاد المستنصر اسمه عبد المجيد ويكنى بابي الميمون ويلقب بالحافظ لدين الله في آخر سنة خمس وعشرين وخمسمائة وقيل هو المجيد بن[48] المستنصر وقيل هو عبد المجيد بن[49] ابي القسم المستعلي بن[50] المستنصر وقيل ولد غير المستعلي للمستنصر فولي الخلافة واجمعوا عليه وانقطع النص من قبل المستعلي واولاده وهو قول الاسماعيلية وان النص في ايامهم متصل من المستنصر الى نزار الى الان وهو مذهبهم وليس احد[51] منهم على الصحيح وبقي الحافظ في الخلافة واستقر وتوطد ملكه

[43] This word is illegible in the Ms.
[44] عشرين is omitted in the Ms.
[45] This word is illegible.
[46] Ms. وقالوا هذا is repeated.
[47] Ms. فاختلفوا
[48] Ms. ابن
[49] Ms. ابن
[50] Ms. ابن
[51] Ms. احدا

وليست[52] خلافة الا في بني العباس لقول النبي صلعم في حق العباس[53] انت ابو الاملاك[54] من امتي الى يوم القيامة واهل مصر والاسماعيلية على الباطل وانما اهل الاغراض والاهواء يقولون ذلك ولا امام ولا خليفة الا ببغداد من آل العباس

قيل وفي سنة خمس وعشرين وخمسمائة ملك الامير داود اسعرد وباهمود وباتاسا وفي (*f. 164b*) سنة اربع[55] وعشرين وخمسمائة لقي آتابك زنكي حسام الدين والامير داود وكسروا على سرجة والتجوا الى دارا وسار زنكي الى الشام وملك حماة وما حولها وحمص وقصد دمشق واخذ دبيس من دمشق وعاد الى الموصل ومعه دبيس مقيدا

قيل وفي سنة ست وعشرين وخمسمائة قصد الخليفة المسترشد[56] في شهر رمضان الموصل ونزل عليها وحاصرها مدة وكان بها نصير الدين جقر واليا فقاتلهم الخليفة وكان حصنها وحفر الخندق[57] وضيق عليها الخليفة ولم ينل منها[58] مقصودا وعاد الى بغداد ودخل في تاسع عشرين ذى القعدة

قيل وفي سنة سبع وعشرين وخمسمائة مات الوزير عبد الملك بميفرقين وولي نظر[59] الديوان الناصح علي بن احمد الآمدى وكان متوليا بآمد فقبضه مؤيد الدين بن نيسان وصادره بثلثين الف دينار وولى موضعه ووصل الى ميفرقين فضم ولده ابو نصر الثمرة[60] واعطى الناصح الوقف فبقي[61] الى ان مات الوزير (و)تولى[62] نظر[63] الديوان

52 Ms. ليس

53 In the margin of the Ms. is written قول الد في حق الـ

54 Ms. *sic.* .i.e., الملوك

55 Ms. اربعة

56 Ms. B adds بالله

57 Ms. B adds دائرة الموصل وبناه after وحفر الخندق

58 Ms. B بها

59 Ms. نضر; Ms. B النظر بالديوان

60 The reading ثمرة is very tentative. Ms. B has the same word فاعطى ابنه ابا نصر الثمرة

61 فبقي is added from Ms. B

62 و has been added. Ms. B وولى

63 Ms. نضر

قيل وفي[64] سنة ثمان وعشرين وخمسمائة وصل المؤيد ابو الحسن بن مخطر الى ميفرقين من الجزيرة وكان صادره الوزير عبد الملك وعاقبه واخذ منه مالا كثيرا وانتقل الى الجزيرة فلما مات الوزير عبد الملك عاد الى ميفرقين وولي الاستيفاء مع الناصح

وفي سنة ثمان وعشرين وخمسمائة وصل شرف الدين حبشي ابو[65] طالب بن حبشي[66] من اهل العراق الى خدمة السعيد حسام الدين واقام عنده على احسن سبيل الضيافة وكان في خدمة صلاح الدين محمد اليغسياني[67] بحماة وكان قبضه وعاقبه وشد معه كلبا في غرارة وكان يضرب الكلب وينهش بدنه واستدار في الغرارة حتى وقع رأس الكلب بين فخذيه وعصر على حلقه حتى مات في الغرارة واطلق فانهزم الى قلعة جعبر واقام عند نجم الدولة[68] مالك بن سالم[69] بن مالك ثم انتقل الى ماردين وبقي عند حسام الدين مدة وولي الوزارة[70] مع السعيد حسام الدين وبلغ من الدولة ما لم يبلغه احد[71] وتحكم اوفى تحكم

وفي هذه السنة وصل[72] الى ماردين المكين[73] ابو البركات بن ابي الفهم[74] الحراني منهزما من بني عمه من حران واقام عند السعيد حسام الدين على سبيل الضيافة

وقيل خرج في شعبان سنة تسع وعشرين وخمسمائة قيل وفي سنة ثمان وعشرين وخمسمائة[75] خرج الخليفة المسترشد من بغداد ولقي

64 وفي has been supplied from Ms. B, which has وفي اخر سنة
65 Ms. ابى
66 Ms.B حبشي بن محمد بن حبشي
67 Ms. اليغساني
68 Ms. B شهاب الدين
69 Ms. مالك بن سالم is not legible.
70 Ms. الوزراة
71 Ms. B غيره; Marsh 333 وبلغ مرتبة لم يبلغها غيره
72 Ms. وفي هذه السنة ووصل
73 Ms. الملكين; Ms. B المكين
74 Ms. الفهر; Ms. B الفهم
75 Ms. B mentions only 528.

السلطان مسعود بباب همذان الى موضع يسمى داى مرك قريب من جبل بهستون ونهب العسكر وكان جمع السلطان خلقا عظيما (*f. 165a*) ومعه صاحب خربرتبت[76] بجيشه وعسكره وكان نفذ له عمه السلطان سنجر عسكرا عظيما فالتقوا وكسروا[77] الخليفة واسروه واسروا ارباب المناصب كلها

ولقد سألت السعيد مؤيد الدين[78] ابا عبد الله محمد بن عبد الكريم الانبارى رحمه الله في سنة اربع وثلثين وخمسمائة ببغداد حين نزلت اليه في هذه السنة عن حال المسترشد والوقعة وما جرى[79] فقال رضي الله عنه كان قد وقع[80] بين السلطان والخليفة في ايام السلطان محمود وخرج وكسره مرتين فلما ولي مسعود استطال نوابه على العراق وعارضوا الخليفة في املاكه فوقعت الوحشة وتجهز المسترشد وعزم على الخروج وجد في ذلك[81] واتفق ان بعض الايام دخل الوزير شرف الدين الزينبي علي بن طراد على الخليفة وانا معه وجمال الدين طلحة صاحب المخزن وكان الخليفة قد طرد اصحاب السلطان عن العراق ورتب صاحب المخزن على دار السلطان للمظالم والبلد فلما دخلنا ذلك اليوم فقال له الوزير شرف الدين يا[82] مولانا في نفس المملوك شيء فهل يأذن له في المقال فقال قل قال يا مولانا الى اين تمضي وبمن تعتضد والى من تلتجئ وبمن تنتصر ومقامنا ببغداد امكن لنا ولا يقصدنا احد والعراق فيه لنا[83] الكفاية فان الحسين بن علي عليه السلم لما خرج الى العراق جرى عليه

[76] Ms. *sic*.
[77] Ms. وكسر
[78] Ms. B adds سديد الدولة after مؤيد الدين
[79] After وما جرى Ms. B adds وسبب ولاية المقتفي وكيف ولي دون غيره
[80] Ms. وقع is written in the margin.
[81] After وجد في ذلك Ms. B adds ووافقه جمال الدين بن طلحة
[82] Ms. يا written above the line.
[83] Ms. ففيه is written on the line and لنا above it.

ما جرى ولو اقام بمكة[84] ما اختلف عليه احد من الناس[85] فقال لي[86] الخليفة ما تقول يا كاتب فقلت يا مولانا الصواب المقام وما رآه الوزير فهو الرأى فلا يقدم[87] علينا احد وليت بقي علينا[88] العراق فقال لصاحب المخزن يا وكيل ما تقول قال في نفسي ما في نفس مولانا وكان هو حمله على الخروج قال المسترشد

واذ لم يكن من الموت بد فمن الغبن[89] ان تموت جبانا[90]

ثم انه جهز وجمع وكان قد حصل في خدمتة جماعة من امراء الاتراك واعطاعهم مالا عظيما ثم خرج وخرجنا فلما قاربنا همذان خرج السلطان مسعود فالتقوا في موضع يسمى داى مرك قريب من جبل بهستون قريب من همذان فلما اصطفت العساكر وهموا بالقتال ففر من معسكرنا جميع الامراء والاتراك الى جانب السلطان فانهزم الخليفة ومن بقي معه ونهب العسكر وقبض الخليفة وارباب المناصب وحمل الوزير وصاحب المخزن وانا ونقيب العلويين الى قلعة سرجهان بالقرب من قزوين[91] والرى ولقد رأيتها في تسع واربعين وخمسمائة لما سافرت الى الرى ورايتها وهي تلوح على راس جبل عال واخذ السلطان المسترشد معه وطاف به في اذربيجان الى ان وصل به الى مراغة فنزل هناك فدخل عليه ثلثة[92] نفر من الملاحدة فقتلوه فرضي الله عنه وقتل (*f. 165b*) معه رجل كان يصلي

[84] Ms. B adds والمدينة after بمكة
[85] After احد من الناس Ms. B adds وكان بايعه جميع الناس
[86] Ms. له
[87] Ms. and Ms. B يقدم
[88] Ms. B لنا
[89] Ms. *sic.*; Ms. B has العجز
[90] Ms. B واذ الم يكن من الموت بد فمن العجز ان يكون جبانا
[91] The Ms. is damaged here. Ms. B قزوين
[92] Ms. ثلث

به يسمى ابن سكينة يوم الخميس سادس عشر[93] ذى القعدة سنة تسع وعشرين وخمسمائة وكانت خلافته سبعة سنة وسبعة شهور ويومين[94]

وكان ولي عهده ولده ابا جعفر المنصور الراشد بالله وكان تخلف ببغداد فلما وصل الخبر الى بغداد بقتله بايعوا الراشد بالخليفة وقيل ان[95] السلطان سنجر نفذ اليه من قتله وقيل ان السلطان مسعود نفذ استأذن عمه سنجر فاذن له في قتله فرتب اولئك[96] فدخلوا عليه فقتلوه ودفن في مدينة المراغة

وكان مع السلطان في معسكره دبيس[97] بن صدقة بن[98] مزيد[99] ورحل السلطان بعد مدة الى باب تبريز وركب بعض الايام ونزل ودخل اليه سيف الدولة دبيس فضرب عنقه وبقي السلطان اياما وتزوج ببنت دبيس وكانت[100] امها شرف خاتون بنت عميد الدولة بن جهير من زبيده بنت نظام الملك[101] وحمل[102] دبيس الى ماردين الى زوجته كهار خاتون فدفن بالمشهد عند نجم الدين الغازى[103] رحمهما الله وكان قد قيل ان دبيس حمل السلطان على قتل المسترشد قال مؤيد الدين لما قتل المسترشد نفذ[104] السلطان مسعود احضرنا عنده فحضر الوزير شرف الدين وجمال الدين صاحب المخزن وانا وكان نقيب العلويين[105] قد مات بقلعة سرجهان ودفن هناك فلما حضرنا عنده[106] قال ما الرأى وما التدبير

93 Ms. سادس عشر Ms. B سادس عشرين
94 Ms. يومان
95 Ms. بل
96 Ms. اوايك
97 Ms. adds سيف الدولة in front of دبيس
98 Ms. ابن
99 Ms. B adds حين قبض الخليفة ويقال انه حمل السلطان على قتله
100 Ms. كان with ت written below the line.
101 Ms. الدين is written on the line, ملك above it. Ms. B adds الحسن بن اسحق
102 Ms. B adds من باب تبريز after حمل
103 Ms. B دفن في مشهد نجم الدين
104 نفذ is best placed here, as in Ms. B. In Ms. A ونفذ is written above مسعود
105 Ms. B النقيب الطاهر
106 Ms. B احضرنا عنده فحضرن

في امر الخلافة من ترون فقال الوزير يا مولانا الخلافة[107] لولي العهد[108] وقد بايعه الناس وجلس واستقر وقد بويع له بولاية العهد والان بعد قتل ابيه فقال ما الى هذا سبيل ابدا ولا اقره عليها فانه يحدث نفسه بالخروج مثل ابيه ونحن كل يوم من حيث ولي المسترشد لم يزل يخرج علينا وكان خرج الى اخي محمود مرتين وعليّ مرة وهذى[109] اخرى ثم تم عليه ما تم وبقيت علينا شناعة عظيمة وسبة الى آخر الدهر ويقولون قتلوا الخليفة وهم كانوا السبب في عود الخلافة الى هذا البيت اريد لا[110] يجلس الا من لا يداخل نفسه[111] في غير امور الدين ولا يجند ولا يتخذ ولا يجمع ولا يخرج علي ولا على اهل بيتي وفي الدار جماعة فاعتمدوا على شيخ منهم صاحب عقل ورأى وتدبير ويلزم نفسه ما يجب من طاعتنا ولا يخرج من داره ولا تعرجوا على هرون بن المقتدى فهو شيخ كبير ولا يرى الفتنة وقد اشار به عمي سنجر[112]

وكان في الدار في ذلك الوقت سبعة اخوة من اولاد المقتدى ولهم اولاد واولاد اولاد وبقي من السبعة الى سنة نيف[113] وخمسين وخمسمائة وكان في الدار من اولاد المستظهر سبعة اخوة منهم الامير ابو عبد الله وابو طالب وابو نصر وابو القسم وابو علي واسماعيل[114] ويحيى ولهم اولاد جماعة وكان للمسترشد اولاد جماعة وللراشد وله مقدار[115] نيف وعشرين ولدا اكبرهم امير الجيش وكان ولد لابيه وهو ابن تسع سنين ولم ير مثل ذلك قط

ولقد حدثني بعض من اثق اليه ببغداد ممن كان يدخل (*f. 166a*)

[107] Ms. من ترون فقال الوزير يا مولانا الخلافة صح is written in the right margin.
[108] After لولى العهد Ms. B adds الراشد
[109] Ms. favours this form.
[110] لا is provided from Ms. B
[111] After لا يداخل نفسه Ms. B has في غير امر الخلافة وامر الدين
[112] Ms. B سلطان العالم سنجر عمي
[113] Ms. B ثلث
[114] Ms. B اعمل
[115] Ms. مقدر

الى دار الخلافة ويطلع عليهم ان المسترشد اشترى[116] للراشد لما كان عمره سبع سنين خمس جوارى[117] وامرهن[118] ان يلاعبنه ويمكنه[119] من انفسهن[120] ويحملنه[121] على ذلك فكن[122] معه[123] على ذلك الى ان صار عمره تسع سنين(و)[124] بلغ مبلغ الرجال وكانت فيهن[125] جارية صفراء حبشية فواقعها ذات يوم فحملت منه فبلغ المسترشد ذلك فانكره واحضرها وهددها فقالت والله ما تقدم اليّ سواه وانه بالغ مثل جميع الرجال فسئل[126] باقي الجوار فقلن[127] مثل ذلك فامر ان تحمل الجارية قطنا ثم وطئها فلما قام عنها اخرجت القطن والمنيّ عليه[128] وكذلك فعل بباقي الجوار[129] فخرج المنيّ ففرح المسترشد بذلك فلما تم حملها وضعت ابنا فسماه المسترشد امير الجيش وسر به سرورا شديدا[130] وهذا ما لم يسمع بمثله الا في الحجاز يقال ان نساء تهامة يحضن لتسع وتبلغ صبيانهم لتسع اقرب ما رأى بين اب وابنه ما رأى بين عمرو بن العاص وبين ابنه عبد الله وكان ولد له وعمره اثنتا عشرة[131] سنة ولم ير مثله الا ما ذكرناه من امر الراشد

وكان الراشد على طريقة ابيه وكان بايعه الناس في آخر سنة تسع

116 Ms. B اتخذ
117 Ms. B جوار
118 Ms. امرهم
119 Ms. يمكنوه
120 Ms. انفسهم
121 Ms. يحملونه
122 Ms. فكانوا
123 After معه Ms. B has وكان ذلك الى ان بلغ
124 و is added.
125 Ms. وكان فيهم
126 Ms. سيل
127 Ms. فقالوا
128 Ms. B فوقه
129 After الجوار Ms. B has وفعل بباقي الجوار واعتبروا فكان المني مع كل واحدة
130 Ms. B جيدا
131 Ms. عشر

وعشرين وخمسمائة وكان شهما من الرجال شريف النفس ذا رأى وهمة فلهذا انحرف السلطان عن توليته الخلافة

قيل وفي ذي الحجة سنة تسع وعشرين وخمسمائة قتل السلطان مسعود صدقة بن دبيس بين يديه صبرا واظنه وهما لان الذى قتله كان قراجا (و)[132] منكورس[133]

قيل ونفذ السلطان مسعود الى عمه سنجر يأخذ اذنه فيمن يولى فنفذ اليه[134] يقول لا تول[135] الا من يضمنه الوزير وصاحب المخزن وابن الانبارى[136] فاجتمع السلطان بهم وشاورهم واشار بهرون[137] وعرفهم ما امرهم السلطان سنجر وقال الوزير اذا كان هذا الامر يلزمنا فنحن نولي من نراه وهو الزاهد العابد الدين الذى ليس في الدار مثله قال السلطان من هو قال الامير عبد الله بن المستظهر فقال وتضمنون ما يجرى منه فقال الوزير نعم

وكان الامير ابو عبد الله صهر الوزير شرف الدين على ابنته فانها دخلت ذات يوم في الدار في زمن المستظهر فرآها الامير ابو عبد الله فطلبها من ابيه فزوجه اياها وكان شرف الدين اذ ذاك نقيب النقباء[138] ودخل بها وبقيت عنده مدة ماتت عنده فقال السلطان ذاك اليكم واكتموا الحال لئلا ينمو الامر فيقتل المقتني ببغداد ثم رحل السلطان والجماعة الى بغداد (*f. 166b*) والوزير ونحن اجمع في صحبته

قيل وكان الراشد بعد قتل ابيه قد بايعه الناس واستبد واستقر ونفذ[139] الى آتابك زنكي الى الموصل واستدعاه وضمن له ان تكون

[132] و has been added
[133] Ms. *sic.*
[134] Ms. B has فوصله الجواب instead of فنفذ اليه
[135] Ms. لا توالى
[136] After لا تول Ms. B has الا من يقع عليه راى الوزير وصاحب المخزن وكاتب الانشاء ويضمنون ما جرى منه ويكون الجواب عليهم
[137] Ms. B اشار السلطان بولاية هرون
[138] Ms. B adds ثم انتقل الى الوزارة after نقيب النقباء
[139] Ms. B انفذ

السلطنة في[140] الملك آلب آرسلان بن محمود الذى عند آتابك[141] وتكون الآتابكية والخلافة بحكمه فنزل آتابك الى بغداد ونزل بالجانب الشرقي[142] في احدى[143] دور السطلنة وبقي الى ان وصله ان السلطان قد طلب بغداد فخيم في الجانب الغربي

ولما قرب السلطان من بغداد ونزل قريبا من النهروان حقق الراشد الحال وانه[144] لا بد من تولية غيره فجمع الامرء باسرهم الذين كانوا في الدار من بني الخلفاء في سرداب[145] فتقدم بان يطبق السرداب[146] ولقد حدثني زين الدولة ابو القسم علي بن الصاحب وكان هو حاجب الباب هو وابوه وجده وكان بين يدى الراشد قال لما جمع الراشد الامراء في السرداب استدعاني وقال يا علي خذ هذا السيف وكان بيده سيف[147] وقال احذر ان يسبق سيفي سيفك[148] فاني اريد اخرج كل من في السرداب واقتل الجميع حتى لا يبقى من يصلح للخلافة فان هؤلاء[149] ربما دخلوا وغيروا وولوا غيرى ثم امر بفتح السرداب فالصائح جاءه فقال ما الخبر فقال ان آتابك زنكي نهب الحريم الطاهرى[150] وطلب الموصل في ذى القعدة واما السلطان فوصل وعبر النهروان ولما حقق آتابك نزول السلطان بالنهروان انهزم فرمى السيف من يده ودخل الى الدار واخذ معه من الجواهر ما لا تعرف[151] لها قيمة واعطاني منها مثل ذلك فخرج واخرج معه قاضي القضاة الزينبي وكان قد استوزر

140 After السلطنة في Ms. B has احد الملكين الذين (*sic.*) كانا معه من اولاد محمود

141 Ms. B has ويوليه الاتابكية للسلطنة والخلافة after عند آتابك

142 Ms. B الغربي

143 Ms. احد

144 After الحال Ms. B has ان اليوم واصلون وعزمهم ان يولون غيره

145 On the four occasions this word is used, it is spelt سرذاب

146 Ms. B سجنهم فيه

147 Ms. سيفا

148 Ms. B يدى ويدك

149 Ms. هآولاء

150 Ms. الطاهر; Ms. B طاهرى

151 Ms. يعرف

جلال الدين ابا[152] الرضا (بن)[153] صدقة فخرج وخرجنا ولحق آتابك[154] زنكي على طريق الموصل

قال السعيد مؤيد الدين رحمه الله فلما كان بكرة ذلك اليوم دخل السلطان بغداد ودخلنا معه فنزل في داره ونزلنا نحن في دورنا وكان دخولنا عاشر ذي القعدة سنة ثلثين وخمسمائة فلما كان من الغد مضى الوزير الى دار السلطنة[155] ونحن معه واستأذنه فيما يفعل فاخذ خطه وخطوطنا بالضمان ثم عدنا الى دورنا واصبحنا يوم الاثنين سابع عشر ذي القعدة سنة ثلثين وخمسمائة وحضرنا عند الامير ابي[156] عبد الله وتحدث الوزير معه وتحدثنا معه وشرط عليه القيام بامر الخلافة وطاعة السلطان[157] واعلمناه اننا قد ضمنا ذلك من السلطان جميع ما اقترحه عليك فرضي بذلك وانفصلنا عنه ومضينا[158] الى السلطان واعلمناه ما جرى وانه رضي بما شرط[159] عليه (*f. 167a*) فقال السلطان اذا كان من الغد[160] فبايعوه، فلما اصبحنا صعدنا الى الدار[161] واخرجنا من الدار اشياء من الالات[162] التي تصلح للغناء واشياء لا تليق[163] وشهد جماعة من اهل الدار انه شرب الخمر فافتى العلماء بخلعه واعتنق ذلك القاضي عماد الدين شرف القضاة ابو طاهر احمد بن الكرخي المحتسب[164] وكان قاضي اصحاب الشافعي رحمه الله واجتمع العلماء والاكابر فخلعوه

152 Ms. ابو
153 بن has been added.
154 Ms. B has وسار سعى آتابك instead of لحق آتابك
155 Ms. السلطنة is illegible.
156 Ms. ابو
157 Ms. B والاكرام وطاعة السلطان
158 Ms. adds من غدوه
159 Ms. شرطت
160 Ms. B اذاكان من غد وهو الثلثاء ثالث عشر ذى القعدة سنة ثلثين وخمسمائة
161 Ms. B دار الراشد
162 Ms. B الات
163 Ms. يليق
164 Ms. B فتى الفقهاء بخلعه وانه لا يصلح لذلك وكان المعتنق لذلك شرف القضاة ابن الكرخي

ودخل اليه الوزير وصاحب المخزن وانا وتحدثنا وناولته رقعة فيها ما يسمى[165] به من اللقب وكان فيها لامقتني لامر الله والمستضيء بامر[166] الله المستنجد بالله فقال ذلك اليكم فقال لي الخليفة[167] ما ترى فقلت المقتني لامر الله فقال مبارك ثم مد يده فاخذها الوزير وقبلها وقال بايعت سيدنا ومولانا المقتفي لامر الله امير المؤمنين على كتاب الله وسنة رسول الله واجتهاده ثم اخذها صاحب المخزن وقبلها[168] وبايعه على مثل ذلك ثم اخذت يده وقلت بعد ان قبلتها بايعت سيدنا ومولانا الامام المقتفي لامر الله امير المؤمنين على ما بايعت عليه اباه واخاه وابن اخيه في ولاية عهده وكنت بايعت الامام المستظهر بالله لما خدمته في وكالة الدار سنة . . .[169] وتسعين وبقيت الى سنة سبع وخمسمائة لما وليت ديوان الانشاء وبايعت المسترشد والراشد ثم قمنا من عنده ودخل الى الدار وبايعه الناس[170] ودخل العلماء والفقهاء والقضاة واكابر الناس[171] اجمع فبايعوه وحضر السلطان مسعود بعد ثلثة ايام وبايعه وبايعه جميع اصحابه من خواجة[172] والامير حاجب[173] وجميع ارباب دولته واستبد له الامر واستقر في الخلافة

قيل وفي سنة تسع وعشرين وخمسمائة مات نجم الدولة ابن مالك بالقلعة وولي ولده وفيها اخذ آتابك زنكي الرقة من مسيب بن مالك

وكان وزر للمسترشد في ايامه جماعة منهم امين الدين خواجة[174]

165 Ms. يسم

166 Ms. B بنور الله

167 Ms. B فقال له الوزير لي (*sic.*)

168 Ms. B adds وقام

169 Ms. has a lacuna here.

170 الناس is supplied from Ms. B

171 Ms. B والمقدمون

172 Ms. اخواجة

173 Ms. B adds تتار

174 Ms. اخواجا

احمد بن نظام الملك[175] مرتين وشرف الدين انوشروان مرتين وجلال الدين ابو علي بن صدقة الى ان مات ووزر له[176] شرف الدين الزينبي[177] الى ان قتل واسر معه على ما ذكرناه

واما ما كان من الراشد فانه خرج مع آتابك زنكي في صفر سنة احدى[178] وثلثين وخمسمائة الى الموصل ومعه قاضي القضاة الزينبي وجلال الدين ابو الرضا بن صدقة ابن اخي[179] الوزير ابي علي[180] وبقي عنده مدة فوصل معه الى باب نصيبين واقام اياما[181] ثم انفصل عنه ومضى الى السلطان مسعود ليدخل عليه ويمضي الى السلطان سنجر[182]

وقيل قصد السلطان داوود[183] ودخل عليه حتى يرده الى الخلافة فلما قارب اصفهان[184] خرج عليه من الملاحدة ودخلوا عليه فقتلوه في شهر رمضان سنة اثنتين وثلثين وخمسمائة وحمل الى اصفهان فدفن بها في مدينة شهرستان من اصفهان على فرسخ ويقال انها من ابنية[185] ذى القرنين على ماء يعرف بززراود[186] على القنطرة وكانت خلافته من حيث بويع له بعد قتل ابيه الى ان بويع للمقتني[187] احد عشر شهرا زائدا فناقصا وقيل ان السلطان نفذ من دخل عليه وقتله[188] وخلف له في الدار نيفا وعشرين ولدا منهم الكبير امير الجيش ويقال انه ولاه العهد

[175] Ms. B نظام الدين ابو نصر احمد

[176] Ms. B adds نقيب النقباء

[177] Ms. B adds علي بن طراد

[178] Ms. احد

[179] Ms. اخ

[180] Ms. b. وكان قد استوزر جلال الدين ابا الرضا بن صدقة ببغداد

[181] Ms. B وعاد الى الموصل

[182] Ms. B وسار يطلب السلطان حتى يستأذنه ويدخل الى خراسان

[183] Ms. *sic*.

[184] Ms. has اصبهان with ف written above the line.

[185] Ms. B بنيه

[186] Ms. *sic*.; Ms. B زيدارد

[187] Ms. المقتني

[188] Ms. B adds وجعل الاسم الملاحدة

قبل خروجه من بغداد[189] واما قاضي القضاة الزينبي رحمه الله فانه عاد ونزل الى بغداد وعاد الى منصبه واما جلال الدين ابو الرضا بن[190] صدقة فانه وزر لآتابك زنكي مدة وعزل وعاد الى بغداد وكان وزر لآتابك بعد موت ضياء الدين ابي سعيد الكفرتوثي واستقر المقتفي في الخلافة وتوطد امره

قيل وفي سنة اثنتين وثلثين حاصر السلطان سلجوق شاه خلاط مدة ورحل عنها . . .[191] وفي سنة ثلث وثلثين خطب الامير داود للمقتفي الجمعة ثالث عشرين المحرم

وفي سنة[192] وثلثين اسر[193] السناسنة صاحب الاخلاط واعطوا خوويت[194] واطلق[195] بسفارة حسام الدين في جمادى الاولى سنة ثلث وثلثين

قيل وفي سنة تسع وعشرين وخمسمائة مات الملك طغربك[196] بباب دمشق وحمل الى العراق قيل[197]

وفي سنة تسع وعشرين وخمسمائة سافرت من ميفرقين الى ماردين ولم اكن قبل ذلك خرجت من ميفرقين وبقيت بها مدة (و)[198] وصل تابوت دبيس وانا بماردين ودفن بالمشهد وهذه السنة ماتت فيها زوجة الامير شهاب الدين محمد بن[199] الياس وكانت زوجة الامير حسام الدين واولدت منه صفية خاتون وكنت بماردين هذه السنة وتزوج

189 Ms. B adds وبقي قاضي القضاة وجلال الدين بالموصل بعد انفصاله
190 Ms. ابن
191 Ms. has a lacuna here. Perhaps it should read قيل
192 A number has been omitted here.
193 Ms. اسروا
194 Ms. اخويت
195 Ms. has واطلق صح in the margin.
196 Ms. *sic*.
197 Ms. *sic*.
198 و has been added.
199 Ms. ابن

السعيد حسام الدين بالملكة . . .[200] خاتون بنت الملك رضوان وكانت وصلت تلك السنة من حلب وكانت زوجة بدر الدولة سليمن بن عبد الجبار ابن ارتق وماتت بماردين ووصلت من حلب ومعها ولد اسمه كبك ويلقب بمجد[201] الملوك فبقيت مدة وتزوجها السعيد حسام الدين وكان وصل هذه السنة تاج الدين ابو سالم بن نباتة رضي الله عنه الى ماردين

قيل وكان في سنة ثمان وعشرين وخمسمائة نازل آتابك زنكي وحسام الدين قلعة الصور فاخذها حادى عشرين رجب وسلمها الى السعيد حسام الدين وقتل جندال[202] بن اسلم وكان اميرا مقداما[203] من اصحاب الامير داود وكان امير الصور للامير داود وفيها (*f. 168a*) وصل آتابك زنكي الى تل شيخ (و)[204] اجتمع بحسام[205] الدين ولقوا داود بباب آمد وكسروه ودخل الى الصور واخذها وفيها ملك آتابك زنكي طنزى ومن تل الشيخ (و)[206] وزر ضياء[207] الدين ابو سعيد بن الكفرتوثي لآتابك زنكي وحصل في خدمته وفي تلك السنة مات شمس الدولة الاحدب

وقيل وفي سنة ثلثين امر حسام الدين بنقض الربض والمحدثة فنقضا[208] وكان قد وقع الخلف بين السعيد حسام الدين والامير داود (و)[209] آتابك مع الامير حسام الدين فكسروا الامير داود على باب

[200] Ms. has a lacuna here.
[201] Ms. مجد
[202] Ms. B حمدان; Marsh 333 (f. 103a) حمدان Ms. *sic.*
[203] Ms. مقدما
[204] و is added.
[205] حسام
[206] و is added.
[207] Ms. ضيها
[208] Ms. B فابتدى في نقضه في الجمعة تاسع المحرم
[209] و is added.

آمد وساروا فملكوا جبل جور وبالقرنين[210] والسيوان اخذت من الامير آرسلان بن عبد الجبار بن ارتق وسلمها آتابك الى السعيد حسام الدين وانهزم الامير آرسلان[211] الى خدمة الامير داود

قيل وفي سنة ثمان وعشرين نهب الامير داود ربض طنزى وسبى[212] كل من فيها[213] ونهب اموالهم وهتك النساء[214] بحيث لو غزت الافرنج ما فعلت اكثر من ذلك[215] وفي سنة ثمان وعشرين ملك السعيد حسام الدين الهتاخ على ما كرناه واخذها من الامير شمس الدولة عيسى بن احمد بن نظام الدين بن[216] مروان

قيل وفي سنة احدى وثلثين وخمسمائة وصل السعيد حسام الدين الى ميفرقين ومعه حبشي بن[217] حبشي وعمل حساب العمال والمتصرفين وصادر اهلها وقلعهم واجحف باهلها ولقي الناس منه شدة لا توصف من الشتم والجور الظلم وسلك بهم اصعب الطرق من الخيف والقهر وقبض الناصح الآمدى وكان متوليا بديوان ميفرقين وقبض ابنه ابا نصر وكان المؤيد بن مخطر متوليا فانهزم من يد حبشي ومضى الى الجزيرة وقبض اخاه ابا سعيد واخرج العميد ابا طاهر بن المحتسب من الحبس وكان له مدة محبوسا وولاه . . .[218] الناس ولقي الناس منه شدة ومشقة لا توصف

وكنت في هذه السنة بالجزيرة واقمت بها مدة وعدت الى ميفرقين واجتزت بنصيبين ورايت آتابك زنكي بنصيبين

قيل وفي سنة تسع وعشرين مات نجم الدولة مالك بن مالك

[210] Ms. *sic.*
[211] Ms. B رسلان
[212] Ms. سبا
[213] Ms. فيه; Ms. B كلها فيه
[214] Ms. B هتكت الحرم
[215] Ms. B ما صنعت بالمسلمين
[216] Ms. ابن
[217] ابن
[218] The Ms. is damaged is here. The terminal ساب is visible. (?) احتساب

بالقلعة واخذ آتابك زنكي الرقة من الامير مسيب وسار الى دمشق وحاصرها مدة ثم دخل فيها وفي القلعة ولده بدران مدة وبقي (الى)[219] ان دخل سنة ثلثين وقتله اخوه الامير علي بن مالك وولي القلعة

قيل وفي سنة ثمان وعشرين وخمسمائة ظهر عبد المؤمن بالمغرب وانا اذكر من حاله وما وصل اليّ من امره وهو ان محمد بن تومرت كان من المصامدة وخرج الى بلاد المشرق وهو شيخ عبد المؤمن بن علي الكومي من جبال السوس الاقصى بالمغرب وكان محمد بن تومرت الادريسي الحسيني خرج (*f. 168b*) الى المشرق وبقي مدة ثم عاد الى المغرب في سنة تسع عشرة[220] وخمسمائة واقام بمروكش[221] واجتمع اليه جماعة من الفقهاء فناظرهم فجرى بينهم اشياء غير ما جرت به عادة المغاربة وخارجا عن طريقهم[222] فانكر عليهم وانكروا عليه ثم انهم اجتمعوا الى امير المسلمين الي ابن يوسف بن تاشفين وقالوا له تخرج هذا من بيننا والا افسد الناس واهلكم فتقدم اليه بالخروج فخرج في سنة عشرين وخمسمائة فنفاه الى الجبل الى المصامدة وهم جنس من البربر وكانوا عشيرته فاقام بينهم وحملهم على ترك طاعة امير[223] المسلمين[224] فخرج اليه امير المسلمين فلقيه فكسره وقتل رأس العسكر عبد الله بن ماوية فخرج امير المسلمين بنفسه وجمع الجموع فلقيه وكسره وتمكن في الجبل وهو مسيرة شهر في شهر وهو جبل درن[225] بولاية مركوش[226] والسوس واجتمع اليه خلق كثير عظيم وبقي الى سنة ثلث وعشرين وخمسمائة ومات محمد بن تومرت وولي موضعه علي

219 الى has been added.
220 Ms. تسعة عشر
221 Ms. *sic.*; Ms. B *sic.*
222 Ms. B فرأوه خارجا عن مذهب المغاربة وطريقتهم
223 Ms. الامير للمسلمين
224 Ms. B adds وامتنعوا من اداء ما كان عليهم فجمع الجيوش
225 Ms. ارن; Ms. B ارن
226 Ms. *sic.*

الورنشي وجهز العساكر وحاصر مركوش[227] في سنة اربع[228] وعشرين وخمسمائة فكسره امير المسلمين وازاحه من مركوش[229] فانهزم الى الجبل وتحصن به وبقي الامر بينه وبين امير المسلمين يزيد وينقص الى سنة ثمان وعشرين وخمسمائة ومات علي الورنشي

وتولى موضعه عبد المؤمن بن علي الكومي[230] وكان من جملة اصحاب محمد بن تومرت وتلامذته واصحابه ومعاضدته[231] فجمع ولقي امير المسلمين وكسره وملك الجبل باسره وملك ولاية اخرى ونزل في سنة ثلثين[232] وخمسمائة الصحراء وفتح اكثر بلاد امير المسلمين وكانت له البقاع وفتح اكثر افرقية وبلادا من الاندلس وفتح اكثر بلاد امير المسلمين وفتح من الافرنج مواضع[233] كثيرة وبقي الى سنة اربعين وخمسمائة ولقي امير المسلمين تاشفين[234] بن[235] علي بن يوسف وكسره وقتل خلقا كثيرا واسره وقتله وتوطدت له البلاد وفتح اكثر المغرب وهابه الناس[236] وكان لا يفتح مدينة الا قتل كل من فيها وكان يقول انا صاحب الزمان وملك في سنة اثنتين واربعين مدينة تونس وهي من اعظم مدن المغرب وقد ذكرت في كتاب المسالك والممالك ان دور سورها احد وعشرين ميلا

وفي سنة احدى وثلثين في رابع ذى القعدة تسلم الامير داود حاني من الامير شاروخ واعطاه اقطاعا واقام في خدمته[237] (في)[238] ربض حاني الى ان مات ودفن في حاني

227 Ms. *sic*.
228 Ms. اربعة
229 Ms. *sic*.
230 Ms. adds (*sic*.) من اهل عرعرا
231 Ms. B adds وهو بربرى الجنس
232 Ms. ثلث
233 Ms. مواضعا
234 Ms. تاشعين
235 Ms. ابن
236 Ms. B adds وكثر في اعينهم
237 Ms. خدمته written in left margin.
238 في has been added.

قيل وفي سنة احدى واربعين وخمسمائة ملك عبد المؤمن من ولاية بني حماد واجلاهم عنها[239] وفي سنة اثنتين وثلثين وخمسمائة فتح المهدية وملكها ولم يبق له منازع ولا من يناويه ولا من يقاومه وبنى مدينتين عظيمتين احدهما[240] برينى[241] وسماها المهدية *(f. 169a)* والاخرى برينى[242] واستقر في ملكه وبقي يفتح من بلاد الافرنج طرفا فطرفا[243] الى ان مات في سنة اربعين[244] وخمسمائة وبقي اولاده من بعده في الملك ويقال انه خلف نيفا واربعين ولدا ذكورا

قيل وفي سنة اثنتين وثلثين وخمسمائة خرج ملك الروم من القسطنطنية الى الشام وملك بزاعة وانه حمل اهلها باسرهم وسبى[245] كل من فيها ونهب ما كان بها وحط على حلب وحاصرها ولقيه آتابك زنكي وبقي في وجهه وسارت اليه عساكر ديار بكر وديار ربيعة اجمع ونفذ الامير داود ولده معه عساكر التركمان فرحل من حلب وعاد الى بلاده

وفي هذه السنة مات بهاء الدين ابو الحسن بن علي ابن الشهرزورى بالرقة ودفن بها[246] وصلت[247] نعية الى الجزيرة وكنت بالجزيرة وفي هذه السنة اقمت بها مدة وعدت الى ميفرقين وفي سنة اثنتين وثلثين اصطلح زنكي مع صاحب دمشق وتزوج بامه وفيها تسلم زنكي حمص وقتل قرخان صاحبها وفيها قتل شهاب الدين صاحب دمشق وولي ابنه

239 Ms. B adds وقتل من اكابرهم جماعة
240 Ms. احدهما
241 Ms. *sic.*; Ms. B في برينى
242 Ms. B . . . والاخرى في برينى وسماها
243 Ms. B وهو الى الان في يد الافرنج من المغرب يفتح
244 Ms. اربعون
245 Ms. سبا
246 Ms. B وولى ولده نجم الدين قضا القضاة
247 Ms. وصل

قيل وفي سنة ثلث وثلثين وخمسمائة نهب الامير داود ارزن وسبى[248] اهلها ونهب اموالهم واباح الجند كلها[249] وكان بها وجرى عليهم اكثر مما جرى على اهل طنزى ولقي الناس منه ما لا يوصف ووصل السعيد حسام الدين الى ميفرقين ووصل اليه حسام الدولة قرتي بن[250] الاحدب صاحب ارزن

قيل وفي شوال سنة ثلث وثلثين توفي سوتكين المرجي صاحب حران وقصدها آتابك وتسلمها وفي هذه السنة كسر حسام الدين الافرانج في شبختان واخذ القافلة من باب الرها وكنت في هذه السنة بآمد وفي هذه السنة اصطلح السعيد حسام الدين وآتابك زنكي فاخذ دارا[251] وتزوج بصفية خاتون بنت السعيد حسام الدين وحملت في سنة اربع وثلثين وخمسمائة الى الموصل وكنت بها

واقمت بميافارقين الى اخر سنة ثلث (وثلثين)[252] وخمسمائة وانحدرت الى بغداد واجتمعت بالسعيد مؤيد الدين ابي عبد الله محمد بن الانبارى رحمه الله ووصلتها في شهر ربيع الاول سنة اربع وثلثين وخمسمائة لانني كنت اقمت بالجزيرة والموصل مدة واقمت ببغداد مدة سنة اشهر ورأيت الخليفة المقتفي لما بايعه خواجة[253] عز الملك ودخل الخليفة المقتفي باخت السلطان فكنت ببغداد وحضرت باب الحجرة واملاك السلطان مسعود بابنة الخليفة المقتفي وخطب قاضي القضاة الزينبي رحمه الله وكان الوزير شرف الدين علي بن طراد[254] الزينبي وكمال الدين صاحب المخزن

[248] Ms. سبا
[249] Ms. B واباح العسكر الناس واموالهم ونساءهم
[250] Ms. ابن
[251] Ms. B وصعد صلاح الدين الى ماردين وقرر امر الصلح بينهما فسلم اليه دارا
[252] وثلثين has been added.
[253] Ms. اخواجا
[254] Ms. حراد

ورأيت جماعة من كبار اهل العراق وقرأت على الشيخ ابي المظفر بن الشهرزورى العطار (*f. 169b*) الفرائض[255] وقرأت الفصيح والعمدة على الشيخ[256] ابي منصور الجواليقي وقرأت التنبيه على الشيخ ابي حسن[257] ابن الخل ولقيت الشيخ ابا منصور الرزاز وجماعة من[258] الفقهاء منهم[259] الشيخ عبد القادر ابن النراوى واولاد قاضي القضاة الدمغاني ويوسف الدمشقي وجماعة من اصحاب الحديث منهم القاضي ابو بكر قاضي البيمارستان وابن السمرقندى وعبد الوهاب الانماطي وجماعة كثيرة وسمعت عليهم وقرأت على الشيخ ابي محمد بن نبت الشيخ القرآن وعلى الشيخ عبد الوهاب الخفاف واقمت ببغداد وزرت جميع المشاهد بها ونزلت الى المداين وزرت قبر سلمان الفارسي واقمت ببغداد الى خامس محرم سنة خمس وثلثين وخمسمائة

وكان شرف الدين الزينبي في الوزارة فغضب في اخر سنة اربع[260] وثلاثين وخمسمائة ومضى الى دار السلطان مغضبا واقام بها[261] ونفذ الخليفة الى السلطان خادما اسمه نجاح استأذن في عزله وناب في الوزارة[262] قاضي القضاة الزينبي مدة وناب بعده مؤيد الدين سديد الدولة ووصل امر السلطان بعزله في سنة خمس وثلثين وخمسمائة وولي الوزارة[263] نظام الدين ابا المظفر بن الزعيم بن جهير وكان استاذ الدار واستقر بها

قيل وفي سنة اربع وثلثين وخمسمائة ملك آتابك زنكي قلعة بعلبك ونزل على دمشق وحاصرها مدة ثم سلموا اليه قلعة بصرى قيل واستقال

[255] Ms. الفرايض
[256] Ms. للشيخ
[257] Ms. الشيخ ابي حسن صح written in the right margin.
[258] Ms. وجماعة الفقها من الشيخ The من is misplaced.
[259] Ms. منهم has been added.
[260] Ms. اربعة
[261] Ms. ونزل بدار نجم الدين رشيد الجامدار
[262] Ms. الوزارة
[263] Ms. الوزارة

صاحب المخزن كمال الدين ومضى الى مكة وولي موضعه قوام الدين بن[264] صدقة ولزم شرف الدين الزينبي داره وكان صاحب الديوان صفي الدين بن[265] الزوان الهاشمي واستقر نظام الدين في الوزارة ثم عدت الى ميفرقين في اوائل[266] محرم سنة خمس وثلثين وخمسمائة وعبرت بالموصل وحصن كيفا فصادفت الامير داود قد وقع بينه وبين السعيد حسام الدين ونهب بلد ميفرقين في محرم سنة ست وثلثين ونزل على باب المدينة واقام بها ثمانية ايام ثم رحل وكان قد اغار على جميع البلد ورحل الى تل شيخ واخذها واقطع البلد وكان السعيد[267] حسام الدين قد خرب قلعة بشاط[268] واخذها وبنى[269] بها واقطع الجبل جميعه وبقي كل يوم يغير من الموضعين الى باب المدينة وتؤخذ ثياب الناس في النهار[270] وكان[271] حبشي في البلاد والحاجب يوسف ينال في الولاية وساس الناس وحفظ . . .[272] وبقي الامر كذلك الى آخر سنة خمس وثلثين وخمسمائة وفي سنة ست وثلثين اصطلح الامير داود والسعيد حسام الدين ووصل الامير داود الى ميفرقين ودخل باب القصر واتفق ان وقع الاتفاق بينهما

قيل وفي منتصف جمادى الاولى[273] سنة ست وثلثين وخمسمائة مات الامير (*f. 170a*) سعد الدولة بالبلدى[274] ابن ابراهيم صاحب آمد وكان

[264] Ms. ابن
[265] Ms. ابن
[266] Ms. اوايل
[267] Ms. كان السعيد illegible.
[268] Ma. فشاط
[269] Ms. بنا
[270] Ms. B النهر; Marsh 333 (f. 103b) النهر
[271] Ms. B adds شرف الدين
[272] The Ms. is damaged here. It appears to read الكـ . . . و. A likely word would be فدبر حبشي امر العسكر والبلد Ms. B الرعايا
[273] Ms. الاول
[274] Ms. *sic*. The usual form in this Ms. is ايللدى

مؤيد الدين[275] متولي آمد فرتب ولده شمس الملوك محمود في الامارة وقررها وكانت امه يمنى خاتون بنت نجم الدين الغازى وكان حسام الدين خاله وكنت في هذه السنة بآمد وكنت في صحبة والدى رحمه الله وقيل في سنة ست وثلثين وخمسمائة قتل[276] شمس الملوك بدمشق

قيل وكان شرف الدين الحبشي والعميد ابو طاهر ابن المحتسب (في الولاية)[277] لما عاد المؤيد ابو الحسن بن المخطر الى خدمة السعيد حسام الدين قبضه حبشي في سنة اربع وثلثين وبقي في القبض وقتل اخاه الرئيس ابا سعيد تحت العقوبة وبقي الى آخر سنة ست وثلثين ونفذ آتابك زنكي الى حسام الدين يقول ان كان رسول يصلني منك يصلك مني لا ينصحوك ولا ينصحوني فان اردت اتفاقنا فنفذ اليّ حبشي فنفذه اليه ومعه الحاجب ناصر ومعه جماعة فلما لقوه انزلهم وبقي ثلثة ايام ثم ولي شرف الدين حبشي الاستيفاء وخلع عليه الجبة الاطلس والبرّكان بالذهب العراقي والفرس بالمركب وعاد الرسل الذين[278] مضوا معه[279] ثم انه تضمن لآتابك زنكي اخذ البلاد[280] وقاطعه في ذلك فقال لي من قد حلف لي ومتى وصلنا الى البلاد سلمتها اليك

وفي هذه السنة قبض السعيد حسام الدين على الاجل ابي[281] الوفا بن[282] السرطان[283] وحبس مدة ثم قلع عينيه ورمى به من رأس قلعة ماردين الى الميدان[284]

قيل وفي سنة سبع وثلثين وخمسمائة صعد آتابك زنكي الى ديار

[275] Ms. B ابن نيسان
[276] Ms. قيل followed by قتل which is deleted.
[277] في الولاية has been added.
[278] Ms. عادت الرسل الذى
[279] Ms. B مضى شرف الدين حبشي الى الموصل برسالة الى اتابك وعادت الامراء الذين مضوا معه
[280] Ms. B قيل ان حبشي رتب في نفس اتابك انه
[281] Ms. ابو
[282] Ms. ابن
[283] Ms. B بن السرطان; Ms. رطان
[284] Ms. B الى ربض ميردين

بكر ودخل الى ولاية الامير يعقوب بن[285] السبع الاحمر فقصد خيران والمعدن وايرون وقطلبس واخذ جميع الولاية وكنت بالموصل في هذه السنة

وفي سنة ثمان وثلثين وخمسمائة قصد آتابك زنكي البلاد ووصل الى بلد ماردين ودخل الى تل بشمى على انه يدخل الى ولاية آمد وميفرقين وكان قد ملك حاني واسعرد وجبل جور وبالقرنين[286] وجميع تلك الولاية اخذها بعد صلح الامير داود ونزل في الزيتون الذى في تل بشمى[287] فلما كان بعض الليالي[288] دخل على حبشي في الخيمة مؤمل[289] الشاقضي ومحمد بن ابي المكارم المحلمي وضرباه بالسيوف واخذا[290] رأسه وسارا[291] به الى السعيد حسام الدين ووقعت[292] الصيحة واختبط الناس والعسكر واصبح آتابك من غدوة فرحل وعاد الى نصيبين

قيل وفي يوم الاحد تاسع عشر محرم سنة تسع وثلثين وخمسمائة مات الامير داود بحاني وحمل الى حصن كيفا وعبر تابوته يوم الاثنين وحط بجامع المحدثة وخرج اليه الناس والقرآء وحمل من غدوة الى حصن كيفا (*f. 170b*) حصن كيفا وملك بعده ولده الامير فخر الدين قرا آرسلان حصن كيفا وخرتبيت وبالوا[293] وملك ولده آرسلان تغمش قلعة ميزكرد وقصد آتابك ولاية الامير داود فملك اسعرد وباهمود وطنزى وباتاسا وجميع الولاية المتصلة بولاية المعدن وعبر الى الولاية الاخرى وذلك

[285] Ms. ابن
[286] Ms. *sic.*
[287] Ms. B ووصل الى تل بشمى وحط بها العسكر
[288] Marsh 333 (f. 104a) في اثنا الليل
[289] The Ms. is illegible here; Ms. B and Marsh 333 (f. 104a) مؤمل
[290] Ms. اخذ; Ms. B اخذا
[291] Ms. سار
[292] Ms. وقع; Ms. B وقعت
[293] Ms. *sic.*

حاني وجبل جور وبالقرنين[294] والسيوان فنزل وملك ارقنين والهالار وتل خوم وجرموك وجميع ذلك غير خرتبيت وبالوا[295] وميزكرد وبقيت بيد اولاد الامير داود

وفي هذه السنة قتل السلطان داود بسوق تبريز وفي هذه السنة تزوج آرسلان تغمش بن[296] داود بهدية خاتون بنت السعيد حسام الدين وحملت اليه الى ميزكرد ووقع الخلف بين آتابك وحسام الدين

ومضى آتابك ونزل الى الرها وحاصرها مدة ثم فتحها عنوة في خامس العشرين من جمادى الاخرة[297] وكان ثالث عشرين كانون الاول تسع وثلثين وخمسمائة وكانت اخذتها الافرنج بعد موت تاج الدولة في سنة اثنتين وتسعين واربعمائة وكان لها بايديهم سبعة واربعين سنة ثم رحل بعدما رتب امرها ونزل الى البيرة وحاصرها مدة وكانت النصارى يقولون ان آتابك يقتل ليلة الميلاد وكانوا منتظرين[298] ذلك وكان فتحها ليلة الميلاد وسلم آتابك وكذبوا قيل وبقي يحاصر البيرة مدة فوصله الخبر بعد ايام بقتل نصير الدين جقر[299] والي الموصل وكان قتله غلمانه في ثامن ذى القعدة سنة تسع وثلثين وخمسمائة فرحل آتابك عن البيرة ونزل الى الموصل وقرر حالها ورتب فيها زين الدين علي كوشك[300] وكان في سنة تسع وثلثين مات الامير كرج غازى صاحب البارعية بآمد وكان لقي الناس من نصير الدين شدة من الجور والظلم والقتل والمصادرات والاقساط فلما ولي زين الدين ازال ذلك جميعه واحسن الى الناس

294 Ms. *sic*.

295 Ms. *sic*.

296 Ms. ابن

297 Ms. الاخر; Ms. B في شهر الله الاصب

298 Ms. منتظرون

299 Ms. ان نصير الدين جقروا وصل الى الموصل وقتل The more coherent version is in Ms. B فوصله الخبر بعد ايام بقتل نصير الدين

300 Ms. B adds بن بكتكين

والرعايا في جميع البلاد ورأى الناس منه كل خير الى (ان)[301] مات في سنة اربع وستين وخمسمائة

وكان في شهر رجب سنة ثمان وثلثين وخمسمائة استدعى علم الدين ابا[302] الفتح محمد بن علي بن نباتة[303] الى ماردين وولاه الامير حسام الدين قضاء ماردين وولى اخاه[304] بهاء الدين خطابة ميفرقين وكان قاضي ماردين مجد الدين داود بن القاضي السديد فعزل في تلك السنة وولي علم الدين وكان المؤيد ابو[305] الحسن بن مخطر المستوفي المتولي لذلك وبعد يومين ولي الخطابة بماردين وكان بميفرقين له الخطابة فولي قضاء ماردين واستقر واقام بها ونقل اهله واولاده الى ماردين وهو بها الى الان

وكان وصل الى ماردين مكين الدولة (*f. 171a*) ابراهيم بن منقذ من اهل مصر فاقام في ضيافة السعيد حسام الدين مدة ثم انه بعد يومين من ولاية علم الدين قضاء ماردين ولاه حسام الدين الوزارة[306] واستناب[307] المهذب البغدادى وكان ناسخا بمشهد ماردين[308] وهو ابو عبد الله محمد العراقي وكان يقول وانا من بيت المعوج من اهل بغداد وكنت في هذه السنة بماردين

وكان السعيد حسام الدين في اول ولايته بميفرقين نقل نجم[309] الدين الغازى وشمس الدولة اخاه من مسجد الامير الى ماردين ثم دفنهما[310] بقلعة ماردين في مسجد الخضر بالقلعة وكان في ذلك الموضع

301 ان has been added.
302 Ms. ابى
303 Ms. B من ميفرقين
304 Ms. اخيه
305 Ms. ابا
306 الوزارة
307 Ms. يستان; Ms. B واستناب
308 Ms. B ميردين
309 Ms. شمش
310 Ms. دفنهم

تربة[311] فيها جماعة من من مات في ايام الغازى فدفن الغازى وشمس الدولة هناك مدة ثم ان السعيد حسام الدين بنى[312] تحت ربض ماردين عند عين باقرى[313] مشهدا[314] مليحا وبنى[315] فيه تربة وغرم عليها مالا عظيما ووقف عليها الوقف وحط المقابر اليها ودفنوا فيها جميع الذين[316] كانوا بالقلعة اولا فاخيرا ونفذ اليها البسط والستور والالات[317] وجمع فيها خزانة كتب وحصل فيها كتب كثيرة[318] وهي الى الان بها

قيل وفي سنة تسع وثلثين وخمسمائة انهدمت عمارة جسر قرامان من سنة ثمان واربعين وفيها انهدمت البدنة داخل ميفرقين وبنيت

قيل وفي سنة اربعين قبض الوزير المصرى وحبس في قلعة ماردين فحصل عنده في الحبس ثياب خام وخرج من الحبس وشدها في وسطه وتدلى من قلعة ماردين[319] وانهزم فلما اصبحوا طلبوه فلم يصادفوه ورأوا الخام مشدودا فطلبوه فوجدوه[320] في طرف الجبل فحملوه الى السعيد حسام الدين فاطلقه قصرفه ولم يسئ اليه

قيل وفي سنة اربعين وخمسمائة كسر السعيد حسام الدين فخر الدين قرا آرسلان على باغين وكان يوما عظيما مشهودا وكانت الكسرة والفتح لشهاب الدين محمد بن الياس بن الغازى فانه كان رأس العسكر مع عمه حسام الدين وفي سنة اربعين وصل آتابك زنكي الى ميفرقين واخذ تل شيخ وضايق ميفرقين مدة ثم سار

قيل وفي سنة اربعين وخمسمائة وصل الشيخ نور الهدى سليمن بن

311 Ms. B وكان لهم تربة بالقلعة
312 Ms. بنا
313 Ms. *sic.*; Ms. B باقيرا
314 Ms. مشهد
315 Ms. بنا
316 Ms. الذى
317 Ms. الات
318 Ma. كتبا كثيرا
319 Ms. B ميردين
320 Ms. B فلما اصبحوا ماجو وركبت الخيل لطلبه فلحقوه

عمر العلوى من اسعرد الى ميفرقين وكان حسام الدين بالبلد فخرج اهل ميفرقين باسرهم ولقوه مقدار[321] فرسخ وخرج الامير فلقيه[322] عند قبة السلطان وكان فاضلا عالما ونزل عند تاج الدين رحمه الله في دار علم الدين وبعد يوم نزل الامير اليه ولم يقم له وجلس في الجامع ووعظ وتكلم وافتتن الناس به وبلغ الامير مبلغا عظيما وكان في اوفى منزلة وحصل اذا كان الامير بميفرقين كان معه واذا سار الى ماردين سار معه وكان يقيم حيث اقام (*f. 171b*) الامير وحصل له الناموس العظيم[323] بحيث انه مدة مقامه عند الامير ما يقم له يوما قط وحصل[324] يبدو[325] منه ما لا يليق بمثله في اعين الناس وسار الى الشام وبقي مدة واخذ قلعة ابي قبيس ووقع بينه وبين الاسماعيلية وعاد الى السعيد حسام الدين واقام مدة وكان اطمع السعيد حسام الدين في عمل الكيميا[326] ولم يصح منه شيء ومضى الى اسعرد واقام بها مدة الى شهر ربيع الاول سنة ست واربعين وخمسمائة فدخل الى الجامع[327] وكان يوم الجمعة فوثب عليه رجلان من الاسماعيلية[328] فضربه احدهما بخنجر فضربه بسيف كان بيده فوثب عليه رجل[329] فضربه بسكين فوقع واختبط الناس وقبض الذى ضربه[330] ورفيقه وبقي الى يومه ومات رحمه الله ودفن باسعرد في مسجد الخضر عليه السلم وقتلوا اللذين قتلاه[331]

321 Ms. مقدر
322 Ms. B ولقيه الامير والجماعة
323 Ms. B وحصل له من الناموس والحرمة ما ليس بالقليل ويحكم على الامير اوفى تحكم
324 Ms. B adds ثم انه يغير عن الطريقة واخذ الخدم
325 Ms. يبدوا
326 Ms. الكيما
327 Ms. B adds ليصلي
328 Ms. الاسماعلية
329 Ms. B فوثب عليه آخر
330 Ms. B adds (*sic.*) وكان من الاسميعيلية
331 Ms. الذين قتلوه

قيل وفي سنة اربعين وخمسمائة اتصل المولى نجم الدين المالك الى خاتون بنت الامير[332] احمد بن سكمان صاحب خلاط وكانت اخت شاه ارمن لامه وبنت عمه ووصل صفي الدين بن رشيق واثير الدين عباد[333] بن ابي الفتوح وسراج الدين بن كامل غازى وجماعة من اكابر دولة[334] سكمان واقاموا اياما بميفرقين وساروا الى ماردين[335] وعادوا ومضى القاضي علم الدين ابو الفتح محمد ابن نباتة ومعه اكابر الدولة[336] الى خلاط في سنة احدى واربعين وخمسمائة واحضروا الخاتون وكان العرس بماردين وحضر اكابر دولة خلاط

قيل وفي سنة احدى واربعين وخمسمائة شرع السعيد[337] حسام الدين رحمه الله في بناء جسر اقرامان على القنطرة[338] بتولي الزاهد ابن الطويل واستقرت[339] قواعده من الجانب الشرقي[340] وقلعه المد واخربه لضعف[341] عمله واخرجه والزمه الزاهد الغمارة[342] فاخرج عليه ثم وليه الامير سيف الدين شير باريك ممدود بن علي بن ارتق[343] وشرع في عمارته بتولي ابي الخير الفاسول[344] واحضر اخشابا لم ير مثلها وابتدأ في عمارته[345] وهو من العجائب التي بنيت[346] في هذا الزمان وبقي العمل فيه[347]

[332] Ms. B adds قطب الدين

[333] Ms. B ابن عباد

[334] Ms. بيت written on the line, دولة above it.

[335] Ms. B خلاط

[336] Ms. B وساروا الى ماردين ولقوا الصاحب وتقرر الحال

[337] Ms. العميد

[338] Ms. *sic.*; Ms. B بالقيطوم

[339] Ms. استقر; Ms. B اسس

[340] Ms. B من الجانبان (*sic.*); Marsh 333 من الجانبين

[341] Ms. B لضعف; Ms. وضعف

[342] Ms. بعمارته; Ms. B and Marsh 333 الغرامة

[343] Ms. *sic.* It should read بن علي بن الب يارق بن ارتق

[344] Ms. B ابي الخير بن الحكيم الفاسول

[345] Ms. B فعمله الى سنة ثمان واربعين وخمسمائة

[346] Ms. الذى بنى

[347] Ms. B وبقي شيء يسير

وفي سنة احدى واربعين وخمسمائة نازل آتابك زنكي قلعة جعبر وفيها سيف الدولة ابو الحسن علي بن مالك وضايقها مضايقة شديدة واشرفت على الاخذ وكان جمال الدين سربي ولد السعيد حسام الدين في خدمته ومعه عسكر وكان قبضه وحسبه في بيعة ربض القلعة

ولقد سألت الوالي المصدر الكامل قاضي القضاة كمال الدين ابا الفضل محمد بن عبد الله الشهرزورى ادام الله ظله في سنة اربع واربعين وخمسمائة بالموصل عن قتل (*f. 172a*) آتابك وما جرى فقال كنا نازلنا القلعة مدة فلما كان بعض الايام خرج الامير حسان المنبجي[348] وصاح اريد اكلم الامير علي[349] فتراءى[350] له من على السور[351] وقال له تعلم ما بيني وبينك[352] واتابك تعرف ايش هو[353] مالك من تلتجئ اليه ولا من يصرفه عنك[354] والراى[355] ان تسلم والا ان اخذها بالسيف يجرى ما لا تقدر على دفعه[356] وبعد هذا ايش تنتظر فقال له يا امير حسان انتظر الفرج من الله تعالى وما انتظرت على منبج لما حاصرها الامير بلك وكفاك الله امره فقال كمال الدين والله ما كان الا تلك الليلة نصف الليل وكان ذلك اليوم الاربعاء خامس شهر ربيع الاخر وقيل تاسعة سنة احدى واربعين وخمسمائة والصايح[357] من القلعة[358] يصيح قتل آتابك يا ابن حسام الدين لك البشرى واختبط الناس وماجوا وكان سبب ذلك ان الامير آتابك كان يبيت في الخيمة وعنده خادم فما

[348] Ms. حسام الدين المنبجي; Ms. B حسان المنبجي
[349] Ms. B اريد يكلمني الامير علي
[350] Ms. فترايا
[351] Ms. الصور; Ms. B السور
[352] Ms. B adds من الصداقة
[353] Ms. B وانت تعرف اتابك وما هو عليه
[354] Ms. B وما لك ظهر مستند اليه
[355] Ms. B الواجب
[356] Ms. B لا تريد
[357] Ms. B جاءنا
[358] Ms. B الى القلعة

كان يبيت عنده غيره فلما نام تلك الليلة قتله الخادم في الخيمة فاخذ السكين بالدم وخرج وطلع الى الربض الى تحت القلعة وصاح اليهم قتلت آتابك فلم يصدقوه فأراهم السكين وعلامة اخرى كان اخذها من عنده فاصعدوه اليهم وحققوا الحال منه وصاحوا فاختبط الناس واختلفوا وقصد[359] الناس مخيم جمال الدين الوزير[360] فنهب وانهزم وجاء اليّ[361] وقصدني[362] الامراء والكبار وركبت[363] وقالوا ما رأى الملك فقصدوا وقصدت خيمة الملك آلب عسلان[364] بن محمود وقلت انا والناس وآتابك غلمان الملك والبلاد له والكل خدمه ومماليك السلطان[365] فاجتمع الناس على الملك واطلق جمال الدين سربي من البيعة وسيروه[366] الى ماردين[367]

وتفرق الناس فريقين فاخذ صلاح الدين محمد[368] ابن ايوب اليغسياني[369] نور الدين محمود بن آتابك وعسكر الشام ومضوا الى الشام فملك حلب وحماة ومنبج وحران وحمص وجميع ما بيد آتابك من الشام واستقر به وسرنا نحن و الملك وعساكر ديار ربيعة فطلبنا الموصل فوصلنا الى سنجار فانهزم الملك وطلب الجزيرة فلحقه اخي تاج الدين ابو طاهر يحيى رحمه الله وعز الدين ابو بكر الدبيسي وحلفا له ورداه الى المعسكر ونزلنا الى الموصل ووصل سيف الدين غازى بن آتابك من بلد شهرزور وكانت اقطاعه من السلطان فملك ديار ربيعة

359 Ms. قصدوا
360 Ms. B المستوفي
361 Ms. B فاخفيته عند بعض اصحابي
362 Ms. وقصدوني
363 Ms. B adds فقلت الملك
364 Ms. *sic.*; Ms. B آرسلان
365 Ms. B وقلت ايش كان اتابك والكل مماليك السلطان
366 Ms. B سير
367 Ms. B الى ابيه
368 Ms. محمود; Ms. B محمد
369 Ms. B الاغسياني

باسرها وحمل الملك الى قلعة الثلو عند سنجار[370] وملك الموصل وجميع البلاد وسيف الدين غازى استوزر جمال الدين محمد بن الاصفهاني وكان مستوفي ديوان ابيه (*f. 172b*) واقطع[371] الجزيرة لعز الدين ابي[372] بكر الدبيسي[373] واستقر في البلاد

وتولى امير نور الدين صلاح الدين[374] واسد الدين شيركوه واحتجب مجد الدين ابا بكر بن[375] الداية وكانت امه داية نور الدين وهي رتبة وكان مجد الدين يخدمه من صباه فلما ولي الامير رد اليه الامر وولاه حلب واستقر في الشام

وبعد ايام من قتل آتابك وثب اهل الرها من الارمن على من كان بها من المسلمين وقتلوا جماعة[376] ووصل عز الدين الدبيسي وحسان صاحب منبج وجماعة من التركمان وتكاثروا عليها ونهبوها وفتحوها وقتل منها خلق كثير[377] واقام بها جماعة

وكان عند قتل آتابك السعيد حسام الدين بميفرقين فوصله الخبر العصر وهو في بستان المحوط فسار من وقته[378] وكان قبل ذلك اليوم وصله الخبر بقبض ولده جمال الدين فضاق صدره ثم وصله الخبر بقتله وسار الى حاني فنازلها وبقي عليها مدة ثم اخذها وكان فيها الامير غازى ابن المهرى فتحها ثالث عشرين شهر ربيع الاخر سنة احدى اربعين وخمسمائة وسار فاخذ السيوان وجبل جور وبالقرنين[379] ونزل ثم اخذ

370 Ms. B ويقال انه قتل الملك
371 Ms. وقطع
372 Ms. ابو
373 Ms. B adds وولى سيف الدين غازى زين الدين علي بن بكتكين وعز الدين الدبيسي
374 Ms. B adds وولده الاكبر
375 Ms. ابن
376 Ms. B adds وملكوها ونفذوا يستدعون الافرنج فاجتمع اليها خلق من المسلمين
377 Ms. خلقا كثيرا
378 Ms. B من ليلته
379 Ms. *sic*.

شبختان (و)[380] الموزّر وتل موزن وجملين ورأس عين الخابور وعاد وكنت في هذه السنة بماردين[381]

وسار فخر الدين قر آرسلان[382] وملك ارقنين وجرموك وتل خوم[383] والهالار وجميع الحصون التي كان اخذها[384] آتابك من ابيه الامير داود وملك جانب اسعرد الشرقي[385] وبهمود[386] وباتاسا وطنزى والروق وقطلبس وبلد صاف وقلعة الهيثم التي في جبل طور عبدين ونزل صاحب اخلاط شاه ارمن فملك خيزان والمعدن وايرون وجميع الولاية التي اخذها[387] آتابك من الامير يعقوب

وفي هذه السنة وهي سنة اثنتين واربعين وخمسمائة ضرب[388] السعيد حسام الدين الفلوس الصفار ومضيت الى المعدن واشتريت صفرا برسم الفلوس

وفي سنة ثلث واربعين مات عسلان[389] تغمش بن الامير داود[390] ونازل السعيد حسام الدين اسعرد اياما واخذها وصل الى خدمته جمال الدين محمود صاحب آمد وجمال الدين ابو القاسم بن[391] نيسان[392] وكان معه على اسعرد فلما اخذها عاد الى ميفرقين وبعد مدة ردها الى فخر الدين وفي هذه المدة ملك[393] فخر الدين قرا آرسلان ميزكرد وعادت هدية خاتون الى ميفرقين وفي هذه السنة وقع الخلف بين

380 و has been added.
381 Ms. B بميردين ودنيسر
382 Ms. *sic.*
383 Ms. تل خرم
384 Ms. اخذ
385 Ms. جانب الشرقي اسعرد; Ms. B حصل له من جائب الحصن اروق
386 Ms. B باهمود
387 Ms. اخذ
388 Ms. B صرف
389 Ms. *sic.*
390 Ms. B adds وخلف ابنا من ابنة الامير عاش بعده اياما قلائل ومات
391 Ms. ابن
392 Ms. سيان
393 Ms. omits a verb; Ms. B ملك

السعيد حسام الدين وابن آتابك سيف الدين غازى ونهب بلد ماردين ونهب مماليك[394] جماعة

وفي هذه السنة وصلت الخاتون بنت عز الدين سلتق صاحبة اخلاط الى حصن كيفا طلبت[395] الحجاز فانزلها فخر الدين قر آرسلان واحسن في اكرامها[396] (*f. 173a*) ووصل بهاء الدين[397] الوزير واثير الدين عباد وعلم الدين بن طبن قاضي ارجيش ونزلوا في دار المؤيد[398] بن مخطر بميفرقين واقاموا اياما ونفذ السعيد حسام الدين الى فخر الدين ومنعوا الخاتون من المسير الى الحجاز[399] وكان شاه ارمن سألهم ذلك فسألوا الخاتون حتى عادوا جميعا الى خلاط

وفي هذه السنة مات المؤيد المستوفي ابو الحسن المبارك بن مخطر وكان متولي الديوان وكان معه المهذب العراقي مشرفا ودفن في ماردين في البيعة التي بناها وولي موضعه ولده الاجل كريم الدولة ابو منصور خالد ويلقب بلقب[400] ابيه مؤيد الدولة كريم الملك واقام بشرائط الخدمة وتابع ما فوض اليه واستقل وزاد على ما يرجو منه وحصل الامور كلها بحكمه

قيل وفي سنة اثنتين واربعين وخمسمائة مات الخليفة الحافظ بمصر وولي موضعه ولده المنصور اسماعيل ويلقب بالظافر وكان السلطان امير الجيوش العادل السلار من المختبي وقرر امر الدولة ورتب العساكر واستقر الظافر بالخلافة

قيل في سنة اثنتين واربعين وخمسمائة قبض آتابك غازى على

[394] Ms. مماليكا
[395] Ms. B فطلب الحج; Ms. طالبت
[396] Ms. اكراحها (*sic.*).
[397] Ms. B adds اوس ابن ابي معاذ (*sic.*).
[398] Ms. B المستوفي
[399] Ms. B ورد فخر الدين الى خلاط ولم يمكنها من المسير الى الحجاز
[400] Ms. لقب

القاضي كمال الدين وتاج الدين ابني عبد الله الشهرزوری وکان امر الدولة من حيث قتل آتابك زنكي اليه فسعى جمال الدين الوزير وزين الدين في ذلك [401] وقبض[402] عليهما ورفعا الى قلعة الموصل واستحضر[403] القاضي نجم الدين ابا علي بن بهاء الدين ابن الحسن بن علي بن القسم الشهرزورى من الرحبة وكان بها متولي القضاء فانه لما مات بهاء الدين الشهرزورى في سنة اثنتين وثلثين وخمسمائة بالرقة على ما ذكرناه ولي قضاء بلاد آتابك اجمع ولده القاضي نجم الدين ابو الحسن بن علي وولي ابن اخيه شمس الدين ابو احمد الموصل وولي كمال الدين قضاء نصيبين والعسكر وولي تاج الدين ابو طاهر قضاء الجزيرة وولي شرف الدين اخو بهاء الدين سنجار وكل منهم ولي مستقلا من غير نيابة فانهم كانوا جميعهم في هذى[404] المواضع نيابة عن بهاء الدين فلما مات تولى هؤلاء[405] هذه البلاد

وولي نجم الدين ولد بهاء الدين باقي البلاد اجمع فيها القضاة نوابه وبقي الى سنة ثلث وثلثين وخمسمائة وتولى شمس الدين ابو احمد موضع قاضي القضاة بالموصل وخدم نجم الدين فاخذ قضاء الموصل مضافا الى ما كان بيده وبقي الى سنة خمس وثلثين وخمسمائة وقبض نجم الدين متوالي نصيبين وصودر وحبس وعوقب عقوبة (*f. 173b*) عظيمة واخذ منه مصادرة ما يقارب مائة الف وثلثين الف دينار آمرية وولي كمال الدين ابو الفضل محمد بن عبد الله الشهرزورى البلاد جميعها واستقل بالامر وحصلت الولاية من القضاء والبلاد العساكر وجميع الامور مردودة الى كمال الدين الى ان قتل آتابك على ما ذكرناه

وبقي نجم الدين في الحبس مدة اربع سنين ثم ان القاضي كمال الدين

[401] Ms. في ذلك صح written on left margin.

[402] Ms. فقبضا

[403] Ms. استحضروا

[404] Ms. *sic*. The scribe often prefers this form.

[405] Ms. هاولاء

توصل في اخراجه وولاه قضاء الرحبة فانه كان في ايام ابيه بهاء الدين وبقي فيه الى ان قبض كمال الدين على ما ذكرناه وحضر وولي الموصل ورتب ولده الاكبر بهاء الدين على ما ذكرناه بالرحبة واستقر هو بالموصل وبقي كمال الدين وتاج الدين في حبس الموصل بالقلعة مدة فنفذ الامام المقتفي الخليفة رحمه الله عليه جماعة . . .[406] رسلا الى الموصل فتوصلوا في اخراجهما الى دورهما ورتب على باب كل واحد منهما رجلين خراسانيين[407] بحيث لا يدخلون ولا يخرجون واخذ ولد كمال الدين ابو احمد الجلال و(ولد)[408] تاج الدين ابو الفضائل[409] الضياء وحبسا في قلعة الموصل فاستبد نجم الدين بقضاء الموصل واقطع عز الدين ابا[410] بكر الدبيسي الجزيرة ورتب فيها قاضيا يعرف بابن حمزة من اهل دقوقا مدة[411]

قيل وكان في سنة ست وثلثين وخمسمائة ولي الوزير نظام الدين ابو جعفر وقيل المظفر محمد بن الزعيم بن جهير وزارة الخليفة بعد ما عاد الاذن من السلطان مسعود بعزل شرف الدين الزينبي وولي قوام الدين بن صدقة المخزن على ما ذكرناه وبقي الوزير الى سنة احدى واربعين وخمسمائة في الوزارة ومضى الى مكة وحج وعاد الى بغداد وفي هذه السنة حج بهاء الدين ابو طاهر بن عقيل بن طاهر بن نباتة من ميفرقين ودخل الى بغداد وحضر دار الخلافة واورد فصلا بحضور الوزير نظام الدين ورشيد الدولة ابن الانبارى رحمهما الله وجمع ارباب دولة الخليفة وعاد وخلع عليه الخليفة وكان صحبه[412] غير القضاة ابو الفتح ابن العمران وبعد عود الوزير الى بغداد بقي مدة وعزل من الوزارة

[406] Ms. There is a lacuna here.
[407] Ms. خراسينية
[408] ولد has been added.
[409] Ms. الفضايل
[410] Ms. ابو
[411] Ms. B وولى الجزيرة الدقوقي
[412] Ms. صحبه

وولي قوام الدين بن صدقة الوزارة[413] وولي المخزن زعيم الدين بن جعفر وولي الديوان الاجل جمال الدين ابو المظهر بن هبة

قيل وفي سنة ثلث واربعين وخمسمائة ماتت الخاتون فاطمة زوجة الخليفة المقتفي ببغداد وفي سنة ثلث واربعين وخمسمائة حضر الشيخ شرف الدين بن سعد بن[414] عصرون من الموصل وعقد على زمرد خاتون بنت السعيد حسام الدين (*f. 174a*) لاتابك[415] غازى وكان الاملاك بقصر ميافارقين على عشرين الف دينار وكان الوالي[416] الشيخ عز الشيوخ ابو القاسم بن[417] حبشي

وفي شعبان سنة ثلث[418] واربعين وخمسمائة وصل عز الدولة ابو نصر بن[419] نيسان الى ميفرقين وعقد على صفية خاتون بنت السعيد حسام الدين لجمال الدين شمس الملوك محمود بن ايلدى[420] صاحب آمد على خمسة[421] الاف[422] دينار[423] وكان الوالي[424] الخطيب تاج العلماء الحصلقي[425] وحملها في الخمس الاواخر من شعبان الى آمد

وفي سنة ثلث واربعين وخمسمائة حضر الامير بهاء الدين سيونج بن كهمش (و)[426] الوزير ضياء الدين[427] من عند الامير فخر الدين دولت شاه بن طغان آرسلان صاحب ارزن وبدليس وعقدا على نورة خاتون

413 Ms. الوزارة
414 Ms. ابن
415 Ms. اتابك
416 Ms. (*sic.*) الولي (?).
417 Ms. ابن
418 Ms. ثلث written above the line, اثنين on it.
419 Ms. ابن
420 Ms. *sic.*
421 Ms. خمس
422 Ms. الف
423 Ms. B خمسين الف دينار
424 Ms. *sic.* الولي (?).
425 Ms. *sic.* (?).
426 و has been added.
427 Ms. adds ايوب

بنت السعيد حسام الدين[428] على خمسين الف دينار وكان الوالي[429] وكان العقد بميفرقين

وكان في سنة ثمان وثلثين وخمسمائة مات حسام الدولة قرتى[430] بارزن وولي الامارة اخوه شمس الدين ياقوت آرسلان الى سنة اربعين وخمسمائة ونفذ اخاه دولت شاه الى خدمة آتابك زنكي لما عبر واخذ بلاد الامير داود بعد موته ثم مات ياقوت آرسلان يوم السبت مستهل شهر رمضان سنة اربعين وخمسمائة وسار ضياء الدين ايوب[431] الى معسكر آتابك فجابوا[432] الامير دولت شاه ويلقب بفخر[433] الدين وعبر به على باب ميفرقين وسار الى ارزن وملك البلاد واستبد بالامارة وملك جميع ولاية ابيه واخوته[434] وكان ضياء الدين ايوب تزوج امه وانتقل[435] الى السعيد حسام الدين وفي ذى الحجة وصلوا الى ميفرقين واخذوا الخاتون وساروا بها الى ارزن وعمل العرس بميفرقين[436]

وفي سنة ثلث واربعين وخمسمائة سار تاج الدين ابو سالم طاهر بن نباتة الى الحجاز ودخل بغداد وحضر ديوان الخلافة وفي سنة ثلث واربعين وخمسمائة عاد الوزير مكين الدين المصرى الى ميفرقين وولاه السعيد حسام الدين الوزارة وبقي اياما وكنت في هذه السنة متولي اشراف ظاهر بلد ميفرقين وبقي مدة ثم انه قبض المؤيد والمهذب وعاقبهما بالقصر اياما ثم انه رتب العميد بن[437] ابي طاهر بن المحتسب في عمل حساب الديوان فجلس يومين لا غير ورسم السعيد حسام الدين بعزله

428 Ms. B adds لفخر الدين دولت شاه بن طغان آرسلان
429 Ms. *sic*. الولي (?).
430 Ms. قوتى
431 Ms. B adds وكان زوج امه
432 Ms. *sic*.; Ms. B وعاد به الى ارزن
433 Ms. فخر
434 Ms. B اخيه
435 Ms. B انتقل; Ms. اتصل
436 Ms. B ووصل بهاء الدين سونج بن . . . واخذها وسار الى ارزن وبقيت عنده مدة
437 Ms. ابن

وصفعه وحلق لحيته وركب حمارا ودوروا به في البلد ونفي واصرف عن البلد وبقي الوزير اياما ثم خرج بعد العصر وغلامه خلفه وسير حول البلد ثم طلب طريق حصن كيفا ومضى فقيل للسعيد حسام الدين قد هرب فقال ما اخذ منا شيأ فلا تطلبوه فمضى وفي بكرة الغد اعيد المؤيد والمهذب الى الديوان واستقر امرهما وعادا الى اوفى منزلة

قيل وفي سنة اربع واربعين وخمسمائة خرج ابن آتابك غازى الى باب نصيبين ونفذ الامير جلدك الخليفتي الى ماردين واخذ (*f. 174b*) زمرد خاتون الى باب نصيبين ونزل معها صمصام الدين ومرض ابن[438] آتابك سيف الدين غازى فحملت الى الموصل ونزلت في درب دراج وفي دار الخاتون بنت سكمان زوجة آتابك زنكي ودخل سيف الدين غازى وهو مريض على شدة واقام بالموصل وقد نفذ الى بغداد فاحضروا الحكيم ابا البركات فحضر وعالجه اياما ومات في صفر سنة اربع[439] واربعين وخمسمائة وولي الامارة اخوه قطب الدين مودود[440] بن[441] آتابك واستقر في الامارة ورتب الدولة جمال الدين الوزير وزين الدين وعز الدين[442] ودفن سيف الدين غازى في المدرسة العمادية[443]

وبعد موت سيف الدين[444] اطلق القاضي كمال الدين واخوه من دورهما[445] واستدعيا الى الميدان[446] وكنت في هذه السنة بالموصل في خدمة السعيد حسام الدين في بيع الحديد وكنت حاضرا بالميدان وكان نفذ الوزير جمال الدين لهما بغلتين فركبا وحضرا الميدان داخل الموصل فلما

[438] Ms. بن written above the line.
[439] Ms. اربعة
[440] Ms. B مودود; Ms. ممدود
[441] Ms. ابن
[442] Ms. B واستقر بوساطة زين الدين والدبيسي وجمال الدين الوزير
[443] Ms. B adds بالموصل
[444] Ms. B adds باربعة ايام
[445] Ms. دورهم
[446] Ms. B adds بباب الدار الاتابكية

دخلا باب الميدان وقد غيرا ثيابهما وركبا بغير طرحات ترجلا فلما رأهما آتابك قطب الدين طلبهما وترجل لهما ولقياه[447] وعزياه عن اخيه وهناءه[448] بالامارة وركبا[449] ووقفا من ناحية وبقيا[450] ساعة وعادا الى مقرهما وازالوا الاجناد من على ابوابهما وحصلا يركبان ويمطيان[451] في كل اسبوع الى خدمة آتابك وزين الدين وجمال الدين وبعد مدة نفذوا وقرروا الحال مع السعيد حسام الدين[452] وعقد لآتابك قطب الدين الى زمرد خاتون بعد انقضاء مدة الوفاء[453] ودخل بها بالموصل

وفي آخر سنة اربع[454] واربعين نازل السعيد حسام الدين مدينة دارا وامتنع الوالي من تسليمها . . .[455] فحاضرها مدة ثم سلمها اليه يوم الاربعاء ثاني عشر ذى[456] الحجة وملكها ورتب فيها واليا الحاجب ابن بقش الدنيسرى وكنت بالمعسكر[457] حتى فتحها في خدمة السعيد حسام الدين وفي هذه السنة سنة اربع واربعين احترق سوق القبة بميافارقين وفي هذه السنة في ذى الحجة وقع الخلف بين اولاد العميد تاج الدين ابي سالم بن[458] نباتة وسار ضياء الدين الى دارا فلقي السعيد حسام الدين وخدم واخذ القضاء وعاد الى ميفرقين وفي[459] ثاني عشر محرم سنة اربع[460] واربعين وخمسمائة ولد قطب الدين[461] ايل غازى ولد المالك نجم الدين دام ظلهما

447 Ms. B وعانقهم
448 Ms. هناه
449 Ms. B وركب وركبا
450 Ms. وبقوا
451 Ms. يمطيان صح in left margin.
452 Ms. B. فتقرر ذلك على مدينة دارا (?).
453 Ms. الوفاة
454 Ms. اربعة
455 The Ms. has a lacuna here اليه (?).
456 Ms. ذو
457 Ms. B adds وكنت اذ ذاك بالمعسكر
458 Ms. ابن
459 Ms. في سنة ثاني (*sic.*).
460 Ms. اربعة
461 Ms. ابن ايل غازى

وفي سنة اربع[462] واربعين وخمسمائة اخذت الافرنج المرية (*f. 175a*) من المسلمين ونهب وحمل نهبها وبيع[463] بديار مصر والساحل والشام

وفي سنة خمس واربعين وخمسمائة املك صمصام الدين بهرام بن[464] السعيد حسام الدين ببنت آتابك اخت قطب الدين وكنت وقت الاملاك في الموصل

وفي[465] سنة خمس واربعين وخمسمائة نهب العرب بنو زعب وغيرهم[466] وذباب وبطران آخر الحاج واخذوا جميع ما كان معهم بين مكة والمدينة عند موضع يسمى سد وتلف خلق كثير عظيم[467] ولم يسمع بذلك الا من سنين بعيدة ولم يسلم الا الاقل من الناس وكنت في هذه السنة بالموصل مقيما

وملك حسام الدين باولاده جميع امراء[468] ديار بكر وديار ربيعة وارمنية واتصاله بهم[469] ولم يبق بعد آتابك زنكي امير مستقل بنفسه من غير معارض ولا منازع ولا من يحكم عليه غير السعيد حسام الدين[470]

وفي سنة خمس واربعين وخمسمائة مات معين الدين انر بدمشق وفيها[471] لقي نور الدين محمود بن زنكي ملك الشام الافرنج وكسرهم اقبح كسرة واسر ابن جوسلين صاحب الرها وما حولها وملك بلاده جميعها وملك نور الدين تل باشر وما حولها وتل خالد وما يليها[472]

462 Ms. اربعة
463 Ms. ابيع; Ms. B بيع
464 Ms. ابن
465 Ms. B adds في المحرم
466 Ms. B نهب العرب الحاج
467 Ms. عظيم written above the line; Ms. B تلف خلق عظيم
468 Ms. B ملوك
469 Ms. B امراءها باتصاله اليهم; Ms. *sic.*
470 After باتصاله اليهم Ms. B has لم يبق بعد اتابك زنكي اميرا مستقل بنفسه يحكم (*sic.*) في ولايته في غير معارض ولا منازع ولا يفعل الا ما يأمره غيره
471 Ms. B في المحرم
472 Ms. B has ولاية كثيرة instead of ما يليها

وملك السعيد حسام الدين سميساط وفي سادس شهر ربيع الاول سنة خمس واربعين وخمسمائة ملك البيرة وفي سنة ست واربعين قتل في هذه الكسرة الحاجب عمر الخاص وكان في خدمة نور الدين وملك فخر الدين قر[473] آرسلان من ولاية ابن جوسلين حصن منصور وبابلوا واخذ من الارمن قلعة كركر وملك السلطان قليج آرسلان مرعش وكيسوم وما جاورها ولم يبق لابن جوسلين من الولاية غير قلعة الروم[474] ولو عاش السعيد حسام الدين كان ملكها[475]

وفي سنة خمس واربعين وخمسمائة مات معين الدين انر بدمشق

وفي سنة ست واربعين سافرت الى خلاط وعدت انحدرت الى بغداد فوصلتها سابع عشرين شهر رمضان واقمت بها وفي سنة ست واربعين طهر السعيد حسام الدين اولاد الامير جمال الدين سربي بميفرقين

وفي سبع واربعين وصل الى السعيد حسام الدين منشور من السلطان والخليفة وقرئ على المنبر بالبلاد[476] ووصلت[477] الخلع وبعد ليلتين وهي ليلة الاثنين ثاني عشرين شهر ربيع الاول سنة سبع واربعين انهدم الجامع بميفرقين موضع المنبر والاروقة[478] وكنت ببغداد واجتمعت ببغداد بقطب الدين العبادى الواعظ وصحبته مدة وكتبت عنه شيئا كثيرا من مجالس

وكان سنة اربع واربعين في آخرها ولي الوزارة عون الدين المظفر محمد بن يحيى بن[479] هبيرة وعزل قوام الدين بن[480] صدقة من الوزارة

473 Ms. *sic.*; Ms. B فرا آرسلان

474 Ms. B has ولم يبق على الفرات موضع ليس هو للمسلمين غير قلعة الروم

475 Ms. وكان ملكها; Ms. B كان قد ملكها

476 Ms. B adds واجتمع الناس

477 وصلت is supplied from Ms. B

478 Ms. B ووقع موضع المنبر والاروقة ونقض الباقي وحفر اساس

479 Ms. ابن

480 Ms. بن provided from Ms. B

واستقر عون الدين فيها وكان اليه ديوان الزمام والاستيفاء وولي ديوان الزمام[481] جلال الدين (*f. 175b*) ابن جعفر اخو صاحب المخزن وكان ابوهما من اهل قرية باعقوبا[482] وكان وزر لمجاهد الدين بهروز مدة حياته وبقي الخليفة مستقر الاحوال

وفي سنة ست واربعين وصل السلطان مسعود الى بغداد واقام بها جميع الشتوة[483] قرأيته في هذه السنة ببغداد ورأيت الفيل والببغة والقرد وسار السلطان الى باب همذان فمرض في جمادى[484] الاولى سنة سبع واربعين وبقي الى حادى عشر جمادى[485] الاخرة[486] ومات بباب همذان وحمل الى اصفهان فاقمت ببغداد الى اول رجب من السنة وسرت ميفرقين فلما وصلنا الى تكريت وقع الخبر بان[487] السطان قد مات فاختبط الناس وسرنا الى الموصل

وخرج الخليفة ونزل في دار السلطان وملك بغداد[488] وهرب مسعود بلال الى تركيت وكان شحنة بغداد وكان قد عمل امارة الحج سنين ولقي الناس منه كل خير وراحة وجند الخليفة الجنود والعساكر فاسقط المؤن والاعشار[489] التى كان يأخذها اصحاب السلطان واحسن الى الناس وعدل في الرعية وحصل العراق واشتغل ارتفاع العراق جميعه[490] فانه كان للسلطان والخواتين واصحاب السلطان بالعراق معيشة عشرين الف فارس فحصل الجميع للخليفة

ولما مات السلطان مسعود بباب همذان كان السلطان محمد شاه بن

481 Ms. الذمام
482 Ms. با يعقوبا
483 Ms. B adds الى الربيع
484 Ms. جمدى
485 Ms. جمدى
486 Ms. الاخر
487 Ms. ان
488 Ms. B adds وملك العراق واستبد به
489 Ms. B adds والمكوس بأسرها
490 Ms. B حصل جميع العراق بحكمه ونفذ العساكر واخذت الحلة وواسط واشتغل بارتفاع العراق جميعه

محمود[491] وكان صهره على ابنته في خوزستان وكان معه في المعسكر[492] اخوه ملك شاه بن محمود فرتبه خاصبيك بن البلنكرى في السلطنة مدة[493] فلما سمع محمد شاه سار من خوزستان الى همذان واخذ السلطنة[494] وسار اخوه ملك شاه فملك خوزستان والاهواز وطرفا من البصرة وبقي مدة وقتل خاصبيك بن[495] البلنكرى واستبد بالسلطنة محمد شاه وكان السلطان مسعود رحمه الله سلطانا عادلا لين الجانب كبير النفس بحيث انه فرق ولايته اجمع على اصحابه وما كان له غير الاسم من السلطنة وكان مع لين جانبه ما حارب احدا الا ظفر به وقتل من الامراء الكبار ما لا قتل غيره منهم منكوروش وقراجا الساقي صاحب فرس[496] وشيراز وقتل عباس صاحب الرى وقتل الراشد والمسترشد ودبيس وبوزباه[497] وعبد الرحمن بن طغربيك[498] وجماعة من الامراء (و)[499] الاسفهسلارية الكبار وسعد سعادة عظيمة ومات وخلف ثلثة[500] بنين صغار واستقر محمد شاه في السلطنة وملك همذان واصفهان وما حولها[501] من غير خطبة بالعراق

قيل وفي سنة سبع واربعين ملك فخر الدين قرا آرسلان حصن كركر من الارمن (و)[502] في سنة سبع واربعين وخمسمائة تزوج جلال الملوك كبك بن[503] سليمان بن عبد الجبار (*f. 176a*) بن ارتق بهدية

[491] Ms. محمود ابن محمود; Ms. B ملك شاه
[492] Ms. في العسكر
[493] Ms. B فتملك وترتب في السلطنة وبقي مدة
[494] Ms. B has ثم نفذ ابن البلنكرى واحضر اخاه من خوزستان واستقر في السلطنة
[495] Ms. ابن
[496] Ms. برس
[497] Ms. *sic.*
[498] Ms. *sic.*
[499] و is provided from Ms. B
[500] Ms. ثلث
[501] Ms. B has ذلك الجانب instead of ما حولها
[502] و is provided from Ms. B
[503] Ms. ابن

خاتون بنت السعيد حسام الدين بسفارة امه الملكة بنت رضوان زوجة حسام الدين

وفي سنة خمس واربعين كان وصل الى ماردين الوزير زين الدين اسعد بن عبد الخالق اخو المؤيد زين الدين وزير السلطان[504] واقام عند حسام الدين واستوزره وبقي في الديوان ومعه المؤيد المستوفي المهذب[505] واستناب رجلا كاتبا يلقب بالشهاب[506] واستقر في الوزارة الى سنة ست[507] واربعين وخمسمائة وكان في سنة اربع واربعين وخمسمائة ماتت صفية خاتون بآمد

وفي اول سنة ست واربعين خرج السعيد حسام الدين ونازل آمد[508] وطالبهم بصداق صفية خاتون وبقي مدة[509] ورحل عن آمد الى ماردين[510] وبقي اياما ونفذ ابن نيسان رجلين فاقاما بقلعة ماردين يعملان بالفاعل اياما ثم ان الوزير زين الدين ركب ذات يوم وصعد الى القلعة فجاز في موضع ضيق فخرج عليه ذانك[511] الرجلان فضربه احدهما بفأس في رأسه فوقع فطلب جماعة كانوا بين يدى الوزير الرجلين[512] فقالا[513] لهم ما تريدون نحن نصعد معكم الى الامير[514] فصعدا مع القوم الى باب القلعة[515] والناس خلفهما[516] ودخلا القلعة الى بين يدى الامير وقالا نحن قتلنا الوزير فقال ولما فقالا امرنا بذلك واكثر

504 Ms. B اخي المؤيد الذى كان وزير البرسقي وحصل وزير السلطان

505 Ms. B ورتب المؤيد والمهذب معه بالديوان على حالها

506 Ms. B adds وهو الان في ديوان صاحب ارزن

507 Ms. ستة

508 Ms. B adds ونازلها وضايقها واقطع البلد

509 Ms. B adds على جسر الحوّ

510 Ms. B ثم رحل الى تل العلوية وجرى بينهم خطاب عظيم واخذ الغلة تلك السنة ثم ان ابن نيسان دبر امره ورحل الامير عنه

511 Ms. اوليك (*sic*).

512 Ms. الرجل ورفيقه

513 Ms. فقال; Ms. B فقال

514 Ms. B adds ونخبره اننا قتلناه

515 Ms. B adds وقالا للاسفهسلار اعلم الامير اننا قد قتلنا الوزير

516 Ms. خلفهم

الناس قالوا ان ابن نيسان دس عليه[517] وقتله فامر الامير حسام الدين بضرب رقابهما على قبره وكان دفن بماردين وكان الرجلان من الملاحدة وعاد حسام الدين نزل[518] على آمد وضايقها فحضر بهاء الدين اوس وزير اخلاط فاجتمع بالسعيد حسام الدين على باب آمد[519] وتحدث معه وسأله فيهم ثم دخل الى آمد واجتمع بمؤيد الدين ابن نيسان وقرر معه الحال فخرج مؤيد الدين الى الامير واستقر الصلح وخرج[520] الآمدية الى السعيد حسام الدين وحصلوا من جملته وتحت امره[521] ورحل عنهم

وفي العشر الاواخر[522] من شهر رجب سنة ست واربعين وخمسمائة ماتت نورة خاتون بنت حسام الدين عند صاحب ارزن وخلفت ابنا عاش بعدها اياما ومات ودفنت بارزن وضاق صدر السعيد حسام الدين لموتها[523] وبقي حسام الدين بعد قتل الوزير زين الدين بغير وزير واكتفى بالاجل مؤيد الدولة[524] ابي منصور خالد بن[525] المبارك بن مخطر الى ان مات فقام بما رفض اليه احسن القيام

وبقي السعيد حسام الدين في الولاية[526] الى يوم الخميس ثاني ذى القعدة سنة ثمان واربعين وخمسمائة وتوفي بماردين وكان مرضه من يوم السبت الى يوم الخميس[527] ثاني ذى القعدة ودفن بالمشهد تحت ماردين

517 Ms. B من قتله
518 Ms. B فنزل
519 Ms. B على ولاية آمد
520 Ms. B خرجوا
521 Ms. B وخرجوا الآمدية الى خدمته وحصلوا في خدمته وخرج اليه مؤيد الدين في النوبة الاولى وعاد رده الى آمد وخرج من بكرة الامير والخاتون واولاد الامير واولاد الرئيس واستقرت قاعدتهم
522 Ms. الاخر; Ms. B الاخر
523 Ms. B ولحق الامير عليها امر عظيم
524 Ms. B adds كريم الملك
525 Ms. ابن
526 الامارة
527 Ms. B adds وجميع مرضه من يوم السبت وانقطع من الاحد الى الخميس

وكانت ولايته ميفرقين ثلثين سنة وماردين اثنتين وثلثين سنة (*f. 176b*) فرضي الله عنه وكان اميرا عالما مطلعا على جميع العلوم يحب اهل العلم ويخالطهم ويكرم ارباب الفضل من كل صناعة وكان كريما جوادا مفضالا لا يرى القتل الا عند الضرورة وكان له من الذمة الجوار ما لا كان للعرب العرباء[528] ولقد قصده الامير ابو[529] بكر صاحب نصيبين منهزما من آتابك زنكي فذم له وطلبه آتابك ولم يسلمه اليه وجرى بينهما امر عظيم[530] واخذ آتابك دارا ونهب البلاد وخرج عن يد السعيد حسام مال عظيم[531] ولم يسلمه وهو كان سبب الوحشة بين السعيد وبين آتابك ثم انفصل عنه ومضى الى السلطان مسعود فقبضه السلطان ونفذه الى آتابك[532] فقتله[533]

وكان السعيد حسام الدين رحمه الله يراعي ارباب البيوت وينظر في احوالهم ولا يرى قلع البيوت الكبار[534] وكان اذا قصده رجل من اصحاب العمائم والعلوم[535] انزله واكرمه واحسن اليه وافضل اليه جميع ما يحتاج اليه[536] وكان اذا تحقق في رجل شيئا من اى العلوم كان قربه وادناه واعطاه وسأله[537] عما يعلمه من علم وصناعة

وكنت لما مات بولاية الكرج في خدمة ملك الابخاز ديمطرى بن داود ملك الولاية باسرها فاني كنت دخلت في سنة ثمان واربعين الى تفليس ووصلت الى خدمته وسرت معه الى ولاية الان[538] والابخاز

528 Ms. للعرباء Ms. B وكان له من الذمة وحسن الجوار ما لا كان للعرب

529 Ms. ابا

530 Ms. adds لاجله

531 Ms. مالا عظيما

532 Ms. B فنفذ آتابك في طلبه فتسلمه اليه فحمله الى اتابك

533 Ms. فقتله written on the left margin.

534 Ms. B قلع بيت قديم

535 Ms. B وكان يقصده جماعة من ارباب البيوتات من جميع البلاد

536 Ms. B ويعطيهم ويقيم عليهم الاقامة والراتب مدة مقامهم في خدمته

537 Ms. سله

538 Ms. *sic.*

والدربند وكنا ذات يوم قريبا من بلد الدربند وكان ذلك اليوم رابع المحرم سنة تسع واربعين وخمسمائة فاستدعاني وقال ان صاحبكم حسام الدين قد مات وقد وصلني الخبر في هذا اليوم[539]

وكان ولي ميفرقين في ايامه جماعة من الولاة منهم الحاجب ابو بكر وبيرم وعثمن[540] بن[541] خمرتاش الحاج كل منهم مرة الا[542] الحاجب بيرم فولي مرتين ثم ولي الحاجب عبد الكريم ثم عزل وولي الحاجب يوسف ينال ثم عزل واعطي تحت دارا اقطاعا[543] واخذها منه آتابك زنكي وولي ميفرقين مملوكا كان للامير اسمه قزغلي مدة ومات وجلس في القصر الامير قيماز الخادم والحاجب مدة ثم ولي الحاجب برنقش مدة[544] وعاد الحاجب يوسف ينال مرة ثانية وبقي في الولاية الى[545] ثالث رجب سنة تسع وثلثين ومات ودفن بميفرقين ثم ولي ناصر الدولة صندل في ذى القعدة سنة تسع وثلثين وبقي الى[546] شهر ربيع الاول سنة ثلث واربعين ومات وبقي ولده غرس الدولة ينال ببرج الملك وجلس الحاجب بيرم في القصر مدة واستقل ينال بالولاية وبقي واليا الى ان مات السعيد حسام الدين رحمه الله على ما ذكرناه ان شاء الله تعالى

539 Ms. B وقال وصلني الخبر بموت صاحبكم
540 Ms. *sic.*; Ms. B عثمان
541 Ms. B بنو
542 Ms. الى; Ms. B الا
543 Ms. B قلعة سرجة
544 Ms. B برنقش الحسامي
545 Ms. B adds الجمعة
546 Ms. B adds الى الخميس في

وانا اذكر نسب الارتقين[1]

وما وصل الي من احوالهم ومن بقي من نسل (*f. 177a*) الامير ارتق رحمه الله قيل لما مات الامير ارتق خلف اولادا جماعة منهم الامير سكمان ونجم الدين غازى[2] وبهرام وعبد الجبار وسياويش[3] وآلب يارق وابنا آخر نذكر اسمه[4] بكداش وابنا آخر اسمه آلبتاش وهؤلاء[5] الذين اعقبوا وبقي نسلهم الى الان بديار بكر وخلف غير هؤلاء[6] وما سمعت بان[7] لهم الان عقبا[8] فاهملت ذكرهم

فاما سكمان فانه ملك حصن كيفا وبقي مدة ومات سنة ست وخمسمائة وخلف الامير ركن الدولة داود والامير ابراهيم وملك حصن كيفا بعد ابيه مدة ومات وملكها بعده ركن الدولة داود وازر خاتون وملك ركن الدولة[9] حصن كيفا بعده وملك غيرها بعد ذلك واولد اربعة[10] بنين هم[11] آرسلان تغمش وقر آرسلان وسليمن ومحمود واما آرسلان تغمش فمات وكان ملك ميزكرد وكان ملكها بعد ابيه وخلف ابنا من ابنة السعيد حسام الدين ومات بعد ابيه بمدة يسيرة واما سليمن فانه مات وخلف ابنا اسمه يعقوب هو الان في خدمة المالك[12]

[1] Ms. B ونحن نذكر الامراء الذين من نسل ارتق
[2] Ms. B الغازى
[3] Ms. B ساوس
[4] Ms. نسله is written as an alternative above اسمه
[5] Ms. هاولا
[6] Ms. هاولا
[7] Ms. ان
[8] Ms. عقب
[9] Ms. وملك حصن كيفا بعد ابيه مدة ومات وملكها بعده ركن الدولة ازر خاتون وملك ركن الدولة صح This lengthy omission is written along most of the left margin
[10] Ms. اربع
[11] Ms. هما
[12] Ms. الملك

نجم الدين وابنا آخر هو في خدمة جمال الدين في حاني واما محمود فملك[13] طنزى والقريشة[14] ومات وخلف ابنا يسمى داود وهو في خدمة اولاد عمه فخر الدين بحصن كيفا واما فخر الدين قر آرسلان فانه ملك البلاد جميعها التي كانت لابنه بعد موته على ما ذكرناه ومات وخلف ابنين هما نور الدين محمد[15] وعماد الدين ابو بكر وولي الامر[16] بعده نور الدين وهو الان في الملك وخلف بناتا جماعة

واما الامير بهرام بن[17] ارتق فانه خلف الامير نور الدولة بلك وملك خرتبيت وبالوا[18] وما حولها واخذها منه شمس الدولة سليمن بن[19] الغازى واخذها بعد ذلك الامير داود بعد موت سليمن وكان تزوج بالملكة فرخندا خاتون بنت الملك رضوان بعد نجم الدين الغازى وهو دخل بها وملك طرفا من قرب الفرات وكان يغزو[20] الافرنج وقتل على منبج على ما ذكرناه وخلف بنتا تزوجها فخر الدين قرا آرسلان ومات عنها

واما سياويش بن ارتق فانه خلف الامير يونس الحرامي ورأيته في خدمة السعيد حسام الدين[21] رحمه الله واولد اولادا منهم في خدمة اولاد فخر الدين بحصن كيفا والامير سيونج وهو في حاني في خدمة جمال الدين اخي[22] المالك[23] نجم الدين وتزوج ببنت الامير شيرباريك واولد منها ابنا اسمه شاه ملك وماتت وتزوج باخت لها اخرى

[13] Ms. ملك
[14] Ms. *sic.*
[15] Ms. محمود
[16] Ms. الامير
[17] Ms. ابن
[18] Ms. *sic.*; Ms. B بالود
[19] Ms. ابن
[20] Ms. يغزوا
[21] Ms. B adds ومات في خدمته
[22] Ms. اخو
[23] Ms. الملك

واما آلب يارق بن ارتق فانه خلف اولادا منهم الامير علي ملك جبل جور واولد الامير ممدود وهو شيرباريك وابنا آخر مات اسمه محمود واولد ابنا اسمه . . .[24] وهو في خرتبيت وتزوج شاه ملك ببنت شيرباريك في سنة سبع وخمسمائة واولد شيرباريك سيونج واسمعيل وطغربك[25] وبناتا جماعة واولد ابنا من جارية اسمه زنكي (*f. 177b*) وبقي في خدمة ابيه مدة ومضى الى مصر وتوفي بها في ايام شاور واما طغربك[26] فمات بحصن كيفا وحمل الى ميفرقين واما سيونج وكان اكبرهم فتزوج[27] بصفية خاتون بنت الملك رضوان ومات ولم يعقب واما اسمعيل فله ولدان ذكران[28] وهو في خدمة المالك[29] نجم الدين وبقي شيرباريك في خدمة المالك[30] حسام الدين الى ان مات وانتقل الى خدمة فخر الدين قرا آرسلان وبقي عنده مدة وعاد الى خدمة المالك نجم الدين ومات في رجب سنة ست وستين وخمسمائة ودفن في قرية لهم في اسفل المقابر

واما عند الجبار بن[31] ارتق فانه خلف ثلثة[32] بنين اغسيان وآرسلان[33] وسليمن فاما اغسيان[34] فانه انتقل وخدم بولاية اخلاط مع بنت سكمان واولد هناك ولدين الامير احمد والاخر يلقب بعز[35] الدين وانتقل الى خدمة فخر الدين قر آرسلان بحصن كيفا وحصل عنده في

[24] Ms. has a lacuna here.
[25] Ms. *sic*.
[26] Ms. *sic*.
[27] Ms. وتزوج
[28] Ms. ولدين ذكور
[29] Ms. الملك
[30] Ms. الملك
[31] Ms. ابن
[32] Ms. ثلث
[33] Ms. رسلان
[34] Ms. اعيان
[35] Ms. عز

اوفى درجة وزوجه ببنت اخيه آرسلان[36] تغمش ومات بالصرع وخلف ابنا له هو في خدمة اولاد فخر الدين

واما آلبتاش فانه خلف الامير علي الحرامي ومات في خدمة حسام الدين وخلف ولدين احدهما ابو[37] بكر وقد لبس الصوف وهو فقير وعمر وهو في خدمة اولاد فخر الدين بحصن كيفا

واما الامير آرسلان بن[38] عبد الجبار فانه ملك جبل جور وبالقرنين[39] والسيوان وبقي مدة واخذها منه السعيد حسام الدين وانتقل الى حصن كيفا الى خدمة ركن الدولة داود ومات في خدمته وخلف اولادا منهم بلاق ومحمود وبناتا وكان زوج بنتا في حياته من الامير زعيم الدولة مسيب بن[40] مالك صاحب الرقة واقام[41] الاولاد في خدمة فخر الدين وانتقل الامير بلاق الى خدمة المالك نجم الدين ومات

واما سليمن كان يلقب ببدر[42] الدولة فانه ملك حلب وتزوج بالخاتون الملكة بنت رضوان التي كانت زوجة الامير بلك واولد منها ابنا سماه كبك ويلقب بجلال الملوك واخذت منه حلب ووصل الى خدمة السعيد حسام الدين واقطعه بلد قلب وحصنها وبقي في خدمته الى ان مات ووصلت الملكة الى ماردين بعد موته ومعها ولده فاقامت بماردين وتزوجها السعيد[43] حسام الدين على ما ذكرناه وزوج ولدها جلال الملوك من ابنة هدية خاتون في سنة سبع واربعين وبقي الى سنة اربع وخمسين وخمسمائة وتوفي بباب نصيبين على ما سنذكره ان شاء الله تعالى

[36] Ms. رسلان
[37] Ms. ابي
[38] Ms. ابن
[39] Ms. *sic.*
[40] Ms. ابن
[41] Ms. اقاموا
[42] Ms. بدر
[43] Ms. للسعيد

واما الابن الاخر وهو بكداش فانه اولد رسلان[44] طغمش وانتقل الى خدمة آتابك طغتكين[45] صاحب دمشق فانه كان عنده في اوفى منزلة وتزوج بعائشة خاتون ابنة اخي الوزير (*f. 178a*) محمد الدويني واقام بدمشق الى سنة ثلث واربعين وخمسمائة في خدمة اولاد طغتكين وقصد الموصل فاقام في خدمة صاحبها مدة يسيرة ثم انتقل الى خدمة السعيد حسام الدين واكرمه واقطعه اقطقعا كثيرة في آخر سنة اربع واربعين عندما ملك دارا وبقي مدة يسيرة ومات وخلف ثلثة بنين احدهم كان يلقب بشمس[46] الدولة عاش في خدمة السعيد بعد ابيه مدة سنتين ومات وبقي الابنان مسعود وبلك وبقي مسعود في خدمة المالك نجم الدين مدة وانتقل الى خدمة فخر الدين قرا آرسلان واما بلك فانه بقي في خدمة المالك نجم الدين الى سنة سبع وستين وتزهد وانقطع وجلس في مسجد ياقوت قريبا من باب الهوّة في رأس الربض وهو الى الان مقيم به

واما نجم الدين الغازى فانه اولد اولادا جماعة احدهم الياس والبزم قتلا في حياته وكهار خاتون واما الياس فانه اولد الامير شهاب الدين محمد بن الياس وبنتا من خاتون . . .[47] تزوجها سعد الدولة ايلدى[48] صاحب آمد وله منها ولد في آمد واما شهاب الدين محمد فانه نشأ في خدمة عمه السعيد حسام الدين واقطعه تل بشمى وكان عنده مكرما الى ان مات وبقي مدة بعد موته وانتقل الى الشام الى خدمة نور الدين فاقطعه اقطاعا كثيرة[49] وبقي في خدمته الى الان وله ثلثة بنين وهم الان في خدمة نور الدين واولد نجم الدين ابنا من جارية اسمه عمر زوجها

[44] Ms. *sic.*
[45] Ms. طعلتكين
[46] Ms. شمس
[47] Ms. has a lacuna here.
[48] Ms. ايلللدى
[49] Ms. كثيرا

بالامير اسفهسلار . . .[50] ومات الولد ولم يعقب واولد ابنا اسمه نصر من جارية زوجها بالحاجب عمر الخاص ومات ولم يعقب وزوج كهار خاتون من سيف الدولة دبيس واولدت منه الامير عز الدين محمد وبقي عندها بماردين الى ان قتل دبيس ومضى الى الحلة وملك مع اخوته وبقي مدة وعاد الى خدمة المالك نجم الدين وتردد مرارا وتوفي بعد امه وكانت[51] توفيت في سنة تسع وخمسمائة ودفنت بماردين وخلف عز الدولة ابنا هو الان في خدمة شهاب الدين محمد بن الياس واولد نجم الدين بنتا سماها عينا خاتون تزوجها الامير ايلدى صاحب آمد واولد منها جمال الدين شمس الملوك محمود وهو الان صاحب آمد وماتت وتزوج بعدها باخت شهاب الدين على ما ذكرناه واولد بنتا اسمها سفرى خاتون تزوجها حسام الدولة قرتى بن[52] طغان آرسلان صاحب ارزن وبدليس وماتت[53] وخلفت ابنا اسمه ياغي بسان (*f. 178b*) وهو في خدمة فخر الدين دولت شاه عمه واولد شمس الدولة سليمن وملك ميفرقين بعد ابيه وتوفي وخلف ابنا اسمه محمود ورايته في ماردين وهو في اسوأ حال[54] وما عالم ما كان منه واولد السعيد حسام الدين تمرتاش وكان عين البيت وسيد الاولاد فملك ماردين على ما ذكرناه بعد ابيه وملك ميفرقين بعد اخيه وبقي الى ان مات وخلف من الاولاد المالك نجم الدين آلبي وملك الملك بعد ابيه وجمال الدين سربي اعطاه اخوه حاني والسيوان وحصن قلب وصمصام الدين بهزام ملك دارا وهدية خاتون هي عند اخيها جمال الدين بحاني وزمرد خاتون بالموصل مات عنها قطب الدين مودود بن زنكي وخلف منها اربعة اولاد ملك الملوك

[50] Ms. illegible امروه or امرو (?).

[51] Ms. كان

[52] Ms. ابن

[53] Ms. مات

[54] Ms. اسو حال; Ms. B سوء حال

سيف غازى بن مودود[55] على ما سنذكره ان شاء الله ومات في حياته صفية خاتون زوجة صاحب آمد ونورة خاتون زوجة صاحب ارزن على ما ذكرناه فرحمة الله عليه ورضوانه لديه فهذا ما وصل اليّ من نسب من بقي من الارتقية والله اعلم بالصواب

[55] Ms. ممدود

Appendix A

Chronological Lists of Rulers Contemporary with the Artuqids and a Genealogical Table of the later Saljuqs

Tables showing the reigns of neighbouring rulers

'Abbāsid Caliphs

al-Mustaẓhir	487/1094
al-Mustarshid	512/1118
al-Rāshid	529/1135
al-Muqtafī	530/1136
al-Mustanjid	555/1160

Great Saljuqs

Malik-Shāh	465/1072
Maḥmūd	485/1092
Berk-Yaruk	487/1094
Malik-Shāh II	498/1104
Muḥammad	498/1104
Sanjar	511/1117 (until 552/1157)

Saljuqs of Iraq

Maḥmūd	511/1117
Dā'ūd	525/1131
Ṭoghrïl	526/1132
Mas'ūd	527/1133
Malik-Shāh	547/1152

Muḥammad	548/1153
Sulaimān-Shāh	555/1160

Kings of Georgia

David	482/1089
Dimitri	519/1125
Giorgi III	551/1156

Fāṭimids

al-Mustanṣir	427/1036
al-Musta'lī	487/1094
al-Āmir	495/1101
al-Ḥāfiẓ	525/1131
al-Ẓāfir	544/1149
al-Fā'iz	549/1154
al-'Āḍid	555/1160

The Almoravids

Yūsuf b. Tāshufīn	453/1061
'Alī	500/1106
Tāshufīn	537/1142
Ibrāhīm	540/1146
Isḥāq	540-1/1146-7

The Almohads

Muḥammad b. Tūmart	(d.524/1130)
'Abd al-Mu'min	524/1130
Abū Ya'qūb Yūsuf	558/1163

The Dānishmendids

Amīr Ghāzī Gümüsh-Tegin	477/1084
Malik Muḥammad	529/1134

The Zangids
a) At Mosul

'Imād al-Dīn Zangī	521/1127
Saif al-Dīn Ghāzī	541/1146

Quṭb al-Dīn Maudūd	544/1149
Saif al-Dīn Ghāzī II	564/1169

b) At Damascus and Aleppo

Nūr al-Dīn	541/1146 - 569/1174

Rulers of Arzan and Bitlīs

Ṭoghan Arslan	498/1104
Ḥusām al-Dīn Qurtï	532/1137
Yāqūt Arslan	538/1143
Fakhr al-Dīn Daulat-Shāh	540/1145 - 588/1192

Rulers of Āmid

Fakhr al-Daula Ibrāhīm	492/1098
Sa'd al-Daula Īl-aldï	504/1110
Jamāl al-Dīn Maḥmūd	536/1142 - 579/1183

Rulers of Akhlāṭ

Sukmān al-Quṭbī	493/1100
Ẓāhir al-Dīn Ibrāhīm	506/1112
Aḥmad b. Sukmān	521/1127
Naṣīr al-Dīn Sukmān	522/1128 - 581/1185-6

The Mazyadids of Ḥilla

Saif al-Daula Ṣadaqa	479/1086
Nūr al-Daula Dubais	501/1108
Saif al-Daula Ṣadaqa	529/1135
Muḥammad	532/1138
'Alī	540-5/1145-50

The Būrids

Ẓāhir al-Dīn Ṭogh-Tegin	497/1103
Tāj al-Mulūk Būrī	522/1128
Shams al-Mulūk Ismā'īl	526/1132
Shihāb al-Dīn Maḥmūd	529/1135
Jamāl al-Dīn Muḥammad	533/1139 (deposed 549/1154-5)

Mujīr al-Dīn Abaq	534/1140 (deposed 549/1154 by Maḥmūd b. Zangī)

The Saljuqs of Rūm

Qïlïch Arslan	485/1092
Malik-Shāh	500/1107
Rukn al-Dīn Mas'ūd	510/1116
'Izz al-Dīn Qïlïch Arslan	551/1156

The Saltuqids of Erzerum

Abu'l-Qāsim Saltuq	465/1072
'Alī	496/1102
Abu'l-Muẓaffar Ghāzī	518/1124
'Izz al-Dīn Saltuq	527/1132 - 564/1168

Notes on the genealogical table of the later Saljuqs

Only names important to an understanding of Ibn al-Azraq's account of the history of the Jazīra in the first half of the sixth/twelfth century have been mentioned.

Ibn al-Azraq's own genealogy of the Saljuqs is found on ff.163-164a. This has been assessed against the genealogical information found in secondary sources.[1]

Those persons mentioned by Ibn al-Azraq in this part of his text are marked with an asterisk.

Apart from a few errors, Ibn al-Azraq has managed to produce a reasonably accurate genealogy.

1. i) Zambaur, *op.cit.*, 221-2.
ii) F. Justi, *Iranisches Namenbuch* (repr. Hildesheim, 1963), 452-3.
iii) C. E. Bosworth, *The Islamic Dynasties* (Edinburgh, 1967), 115-8.

Appendix B

Genealogical Table of the Artuqids with Commentary

Notes on the genealogical table

The genealogy of the Artuqids provided by Ibn al-Azraq in his history is the earliest extant. For this reason, his information has been used as the principal basis for the table given in this appendix.

Other tables have been consulted, including those of Turan,[1] Artuk[2] and Zambaur.[3] By far the fullest and best one is that of Cahen.[4] Where there is a disagreement with Cahen's reading of Ibn al-Azraq's information, this has been recorded in the footnotes.

It should be noted that Ms.A has been used since its account is much fuller than that found in Ms.B,[5] which omits entirely any mention of Alp-Tash and Bektash, two of the sons of Artuq, and their descendants. Ms.B also attributes the descendants of Alp-Yaruq to Siyāwush and confuses the two people mentioned in the text of Ms.A as Shams al-Daula. Ms.B also gives no genealogy for İl-Ghāzī himself.

A common error amongst the chronicles is the confusion between Sukmān b. Artuq of Ḥiṣn Kaifā and Sukmān al-Quṭbī of Akhlāṭ. This mistake is made by Ibn al-Azraq, who thereby contradicts himself. On f.160b he states correctly that Sukmān b. Artuq died in 498/1104-5. On f.177a, however, he writes that the death of Sukmān b. Artuq occurred in 506/1112-3.

Sukmān al-Quṭbī died in 504/1110-1 or 506/1112-3 (Ibn al-

1. O. Turan, *Doğu Anadolu Türk Devletleri Tarihi* (Istanbul, 1973). His table is on the last page which is unnumbered.
2. *Op.cit.* The table is also attached to the last page.
3. *Op.cit.*, 230.
4. *Op.cit.*, 268.
5. Ms.B, ff.105b-106b.

Qalānisī, *Dhail,* 174-5; Ibn al-Athīr, *al-Kāmil* X, 340-1 and *Atab.*, 18).

Ibn Taghribirdī makes a similar error in the *Nujūm al-Ẓāhira* (*Recueil,* III, 495-6). Under the year 503/1109-10 he refers to Sukmān b. Artuq (who had died in 498/1104-5) as lord of Armenia, Akhlāṭ and Mayyāfāriqīn. These territories were of course ruled at that time by Sukmān al-Quṭbī. Under 504/1110-1 he mentions the death of Quṭb al-Dīn Sukmān b. Artuq (*sic*) who was buried at Akhlāṭ. He then gives a false genealogy for Sukmān al-Quṭbī, relating him to İl-Ghāzī and Artuq.

The following notes summarise Ibn al-Azraq's information in Ms.A, with other comments, where necessary, from either Ms.B or other sources. The aim has not been to include genealogical information provided in the last part of Ibn al-Azraq's work, which is outside the historical period treated in this book, but rather to facilitate a reading of ff.177a-178b. Except where indicated, the information given in the notes which follow comes from these two folios. The reading of these folios is best accompanied by the visual aid of the table since the ambiguity of the personal pronouns renders the genealogy difficult to follow.

1. *Ibrāhīm*

   He is omitted in Ms.B.

2. *Arslan Ṭoghmïsh*

   He ruled Mīzgard after his father's death.

3. *Sulaimān*

   There is no information about this son of Dā'ūd.

4. *Maḥmūd*

   He took Ṭanzī and Qarshiyya.

5. *Ya'qūb*

   He was in the service of Najm al-Dīn Alpï.

6. *Unnamed son of Sulaimān b. Dā'ūd*

   He was in the service of Jamāl al-Dīn b. Temür-Tash at Ḥānī.

7. *Dā'ūd*

   He was in the service of the sons of his uncle Qara Arslan at Ḥiṣn Kaifā.

8. *Nūr al-Dīn Muḥammad*

   He succeeded his father, Qara Arslan, at Ḥiṣn Kaifā.

9. *Balak*

   A very significant member of the Artuqid family who is virtually ignored by Ibn al-Azraq. Fortunately, other sources give ample coverage of his career.

10. *Balak's daughter*

    She married Fakhr al-Dīn Qara Arslan.

11. *Yūnus al-Ḥarāmī*
He worked for Temür-Tash (Ms.A). The author met him personally (Ms.B).

12. *Sevinch*
He was in the service of Jamāl al-Dīn b. Temür-Tash at Ḥānī. He married the daughter of Shīrbārīk by whom he had a son, Shāh Malik. He later married another daughter of Shīrbārīk.

13. *Alp-Yaruq*
Ms.B omits any mention of this son of Artuq. His descendants, whom Ms.A enumerates, are attributed in Ms.B to Siyāwush. There is still justifiable confusion over the genealogy of Alp-Yaruq and especially over that of Yāqūtī. For example, Edhem, in his table of the Artuqids, has Yāqūtī as the son of Artuq, not the grandson (H. Edhem, *Düvel-i Islâmiye* [Istanbul, 1927], 241).

14. *'Alī*
He held Jabal Jūr after losing Mārdīn (Ms.A).

15. *Shīrbārīk*
He worked for Temür-Tash until the latter died. He moved to the service of Fakhr al-Dīn Qara Arslan, then returned to work for Najm al-Dīn Alpï (Ms.A).

16. *Unnamed son of 'Alī b. Alp-Yaruq*
He lived in Khartabirt (Ms.A).

17. *Sevinch*
He was the eldest son of Shīrbārīk. He died, leaving no issue. He married Ṣafiyya Khātūn, daughter of Malik Riḍwān (Ms.A). Cahen records this fact without comment. It is just conceivable that such a marriage took place but Riḍwān, a contemporary of Artuq's sons, died in 507/1113-4 and Sevinch was the great-great-grandson of Artuq. Maybe this is a confused reference to Sevinch b. Siyāwush (cf. n.12 above).

18. *Ismā'īl*
He was in the service of Najm al-Dīn Alpï (Ms.A).

19. *Ṭoghrïl*
(Known as Ṭoghr Beg in Ms.A). He died in Ḥiṣn Kaifā and was buried in Mayyāfāriqīn (Ms.A).

20. *The daughters of Shīrbārīk*
One daughter married Sevinch. On her death, he married her sister (Ms.A).

21. *Zangī b. Shīrbārīk*
His mother was a slave-girl. He stayed with his father for a while, then went to Egypt to serve Shāwar (Ms.A).

22. *Yaghï-Sïyan*
He served at Akhlāṭ with the daughter of Sukmān (al-Quṭbī).

There he had two sons. He then moved to the service of Qara Arslan in Ḥiṣn Kaifā. He married a daughter of Arslan Ṭoghmïsh. He died of epilepsy, leaving a son in the service of the sons of Qara Arslan (Ms.A). Cahen says it was his son 'Izz al-Dīn who died of epilepsy, though Ibn al-Azraq clearly says that it was the father who died in this way (Ms.A, f.177b).

23. *Badr al-Daula Sulaimān*
When he lost Aleppo, he joined the service of Temür-Tash who gave him Qalb as an *iqṭā'*. He remained until his death in the service of Temür-Tash (Ms.A).

24. *Arslan b. 'Abd al-Jabbār*
He took Jabal Jūr, Dhu'l-Qarnain and al-Sīwān and held them until Temür-Tash wrested them from him. He then moved to the service of Dā'ūd in Ḥiṣn Kaifā where he died (Ms.A). Cahen does not mention this information but states that Arslan joined the service of Temür-Tash and Alpï, after the death of Dā'ūd.

25. *Unnamed son of Yaghï-Sïyan*
He worked for the sons of Qara Arslan (Ms.A).

26. *Köpek*
He was brought to Mārdīn after his father's death by his mother, whom Temür-Tash subsequently married. Köpek married Hadiyya Khātūn and died in 554/1159-60 outside Naṣībīn (Ms.A). Cahen says he died outside Mārdīn, but gives no source for this information.

27. *Unnamed daughter of Arslan b. 'Abd al-Jabbār*
She married Za'īm al-Daula Musayyib b. Mālik, lord of al-Raqqa (Ms.A).

28. *Bulāq (B.lāq)*
He was in the service of Najm al-Dīn Alpï until he died (Ms.A).

29. *'Alī al-Ḥarāmī*
He died in the service of Temür-Tash (Ms.A).

30. *Abū Bakr*
He became a *Ṣūfī* and a *faqīr*. He had a long life. He was in the service of the sons of Qara Arslan in Ḥiṣn Kaifā (Ms.A).

31. *Arslan Ṭoghmïsh*
He worked for Ṭogh-Tegin of Damascus. He married 'Ā'isha Khātūn, the daughter of the brother of the vizier, Muḥammed al-Dvīnī. He stayed with the Būrids until 543/1148-9; he then went to Mosul and moved to the service of Temür-Tash, who gave him a number of *iqṭā's* in 544/1149-50. He died shortly afterwards (Ms.A).

32. *Shams al-Daula*

He died two years after his father in the service of Temür-Tash (Ms.A). Ms.B confuses this Shams al-Daula Sulaimān with the better-known man of the same name who was the son of İl-Ghāzī. It was İl-Ghāzī's son, Sulaimān, who had a son - Maḥmūd - whose scandalous way of life Ibn al-Azraq deplored.

33. *Mas'ūd*

He stayed in the service of Alpï, then moved to work for Qara Arslan (Ms.A). Cahen calls him Mahmūd.

34. *Balak*

He remained with Alpï until (5)67/1171-2 and then became an ascetic. He was still alive when Ibn al-Azraq wrote his account (Ms.A).

35. *'Umar*

His mother was a slave-girl. He died, leaving no issue. İl-Ghāzī married 'Umar's mother to one of his supporters (Ms.A).

36. *Naṣr*

His mother was also a slave-girl, whom İl-Ghāzī married to the *ḥājib* 'Umar al-Khāṣṣ. Naṣr died without leaving any issue (Ms.A).

37. *Ayāz*

He was sent by İl-Ghāzī to fight with the troops from Mosul in 504/1110-1 (Ibn al-Qalānisī, *Dhail,* 174-5; Ibn al-Athīr, *al-Kāmil,* X, 340-1 and *Atab.,* 18). He was killed in 509/1115-6 by the men whom Bursuq had appointed to guard him (Ibn al-Athīr, *al-Kāmil,* X, 358).

38. *Guhar Khātūn*

She married Dubais, by whom she had a son, 'Izz al-Dīn Muḥammad. He stayed with her until Dubais was killed. He then spent time both at al-Ḥilla with his brothers and at Mārdīn, where he served Alpï. Guhar Khātūn died in 559/1163-4 and was buried at Mārdīn (Ms.A).

39. *Al-Bazm*

He was killed in İl-Ghāzī's lifetime (Ms.A). Artuk calls him Elbazmi, Cahen Al-Bazm/Bazmiš.

40. *Sulaimān*

He ruled Mayyāfāriqīn after his father (Ms.A).

41. *Safra Khātūn*

She married Qurtï, the lord of Arzan and Bitlīs. She had a son Yaghï-Basan, who at the time Ibn al-Azraq was writing was in the service of his uncle, Daulat-Shāh (Ms.A). She is not mentioned by Cahen.

42. *Yumna Khātūn*

A daughter of such a name is not mentioned in the genealogical account of Ms.A., which speaks of 'Aina Khātūn. But elsewhere in Ms.A (f. 170a), the wife of İl-aldï of Āmid is called Yumna Khātūn. She was the mother of Shams al-Mulūk Maḥmūd, who was lord of Āmid in Ibn al-Azraq's time.

43. *Shihāb al-Dīn Muḥammad*

He grew up in the service of Temür-Tash, who gave him Tall Bashmī as an *iqṭā'*. He ended up in Syria in the service of Nūr al-Dīn, who gave him many *iqṭā's*. He was still alive in Ibn al-Azraq's time (Ms.A).

44. *Shāh Malik*

He married the daughter of Shīrbārīk in 507/1113-4 (*sic*) (Ms.A). This date is much too early and is probably due to a scribal error.

45. *Maḥmūd*

The author met him in Mārdīn (Ms.A; cf. no. 32 *supra*). Cahen says he was governor of Mārdīn and was then exiled to the Sāḥil.

46. *Jamāl al-Dīn Qurtï (?)*

Temür-Tash gave him Ḥānī, al-Sīwān and Qalb (Ms.A). Ṭughrati is the version of the name given by Artuk. Cahen prefers Tafrati, whilst Turan avoids the problem by omitting that part of the name. Qurtï is at least a name widespread amongst the Turcomans and Kurds of this time.

47. *Ṣamṣam al-Dīn Bahrām*

He was the lord of Dārā (Ms.A).

48. *Hadiyya Khātūn*

She lived in Ḥānī with her brother (Ms.A).

49. *Zumurrud Khātūn*

She married Quṭb al-Dīn Maudūd b. Zangī. She had four sons by him (Ms.A).

50. *Ṣafiyya Khātūn*

She married the lord of Āmid (Ms.A).

51. *The sons of Shihāb al-Dīn Muḥammad*

They served Nūr al-Dīn (Ms.A).

52. *Nūra Khātūn*

She was the wife of the lord of Arzan (Ms.A).

Bibliography

Primary Sources

Abu'l-Fidā', 'Imād al-Dīn Ismā'īl b. 'Alī, *Al-Mukhtaṣar fī akhbār al-bashar* III (Cairo, n.d.).

Anonymous Syriac Chronicle, tr. A. S. Tritton as "The First and Second Crusades from an Anonymous Syriac Chronicle", with notes by H. A. R. Gibb, *JRAS* 1933, 69-101, 273-305.

Bar Hebraeus (Abu'l-Faraj), *The Chronography of Gregory Abū'l Faraj, the Hebrew Physician, commonly known as Bar Hebraeus*, facsimile ed. and tr. E. A. W. Budge, 2 vols., (London, 1932).

al-Bundārī, al-Fatḥ b. 'Alī, *Zubdat al-nuṣra wa nukhbat al-'uṣra*, ed. M. T. Houtsma in *Recueil de textes relatifs à l'Histoire des Seljoucides* II (Leiden, 1889).

al-Ḥusainī, Ṣadr al-Dīn Abu'l-Ḥasan 'Alī b. Nāṣir, *Akhbār al-Daula al-Saljūqiyya*, ed. M. Iqbāl (Lahore, 1933).

Ibn al-'Adīm, Kamāl al-Dīn Abu'l-Qāsim 'Umar, *Bughyat al-ṭalab fī tārīkh Ḥalab*, ed. A. Sevim (Ankara, 1976).

----, *Zubdat al-ḥalab min tārīkh Ḥalab II*, ed. S. Dahān (Damascus, 1954).

Ibn al-Athīr, 'Izz al-Dīn Abu'l-Ḥusain 'Alī, *al-Kāmil fi'l-tārīkh*, ed. C. J. Tornberg (Leiden and Uppsala, 1851-76).

----, *Tārīkh al-daula al-atābakiyya: mulūk al-Mauṣil* (*Al-tārīkh al-bahr fi'l-daulat al-atābakiyya (bi'l-Mauṣil)*), ed. A. Ṭulaimāt (Cairo, 1963).

Ibn al-Azraq, *Tārīkh al-Fāriqī*, ed. B. A. L. 'Awaḍ, rev. M. S. Ghorbal (Cairo, 1959).

Ibn Baṭṭūṭa, *The travels of Ibn Baṭṭūṭa A.D. 1325-1354*, tr. H. A. R. Gibb (Cambridge, 1958-62).

Ibn al-Furāt, *Tārīkh al-Duwal wa'l-Mulūk*, Oesterreichische Nationalbibliothek, Vienna, MS. A. F. 118 (Flügel 814, II).

Ibn Ḥauqal, Abu'l-Qāsim b. 'Alī al-Naṣībī, *Kitāb ṣūrat al-'arḍ*, ed. J. H. Kramers (Leiden, 1938-9); tr. J. H. Kramers and G. Wiet as *La Configuration de la Terre*, 2 vols. (Beirut and Paris, 1964).

Ibn al-Jauzī, Abu'l-Faraj 'Abd al-Raḥmān, *Al-Muntaẓam fī tārīkh al-mulūk wa'l-umam* X (Hyderabad, 1940) (editor unidentified).

Ibn Khallikān, Aḥmad b. Muḥammad, *Kitāb Wafayāt al-A'yān: Ibn Khallikan's Biographical Dictionary*, 4 vols., tr. Baron W. M. de Slane (Paris, 1843-71).

----, *Wafayāt al-a'yān wa anbā' ibnā' al-zamān* 2 vols. (Cairo, 1299/1881-2).
Ibn Khurdādhbih, Abu'l-Qāsim 'Ubaidallāh b. 'Abdallāh, *Kitāb al-masālik wa'l-mamālik*, ed. M. J. de Goeje (Leiden, 1889).
Ibn al-Qalānisī, Ḥamza b. Asad Abū Ya'lā, *Dhail tārīkh Dimishq*, ed. H. F. Amedroz (Leiden, 1908).
----, *Dhail tārīkh Dimishq* tr. H. A. R. Gibb as *The Damascus Chronicle of the Crusades* (London, 1932).
----, *Dhail tārīkh Dimishq*, tr. R. Le Tourneau as *Damas de 1075 à 1154* (Damascus, 1952).
Ibn Ṣaṣrā, Muḥammad b. Muḥammad, *Kitāb al-Durra al-Muḍī'a fi'l-Daula al-Ẓāhiriyya*, ed. and tr. W. M. Brinner as *A Chronicle of Damascus 1389-1397* 2 vols. (Berkeley, Los Angeles and London, 1963).
Ibn Shaddād, 'Izz al-Dīn, *Al-a'lāq al-khaṭīra fī dhikr umarā' al-Shām wa'l-Jazīra*, ed. S. Dahān (Damascus, 1963).
----, *Al-a'laq al-khaṭīra fī dhikr umarā' al-Shām wa'l-Jazīra*, Bodleian MS. Marsh 333.
Ibn Taghribirdī, Abu'l-Maḥāsin Yūsuf, *Kitāb nujūm al-zāhira fī mulūk Miṣr wa'l-Qāhira*, extracts ed. and tr. *RHC/HO* III, 477-509.
Ibn al-Ṭiqṭaqā, Jalāl al-Dīn Abū Ja'far Muḥammad b. 'Alī, *Al-Fakhrī fi'l-ādāb al-sulṭāniyya wa'l-duwal al-islāmiyya*, tr. E. Amar (Paris, 1910).
Ibn Wāṣil, Jamāl al-Dīn Muḥammad b. Sālim, *Mufarrij al-kurūb fī akhbār Banī Ayyūb* I, ed. Jamāl al-Dīn al-Shayyāl (Cairo, 1953).
al-Marrākushī, 'Abd al-Wāḥid, *Al-mu'jib fī talkhīṣ akhbār al-Maghrib*, ed. R. P. A. Dozy (Leiden, 1847).
Matthew of Edessa, *Parmut'iwn,* tr. E. Dulaurier as *Chronique de Matthieu d'Edesse (962-1136) avec la continuation de Grégoire le Prêtre jusqu'en 1162* (Paris, 1858).
Michael the Syrian, facsimile ed. and tr. J.-B. Chabot as *Chronique de Michel le Syrien* (Paris, 1899-1914).
al-Qalqashandī, Shihāb al-Dīn Abu'l-'Abbās b. 'Alī (?'Abdallāh), *Ṣubḥ al-a'shā fī ṣinā'at al-inshā'*, ed. Muḥammad 'Abd al-Rasūl Ibrāhīm (Cairo, 1913-20).
al-Qazwīnī, Ḥamdallāh Mustaufī, *Tārīkh-i Guzīda*, tr. C. Defrémery as "Histoire des Seldjoukides", *JA* April-May 1848, 417-62; September 1848, 259-79; October 1848, 334-70.
----, *The geographical part of the Nuzhat-al-Qulūb composed by Ḥamd-Allāh Mustawfī of Qazwīn in 740 (1340)*, tr. G. Le Strange (London, 1919).
al-Rāwandī, Muḥammad b. 'Alī, *Rāḥat al-ṣudūr wa āyat al-surūr*, ed. M. Iqbāl (London, 1921).

Recueil des historiens des Croisades. Historiens orientaux. I-V (Paris, 1872-1906).

Sibṭ b. al-ʿAjamī, *Kunūz al-dhahab fī tārīkh Ḥalab*, tr. J. Sauvaget as "*Les Trésors d'Or" de Sibṭ Ibn al-ʿAjami. Matériaux pour servir à l'histoire de la ville d'Alep* II (Beirut, 1950).

Sibṭ b. al-Jauzī, Shams al-Dīn Abu'l-Muẓaffar Yūsuf (attrib.), *Kanz al-mulūk fī Kaifiyyat al-Sulūk*, ed. G. Vitestam (Lund, 1970).

----, *Mir'āt al-zamān fī tārīkh al-aʿyān* VIII/I (Hyderabad, 1951) (editor unidentified).

----, *Mukhtaṣar Mir'āt al-Zamān*, ed. J. R. Jewett (Chicago, 1907).

Tihrānī, Abū Bakr, *Kitāb-i Diyārbakriyya*, 2 vols., ed. N. Lugal and F. Sümer (Ankara, 1962).

Usāma b. Munqidh, *Kitāb al-iʿtibār*, tr. P. K. Hitti as *Memoirs of an Arab-Syrian Gentleman* (repr. Beirut, 1964).

Yāqūt b. ʿAbdallāh al-Ḥamawī, *Muʿjam al-buldān*, tr. C. A. C. Barbier de Meynard as *Dictionnaire géographie, historique et littéraire de la Perse et des contrées adjacentes* (Paris, 1861).

Secondary Sources

Abun-Nasr, J. M., *A History of the Maghrib* (Cambridge, 1971).

Altun, A., *Mardin'de Türk Devri Mimarisi* (Istanbul, 1971).

Amedroz, H. F., "Three Arabic MSS. on the History of the City of Mayyāfāriqīn", *JRAS* 1902, 785-812.

Artuk, I., *Mardin Artukoğullarï Tarihi* (Istanbul, 1944).

Ayāz, Q., *An unexploited source for the history of the Saljūqs: a translation and critical commentary on the Akhbār al-Dawlat al-Saljūqiyya* (unpublished Ph.D thesis, Edinburgh, 1985).

Barbier de Meynard, C. A. C., *Dictionnaire géographique de la Perse*, see Yāqūt.

Bausani, A., "Religion in the Saljuq period", in *The Cambridge History of Iran. 5. The Saljuq and Mongol Periods*, ed. J. A. Boyle (Cambridge, 1968), 283-302.

Blair, S. S., "The Inscription from the Tomb Tower at Basṭām", in *Art et Société dans le Monde Iranien*, ed. C. Adle (Paris, 1982), 263-86.

Blau, J., "The Importance of Middle Arabic Dialects for the History of Arabic", in *Scripta Hierosolymitana. IX. Studies in Islamic History and Civilisation*, ed. U. Heyd (Jerusalem, 1961),

An important study on the Artuqids came to my notice only after this book was in press:

G. Väth, *Die Geschichte der artuqidischen Fürstentümer in Syrien und der Ğazira'l-Furātīya (496-812/1102-1409)* (Islamkundliche Untersuchungen, Bd. 121) (Berlin, 1987).

Bosworth, C. E., *The Islamic dynasties. A chronological and genealogical handbook* (Edinburgh, 1967).

----, *The Ghaznavids. Their empire in Afghanistan and eastern Iran. 994:1040* (Edinburgh, 1963).

----, "The political and dynastic history of the Iranian world (A.D. 1000-1217)", in *The Cambridge History of Iran. 5. The Saljuq and Mongol Periods*, ed. J. A. Boyle (Cambridge, 1968), 1-202.

----, "Al-Ḥusainī", *Supplement, EI*^{2}.

Brinner, W. M., *A Chronicle of Damascus 1389-1397*, see Ibn Ṣaṣrā.

Brockelmann, C., *Geschichte der arabischen Literatur*, 2 vols. (Leiden, 1943-9; *Supplementband*, 3 vols. Leiden, 1937-42).

Brosset, M. F., *Histoire de la Géorgie depuis l'antiquité jusqu'au XIXe siècle. I. Histoire ancienne jusqu'en 1469 de J. C.* (St. Petersburg, 1849).

Cahen, C., "Artuḳids", *EI*^{2}.

----, "Balak", *EI*^{2}.

----, and Canard, M., "Diyār Bakr", *EI*^{2}.

----, "Ibn Djahīr", *EI*^{2}.

----, "La chronique abrégée d'al-'Azīmī", *JA* CCXXX (1938), 353-448.

----, "La Djazira au milieu du treizième siècle d'après 'Izz al-Dīn Ibn Chaddad", *Revue des Etudes Islamiques* VIII (1934), 109-28.

----, *La Syrie du Nord à l'époque des Croisades et la principauté franque d'Antioche* (Paris, 1940).

----, "Le Diyār Bakr au temps des premiers Urtuḳides", *JA* CCXXVII (1935), 219-76.

----, *Pre-Ottoman Turkey*, tr. J. Jones-Williams (London, 1968).

----, "The Historiography of the Seljuqid Period", in *Historians of the Middle East*, eds. B. Lewis and P. M. Holt (London, 1962), 59-78.

----, "The Turkish Invasion: The Selchükids", in *A History of the Crusades* I, eds. K. M. Setton and M. W. Baldwin (Madison, Milwaukee and London, 1969), 135-76.

Canard, M., *Histoire de la dynastie des H'amdanides de Jazîra et de Syrie* I (Paris, 1953).

Clauson, G. L. M., *An etymological dictionary of pre-thirteenth century Turkish* (Oxford, 1972).

Crawford, R. W., "Riḍwān the maligned", in *The World of Islam. Studies in honor of P. K. Hitti*, eds. J. Kritzeck and R. B. Winder (Princeton, 1959), 135-44.

Dahan, S., "The origin and development of the local histories of Syria", in *Historians of the Middle East*, eds. B. Lewis and P. M. Holt (London, 1962), 108-17.

Dolapönü, M. H., *Tarihte Mardin* (Istanbul, 1972).

Dowsett, C. J. F., "A twelfth-century Armenian inscription at Edessa", *Iran and Islam. In memory of the late Vladimir Minorsky*, ed. C. E. Bosworth (Edinburgh, 1971), 197-227.

Dozy, R. P. A., *Supplément aux dictionnaires arabes*, 2 vols. (Leiden, 1881).

Eddé, A.-M., *La description de la Syrie du Nord de 'Izz al-Dīn Ibn Šaddād.* (Damascus, 1982).

Elisséeff, N., *Nūr al-Dīn. Un grand prince musulman de Syrie au temps des Croisades*, 3 vols. (Damascus, 1967).

Elshayyal, M. F., *A critical edition of Volume II of Tārīkh al-Duwal wa'l-Mulūk by Muḥammad b. 'Abd al-Raḥīm b. 'Alī Ibn al-Furāt* (unpublished Ph.D thesis, Edinburgh, 1986).

Fink, H. S., "Mawdūd of Mosul, Precursor of Saladin", *The Muslim World* XLIII (1953), 18-27.

Fück, J.,*'Arabīya. Recherches sur l'histoire de la langue et du style arabe*, French tr. by C. Denizeau (Paris, 1955).

Gabriel, A., *Voyages archéologiques dans la Turquie orientale. Avec un recueil d'inscriptions arabes par Jean Sauvaget* (Paris, 1940).

Gabrieli, F., "The Arabic historiography of the Crusades", in *Historians of the Middle East*, eds. B. Lewis and P. M. Holt (London, 1962), 98-107.

Gaudefroy-Demombynes, M., *La Syrie à l'époque des mamelouks* (Paris, 1923).

Gibb, H. A. R., "Notes on the Arabic Materials for the History of the Early Crusades", *BSOS* VII (1933-5), 739-54.

----, *Saladin* (Oxford, 1971).

----, "The Career of Nūr-ad-Dīn", in *A History of the Crusades* I, eds. K. M. Setton and M. W. Baldwin (Madison, Milwaukee and London, 1969), 513-27.

----, *The Damascus Chronicle of the Crusades*, see Ibn al-Qalānisī.

----, "The Rise of Saladin 1169-1189", in *A History of the Crusades* I, eds. K. M. Setton and M. W. Baldwin (Madison, Milwaukee and London, 1969), 563-89.

Goldziher, I., *Muslim Studies* II, ed. S. M. Stern, tr. C. R. Barber and S. M. Stern (London, 1971).

Graf, G., *Der Sprachgebrauch der ältesten christlich-arabischen Literatur. Ein Beitrag zur Geschichte des vulgär-arabisch* (Leipzig, 1905).

Grousset, R., *Histoire des croisades et du royaume franc de Jérusalem* I (Paris, 1934).

Guseynov, R. A., "Sultan i khalif (Iz istorii syuzereniteta i vassaliteta na Blizhnem Vostoke XI-XII vv.)", *Palestinskiy Sbornik* 19 (82, 1969), 24-43.

Herzfeld, E. E., "Eine Bauinschrift von Niẓâm al-mulk", *Der Islam* XII (1921), 98-101.

Hillenbrand, C., "Marwānids", *EI*².

----, "Mayyāfāriḳīn", *EI*².

----, "Some medieval Islamic approaches to source material", *Oriens* 27-28 (1981), 197-225.

----, "The career of Najm al-Dīn İl-Ghāzī", *Der Islam* 58/2 (1981), 250-292.

----, "The establishment of Artuqid power in Diyār Bakr in the twelfth century", *Studia Islamica*, LIV, (1981), 129-53.

----, "The History of the Jazīra, 1100-1250: A Short Introduction", in *The Art of Syria and the Jazīra 1100-1250*, ed. J. Raby (Oxford, 1985), 1-19.

Hodgson, M. G. S., *The Order of the Assassins* (The Hague, 1955).

Honigmann, E., *Die Ostgrenze des byzantinischen Reiches von 363 bis 1071* (Brussels, 1935).

----, "Naṣībīn", *EI*¹.

----, "Ortoḳids", *EI*¹.

Horst, H., *Die Staatsverwaltung der Grossselǧūqen und Ḫōrazmšāhs (1038-1231). Eine Untersuchung nach Urkundenformularen der Zeit* (Wiesbaden, 1964).

Houtsma, M. H., *Ein Türkisch-Arabisches Glossar* (Leiden, 1894).

----, "Mas'ūd", *EI*¹.

Huart, C., "Khil'a", *EI*¹.

Ilisch, L., *Geschichte der Artuqidenherrschaft von Mardin zwischen Mamluken und Mongolen 1260-1410 A.D.*, Münster, 1984.

----, "Die älteste artuqidische Kupferprägung", *Münstersche Numismatische Zeitung*, November, 1976.

İlter, F., "Eine Gruppe der frühtürkischen Brücken in Südostanatolien", *IVème Congrès International d'Art Turc. Etudes historiques 3* (Aix and Paris, 1976), 97-103.

Julien, C.-A., *History of North Africa. Tunisia. Algeria. Morocco. From the Arab Conquest to 1830*, French text ed. and rev. R. Le Tourneau; tr. J. Petrie, ed. C. C. Stewart (London, 1970).

Justi, F., *Iranisches Namenbuch* (repr. Hildesheim, 1963).

Klausner, C. L., *The Seljuk vezirate. A study of civil administration 1055-1194* (Cambridge, Mass., 1973).

Köprülü, M. F., "Artuk Oğullari", *IA*, 617-25.

----, review of C. Cahen, "Le Diyār Bakr au temps des premiers Urtuḳides", *Belleten*, sayï 1 (1937), 283-8.

Kritzeck, J., "Ibn-al-Ṭiqṭaqa and the fall of Baghdād", in *The World of Islam. Studies in honor of P. K. Hitti*, eds. J. Kritzeck and R. B. Winder (Princeton, 1959), 159-84.
Lambton, A. K. S., "The internal structure of the Saljuq empire", in *The Cambridge History of Iran. 5. The Saljuq and Mongol Periods*, ed. J. A. Boyle (Cambridge, 1968), 203-82.
Lane, E. W., *An Arabic-English Lexicon* (London, 1872).
Lane-Poole, S., *Catalogue of oriental coins in the British Museum III. The coins of the Turkmán Houses of Saljook, Urtuk, Zengee, etc.*, ed. R. S. Poole (London, 1877).
----, *Saladin and the Fall of the Kingdom of Jerusalem* (London and New York, 1898).
Lang, D. M., *Studies in the Numismatic History of Georgia in Transcaucasia* (New York, 1955).
----, *The Georgians* (London, 1966).
Lehmann-Haupt, C. F., *Armenien einst und jetzt. Reisen und Forschungen* (Berlin, 1910).
Le Strange, G., *Baghdad during the Abbasid caliphate* (Oxford, 1900).
----, *Palestine under the Moslems* (London, 1890).
----, *The lands of the eastern caliphate* (Cambridge, 1905).
Le Tourneau, R., *Damas de 1075 à 1154*, see Ibn al-Qalānisī.
Lévi-Provençal, E., "'Abd al-Mu'min", *EI*².
----, "Rabaḍ", *EI*¹.
----, "Rabāṭ", *EI*¹.
Levy, R., *A Baghdad chronicle* (Cambridge, 1929).
----, *The social structure of Islam* (Cambridge, 1971).
Luther, K. A., "A New Source for the History of the Iraq Seljuqs: The *Tārīkh al-Vuzarā*'", *Der Islam* 45 (1969), 117-28.
----, *The political transformation of the Seljuq sultanate of Iraq and western Iran 1152-1187* (unpublished Ph.D. thesis, Princeton, 1964).
Lynch, H. F. B., *Armenia. Travels and Studies* (repr. Beirut, 1965).
Marçais, G., "al-Mahdīya", *EI*¹.
Markwart, J., *Südarmenien und die Tigrisquellen nach griechischen und arabischen Geographen* (Vienna, 1930).
Minorsky, V. F., *A history of Sharvān and Darband in the 10th-11th centuries* (Cambridge, 1958).
----, "Alan", *EI*².
----, "Caucasica in the History of Mayyāfāriqīn", *BSOAS* XIII/4 (1949), 27-35.
----, "Kurds", *EI*¹.
----, "Mārdīn", *EI*¹.
----, review of H. Ḥasan, *Falakī-i-Shīrwānī* I and II, *BSOS* V (1928-30), 903-10.

----, *Studies in Caucasian History* (London, 1953).

Miranda, A. H., *Historia Politica del Imperio Almohade*, 2 vols. (Tetuan, 1956).

Pedersen, J., "Masdjid", *EI*[1].

Quatremère, M. E., *Histoire des Mongols de la Perse* I (Paris, 1836) (ed. and tr. of Rashīd al-Dīn Faḍlallāh, *Jāmiʿ al-Tawārīkh).*

----, *Histoire des sultans mamlouks, de l'Egypte* I-II, tr. of Maqrīzī, *Al-Sulūk fī maʿrifāt duwal al-mulūk* (Paris, 1837-45)

----, "Notice historique sur les Ismailiens", in *Fundgruben des Orients* IV, ed. Graf W. Rzewusky (Vienna, 1818).

Röhricht, R., *Geschichte des Königreichs Jerusalem (1100-1291)* (Innsbruck, 1898).

Runciman, S., *A History of the Crusades. I. The Kingdom of Jerusalem and the Frankish East 1100-1187* (Cambridge, 1954).

Sanaullah, M. F., *The decline of the Saljūqid Empire* (Calcutta, 1938).

Sauvaget, J., "La Tombe de l'Ortoḳide Balak", *Ars Islamica V* (1938), 207-15.

----, "Noms et surnoms de Mamelouks", *JA* CCXXXVIII (1950), 31-58.

Setton, K. M. and Baldwin, M. W., eds., *A History of the Crusades. I. The First Hundred Years* (Madison, Milwaukee and London, 1969).

Sevim, A., "Artuklularïn Soyu ve Bey'in Siyase Faaliyetleri", *Belleten* XXVI, sayï 101 (1962), 121-47.

----, "Artuk Oğlu İlgazi", *Belleten* XXVI, sayï 104 (1962), 649-91.

----, "Artukoğlu Sökmen'in Siyasi Faaliyetleri", *Belleten* XXVI, sayï 103 (1962), 501-20.

Siddiqi, A. H., *Caliphate and Kingship in Medieval Persia* (Lahore, 1942).

Sivan, E., *L'Islam et la Croisade. Idéologie et Propagande dans les Réactions Musulmanes aux Croisades* (Paris, 1968).

Socin, A., "Der arabische Dialekt von Mōṣul und Märdīn", *Zeitschrift der Deutschen Morgenländischen Gesellschaft* XXXVI (1882), 1-53.

Sourdel-Thomine, J., "Buzāʿa", *EI*[2].

Spuler, B., *Iran in früh-islamischer Zeit. Politik, Kultur, Verwaltung und öffentliches Leben zwischen der arabischen und der seldschukischen Eroberung 633 bis 1055* (Wiesbaden, 1952).

Steingass, F., *A Comprehensive Persian-English Dictionary* (London, n.d.).

Stern, S. M., "The Succession to the Fatimid Imam al-Āmir, the Claims of the Later Fatimids to the Imamate and the Rise of Ṭayyibī Ismailism", *Oriens* 4 (1951), 193-255.

Stevenson, W. B., *The Crusaders in the East* (Cambridge, 1907).

Süssheim, K., "Ilghāzī", *EI*[1].

Taylor, J. G., "Travels in Kurdistan, with Notices of the Sources of the Eastern and Western Tigris, and Ancient Ruins in their Neighbourhood", *The Journal of the Royal Geographical Society* 35 (1865), 21-58.
T'seret'heli, G. V., *Arabuli Krest'omathia* (Tiflis, 1949).
Turan, O., *Doğu Anadolu Türk Devletleri Tarihi* (Istanbul 1973).
----, *Selçuklular Tarihi ve Türk-İslâm Medeniyeti* (Ankara, 1965).
----, *Selçuklular Zamaninda Türkiye. Siyâsi Tarih Alp Arslan'dan Osman Gazi'ye (1071-1318)* (Istanbul, 1971).
Tyan, E., *Institutions du droit public musulman*, 2 vols. (Paris, 1954-6).
Ünal, R. H., *Les monuments islamiques anciens de la ville d'Erzerum et de sa région* (Paris, 1968).
Uzunçarşili, İ. H., *Osmanli devleti teşkilâtina medhal* (Istanbul, 1941).
Van Berchem, M., "Arabische Inschriften", in Max Freiherr von Oppenheim, *Inschriften aus Syrien, Mesopotamien, und Kleinasien* (Leipzig, 1909).
----, and Strzygowski, J., *Amida* (Heidelberg, 1910).
Vryonis, S., Jr., *The Decline of Medieval Hellenism in Asia Minor and the Process of Islamization from the Eleventh through the Fifteenth Century* (Berkeley, Los Angeles and London, 1971).
Weil, G., *Geschichte der Chalifen* III (Mannheim, 1851).
Wilken, F. *Geschichte der Kreuzzüge* (Leipzig, 1807-32).
Wüstenfeld, F. *Geschichte der Fatimiden-Chalifen. Nach Arabischen Quellen* (Göttingen, 1881).
----, "Jâcût's Reisen, aus seinem geographischen Wörterbuche beschrieben", *ZDMG* XVIII (1864), 397-493.
----, *Ueber die Quellen des Werkes Ibn Challikani vitae illustrium hominum* (Göttingen, 1837).
Yinanc, M. H., "Diyarbekir", *IA*.
Zakkar, S., *The Emirate of Aleppo 1004-1094* (Beirut, 1971).
Zambaur, E. de, *Manuel de Généalogie et de Chronologie pour l'Histoire de l'Islam* (Hanover,1927).

Introduction to the Footnotes

General Comments

The commentary on the edition and translation of Ibn al-Azraq's text is inevitably long. The linguistic problems raised by a translation of the text require discussion. Moreover, the author's chaotic chronology and unexplained allusions necessitate constant reference to other primary sources which deal with the historical period under discussion.

Place-names present a major problem for an understanding of this text. Explanations or references to geographical works have been given wherever possible. It must be admitted, however, that the exact location of some of the places mentioned by Ibn al-Azraq remains unknown, as Cahen pointed out in his pioneer article on the Artuqids in 1935.

In the footnotes, frequent reference has been made to the unpublished section of the historical geography of Ibn Shaddād, which deals with the Jazīra and which concentrates, therefore, on the same areas as Ibn al-Azraq.[1] It is true that Ibn Shaddād does not offer precise information on the location of many of the places which both he and Ibn al-Azraq mention, but since Ibn Shaddād's work is a virtually unexploited source it seemed appropriate to record his comments in some detail.

It is unfortunate that so many explanatory notes should be necessary in the first few pages of the footnotes - i.e. those which deal with Ibn al-Azraq's account of the reign of İl-Ghāzī. It is quite apparent that the information on this period available to Ibn al-Azraq is far from complete and that he himself only partially understands it. For further information not given in the footnotes in this section of the commentary, reference should be made to the extended discussion of this period in my article on İl-Ghāzī.[2]

1. Claude Cahen summarised the contents of Ibn Shaddād's work on the Jazīra in his article, "La Djazira au milieu du treizième siècle d'après 'Izz al-din Ibn Chaddad", *Revue des Etudes Islamiques* VIII (1934), 109-16. He did not, however, make full use of the information nor did he link it to the text of Ibn al-Azraq.
2. Cf. Hillenbrand, "İl-Ghāzī".

Similarly, the commentary on the genealogical section (ff.177a-178b) is deliberately brief in order to avoid duplication of the discussion in the notes to the genealogical table.

Another difficulty inherent in Ibn al-Azraq's text is its administrative terminology. With increasing political fragmentation at the beginning of the sixth/twelfth century and the rise of semi-independent dynasties centred in a major city, e.g. the Artuqids at Mārdīn and the Zangids at Mosul, it is difficult to determine the exact meaning of the administrative terms used in connection with these rulers in the chronicles. The actual titles are inherited from the administrative system of the Great Saljuqs but often offices are merged. Ibn al-Azraq uses administrative terms freely but does not see the need to define them. The offices he mentions are discussed wherever possible in the footnotes.

List of abbreviations used in the footnotes

For full details of these titles, see the bibliography.

Abu'l-Fiḍā', *Mukhtaṣar* = *Al-Mukhtaṣar fī akhbār al-bashar* III

Anon. Syr. Chron. = Anonymous Syriac Chronicle, tr. Tritton, *JRAS*, 1933

'Awaḍ = Ibn al-Azraq, *Tārīkh al-Fāriqī*, ed. 'Awaḍ

al-'Aẓīmī, "Chronique" = Cahen (ed.), "La chronique abrégée d'al-'Azīmī", *JA*, 1938

Bar Hebraeus, *Chronography* = *The Chronography of Gregory Abû'l Faraj*, tr. Budge

Bosworth, "Iranian World" = Bosworth, "The political and dynastic history of the Iranian world (A.D. 1000-1217)", *Cambridge History of Iran* 5

al-Bundārī, *Zubdat* = *Zubdat al-nuṣra*, ed. Houtsma

Cahen, "Diyār Bakr" = Cahen, "Le Diyār Bakr au temps des premiers Urtuḳides", *JA*, 1935

Cahen, *Syrie* = Cahen, *La Syrie du Nord*, 1940

Canard, *H'amdanides* = Canard, *Histoire de la dynastie des H'amdanides*, 1953

CHI 5 = *The Cambridge History of Iran*, Vol. 5, 1968

Dozy, *Supplément* = Dozy, *Supplément aux dictionnaires arabes*, 1881

Eddé, *Description* = Eddé, *La description de la Syrie du Nord de 'Izz al-Dīn Ibn Shaddād*, 1982

Elshayyal, *Ibn al-Furāt (Shayyāl)* = Elshayyal, *A critical edition of Volume II of Tārīkh al-Duwal wa'l-Mulūk by Muḥammad b. 'Abd al-Raḥīm b. 'Alī Ibn al-Furāt*, 1986

Hillenbrand, "Approaches" = Hillenbrand, "Some medieval Islamic approaches to source material", *Oriens*, 1981

Hillenbrand, "Establishment" = Hillenbrand, "The establishment of Artuqid power in Diyār Bakr in the twelfth century", *SI*, 1981

Hillenbrand, "İl-Ghāzī" = Hillenbrand, "The career of Najm al-Dīn İl-Ghāzī", *Der Islam*, 1981

Honigmann, *Ostgrenze* = Honigmann, *Die Ostgrenze des byzantinischen Reiches*, 1935

Horst, *Staatsverwaltung* = Horst, *Die Staatsverwaltung der Grossselǧūqen*, 1964

al-Ḥusainī, *Akhbār* = al-Ḥusainī, *Akhbār al-Daula al-Saljuqiyya*, ed. Iqbāl, 1933

Ibn al-ʿAdīm, *Bughyat* = Ibn al-ʿAdīm, *Bughyat al-ṭalab*, ed. Sevim, 1976

Ibn al-ʿAdīm, *Zubda* = Ibn al-ʿAdīm, *Zubdat al-ḥalab*, ed. Dahān, 1954

Ibn al-Athīr, *al-Kāmil* = Ibn al-Athīr, *al-Kāmil fi'l-tārīkh*, ed. Tornberg, 1851-76

Ibn al-Athīr, *Atabegs* = Ibn al-Athīr, *Tārīkh al-daula al-atābakiyya*, ed. Ṭulaimāt, 1963

Ibn al-Furāt, *Duwal* = Ibn al-Furāt, *Tārīkh al-Duwal*, Vienna Ms II

Ibn al-Jauzī, *Muntazam* = Ibn al-Jauzī, *al-Muntazam fī tārīkh al-mulūk wa'l-umam* X, 1940

Ibn Khallikān, *Wafayāt* = Ibn Khallikān, *Wafayāt al-aʿyān*, tr. de Slane, 1843-71

Ibn al-Qalānisī, *Dhail* = Ibn al-Qalānisī, *Dhail tārīkh Dimishq*, ed. Amedroz, 1908

Ibn Shaddād, *Jazīra,* Ibn Shaddād, *al-Aʿlaq al-khaṭīra*, Bodleian Ms Marsh 333

Ibn al-Ṭiqṭaqā, *al-Fakhrī* = Ibn al-Ṭiqṭaqā, *al-Fakhrī fi'l-ādāb al-sulṭāniyya*, tr. Amar, 1910

Ilisch, *Geschichte* = Ilisch, *Geschichte der Artuqidenherrschaft von Mardin zwischen Mamluken und Mongolen 1260-1410 A.D.*,1984

Le Strange, *Baghdad* = Le Strange, *Baghdad during the Abbasid Caliphate*, 1900

Le Strange, *Lands* = Le Strange, *Lands of the Eastern Caliphate*, 1905

Markwart, Südarmenien = Markwart, *Südarmenien und die Tigrisquellen*, 1930

Matthew of Edessa, *Chronique* = Matthew of Edessa, *Chronique,* tr. Dulaurier, 1858

Michael the Syrian, *Chronique* = Michael the Syrian, *Chronique,* tr. Chabot, 1899-1914

Minorsky, "Causcasica I" = Minorsky, "Caucasica in the History of Mayyāfāriqīn", *BSOAS*, 1949

Minorsky, *Studies* = Minorsky, *Studies in Caucasian History* 1953

Mustaufī, *Guzīda* = Ḥamdallāh Mustaufī al-Qazwīnī, *Tārīkh-i Guzīda*, tr. Defrémery, *JA*, 1848

Rāwandī, *Rāḥat* = Rāwandī, *Rāḥat al-ṣudūr*, ed. Iqbāl, 1921

Turan, *Doğu Anadolu* = Turan, *Doğu Anadolu Türk Devleteri Tarihi*, 1973

Usāma, *Memoirs* = Usāma, *Memoirs*, tr. Hitti, repr. 1964

Uzunçarşïlï, *Osmanlï devleti* = Uzunçarşïlï, *Osmanlï devleti teşkilātïna medhal*, 1941

Yāqūt, Reisen = Wüstenfeld, "Jacuts Reisen", *ZDMG*, 1864

Introductory comments to the index

The index provided for this book is more detailed than the indices of most books on Islamic subjects and the quantity of cross-referencing may seem excessive. The sole aim of this procedure, however, has been to make information in the text more easily traceable. Moreover, Ibn al-Azraq frequently refers to the same person under several names - *kunya, laqab, ism,* or parts and combinations of any of these, and apparently assumes that his readers will easily identify the person in question. When a full name has been broken up in this way its constituent parts are separately indexed and cross-referenced. This system admittedly produces certain anomalies: thus Ṣadaqa, the father of Dubais, occurs in the index as a separate name although in the text proper he appears only as part of the name of his son. The result of including such entries is that the index is more detailed than might be expected; however, the system not only helps the reader to track down information quickly but also links the text to the translation and footnotes where many of the names recur under several forms. The wealth of names in the text itself makes an index desirable but it is doubly valuable in view of the muddled chronology of Ibn al-Azraq. A detailed index of proper names to some extent compensates for this deficiency.

The cross-references allow a person to be traced via his *ism* or his *laqab*. Either may be used as the basis of the main entry in the index, but the principle is that a person is recorded under the name that is most often used. In cases of doubt the father's name is added to the *ism* or *laqab* in the index entry. When a genealogy, complete with titles, is given at length in the index it is in order to enable the reader to trace the person in question more easily. Ibn al-Azraq frequently gives names in shorthand form and only on subsequent (often much later) occasions does he give the name in full; e.g. the name Tāj al-Dīn Abū Sālim Ṭāhir b. Nubāta first appears in full as late as f.174a.

Names spelt variously within the same manuscript are given a single "standard" form in the index. Some inconsistencies may therefore be detected between the form of a name in the index and a given occurrence in the text. This is particularly likely to happen over the introduction or omission of *ibn* in a name. Where the text itself is inconsistent in this matter the more common form of the name appears in the index.

Names which span two pages, or two folios, occur in the index under both pages or folios.

In general, where a person is known by his office, that office is given after his name in the index entry. However, where the text refers to a person by his office only and not by any element of his name (e.g. "the sulṭān") these references do not appear in the index. *Nisbas* are usually recorded separately and cross-referenced.

For the purposes of alphabetical order, *al-* as the first element of a name should be ignored. Where it appears elsewhere in a name, e.g. Abu'l-Ḥasan, it is however subject to strict alphabetical order. Mayyāfāriqīn does not appear in the index as it is by far the commonest of the proper names in the text.

Where references occur in brackets, the names in question have been incorporated into the translation for the sake of clarity. They do not occur in the Arabic text.

INDEX

A

B

C

D

E

F

G

H

I

J

K

L

M

N

O

P

Q

R

S

T

U

W

Y

Z

ORIENTALISTE, P.B. 41, B-3000 Leuven